The C# Programming Language

Microsoft .NET Development Series

John Montgomery, *Series Advisor*
Don Box, *Series Advisor*
Martin Heller, *Series Editor*

The **Microsoft .NET Development Series** is supported and developed by the leaders and experts of Microsoft development technologies including Microsoft architects and DevelopMentor instructors. The books in this series provide a core resource of information and understanding every developer needs in order to write effective applications and managed code. Learn from the leaders how to maximize your use of the .NET Framework and its programming languages.

Titles in the Series

Brad Abrams, *.NET Framework Standard Library Annotated Reference Volume 1*, 0-321-15489-4

Keith Ballinger, *.NET Web Services: Architecture and Implementation*, 0-321-11359-4

Don Box with Chris Sells, *Essential .NET, Volume 1: The Common Language Runtime*, 0-201-73411-7

Mahesh Chand, *Graphics Programming with GDI+*, 0-321-16077-0

Anders Hejlsberg, Scott Wiltamuth, Peter Golde, *The C# Programming Language*, 0-321-15491-6

Alex Homer, Dave Sussman, Mark Fussell, *A First Look at ADO.NET and System.Xml v. 2.0*, 0-321-22839-1

Alex Homer, Dave Sussman, Rob Howard, *A First Look at ASP.NET v. 2.0*, 0-321-22896-0

James S. Miller and Susann Ragsdale, *The Common Language Infrastructure Annotated Standard*, 0-321-15493-2

Fritz Onion, *Essential ASP.NET with Examples in C#*, 0-201-76040-1

Fritz Onion, *Essential ASP.NET with Examples in Visual Basic .NET*, 0-201-76039-8

Ted Pattison and Dr. Joe Hummel, *Building Applications and Components with Visual Basic .NET*, 0-201-73495-8

Chris Sells, *Windows Forms Programming in C#*, 0-321-11620-8

Chris Sells and Justin Gehtland, *Windows Forms Programming in Visual Basic .NET*, 0-321-12519-3

Damien Watkins, Mark Hammond, Brad Abrams, *Programming in the .NET Environment*, 0-201-77018-0

Shawn Wildermuth, *Pragmatic ADO.NET: Data Access for the Internet World*, 0-201-74568-2

The C# Programming Language

- **Anders Hejlsberg**
  Scott Wiltamuth
  Peter Golde

✚✚Addison-Wesley

Boston • San Francisco • New York • Toronto • Montreal
London • Munich • Paris • Madrid
Capetown • Sydney • Tokyo • Singapore • Mexico City

The publisher offers discounts on this book when ordered in quantity for special sales. For more information, please contact:

U.S. Corporate and Government Sales
(800) 382-3419
corpsales@pearsontechgroup.com

For sales outside of the U.S., please contact:

International Sales
(317 581-3793)
international@pearsontechgroup.com

Visit Addison-Wesley on the Web: www.awprofessional.com

Library of Congress Cataloging-in-Publication Data
Hejlsberg, Anders.
 The C# programming language / Anders Hejlsberg, Scott Wiltamuth, Peter Golde.
  p. cm.
 Includes bibliographical references and index.
 ISBN 0-321-15491-6 (alk. paper)
 1. C# (Computer program language) I. Wiltamuth, Scott. II. Golde, Peter. III. Title.

 QA76.76.C154H45 2003
 005.13'3—dc21   2003056094

ISBN 0-321-15491-6
Text printed on recycled paper
1 2 3 4 5 6 7 8 9 10—CRW—0706050403
First printing, October 2003

Contents

Preface

The C# project started almost five years ago, in December 1998, with the goal to create a simple, modern, object-oriented, and type-safe programming language for the new and yet to be named .NET platform. Since then, C# has come a long way. The language is now in use by hundreds of thousands of programmers, it has been standardized by both ECMA and ISO/IEC, and the development of a second version of the language with several major new features is close to completion.

This book is a complete technical specification of the C# programming language. The book is divided into three parts. Part I, "C# 1.0," includes Chapters 1–18 and describes the C# 1.0 language, as delivered in Visual Studio .NET 2002 and 2003. Part II, "C# 2.0," includes Chapters 19–23 and describes the four major new features of C# 2.0: generics, anonymous methods, iterators, and partial types. Part III, "Appendixes," describes documentation comments and summarizes the lexical and syntactic grammars found in Part I of the book. As of this writing, C# 2.0 is close to entering beta testing. Because C# 2.0 is still a work in progress, some of the new features described in the second part of the book might change in the final release. We do, however, expect any such changes to be minor.

Many people have been involved in the creation of the C# language. The language design team for C# 1.0 consisted of Anders Hejlsberg, Scott Wiltamuth, Peter Golde, Peter Sollich, and Eric Gunnerson. For C# 2.0, the language design team consisted of Anders Hejlsberg, Peter Golde, Peter Hallam, Shon Katzenberger, Todd Proebsting, and Anson Horton. Furthermore, the design and implementation of generics in C# and the .NET Common Language Runtime is based on the "Gyro" prototype built by Don Syme and Andrew Kennedy of Microsoft Research.

It is impossible to acknowledge all the people who have influenced the design of C#, but we are nonetheless grateful to all of them. Nothing good gets designed in a vacuum, and the constant feedback we receive from our large and enthusiastic user base is invaluable.

C# has been and continues to be one of the most challenging and exciting projects on which we've worked. We hope you enjoy using C# as much as we enjoyed creating it.

Anders Hejlsberg
Scott Wiltamuth
Peter Golde

Seattle, August 2003

Part I

C# 1.0

1. Introduction

C# (pronounced "See Sharp") is a simple, modern, object-oriented, and type-safe programming language. C# has its roots in the C family of languages and will be immediately familiar to C, C++, and Java programmers. C# is standardized by ECMA International as the *ECMA-334* standard and by ISO/IEC as the *ISO/IEC 23270* standard. Microsoft's C# compiler for the .NET Framework is a conforming implementation of both of these standards.

C# is an object-oriented language, but C# further includes support for *component-oriented* programming. Contemporary software design increasingly relies on software components in the form of self-contained and self-describing packages of functionality. Key to such components is that they present a programming model with properties, methods, and events; they have attributes that provide declarative information about the component; and they incorporate their own documentation. C# provides language constructs to directly support these concepts, making C# a very natural language in which to create and use software components.

Several C# features aid in the construction of robust and durable applications: *Garbage collection* automatically reclaims memory occupied by unused objects; *exception handling* provides a structured and extensible approach to error detection and recovery; and the *type-safe* design of the language makes it impossible to have uninitialized variables, to index arrays beyond their bounds, or to perform unchecked type casts.

C# has a *unified type system*. All C# types, including primitive types such as `int` and `double`, inherit from a single root `object` type. Thus, all types share a set of common operations, and values of any type can be stored, transported, and operated upon in a consistent manner. Furthermore, C# supports both user-defined reference types and value types, allowing dynamic allocation of objects as well as in-line storage of lightweight structures.

To ensure that C# programs and libraries can evolve over time in a compatible manner, much emphasis has been placed on *versioning* in C#'s design. Many programming languages pay little attention to this issue, and, as a result, programs written in those languages break more often than necessary when newer versions of dependent libraries are introduced. Aspects of C#'s design that were directly influenced by versioning considerations include the separate `virtual` and `override` modifiers, the rules for method overload resolution, and support for explicit interface member declarations.

The rest of this chapter describes the essential features of the C# language. Although later chapters describe rules and exceptions in a detail-oriented and sometimes mathematical manner, this chapter strives for clarity and brevity at the expense of completeness. The intent is to provide the reader with an introduction to the language that will facilitate the writing of early programs and the reading of later chapters.

1.1 Hello World

The "Hello, World" program is traditionally used to introduce a programming language. Here it is in C#:

```
using System;

class Hello
{
    static void Main() {
        Console.WriteLine("Hello, World");
    }
}
```

C# source files typically have the file extension .cs. Assuming that the "Hello, World" program is stored in the file hello.cs, the program can be compiled with the Microsoft C# compiler using the command line

```
csc hello.cs
```

which produces an executable assembly named hello.exe. The output produced by this application when it is run is

```
Hello, World
```

The "Hello, World" program starts with a using directive that references the System namespace. Namespaces provide a hierarchical means of organizing C# programs and libraries. Namespaces contain types and other namespaces—for example, the System namespace contains a number of types, such as the Console class referenced in the program, and a number of other namespaces, such as IO and Collections. A using directive that references a given namespace enables unqualified use of the types that are members of that namespace. Because of the using directive, the program can use Console.WriteLine as shorthand for System.Console.WriteLine.

The Hello class declared by the "Hello, World" program has a single member, the method named Main. The Main method is declared with the static modifier. Unlike instance methods, which reference a particular object instance using the keyword this, static methods operate without reference to a particular object. By convention, a static method named Main serves as the entry point of a program.

The output of the program is produced by the WriteLine method of the Console class in the System namespace. This class is provided by the .NET Framework class libraries, which, by default, are automatically referenced by the Microsoft C# compiler. Note that C# itself does not have a separate runtime library. Instead, the .NET Framework *is* the runtime library of C#.

1.2 Program Structure

The key organizational concepts in C# are *programs*, *namespaces*, *types*, *members*, and *assemblies*. C# programs consist of one or more source files. Programs declare types, which contain members and can be organized into namespaces. Classes and interfaces are examples of types. Fields, methods, properties, and events are examples of members. When C# programs are compiled, they are physically packaged into assemblies. Assemblies typically have the file extension .exe or .dll, depending on whether they implement *applications* or *libraries*.

The example

```
using System;

namespace Acme.Collections
{
    public class Stack
    {
        Entry top;

        public void Push(object data) {
            top = new Entry(top, data);
        }

        public object Pop() {
            if (top == null) throw new InvalidOperationException();
            object result = top.data;
            top = top.next;
            return result;
        }

        class Entry
        {
            public Entry next;
            public object data;

            public Entry(Entry next, object data) {
                this.next = next;
                this.data = data;
            }
        }
    }
}
```

declares a class named Stack in a namespace called Acme.Collections. The fully qualified name of this class is Acme.Collections.Stack. The class contains several members: a field named top, two methods named Push and Pop, and a nested class named Entry. The Entry class further contains three members: a field named next, a field named data, and a constructor. Assuming that the source code of the example is stored in the file acme.cs, the command line

```
csc /t:library acme.cs
```

compiles the example as a library (code without a Main entry point) and produces an assembly named acme.dll.

Assemblies contain executable code in the form of *Intermediate Language* (IL) instructions, and symbolic information in the form of *metadata*. Before it is executed, the IL code in an assembly is automatically converted to processor-specific code by the Just-In-Time (JIT) compiler of .NET Common Language Runtime.

Because an assembly is a self-describing unit of functionality containing both code and metadata, there is no need for #include directives and header files in C#. The public types and members contained in a particular assembly are made available in a C# program simply by referencing that assembly when compiling the program. For example, this program uses the Acme.Collections.Stack class from the acme.dll assembly:

```csharp
using System;
using Acme.Collections;

class Test
{
    static void Main() {
        Stack s = new Stack();
        s.Push(1);
        s.Push(10);
        s.Push(100);
        Console.WriteLine(s.Pop());
        Console.WriteLine(s.Pop());
        Console.WriteLine(s.Pop());
    }
}
```

If the program is stored in the file test.cs, when test.cs is compiled, the acme.dll assembly can be referenced using the compiler's /r option:

```
csc /r:acme.dll test.cs
```

This creates an executable assembly named test.exe, which, when run, produces the output:

```
100
10
1
```

C# permits the source text of a program to be stored in several source files. When a multi-file C# program is compiled, all of the source files are processed together, and the source files can freely reference each other—conceptually, it is as if all the source files were concatenated into one large file before being processed. Forward declarations are never needed in C# because, with very few exceptions, declaration order is insignificant. C# does not limit a source file to declaring only one public type nor does it require the name of the source file to match a type declared in the source file.

1.3 Types and Variables

There are two kinds of types in C#: *value types* and *reference types*. Variables of value types directly contain their data whereas variables of reference types store references to their data, the latter being known as objects. With reference types, it is possible for two variables to reference the same object and thus possible for operations on one variable to affect the object referenced by the other variable. With value types, the variables each have their own copy of the data, and it is not possible for operations on one to affect the other (except in the case of `ref` and `out` parameter variables).

C#'s value types are further divided into *simple types*, *enum types*, and *struct types*, and C#'s reference types are further divided into *class types*, *interface types*, *array types*, and *delegate types*.

The following table provides an overview of C#'s type system.

Category		Description
Value types	Simple types	Signed integral: `sbyte`, `short`, `int`, `long`
		Unsigned integral: `byte`, `ushort`, `uint`, `ulong`
		Unicode characters: `char`
		IEEE floating point: `float`, `double`
		High-precision decimal: `decimal`
		Boolean: `bool`
	Enum types	User-defined types of the form `enum E {...}`
	Struct types	User-defined types of the form `struct S {...}`

continues

Category		Description
Reference types	Class types	Ultimate base class of all other types: `object`
		Unicode strings: `string`
		User-defined types of the form `class C {...}`
	Interface types	User-defined types of the form `interface I {...}`
	Array types	Single- and multi-dimensional, for example, `int[]` and `int[,]`
	Delegate types	User-defined types of the form `delegate T D(...)`

The eight integral types provide support for 8-bit, 16-bit, 32-bit, and 64-bit values in signed or unsigned form.

The two floating point types, `float` and `double`, are represented using the 32-bit single-precision and 64-bit double-precision IEEE 754 formats.

The `decimal` type is a 128-bit data type suitable for financial and monetary calculations.

C#'s `bool` type is used to represent boolean values—values that are either `true` or `false`.

Character and string processing in C# uses Unicode encoding. The `char` type represents a 16-bit Unicode code unit, and the `string` type represents a sequence of 16-bit Unicode code units.

The following table summarizes C#'s numeric types.

Category	Bits	Type	Range/Precision
Signed integral	8	`sbyte`	−128...127
	16	`short`	−32,768...32,767
	32	`int`	−2,147,483,648...2,147,483,647
	64	`long`	−9,223,372,036,854,775,808...9,223,372,036,854,775,807

Category	Bits	Type	Range/Precision
Unsigned integral	8	byte	0...255
	16	ushort	0...65,535
	32	uint	0...4,294,967,295
	64	ulong	0...18,446,744,073,709,551,615
Floating point	32	float	1.5×10^{-45} to 3.4×10^{38}, 7-digit precision
	64	double	5.0×10^{-324} to 1.7×10^{308}, 15-digit precision
Decimal	128	decimal	1.0×10^{-28} to 7.9×10^{28}, 28-digit precision

C# programs use *type declarations* to create new types. A type declaration specifies the name and the members of the new type. Five of C#'s categories of types are user-definable: class types, struct types, interface types, enum types, and delegate types.

A class type defines a data structure that contains data members (fields) and function members (methods, properties, and others). Class types support inheritance and polymorphism, mechanisms whereby derived classes can extend and specialize base classes.

A struct type is similar to a class type in that it represents a structure with data members and function members. However, unlike classes, structs are value types and do not require heap allocation. Struct types do not support user-specified inheritance, and all struct types implicitly inherit from type object.

An interface type defines a contract as a named set of function members. A class or struct that implements an interface must provide implementations of the interface's function members. An interface may inherit from multiple base interfaces, and a class or struct may implement multiple interfaces.

An enum type is a distinct type with named constants. Every enum type has an underlying type, which must be one of the eight integral types. The set of values of an enum type is the same as the set of values of the underlying type.

A delegate type represents references to methods with a particular parameter list and return type. Delegates make it possible to treat methods as entities that can be assigned to variables and passed as parameters. Delegates are similar to the concept of function point-ers found in some other languages, but unlike function pointers, delegates are object-oriented and type-safe.

C# supports single- and multi-dimensional arrays of any type. Unlike other types, array types do not have to be declared before they can be used. Instead, array types are con-structed by following a type name with square brackets. For example, int[] is a single-dimensional array of int, int[,] is a two-dimensional array of int, and int[][] is a single-dimensional array of single-dimensional arrays of int.

C#'s type system is unified such that a value of any type can be treated as an object. Every type in C# directly or indirectly derives from the object class type, and object is the ultimate base class of all types. Values of value types are treated as objects by performing *boxing* and *unboxing* operations. In the following example, an int value is converted to object and back again to int.

```
using System;
class Test
{
    static void Main() {
        int i = 123;
        object o = i;        // Boxing
        int j = (int)o;      // Unboxing
    }
}
```

When a value of a value type is converted to type object, an object instance, also called a "box," is allocated to hold the value, and the value is copied into that box. Conversely, when an object reference is cast to a value type, a check is made that the referenced object is a box of the correct value type, and, if the check succeeds, the value in the box is copied out.

C#'s unified type system effectively means that value types can become objects "on demand." Because of the unification, general-purpose libraries that use type object, such as the collection classes in the .NET Framework, can be used with both reference types and value types.

There are several kinds of *variables* in C#, including fields, array elements, local variables, and parameters. Variables represent storage locations, and every variable has a type that determines what values can be stored in the variable, as shown by the following table.

Type of Variable	Possible Contents
Value type	A value of that exact type
object	A null reference, a reference to an object of any reference type, or a reference to a boxed value of any value type
Class type	A null reference, a reference to an instance of that class type, or a reference to an instance of a class derived from that class type
Interface type	A null reference, a reference to an instance of a class type that implements that interface type, or a reference to a boxed value of a value type that implements that interface type
Array type	A null reference, a reference to an instance of that array type, or a reference to an instance of a compatible array type
Delegate type	A null reference or a reference to an instance of that delegate type

1.4 Expressions

Expressions are constructed from *operands* and *operators*. The operators of an expression indicate which operations to apply to the operands. Examples of operators include +, -, *, /, and new. Examples of operands include literals, fields, local variables, and expressions.

When an expression contains multiple operators, the *precedence* of the operators controls the order in which the individual operators are evaluated. For example, the expression $x + y * z$ is evaluated as $x + (y * z)$ because the * operator has higher precedence than the + operator.

Most operators can be *overloaded*. Operator overloading permits user-defined operator implementations to be specified for operations where one or both of the operands are of a user-defined class or struct type.

The following table summarizes C#'s operators, listing the operator categories in order of precedence from highest to lowest. Operators in the same category have equal precedence.

Category	Expression	Description
Primary	`x.m`	Member access
	`x(...)`	Method and delegate invocation
	`x[...]`	Array and indexer access
	`x++`	Post-increment
	`x--`	Post-decrement
	`new T(...)`	Object and delegate creation
	`new T[...]`	Array creation
	`typeof(T)`	Obtain `System.Type` object for `T`
	`checked(x)`	Evaluate expression in checked context
	`unchecked(x)`	Evaluate expression in unchecked context
Unary	`+x`	Identity
	`-x`	Negation
	`!x`	Logical negation
	`~x`	Bitwise negation
	`++x`	Pre-increment
	`--x`	Pre-decrement
	`(T)x`	Explicitly convert `x` to type `T`
Multiplicative	`x * y`	Multiplication
	`x / y`	Division
	`x % y`	Remainder

Category	Expression	Description
Additive	`x + y`	Addition, string concatenation, delegate combination
	`x - y`	Subtraction, delegate removal
Shift	`x << y`	Shift left
	`x >> y`	Shift right
Relational and type testing	`x < y`	Less than
	`x > y`	Greater than
	`x <= y`	Less than or equal
	`x >= y`	Greater than or equal
	`x is T`	Return `true` if x is a T, `false` otherwise
	`x as T`	Return x typed as T; return `null` if x is not a T
Equality	`x == y`	Equal
	`x != y`	Not equal
Logical AND	`x & y`	Integer bitwise AND, boolean logical AND
Logical XOR	`x ^ y`	Integer bitwise XOR, boolean logical XOR
Logical OR	`x	y`	Integer bitwise OR, boolean logical OR
Conditional AND	`x && y`	Evaluates y only if x is `true`
Conditional OR	`x || y`	Evaluates y only if x is `false`
Conditional	`x ? y : z`	Evaluates y if x is `true`, z if x is `false`
Assignment	`x = y`	Assignment
	`x op= y`	Compound assignment; supported operators are `*= /= %= += -= <<= >>= &= ^= |=`

1.5 Statements

The actions of a program are expressed using *statements*. C# supports several different kinds of statements, a number of which are defined in terms of embedded statements.

A *block* permits multiple statements to be written in contexts where a single statement is allowed. A block consists of a list of statements written between the delimiters { and }.

Declaration statements are used to declare local variables and constants.

Expression statements are used to evaluate expressions. Expressions that can be used as statements include method invocations, object allocations using the new operator, assignments using = and the compound assignment operators, and increment and decrement operations using the ++ and -- operators.

Selection statements are used to select one of a number of possible statements for execution based on the value of some expression. In this group are the if and switch statements.

Iteration statements are used to repeatedly execute an embedded statement. In this group are the while, do, for, and foreach statements.

Jump statements are used to transfer control. In this group are the break, continue, goto, throw, and return statements.

The try-catch statement is used to catch exceptions that occur during execution of a block, and the try-finally statement is used to specify finalization code that is always executed, whether an exception occurred or not.

The checked and unchecked statements are used to control the overflow checking context for integral-type arithmetic operations and conversions.

The lock statement is used to obtain the mutual-exclusion lock for a given object, execute a statement, and then release the lock.

The using statement is used to obtain a resource, execute a statement, and then dispose of that resource.

The following table lists C#'s statements and provides an example for each.

Statement	Example
Local variable declaration	```static void Main() {` ` int a;` ` int b = 2, c = 3;` ` a = 1;` ` Console.WriteLine(a + b + c);` `}```

Statement	Example
Local constant declaration	```static void Main() {
const float pi = 3.1415927f;
const int r = 25;
Console.WriteLine(pi * r * r);
}```
Expression statement	```static void Main() {
int i;
i = 123;   // Expression statement
Console.WriteLine(i);   // Expression statement
i++;   // Expression statement
Console.WriteLine(i);   // Expression statement
}```
if statement	```static void Main(string[] args) {
if (args.Length == 0) {
Console.WriteLine("No arguments");
}
else {
Console.WriteLine("One or more arguments");
}
}```
switch statement	```static void Main(string[] args) {
int n = args.Length;
switch (n) {
case 0:
Console.WriteLine("No arguments");
break;
case 1:
Console.WriteLine("One argument");
break;
default:
Console.WriteLine("{0} arguments", n);
break;
}
}```
while statement	```static void Main(string[] args) {
int i = 0;
while (i < args.Length) {
Console.WriteLine(args[i]);
i++;
}
}```
do statement	```static void Main() {
string s;
do {
s = Console.ReadLine();
if (s != null) Console.WriteLine(s);
} while (s != null);
}```

continues

Statement	Example
| for statement | ```csharp
static void Main(string[] args) {
  for (int i = 0; i < args.Length; i++) {
    Console.WriteLine(args[i]);
  }
}
``` |
| foreach statement | ```csharp
static void Main(string[] args) {
  foreach (string s in args) {
    Console.WriteLine(s);
  }
}
``` |
| break statement | ```csharp
static void Main() {
  while (true) {
    string s = Console.ReadLine();
    if (s == null) break;
    Console.WriteLine(s);
  }
}
``` |
| continue statement | ```csharp
static void Main(string[] args) {
  for (int i = 0; i < args.Length; i++) {
    if (args[i].StartsWith("/")) continue;
    Console.WriteLine(args[i]);
  }
}
``` |
| goto statement | ```csharp
static void Main(string[] args) {
  int i = 0;
  goto check;
  loop:
  Console.WriteLine(args[i++]);
  check:
  if (i < args.Length) goto loop;
}
``` |
| return statement | ```csharp
static int Add(int a, int b) {
  return a + b;
}

static void Main() {
  Console.WriteLine(Add(1, 2));
  return;
}
``` |

Statement	Example
| throw and try statements | ```csharp
static double Divide(double x, double y) {
  if (y == 0) throw new DivideByZeroException();
  return x / y;
}
static void Main(string[] args) {
  try {
    if (args.Length != 2) {
      throw new Exception("Two numbers required");
    }
    double x = double.Parse(args[0]);
    double y = double.Parse(args[1]);
    Console.WriteLine(Divide(x, y));
  }
  catch (Exception e) {
    Console.WriteLine(e.Message);
  }
}
``` |
| checked and unchecked statements | ```csharp
static void Main() {
  int i = int.MaxValue;
  checked {
    Console.WriteLine(i + 1); // Exception
  }
  unchecked {
    Console.WriteLine(i + 1); // Overflow
  }
}
``` |
| lock statement | ```csharp
class Account
{
  decimal balance;

  public void Withdraw(decimal amount) {
    lock (this) {
      if (amount > balance) {
        throw new Exception("Insufficient funds");
      }
      balance -= amount;
    }
  }
}
``` |
| using statement | ```csharp
static void Main() {
  using (TextWriter w = File.CreateText("test.txt")) {
    w.WriteLine("Line one");
    w.WriteLine("Line two");
    w.WriteLine("Line three");
  }
}
``` |

1.6 Classes and Objects

Classes are the most fundamental of C#'s types. A class is a data structure that combines state (fields) and actions (methods and other function members) in a single unit. A class provides a definition for dynamically created *instances* of the class, also known as *objects*. Classes support *inheritance* and *polymorphism*, mechanisms whereby *derived classes* can extend and specialize *base classes*.

New classes are created using class declarations. A class declaration starts with a header that specifies the attributes and modifiers of the class, the name of the class, the base class (if any), and the interfaces implemented by the class. The header is followed by the class body, which consists of a list of member declarations written between the delimiters { and }.

The following is a declaration of a simple class named `Point`:

```
public class Point
{
    public int x, y;
    public Point(int x, int y) {
        this.x = x;
        this.y = y;
    }
}
```

Instances of classes are created using the `new` operator, which allocates memory for a new instance, invokes a constructor to initialize the instance, and returns a reference to the instance. The following statements create two `Point` objects and store references to those objects in two variables:

```
Point p1 = new Point(0, 0);
Point p2 = new Point(10, 20);
```

The memory occupied by an object is automatically reclaimed when the object is no longer in use. It is neither necessary nor possible to explicitly deallocate objects in C#.

1.6.1 Members

The members of a class are either *static members* or *instance members*. Static members belong to classes, and instance members belong to objects (instances of classes).

The following table provides an overview of the kinds of members a class can contain.

Member	Description
Constants	The constant values associated with the class
Fields	The variables of the class
Methods	The computations and actions that can be performed by the class
Properties	The actions associated with reading and writing named properties of the class
Indexers	The actions associated with indexing instances of the class in the same way as an array
Events	The notifications that can be generated by the class
Operators	The conversions and expression operators supported by the class
Constructors	The actions required to initialize instances of the class or the class itself
Destructors	The actions to perform before instances of the class are permanently discarded
Types	The nested types declared by the class

1.6.2 Accessibility

Each member of a class has an associated accessibility, which controls the regions of program text that are able to access the member. There are five possible forms of accessibility. These are summarized in the following table.

Accessibility	Meaning
`public`	Access not limited
`protected`	Access limited to this class and classes derived from this class
`internal`	Access limited to this program
`protected internal`	Access limited to this program and classes derived from this class
`private`	Access limited to this class

1.6.3 **Base Classes**

A class declaration may specify a base class by following the class name with a colon and the name of the base class. Omitting a base class specification is the same as deriving from type object. In the following example, the base class of Point3D is Point, and the base class of Point is object:

```
public class Point
{
    public int x, y;
    public Point(int x, int y) {
        this.x = x;
        this.y = y;
    }
}
public class Point3D: Point
{
    public int z;
    public Point3D(int x, int y, int z): Point(x, y) {
        this.z = z;
    }
}
```

A class inherits the members of its base class. Inheritance means that a class implicitly contains all members of its base class, except for the constructors of the base class. A derived class can add new members to those it inherits, but it cannot remove the definition of an inherited member. In the previous example, Point3D inherits the x and y fields from Point, and every Point3D instance contains three fields, x, y, and z.

An implicit conversion exists from a class type to any of its base class types. Therefore, a variable of a class type can reference an instance of that class or an instance of any derived class. For example, given the previous class declarations, a variable of type Point can reference either a Point or a Point3D:

```
Point a = new Point(10, 20);
Point b = new Point3D(10, 20, 30);
```

1.6.4 **Fields**

A field is a variable that is associated with a class or with an instance of a class.

A field declared with the static modifier defines a *static field*. A static field identifies exactly one storage location. No matter how many instances of a class are created, there is only one copy ever of a static field.

A field declared without the static modifier defines an *instance field*. Every instance of a class contains a separate copy of all the instance fields of that class.

In the following example, each instance of the `Color` class has a separate copy of the r, g, and b instance fields, but there is only one copy of the `Black`, `White`, `Red`, `Green`, and `Blue` static fields:

```
public class Color
{
    public static readonly Color Black = new Color(0, 0, 0);
    public static readonly Color White = new Color(255, 255, 255);
    public static readonly Color Red = new Color(255, 0, 0);
    public static readonly Color Green = new Color(0, 255, 0);
    public static readonly Color Blue = new Color(0, 0, 255);

    private byte r, g, b;

    public Color(byte r, byte g, byte b) {
        this.r = r;
        this.g = g;
        this.b = b;
    }
}
```

As shown in the previous example, *read-only fields* may be declared with a `readonly` modifier. Assignment to a `readonly` field can only occur as part of the field's declaration or in an instance constructor or static constructor in the same class.

1.6.5 Methods

A *method* is a member that implements a computation or action that can be performed by an object or class. *Static methods* are accessed through the class. *Instance methods* are accessed through instances of the class.

Methods have a (possibly empty) list of *parameters*, which represent values or variable references passed to the method, and a *return type*, which specifies the type of the value computed and returned by the method. A method's return type is `void` if it does not return a value.

The *signature* of a method must be unique in the class in which the method is declared. The signature of a method consists of the name of the method and the number, modifiers, and types of its parameters. The signature of a method does not include the return type.

1.6.5.1 *Parameters*

Parameters are used to pass values or variable references to methods. The parameters of a method get their actual values from the *arguments* that are specified when the method is invoked. There are four kinds of parameters: value parameters, reference parameters, output parameters, and parameter arrays.

A *value parameter* is used for input parameter passing. A value parameter corresponds to a local variable that gets its initial value from the argument that was passed for the parameter. Modifications to a value parameter do not affect the argument that was passed for the parameter.

A *reference parameter* is used for both input and output parameter passing. The argument passed for a reference parameter must be a variable, and during execution of the method, the reference parameter represents the same storage location as the argument variable. A reference parameter is declared with the `ref` modifier. The following example shows the use of `ref` parameters.

```
using System;

class Test
{
    static void Swap(ref int x, ref int y) {
        int temp = x;
        x = y;
        y = temp;
    }

    static void Main() {
        int i = 1, j = 2;
        Swap(ref i, ref j);
        Console.WriteLine("{0} {1}", i, j);        // Outputs "2 1"
    }
}
```

An *output parameter* is used for output parameter passing. An output parameter is similar to a reference parameter except that the initial value of the caller-provided argument is unimportant. An output parameter is declared with the `out` modifier. The following example shows the use of `out` parameters.

```
using System;

class Test
{
    static void Divide(int x, int y, out int result, out int remainder) {
        result = x / y;
        remainder = x % y;
    }

    static void Main() {
        int res, rem;
        Divide(10, 3, out res, out rem);
        Console.WriteLine("{0} {1}", res, rem);   // Outputs "3 1"
    }
}
```

A *parameter array* permits a variable number of arguments to be passed to a method. A parameter array is declared with the `params` modifier. Only the last parameter of a method can be a parameter array, and the type of a parameter array must be a single-dimensional array type. The `Write` and `WriteLine` methods of the `System.Console` class are good examples of parameter array usage. They are declared as follows.

```
public class Console
{
    public static void Write(string fmt, params object[] args) {...}

    public static void WriteLine(string fmt, params object[] args) {...}

    ...
}
```

Within a method that uses a parameter array, the parameter array behaves exactly like a regular parameter of an array type. However, in an invocation of a method with a parameter array, it is possible to pass either a single argument of the parameter array type or any number of arguments of the element type of the parameter array. In the latter case, an array instance is automatically created and initialized with the given arguments. This example

```
Console.WriteLine("x={0} y={1} z={2}", x, y, z);
```

is equivalent to writing the following.

```
object[] args = new object[3];
args[0] = x;
args[1] = y;
args[2] = z;
Console.WriteLine("x={0} y={1} z={2}", args);
```

1.6.5.2 *Method Body and Local Variables*
A method's body specifies the statements to execute when the method is invoked.

A method body can declare variables that are specific to the invocation of the method. Such variables are called *local variables*. A local variable declaration specifies a type name, a variable name, and possibly an initial value. The following example declares a local variable i with an initial value of zero and a local variable j with no initial value.

```
using System;

class Squares
{
    static void Main() {
        int i = 0;
        int j;
        while (i < 10) {
            j = i * i;
            Console.WriteLine("{0} x {0} = {1}", i, j);
            i = i + 1;
        }
    }
}
```

C# requires a local variable to be *definitely assigned* before its value can be obtained. For example, if the declaration of the previous i did not include an initial value, the compiler would report an error for the subsequent usages of i because i would not be definitely assigned at those points in the program.

A method can use return statements to return control to its caller. In a method returning void, return statements cannot specify an expression. In a method returning non-void, return statements must include an expression that computes the return value.

1.6.5.3 *Static and Instance Methods*
A method declared with a static modifier is a *static method*. A static method does not operate on a specific instance and can only access static members.

A method declared without a static modifier is an *instance method*. An instance method operates on a specific instance and can access both static and instance members. The instance on which an instance method was invoked can be explicitly accessed as this. It is an error to refer to this in a static method.

The following Entity class has both static and instance members.

```
class Entity
{
    static int nextSerialNo;

    int serialNo;

    public Entity() {
        serialNo = nextSerialNo++;
    }

    public int GetSerialNo() {
        return serialNo;
    }

    public static int GetNextSerialNo() {
        return nextSerialNo;
    }

    public static void SetNextSerialNo(int value) {
        nextSerialNo = value;
    }
}
```

Each Entity instance contains a serial number (and presumably some other information that is not shown here). The Entity constructor (which is like an instance method) initializes the new instance with the next available serial number. Because the constructor is an instance member, it is permitted to access both the serialNo instance field and the nextSerialNo static field.

The `GetNextSerialNo` and `SetNextSerialNo` static methods can access the `nextSerialNo` static field, but it would be an error for them to access the `serialNo` instance field.

The following example shows the use of the `Entity` class.

```
using System;

class Test
{
    static void Main() {
        Entity.SetNextSerialNo(1000);

        Entity e1 = new Entity();
        Entity e2 = new Entity();

        Console.WriteLine(e1.GetSerialNo());        // Outputs "1000"
        Console.WriteLine(e2.GetSerialNo());        // Outputs "1001"
        Console.WriteLine(Entity.GetNextSerialNo()); // Outputs "1002"
    }
}
```

Note that the `SetNextSerialNo` and `GetNextSerialNo` static methods are invoked on the class whereas the `GetSerialNo` instance method is invoked on instances of the class.

1.6.5.4 *Virtual, Override, and Abstract Methods*
When an instance method declaration includes a `virtual` modifier, the method is said to be a *virtual method*. When no `virtual` modifier is present, the method is said to be a *nonvirtual method*.

When a virtual method is invoked, the *runtime type* of the instance for which that invocation takes place determines the actual method implementation to invoke. In a nonvirtual method invocation, the *compile-time type* of the instance is the determining factor.

A virtual method can be *overridden* in a derived class. When an instance method declaration includes an `override` modifier, the method overrides an inherited virtual method with the same signature. Whereas a virtual method declaration *introduces* a new method, an override method declaration *specializes* an existing inherited virtual method by providing a new implementation of that method.

An *abstract* method is a virtual method with no implementation. An abstract method is declared with the `abstract` modifier and is permitted only in a class that is also declared `abstract`. An abstract method must be overridden in every nonabstract derived class.

The following example declares an abstract class, `Expression`, which represents an expression tree node, and three derived classes, `Constant`, `VariableReference`, and

25

Operation, which implement expression tree nodes for constants, variable references, and arithmetic operations.

```csharp
using System;
using System.Collections;

public abstract class Expression
{
    public abstract double Evaluate(Hashtable vars);
}

public class Constant: Expression
{
    double value;

    public Constant(double value) {
        this.value = value;
    }

    public override double Evaluate(Hashtable vars) {
        return value;
    }
}

public class VariableReference: Expression
{
    string name;

    public VariableReference(string name) {
        this.name = name;
    }

    public override double Evaluate(Hashtable vars) {
        object value = vars[name];
        if (value == null) {
            throw new Exception("Unknown variable: " + name);
        }
        return Convert.ToDouble(value);
    }
}

public class Operation: Expression
{
    Expression left;
    char op;
    Expression right;

    public Operation(Expression left, char op, Expression right) {
        this.left = left;
        this.op = op;
        this.right = right;
    }
```

```
    public override double Evaluate(Hashtable vars) {
        double x = left.Evaluate(vars);
        double y = right.Evaluate(vars);
        switch (op) {
            case '+': return x + y;
            case '-': return x - y;
            case '*': return x * y;
            case '/': return x / y;
        }
        throw new Exception("Unknown operator");
    }
}
```

The previous four classes can be used to model arithmetic expressions. For example, using instances of these classes, the expression x + 3 can be represented as follows.

```
Expression e = new Operation(
    new VariableReference("x"),
    '+',
    new Constant(3));
```

The `Evaluate` method of an `Expression` instance is invoked to evaluate the given expression and produce a `double` value. The method takes as an argument a `Hashtable` that contains variable names (as keys of the entries) and values (as values of the entries). The `Evaluate` method is a virtual abstract method, meaning that nonabstract derived classes must override it to provide an actual implementation.

A `Constant`'s implementation of `Evaluate` simply returns the stored constant. A `VariableReference`'s implementation looks up the variable name in the hashtable and returns the resulting value. An `Operation`'s implementation first evaluates the left and right operands (by recursively invoking their `Evaluate` methods) and then performs the given arithmetic operation.

The following program uses the `Expression` classes to evaluate the expression x * (y + 2) for different values of x and y.

```
using System;
using System.Collections;

class Test
{
    static void Main() {

        Expression e = new Operation(
            new VariableReference("x"),
            '*',
            new Operation(
                new VariableReference("y"),
                '+',
                new Constant(2)
            )
        );
```

```
            Hashtable vars = new Hashtable();

            vars["x"] = 3;
            vars["y"] = 5;
            Console.WriteLine(e.Evaluate(vars));  // Outputs "21"

            vars["x"] = 1.5;
            vars["y"] = 9;
            Console.WriteLine(e.Evaluate(vars));  // Outputs "16.5"
        }
    }
```

1.6.5.5 *Method Overloading*

Method *overloading* permits multiple methods in the same class to have the same name as long as they have unique signatures. When compiling an invocation of an overloaded method, the compiler uses *overload resolution* to determine the specific method to invoke. Overload resolution finds the one method that best matches the arguments or reports an error if no single best match can be found. The following example shows overload resolution in effect. The comment for each invocation in the Main method shows which method is actually invoked.

```
class Test
{
    static void F() {
        Console.WriteLine("F()");
    }

    static void F(object x) {
        Console.WriteLine("F(object)");
    }

    static void F(int x) {
        Console.WriteLine("F(int)");
    }

    static void F(double x) {
        Console.WriteLine("F(double)");
    }

    static void F(double x, double y) {
        Console.WriteLine("F(double, double)");
    }

    static void Main() {
        F();                    // Invokes F()
        F(1);                   // Invokes F(int)
        F(1.0);                 // Invokes F(double)
        F("abc");               // Invokes F(object)
        F((double)1);           // Invokes F(double)
        F((object)1);           // Invokes F(object)
        F(1, 1);                // Invokes F(double, double)
    }
}
```

As shown by the example, a particular method can always be selected by explicitly casting the arguments to the exact parameter types.

1.6.6 Other Function Members

Members that contain executable code are collectively known as the *function members* of a class. The preceding section describes methods, which are the primary kind of function members. This section describes the other kinds of function members supported by C#: constructors, properties, indexers, events, operators, and destructors.

The following table shows a class called List, which implements a growable list of objects. The class contains several examples of the most common kinds of function members.

`public class List` `{`	
`    const int defaultCapacity = 4;`	Constant
`    object[] items;` `    int count;`	Fields

`    public List(): this(defaultCapacity) {}`
 	
`    public List(int capacity) {`
`        items = new object[capacity];`
`    }`
	Constructors

`    public int Count {`
`        get { return count; }`
`    }`
`    public string Capacity {`
`        get {`
`            return items.Length;`
`        }`
`        set {`
`            if (value < count) value = count;`
`            if (value != items.Length) {`
`                object[] newItems = new object[value];`
`                Array.Copy(items, 0, newItems, 0, count);`
`                items = newItems;`
`            }`
`        }`
`    }`
	Properties

`    public object this[int index] {`
`        get {`
`            return items[index];`
`        }`
`        set {`
`            items[index] = value;`
`            OnListChange();`
`        }`
`    }`
	Indexer

continues

```public void Add(object item) { if (count == Capacity) Capacity = count * 2; items[count] = item; count++; OnChanged(); } protected virtual void OnChanged() { if (Changed != null) Changed(this, EventArgs.Empty); } public override bool Equals(object other) { return Equals(this, other as List); } static bool Equals(List a, List b) { if (a == null) return b == null; if (b == null || a.count != b.count) return false; for (int i = 0; i < a.count; i++) { if (!object.Equals(a.items[i], b.items[i])) { return false; } } }```	Methods
```public event EventHandler Changed;```	Event
```public static bool operator ==(List a, List b) { return Equals(a, b); } public static bool operator !=(List a, List b) { return !Equals(a, b); }```	Operators
```}```	

1.6.6.1 *Constructors*

C# supports both instance and static constructors. An ***instance constructor*** is a member that implements the actions required to initialize an instance of a class. A ***static constructor*** is a member that implements the actions required to initialize a class itself when it is first loaded.

A constructor is declared like a method with no return type and the same name as the containing class. If a constructor declaration includes a static modifier, it declares a static constructor. Otherwise, it declares an instance constructor.

Instance constructors can be overloaded. For example, the List class declares two instance constructors, one with no parameters and one that takes an int parameter.

Instance constructors are invoked using the `new` operator. The following statements allocate two `List` instances using each of the constructors of the `List` class.

```
List list1 = new List();
List list2 = new List(10);
```

Unlike other members, instance constructors are not inherited, and a class has no instance constructors other than those actually declared in the class. If no instance constructor is supplied for a class, then an empty one with no parameters is automatically provided.

1.6.6.2 *Properties*
Properties are a natural extension of fields. Both are named members with associated types, and the syntax for accessing fields and properties is the same. However, unlike fields, properties do not denote storage locations. Instead, properties have *accessors* that specify the statements to be executed when their values are read or written.

A property is declared like a field, except that the declaration ends with a `get` accessor and/or a `set` accessor written between the delimiters { and } instead of ending in a semicolon. A property that has both a `get` accessor and a `set` accessor is a *read-write property*, a property that has only a `get` accessor is a *read-only property*, and a property that has only a `set` accessor is a *write-only property*.

A `get` accessor corresponds to a parameterless method with a return value of the property type. Except as the target of an assignment, when a property is referenced in an expression, the `get` accessor of the property is invoked to compute the value of the property.

A `set` accessor corresponds to a method with a single parameter named `value` and no return type. When a property is referenced as the target of an assignment or as the operand of ++ or --, the `set` accessor is invoked with an argument that provides the new value.

The `List` class declares two properties, `Count` and `Capacity`, which are read-only and read-write, respectively. The following is an example of use of these properties.

```
List names = new List();
names.Capacity = 100;        // Invokes set accessor
int i = names.Count;         // Invokes get accessor
int j = names.Capacity;      // Invokes get accessor
```

Similar to fields and methods, C# supports both instance properties and static properties. Static properties are declared with the `static` modifier, and instance properties are declared without it.

The accessor(s) of a property can be virtual. When a property declaration includes a `virtual`, `abstract`, or `override` modifier, it applies to the accessor(s) of the property.

1.6.6.3 *Indexers*

An *indexer* is a member that enables objects to be indexed in the same way as an array. An indexer is declared like a property except that the name of the member is this followed by a parameter list written between the delimiters [and]. The parameters are available in the accessor(s) of the indexer. Similar to properties, indexers can be read-write, read-only, and write-only, and the accessor(s) of an indexer can be virtual.

The List class declares a single read-write indexer that takes an int parameter. The indexer makes it possible to index List instances with int values. For example

```
List names = new List();
names.Add("Liz");
names.Add("Martha");
names.Add("Beth");
for (int i = 0; i < names.Count; i++) {
    string s = (string)names[i];
    names[i] = s.ToUpper();
}
```

Indexers can be overloaded, meaning that a class can declare multiple indexers as long as the number or types of their parameters differ.

1.6.6.4 *Events*

An *event* is a member that enables a class or object to provide notifications. An event is declared like a field except that the declaration includes an event keyword and the type must be a delegate type.

Within a class that declares an event member, the event behaves just like a field of a delegate type (provided the event is not abstract and does not declare accessors). The field stores a reference to a delegate that represents the event handlers that have been added to the event. If no event handlers are present, the field is null.

The List class declares a single event member called Changed, which indicates that a new item has been added to the list. The Changed event is raised by the OnChanged virtual method, which first checks whether the event is null (meaning that no handlers are present). The notion of raising an event is precisely equivalent to invoking the delegate represented by the event—thus, there are no special language constructs for raising events.

Clients react to events through *event handlers*. Event handlers are attached using the += operator and removed using the -= operator. The following example attaches an event handler to the Changed event of a List.

```
using System;

class Test
{
    static int changeCount;
```

```
        static void ListChanged(object sender, EventArgs e) {
            changeCount++;
        }
        static void Main() {
            List names = new List();
            names.Changed += new EventHandler(ListChanged);
            names.Add("Liz");
            names.Add("Martha");
            names.Add("Beth");
            Console.WriteLine(changeCount);// Outputs "3"
        }
    }
```

For advanced scenarios where control of the underlying storage of an event is desired, an
event declaration can explicitly provide add and remove accessors, which are somewhat
similar to the set accessor of a property.

1.6.6.5 *Operators*

An *operator* is a member that defines the meaning of applying a particular expression
operator to instances of a class. Three kinds of operators can be defined: unary operators,
binary operators, and conversion operators. All operators must be declared as public and
static.

The List class declares two operators, operator == and operator !=, and thus gives
new meaning to expressions that apply those operators to List instances. Specifically, the
operators define equality of two List instances as comparing each of the contained objects
using their Equals methods. The following example uses the == operator to compare two
List instances.

```
using System;
class Test
{
    static void Main() {
        List a = new List();
        a.Add(1);
        a.Add(2);
        List b = new List();
        b.Add(1);
        b.Add(2);
        Console.WriteLine(a == b);    // Outputs "True"
        b.Add(3);
        Console.WriteLine(a == b);    // Outputs "False"
    }
}
```

The first Console.WriteLine outputs True because the two lists contain the same number of objects with the same values. Had List not defined operator ==, the first

`Console.WriteLine` would have output `False` because a and b reference different `List` instances.

1.6.6.6 *Destructors*

A *destructor* is a member that implements the actions required to destruct an instance of a class. Destructors cannot have parameters, they cannot have accessibility modifiers, and they cannot be invoked explicitly. The destructor for an instance is invoked automatically during garbage collection.

The garbage collector is allowed wide latitude in deciding when to collect objects and run destructors. Specifically, the timing of destructor invocations is not deterministic, and destructors may be executed on any thread. For these and other reasons, classes should implement destructors only when no other solutions are feasible.

1.7 Structs

Like classes, *structs* are data structures that can contain data members and function members, but unlike classes, structs are value types and do not require heap allocation. A variable of a struct type directly stores the data of the struct, whereas a variable of a class type stores a reference to a dynamically allocated object. Struct types do not support user-specified inheritance, and all struct types implicitly inherit from type `object`.

Structs are particularly useful for small data structures that have value semantics. Complex numbers, points in a coordinate system, or key-value pairs in a dictionary are all good examples of structs. The use of structs rather than classes for small data structures can make a large difference in the number of memory allocations an application performs. For example, the following program creates and initializes an array of 100 points. With `Point` implemented as a class, 101 separate objects are instantiated—one for the array and one each for the 100 elements.

```
class Point
{
    public int x, y;

    public Point(int x, int y) {
        this.x = x;
        this.y = y;
    }
}

class Test
{
    static void Main() {
        Point[] points = new Point[100];
        for (int i = 0; i < 100; i++) points[i] = new Point(i, i);
    }
}
```

An alternative is to make `Point` a struct.

```
struct Point
{
    public int x, y;
    public Point(int x, int y) {
        this.x = x;
        this.y = y;
    }
}
```

Now, only one object is instantiated—the one for the array—and the `Point` instances are stored in-line in the array.

Struct constructors are invoked with the `new` operator, but that does not imply that memory is being allocated. Instead of dynamically allocating an object and returning a reference to it, a struct constructor simply returns the struct value itself (typically in a temporary location on the stack), and this value is then copied as necessary.

With classes, it is possible for two variables to reference the same object and thus possible for operations on one variable to affect the object referenced by the other variable. With structs, the variables each have their own copy of the data, and it is not possible for operations on one to affect the other. For example, the output produced by the following code fragment depends on whether `Point` is a class or a struct.

```
Point a = new Point(10, 10);
Point b = a;
a.x = 20;
Console.WriteLine(b.x);
```

If `Point` is a class, the output is `20` because a and b reference the same object. If `Point` is a struct, the output is `10` because the assignment of a to b creates a copy of the value, and this copy is unaffected by the subsequent assignment to a.x.

The previous example highlights two of the limitations of structs. First, copying an entire struct is typically less efficient than copying an object reference, so assignment and value parameter passing can be more expensive with structs than with reference types. Second, except for `ref` and `out` parameters, it is not possible to create references to structs, which rules out their usage in a number of situations.

1.8 Arrays

An *array* is a data structure that contains a number of variables that are accessed through computed indices. The variables contained in an array, also called the *elements* of the array, are all of the same type, and this type is called the element type of the array.

Array types are reference types, and the declaration of an array variable simply sets aside space for a reference to an array instance. Actual array instances are created dynamically at runtime using the new operator. The new operation specifies the *length* of the new array instance, which is then fixed for the lifetime of the instance. The indices of the elements of an array range from 0 to Length - 1. The new operator automatically initializes the elements of an array to their default value, which, for example, is zero for all numeric types and null for all reference types.

The following example creates an array of int elements, initializes the array, and prints out the contents of the array.

```
using System;

class Test
{
    static void Main() {
        int[] a = new int[10];
        for (int i = 0; i < a.Length; i++) a[i] = i * i;
        for (int i = 0; i < a.Length; i++) {
            Console.WriteLine("a[{0}] = {1}", i, a[i]);
        }
    }
}
```

This example creates and operates on a *single-dimensional array*. C# also supports *multi-dimensional arrays*. The number of dimensions of an array type, also known as the *rank* of the array type, is one plus the number of commas written between the square brackets of the array type. The following example allocates a one-dimensional, a two-dimensional, and a three-dimensional array.

```
int[] a1 = new int[10];
int[,] a2 = new int[10, 5];
int[,,] a3 = new int[10, 5, 2];
```

The a1 array contains 10 elements, the a2 array contains 50 (10×5) elements, and the a3 array contains 100 ($10 \times 5 \times 2$) elements.

The element type of an array can be any type, including an array type. An array with elements of an array type is sometimes called a *jagged array* because the lengths of the element arrays do not all have to be the same. The following example allocates an array of arrays of int:

```
int[][] a = new int[3][];
a[0] = new int[10];
a[1] = new int[5];
a[2] = new int[20];
```

The first line creates an array with three elements, each of type int[] and each with an initial value of null. The subsequent lines then initialize the three elements with references to individual array instances of varying lengths.

The new operator permits the initial values of the array elements to be specified using an *array initializer,* which is a list of expressions written between the delimiters { and }. The following example allocates and initializes an int[] with three elements.

```
int[] a = new int[] {1, 2, 3};
```

Note that the length of the array is inferred from the number of expressions between { and }. Local variable and field declarations can be shortened further such that the array type does not have to be restated.

```
int[] a = {1, 2, 3};
```

Both of the previous examples are equivalent to the following:

```
int[] a = new int[3];
a[0] = 1;
a[1] = 2;
a[2] = 3;
```

1.9 Interfaces

An *interface* defines a contract that can be implemented by classes and structs. An interface can contain methods, properties, events, and indexers. An interfaces does not provide implementations of the members it defines—it merely specifies the members that must be supplied by classes or structs that implement the interface.

Interfaces may employ *multiple inheritance.* In the following example, the interface IComboBox inherits from both ITextBox and IListBox.

```
interface IControl
{
    void Paint();
}
interface ITextBox: IControl
{
    void SetText(string text);
}
interface IListBox: IControl
{
    void SetItems(string[] items);
}
interface IComboBox: ITextBox, IListBox {}
```

Classes and structs can implement multiple interfaces. In the following example, the class EditBox implements both IControl and IDataBound.

```
interface IDataBound
{
    void Bind(Binder b);
}

public class EditBox: IControl, IDataBound
{
    public void Paint() {...}
    public void Bind(Binder b) {...}
}
```

When a class or struct implements a particular interface, instances of that class or struct can be implicitly converted to that interface type. For example

```
EditBox editBox = new EditBox();
IControl control = editBox;
IDataBound dataBound = editBox;
```

In cases where an instance is not statically known to implement a particular interface, dynamic type casts can be used. For example, the following statements use dynamic type casts to obtain an object's IControl and IDataBound interface implementations. Because the actual type of the object is EditBox, the casts succeed.

```
object obj = new EditBox();
IControl control = (IControl)obj;
IDataBound dataBound = (IDataBound)obj;
```

In the previous EditBox class, the Paint method from the IControl interface and the Bind method from the IDataBound interface are implemented using public members. C# also supports *explicit interface member implementations*, using which the class or struct can avoid making the members public. An explicit interface member implementation is written using the fully qualified interface member name. For example, the EditBox class could implement the IControl.Paint and IDataBound.Bind methods using explicit interface member implementations as follows.

```
public class EditBox: IControl, IDataBound
{
    void IControl.Paint() {...}
    void IDataBound.Bind(Binder b) {...}
}
```

Explicit interface members can only be accessed via the interface type. For example, the implementation of IControl.Paint provided by the previous EditBox class can only be invoked by first converting the EditBox reference to the IControl interface type.

```
EditBox editBox = new EditBox();
editBox.Paint();                    // Error, no such method
IControl control = editBox;
control.Paint();                    // Ok
```

1.10 Enums

An *enum type* is a distinct value type with a set of named constants. The following example declares and uses an enum type named `Color` with three constant values, `Red`, `Green`, and `Blue`.

```
using System;

enum Color
{
    Red,
    Green,
    Blue
}

class Test
{
    static void PrintColor(Color color) {
        switch (color) {
            case Color.Red:
                Console.WriteLine("Red");
                break;
            case Color.Green:
                Console.WriteLine("Green");
                break;
            case Color.Blue:
                Console.WriteLine("Blue");
                break;
            default:
                Console.WriteLine("Unknown color");
                break;
        }
    }

    static void Main() {
        Color c = Color.Red;
        PrintColor(c);
        PrintColor(Color.Blue);
    }
}
```

Each enum type has a corresponding integral type called the *underlying type* of the enum type. An enum type that does not explicitly declare an underlying type has an underlying type of `int`. An enum type's storage format and range of possible values are determined by its underlying type. The set of values that an enum type can take on is not limited by its enum members. In particular, any value of the underlying type of an enum can be cast to the enum type and is a distinct valid value of that enum type.

The following example declares an enum type named `Alignment` with an underlying type of `sbyte`.

```
enum Alignment: sbyte
{
    Left = -1,
    Center = 0,
    Right = 1
}
```

As shown by the previous example, an enum member declaration can include a constant expression that specifies the value of the member. The constant value for each enum member must be in the range of the underlying type of the enum. When an enum member declaration does not explicitly specify a value, the member is given the value zero (if it is the first member in the enum type) or the value of the textually preceding enum member plus one.

Enum values can be converted to integral values and vice versa using type casts. For example

```
int i = (int)Color.Blue;      // int i = 2;
Color c = (Color)2;           // Color c = Color.Blue;
```

The default value of any enum type is the integral value zero converted to the enum type. In cases where variables are automatically initialized to a default value, this is the value given to variables of enum types. In order for the default value of an enum type to be easily available, the literal 0 implicitly converts to any enum type. Thus, the following is permitted.

```
Color c = 0;
```

1.11 Delegates

A *delegate type* represents references to methods with a particular parameter list and return type. Delegates make it possible to treat methods as entities that can be assigned to variables and passed as parameters. Delegates are similar to the concept of function pointers found in some other languages, but unlike function pointers, delegates are object-oriented and type-safe.

The following example declares and uses a delegate type named `Function`.

```
using System;

delegate double Function(double x);
```

```
class Multiplier
{
    double factor;

    public Multiplier(double factor) {
        this.factor = factor;
    }

    public double Multiply(double x) {
        return x * factor;
    }
}

class Test
{
    static double Square(double x) {
        return x * x;
    }

    static double[] Apply(double[] a, Function f) {
        double[] result = new double[a.Length];
        for (int i = 0; i < a.Length; i++) result[i] = f(a[i]);
        return result;
    }

    static void Main() {
        double[] a = {0.0, 0.5, 1.0};

        double[] squares = Apply(a, new Function(Square));

        double[] sines = Apply(a, new Function(Math.Sin));

        Multiplier m = new Multiplier(2.0);
        double[] doubles =  Apply(a, new Function(m.Multiply));
    }
}
```

An instance of the `Function` delegate type can reference any method that takes a `double` argument and returns a `double` value. The `Apply` method applies a given `Function` to the elements of a `double[]`, returning a `double[]` with the results. In the `Main` method, `Apply` is used to apply three different functions to a `double[]`.

A delegate can reference either a static method (such as `Square` or `Math.Sin` in the previous example) or an instance method (such as `m.Multiply` in the previous example). A delegate that references an instance method also references a particular object, and when the instance method is invoked through the delegate, that object becomes `this` in the invocation.

An interesting and useful property of a delegate is that it does not know or care about the class of the method it references; all that matters is that the referenced method has the same parameters and return type as the delegate.

1.12 **Attributes**

Types, members, and other entities in a C# program support modifiers that control certain aspects of their behavior. For example, the accessibility of a method is controlled using the public, protected, internal, and private modifiers. C# generalizes this capability such that user-defined types of declarative information can be attached to program entities and retrieved at runtime. Programs specify this additional declarative information by defining and using *attributes*.

The following example declares a HelpAttribute attribute that can be placed on program entities to provide links to their associated documentation.

```
using System;

public class HelpAttribute: Attribute
{
    string url;
    string topic;

    public HelpAttribute(string url) {
        this.url = url;
    }

    public string Url {
        get { return url; }
    }

    public string Topic {
        get { return topic; }
        set { topic = value; }
    }
}
```

All attribute classes derive from the System.Attribute base class provided by the .NET Framework. If an attribute's name ends in Attribute, that part of the name can be omitted when the attribute is referenced. For example, the HelpAttribute attribute can be used as follows.

```
[Help("http://msdn.microsoft.com/.../MyClass.htm")]
public class Widget
{
    [Help("http://msdn.microsoft.com/.../MyClass.htm", Topic = "Display")]
    public void Display(string text) {}
}
```

This example attaches a HelpAttribute to the Widget class and another HelpAttribute to the Display method in the class. The public constructors of an attribute class control the information that must be provided when the attribute is attached to a program entity. Additional information can be provided by referencing public read-write properties of the attribute class (such as the reference to the Topic property previously).

The following example shows how attribute information for a given program entity can be retrieved at runtime using reflection.

```
using System;
using System.Reflection;

class Test
{
    static void ShowHelp(MemberInfo member) {
        HelpAttribute a = Attribute.GetCustomAttribute(member,
            typeof(HelpAttribute)) as HelpAttribute;
        if (a == null) {
            Console.WriteLine("No help for {0}", member);
        }
        else {
            Console.WriteLine("Help for {0}:", member);
            Console.WriteLine("  Url={0}, Topic={1}", a.Url, a.Topic);
        }
    }

    static void Main() {
        ShowHelp(typeof(Widget));
        ShowHelp(typeof(Widget).GetMethod("Display"));
    }
}
```

When a particular attribute is requested through reflection, the constructor for the attribute class is invoked with the information provided in the program source, and the resulting attribute instance is returned. If additional information was provided through properties, those properties are set to the given values before the attribute instance is returned.

2. Lexical Structure

2.1 Programs

A C# *program* consists of one or more *source files*, known formally as *compilation units* (§9.1). A source file is an ordered sequence of Unicode characters. Source files typically have a one-to-one correspondence with files in a file system, but this correspondence is not required. For maximal portability, it is recommended that files in a file system be encoded with the UTF-8 encoding.

Conceptually speaking, a program is compiled using three steps:

1. Transformation, which converts a file from a particular character repertoire and encoding scheme into a sequence of Unicode characters

2. Lexical analysis, which translates a stream of Unicode input characters into a stream of tokens

3. Syntactic analysis, which translates the stream of tokens into executable code

2.2 Grammars

This specification presents the syntax of the C# programming language using two grammars. The *lexical grammar* (§2.2.2) defines how Unicode characters are combined to form line terminators, white space, comments, tokens, and preprocessing directives. The *syntactic grammar* (§2.2.3) defines how the tokens resulting from the lexical grammar are combined to form C# programs.

2.2.1 Grammar Notation

The lexical and syntactic grammars are presented using *grammar productions*. Each grammar production defines a nonterminal symbol and the possible expansions of that nonterminal symbol into sequences of nonterminal or terminal symbols. In grammar productions, *nonterminal* symbols are shown in italic type, and `terminal` symbols are shown in a fixed-width font.

The first line of a grammar production is the name of the nonterminal symbol being defined, followed by a colon. Each successive indented line contains a possible expansion of the nonterminal given as a sequence of nonterminal or terminal symbols. For example, the following production

> *while-statement:*
> > while (*boolean-expression*) *embedded-statement*

defines a *while-statement* to consist of the token while, followed by the token (, followed by a *boolean-expression*, followed by the token), followed by an *embedded-statement*.

When there is more than one possible expansion of a nonterminal symbol, the alternatives appear on separate lines. For example, the following production

> *statement-list:*
> > *statement*
> > *statement-list   statement*

defines a *statement-list* to either consist of a *statement* or consist of a *statement-list* followed by a *statement*. In other words, the definition is recursive and specifies that a statement list consists of one or more statements.

A subscripted suffix $_{opt}$ indicates an optional symbol. The following production

> *block:*
> > { *statement-list$_{opt}$* }

is shorthand for

> *block:*
> > { }
> > { *statement-list* }

and defines a *block* to consist of an optional *statement-list* enclosed in { and } tokens.

Alternatives usually appear on separate lines; however, in cases where there are many alternatives, the phrase "one of" may precede a list of expansions given on a single line. This is simply shorthand for listing each of the alternatives on a separate line. For example, the following production

> *real-type-suffix:* one of
> > F   f   D   d   M   m

is shorthand for the following

real-type-suffix:
>   F
>   f
>   D
>   d
>   M
>   m

2.2.2 Lexical Grammar

The lexical grammar of C# is presented in §2.3, §2.4, and §2.5. The terminal symbols of the lexical grammar are the characters of the Unicode character set, and the lexical grammar specifies how characters are combined to form tokens (§2.4), white space (§2.3.2), comments (§2.3.3), and preprocessing directives (§2.5).

Every source file in a C# program must conform to the *input* production of the lexical grammar (§2.3).

2.2.3 Syntactic Grammar

The following chapters and appendices present the syntactic grammar of C#. The terminal symbols of the syntactic grammar are the tokens defined by the lexical grammar, and the syntactic grammar specifies how tokens are combined to form C# programs.

Every source file in a C# program must conform to the *compilation-unit* production of the syntactic grammar (§9.1).

2.3 Lexical Analysis

The *input* production defines the lexical structure of a C# source file. Each source file in a C# program must conform to this lexical grammar production.

input:
>   *input-section*$_{opt}$

input-section:
>   *input-section-part*
>   *input-section input-section-part*

input-section-part:
>   *input-elements*$_{opt}$ *new-line*
>   *pp-directive*

input-elements:
    input-element
    input-elements   input-element

input-element:
    whitespace
    comment
    token

Five basic elements make up the lexical structure of a C# source file: line terminators (§2.3.1), white space (§2.3.2), comments (§2.3.3), tokens (§2.4), and preprocessing directives (§2.5). Of these basic elements, only tokens are significant in the syntactic grammar of a C# program (§2.2.3).

The lexical processing of a C# source file consists of reducing the file into a sequence of tokens that becomes the input to the syntactic analysis. Line terminators, white space, and comments can serve to separate tokens, and preprocessing directives can cause sections of the source file to be skipped, but otherwise these lexical elements have no impact on the syntactic structure of a C# program.

When several lexical grammar productions match a sequence of characters in a source file, the lexical processing always forms the longest possible lexical element. For example, the character sequence / / is processed as the beginning of a single-line comment because that lexical element is longer than a single / token.

2.3.1 Line Terminators
Line terminators divide the characters of a C# source file into lines.

new-line:
    Carriage-return character (U+000D)
    Line-feed character (U+000A)
    Carriage-return character (U+000D) followed by line-feed character (U+000A)
    Line-separator character (U+2028)
    Paragraph-separator character (U+2029)

For compatibility with source code editing tools that add end-of-file markers and to enable a source file to be viewed as a sequence of properly terminated lines, the following transformations are applied, in order, to every source file in a C# program.

- If the last character of the source file is a Control-Z character (U+001A), this character is deleted.

- A carriage-return character (U+000D) is added to the end of the source file if that source file is nonempty and if the last character of the source file is not a carriage return (U+000D), a line feed (U+000A), a line separator (U+2028), or a paragraph separator (U+2029).

2.3.2 White Space

White space is defined as any character with Unicode class Zs (which includes the space character) as well as the horizontal tab character, the vertical tab character, and the form-feed character.

> *whitespace:*
> > Any character with Unicode class Zs
> > Horizontal tab character (U+0009)
> > Vertical tab character (U+000B)
> > Form-feed character (U+000C)

2.3.3 Comments

C# supports two forms of comments: *single-line comments* and *delimited comments*. Single-line comments start with the characters // and extend to the end of the source line. Delimited comments start with the characters /* and end with the characters */. Delimited comments may span multiple lines.

> *comment:*
> > *single-line-comment*
> > *delimited-comment*
>
> *single-line-comment:*
> > // *input-characters*$_{opt}$
>
> *input-characters:*
> > *input-character*
> > *input-characters input-character*
>
> *input-character:*
> > Any Unicode character except a *new-line-character*
>
> *new-line-character:*
> > Carriage-return character (U+000D)
> > Line-feed character (U+000A)
> > Line-separator character (U+2028)
> > Paragraph-separator character (U+2029)

delimited-comment:
    / *   *delimited-comment-characters*$_{opt}$ * /

delimited-comment-characters:
    delimited-comment-character
    delimited-comment-characters delimited-comment-character

delimited-comment-character:
    not-asterisk
    * *not-slash*

not-asterisk:
    Any Unicode character except *

not-slash:
    Any Unicode character except /

Comments do not nest. The character sequences /* and */ have no special meaning within a // comment, and the character sequences // and /* have no special meaning within a delimited comment.

Comments are not processed within character and string literals.

The following example includes a delimited comment.

```
/* Hello, world program
   This program writes "hello, world" to the console
*/
class Hello
{
    static void Main() {
        System.Console.WriteLine("hello, world");
    }
}
```

The following example shows several single-line comments.

```
// Hello, world program
// This program writes "hello, world" to the console
//
class Hello // any name will do for this class
{
    static void Main() { // this method must be named "Main"
        System.Console.WriteLine("hello, world");
    }
}
```

2.4 Tokens

There are several kinds of tokens: identifiers, keywords, literals, operators, and punctuators. White space and comments are not tokens, but they act as separators for tokens.

> *token:*
> > *identifier*
> > *keyword*
> > *integer-literal*
> > *real-literal*
> > *character-literal*
> > *string-literal*
> > *operator-or-punctuator*

2.4.1 Unicode Character Escape Sequences

A Unicode character escape sequence represents a Unicode character. Unicode character escape sequences are processed in identifiers (§2.4.2), character literals (§2.4.4.4), and regular string literals (§2.4.4.5). A Unicode character escape is not processed in any other location (for example, to form an operator, punctuator, or keyword).

> *unicode-escape-sequence:*
> > \u *hex-digit hex-digit hex-digit hex-digit*
> > \U *hex-digit hex-digit hex-digit hex-digit hex-digit hex-digit hex-digit hex-digit*

A Unicode escape sequence represents the single Unicode character formed by the hexadecimal number following the \u or \U characters. Because C# uses a 16-bit encoding of Unicode code points in characters and string values, a Unicode character in the range U+10000 to U+10FFFF is not permitted in a character literal and is represented using a Unicode surrogate pair in a string literal. Unicode characters with code points above 0x10FFFF are not supported.

Multiple translations are not performed. For instance, the string literal \u005Cu005C is equivalent to \u005C rather than \. The Unicode value \u005C is the character \.

The following example shows several uses of \u0066, which is the escape sequence for the letter f.

```
class Class1
{
    static void Test(bool \u0066) {
        char c = '\u0066';
        if (\u0066)
            System.Console.WriteLine(c.ToString());
    }
}
```

The program is equivalent to the following.

```
class Class1
{
    static void Test(bool f) {
        char c = 'f';
        if (f)
            System.Console.WriteLine(c.ToString());
    }
}
```

2.4.2 Identifiers

The rules for identifiers given in this section correspond to those recommended by the Unicode Standard Annex 15, except that an underscore is allowed as an initial character (as is traditional in the C programming language), Unicode escape sequences are permitted in identifiers, and the @ character is allowed as a prefix to enable keywords to be used as identifiers.

identifier:
> *available-identifier*
> @ *identifier-or-keyword*

available-identifier:
> *An identifier-or-keyword that is not a keyword*

identifier-or-keyword:
> *identifier-start-character identifier-part-characters*$_{opt}$

identifier-start-character:
> *letter-character*
> *_ (the underscore character* U+005F*)*

identifier-part-characters:
> *identifier-part-character*
> *identifier-part-characters identifier-part-character*

identifier-part-character:
> *letter-character*
> *decimal-digit-character*
> *connecting-character*
> *combining-character*
> *formatting-character*

letter-character:
> A Unicode character of classes Lu, Ll, Lt, Lm, Lo, or Nl
> *A unicode-escape-sequence* representing a character of classes Lu, Ll, Lt, Lm, Lo, or Nl

combining-character:
>   A Unicode character of classes Mn or Mc
>   A *unicode-escape-sequence* representing a character of classes Mn or Mc

decimal-digit-character:
>   A Unicode character of the class Nd
>   A *unicode-escape-sequence* representing a character of the class Nd

connecting-character:
>   A Unicode character of the class Pc
>   A *unicode-escape-sequence* representing a character of the class Pc

formatting-character:
>   A Unicode character of the class Cf
>   A *unicode-escape-sequence* representing a character of the class Cf

For information on these Unicode character classes, see *The Unicode Standard, Version 3.0*, section 4.5.

Examples of valid identifiers include `identifier1`, `_identifier2`, and `@if`.

An identifier in a conforming program must be in the canonical format defined by Unicode Normalization Form C, as defined by the Unicode Standard Annex 15. The behavior when encountering an identifier not in Normalization Form C is implementation defined; however, a diagnostic is not required.

The prefix @ enables the use of keywords as identifiers, which is useful when interfacing with other programming languages. The character @ is not actually part of the identifier, so the identifier might be seen in other languages as a normal identifier, without the prefix. An identifier with an @ prefix is called a ***verbatim identifier***. Use of the @ prefix for identifiers that are not keywords is permitted but strongly discouraged as a matter of style.

The following example defines a class named `class` with a static method named `static` that takes a parameter named `bool`.

```
class @class
{
    public static void @static(bool @bool) {
        if (@bool)
            System.Console.WriteLine("true");
        else
            System.Console.WriteLine("false");
    }
}
```

```
class Class1
{
    static void M() {
        cl\u0061ss.st\u0061tic(true);
    }
}
```

Note that because Unicode escapes are not permitted in keywords, the token `cl\u0061ss` is an identifier and is the same identifier as `@class`.

Two identifiers are considered the same if they are identical after the following transformations are applied, in order.

- The prefix @, if used, is removed.

- Each *unicode-escape-sequence* is transformed into its corresponding Unicode character.

- Any *formatting-characters* are removed.

Identifiers containing two consecutive underscore characters (U+005F) are reserved for use by the implementation. For example, an implementation might provide extended keywords that begin with two underscores.

2.4.3 Keywords

A *keyword* is an identifier-like sequence of characters that is reserved and cannot be used as an identifier except when prefaced by the @ character.

keyword: one of

abstract	as	base	bool	break
byte	case	catch	char	checked
class	const	continue	decimal	default
delegate	do	double	else	enum
event	explicit	extern	false	finally
fixed	float	for	foreach	goto
if	implicit	in	int	interface
internal	is	lock	long	namespace
new	null	object	operator	out
override	params	private	protected	public
readonly	ref	return	sbyte	sealed
short	sizeof	stackalloc	static	string
struct	switch	this	throw	true
try	typeof	uint	ulong	unchecked
unsafe	ushort	using	virtual	void
volatile	while			

In some places in the grammar, specific identifiers have special meaning but are not keywords. For example, within a property declaration, the `get` and `set` identifiers have special meaning (§10.6.2). An identifier other than `get` or `set` is never permitted in these locations, so this use does not conflict with using these words as identifiers.

2.4.4 Literals

A *literal* is a source code representation of a value.

> *literal:*
> > *boolean-literal*
> > *integer-literal*
> > *real-literal*
> > *character-literal*
> > *string-literal*
> > *null-literal*

2.4.4.1 *Boolean Literals*

There are two boolean literal values: `true` and `false`.

> *boolean-literal:*
> > `true`
> > `false`

The type of a *boolean-literal* is `bool`.

2.4.4.2 *Integer Literals*

Integer literals are used to write values of types `int`, `uint`, `long`, and `ulong`. Integer literals have two possible forms: decimal and hexadecimal.

> *integer-literal:*
> > *decimal-integer-literal*
> > *hexadecimal-integer-literal*
>
> *decimal-integer-literal:*
> > *decimal-digits   integer-type-suffix$_{opt}$*
>
> *decimal-digits:*
> > *decimal-digit*
> > *decimal-digits   decimal-digit*
>
> *decimal-digit:* one of
> > 0   1   2   3   4   5   6   7   8   9

integer-type-suffix: one of
    U u L l UL Ul uL ul LU Lu lU lu

hexadecimal-integer-literal:
    0x *hex-digits integer-type-suffix*$_{opt}$
    0X *hex-digits integer-type-suffix*$_{opt}$

hex-digits:
    hex-digit
    hex-digits hex-digit

hex-digit: one of
    0 1 2 3 4 5 6 7 8 9 A B C D E F a b c d e f

The type of an integer literal is determined as follows.

- If the literal has no suffix, it has the first of these types in which its value can be represented: `int`, `uint`, `long`, `ulong`.

- If the literal is suffixed by `U` or `u`, it has the first of these types in which its value can be represented: `uint`, `ulong`.

- If the literal is suffixed by `L` or `l`, it has the first of these types in which its value can be represented: `long`, `ulong`.

- If the literal is suffixed by `UL`, `Ul`, `uL`, `ul`, `LU`, `Lu`, `lU`, or `lu`, it is of type `ulong`.

If the value represented by an integer literal is outside the range of the `ulong` type, a compile-time error occurs.

As a matter of style, it is suggested that `L` be used instead of `l` when writing literals of type `long` because it is easy to confuse the letter `l` with the digit 1.

To permit the smallest possible `int` and `long` values to be written as decimal integer literals, the following two rules exist.

- When a *decimal-integer-literal* with the value 2147483648 (2^{31}) and no *integer-type-suffix* appears as the token immediately following a unary minus operator token (§7.6.2), the result is a constant of type `int` with the value –2147483648 (-2^{31}). In all other situations, such a *decimal-integer-literal* is of type `uint`.

- When a *decimal-integer-literal* with the value 9223372036854775808 (2^{63}) and no *integer-type-suffix* or the *integer-type-suffix* `L` or `l` appears as the token immediately following a unary minus operator token (§7.6.2), the result is a constant of type `long` with the value –9223372036854775808 (-2^{63}). In all other situations, such a *decimal-integer-literal* is of type `ulong`.

2.4.4.3 *Real Literals*

Real literals are used to write values of types float, double, and decimal.

real-literal:
> *decimal-digits* . *decimal-digits* *exponent-part*_{opt} *real-type-suffix*_{opt}
> . *decimal-digits* *exponent-part*_{opt} *real-type-suffix*_{opt}
> *decimal-digits* *exponent-part* *real-type-suffix*_{opt}
> *decimal-digits* *real-type-suffix*

exponent-part:
> e *sign*_{opt} *decimal-digits*
> E *sign*_{opt} *decimal-digits*

sign: one of
> + −

real-type-suffix: one of
> F f D d M m

If no *real-type-suffix* is specified, the type of the real literal is double. Otherwise, the real type suffix determines the type of the real literal as follows.

- A real literal suffixed by F or f is of type float. For example, the literals 1f, 1.5f, 1e10f, and 123.456F are all of type float.

- A real literal suffixed by D or d is of type double. For example, the literals 1d, 1.5d, 1e10d, and 123.456D are all of type double.

- A real literal suffixed by M or m is of type decimal. For example, the literals 1m, 1.5m, 1e10m, and 123.456M are all of type decimal. This literal is converted to a decimal value by taking the exact value and, if necessary, rounding to the nearest representable value using banker's rounding (§4.1.7). Any scale apparent in the literal is preserved unless the value is rounded or the value is zero (in which, in the latter case, the sign and scale will be 0). Hence, the literal 2.900m will be parsed to form the decimal with sign 0, coefficient 2900, and scale 3.

If the specified literal cannot be represented in the indicated type, a compile-time error occurs.

The value of a real literal of type float or double is determined by using the IEEE "round to nearest" mode.

Note that in a real literal, decimal digits are always required after the decimal point. For example, 1.3F is a real literal but 1.F is not.

2. Lexical Structure

2.4.4.4 *Character Literals*

A character literal represents a single character and usually consists of a character in quotes, as in `'a'`.

> *character-literal:*
>   `'` *character* `'`

> *character:*
>   *single-character*
>   *simple-escape-sequence*
>   *hexadecimal-escape-sequence*
>   *unicode-escape-sequence*

> *single-character:*
>   Any character except `'` (U+0027), `\` (U+005C), and *new-line-character*

> *simple-escape-sequence:* one of
>   `\'` `\"` `\\` `\0` `\a` `\b` `\f` `\n` `\r` `\t` `\v`

> *hexadecimal-escape-sequence:*
>   `\x` *hex-digit* *hex-digit*$_{opt}$ *hex-digit*$_{opt}$ *hex-digit*$_{opt}$

A character that follows a backslash character (`\`) in a *character* must be one of the following characters: `'`, `"`, `\`, `0`, `a`, `b`, `f`, `n`, `r`, `t`, `u`, `U`, `x`, or `v`. Otherwise, a compile-time error occurs.

A hexadecimal escape sequence represents a single Unicode character, with the value formed by the hexadecimal number following `\x`.

If the value represented by a character literal is greater than U+FFFF, a compile-time error occurs.

A Unicode character escape sequence (§2.4.1) in a character literal must be in the range U+0000 to U+FFFF.

A simple escape sequence represents a Unicode character encoding, as described in the following table.

Escape Sequence	Character Name	Unicode Encoding
`\'`	Single quote	0x0027
`\"`	Double quote	0x0022
`\\`	Backslash	0x005C

Escape Sequence	Character Name	Unicode Encoding
\0	Null	0x0000
\a	Alert	0x0007
\b	Backspace	0x0008
\f	Form feed	0x000C
\n	New line	0x000A
\r	Carriage return	0x000D
\t	Horizontal tab	0x0009
\v	Vertical tab	0x000B

The type of a *character-literal* is `char`.

2.4.4.5 *String Literals*
C# supports two forms of string literals: ***regular string literals*** and ***verbatim string literals***.

A regular string literal consists of zero or more characters enclosed in double quotes, as in `"hello"`, and may include both simple escape sequences (such as `\t` for the tab character) and hexadecimal and Unicode escape sequences.

A verbatim string literal consists of an `@` character followed by a double-quote character, zero or more characters, and a closing double-quote character. A simple example is `@"hello"`. In a verbatim string literal, the characters between the delimiters are interpreted verbatim; the only exception is a *quote-escape-sequence*. In particular, simple escape sequences and hex and Unicode escape sequences are not processed in verbatim string literals. A verbatim string literal may span multiple lines.

> *string-literal:*
>   *regular-string-literal*
>   *verbatim-string-literal*
>
> *regular-string-literal:*
>   `"` *regular-string-literal-characters*_{opt}   `"`
>
> *regular-string-literal-characters:*
>   *regular-string-literal-character*
>   *regular-string-literal-characters* *regular-string-literal-character*

regular-string-literal-character:
    single-regular-string-literal-character
    simple-escape-sequence
    hexadecimal-escape-sequence
    unicode-escape-sequence

single-regular-string-literal-character:
    Any character except " (U+0022), \ (U+005C), and *new-line-character*

verbatim-string-literal:
    @ "   *verbatim -string-literal-characters$_{opt}$*   "

verbatim-string-literal-characters:
    verbatim-string-literal-character
    verbatim-string-literal-characters   verbatim-string-literal-character

verbatim-string-literal-character:
    single-verbatim-string-literal-character
    quote-escape-sequence

single-verbatim-string-literal-character:
    Any character except "

quote-escape-sequence:
    " "

A character that follows a backslash character (\) in a *regular-string-literal-character* must be one of the following characters: ', ", \, 0, a, b, f, n, r, t, u, U, x, or v. Otherwise, a compile-time error occurs.

The following example shows a variety of string literals.

```
string a = "hello, world";                    // hello, world
string b = @"hello, world";                   // hello, world

string c = "hello \t world";                  // hello   world
string d = @"hello \t world";                 // hello \t world

string e = "Joe said \"Hello\" to me";        // Joe said "Hello" to me
string f = @"Joe said ""Hello"" to me";       // Joe said "Hello" to me

string g = "\\\\server\\share\\file.txt";     // \\server\share\file.txt
string h = @"\\server\share\file.txt";        // \\server\share\file.txt

string i = "one\r\ntwo\r\nthree";
string j = @"one
two
three";
```

The last string literal, j, is a verbatim string literal that spans multiple lines. The characters between the quotation marks, including white space such as new line characters, are preserved verbatim.

Because a hexadecimal escape sequence can have a variable number of hexadecimal digits, the string literal `"\x123"` contains a single character with hexadecimal value 123. To create a string containing the character with hexadecimal value 12 followed by the character 3, one could write `"\x00123"` or `"\x12" + "3"` instead.

The type of a *string-literal* is `string`.

Each string literal does not necessarily result in a new string instance. When two or more string literals that are equivalent according to the string equality operator (§7.9.7) appear in the same assembly, these string literals refer to the same string instance. For instance, the output produced by the following is `True` because the two literals refer to the same string instance.

```
class Test
{
    static void Main() {
        object a = "hello";
        object b = "hello";
        System.Console.WriteLine(a == b);
    }
}
```

2.4.4.6 *The Null Literal*

null-literal:
    null

The type of a *null-literal* is the null type.

2.4.5 Operators and Punctuators

There are several kinds of operators and punctuators. Operators are used in expressions to describe operations involving one or more operands. For example, the expression a + b uses the + operator to add the two operands a and b. Punctuators are for grouping and separating.

operator-or-punctuator: one of

{	}	[	]	(	)	.	,	:	;
+	–	*	/	%	&	|	^	!	~
=	<	>	?	++	--	&&	||	<<	>>
==	!=	<=	>=	+=	-=	*=	/=	%=	&=
|=	^=	<<=	>>=	->					

2.5 Preprocessing Directives

The preprocessing directives provide the ability to conditionally skip sections of source files, to report error and warning conditions, and to delineate distinct regions of source code. The term "preprocessing directives" is used only for consistency with the C and C++ programming languages. In C#, there is no separate preprocessing step; preprocessing directives are processed as part of the lexical analysis phase.

pp-directive:
    pp-declaration
    pp-conditional
    pp-line
    pp-diagnostic
    pp-region

The following preprocessing directives are available:

- `#define` and `#undef`, which define and undefine, respectively, conditional compilation symbols (§2.5.3)

- `#if`, `#elif`, `#else`, and `#endif`, which conditionally skip sections of source code (§2.5.4).

- `#line`, which controls line numbers emitted for errors and warnings (§2.5.7).

- `#error` and `#warning`, which issue errors and warnings, respectively (§2.5.5).

- `#region` and `#endregion`, which explicitly mark sections of source code (§2.5.6).

A preprocessing directive always occupies a separate line of source code and always begins with a # character and a preprocessing directive name. White space may occur before the # character and between the # character and the directive name.

A source line containing a `#define`, `#undef`, `#if`, `#elif`, `#else`, `#endif`, or `#line` directive may end with a single-line comment. Delimited comments (the `/* */` style of comments) are not permitted on source lines containing preprocessing directives.

Preprocessing directives are not tokens and are not part of the syntactic grammar of C#. However, preprocessing directives can be used to include or exclude sequences of tokens and can in that way affect the meaning of a C# program. For example, when compiled, the following program

```
#define A
#undef B

class C
{
#if A
    void F() {}
#else
    void G() {}
#endif
```

```
#if B
    void H() {}
#else
    void I() {}
#endif
}
```

results in the same sequence of tokens as the following program.

```
class C
{
    void F() {}
    void I() {}
}
```

Thus, whereas lexically the two programs are quite different, syntactically they are identical.

2.5.1 Conditional Compilation Symbols

The conditional compilation functionality provided by the #if, #elif, #else, and #endif directives is controlled through preprocessing expressions (§2.5.2) and conditional compilation symbols.

> *conditional-symbol:*
>   Any *identifier-or-keyword* except `true` or `false`

A conditional compilation symbol has two possible states: *defined* or *undefined*. At the beginning of the lexical processing of a source file, a conditional compilation symbol is undefined unless it has been explicitly defined by an external mechanism (such as a command-line compiler option). When a #define directive is processed, the conditional compilation symbol named in that directive becomes defined in that source file. The symbol remains defined until an #undef directive for that same symbol is processed or until the end of the source file is reached. An implication of this is that #define and #undef directives in one source file have no effect on other source files in the same program.

When referenced in a preprocessing expression, a defined conditional compilation symbol has the boolean value `true`, and an undefined conditional compilation symbol has the boolean value `false`. There is no requirement that conditional compilation symbols be explicitly declared before they are referenced in preprocessing expressions. Instead, undeclared symbols are simply undefined and thus have the value `false`.

The namespace for conditional compilation symbols is distinct and separate from all other named entities in a C# program. Conditional compilation symbols can only be referenced in #define and #undef directives and in preprocessing expressions.

2.5.2 Preprocessing Expressions

Preprocessing expressions can occur in `#if` and `#elif` directives. The operators `!`, `==`, `!=`, `&&`, and `||` are permitted in preprocessing expressions, and parentheses may be used for grouping.

> *pp-expression:*
>> *whitespace$_{opt}$ pp-or-expression   whitespace$_{opt}$*
>
> *pp-or-expression:*
>> *pp-and-expression*
>> *pp-or-expression   whitespace$_{opt}$ || whitespace$_{opt}$ pp-and-expression*
>
> *pp-and-expression:*
>> *pp-equality-expression*
>> *pp-and-expression   whitespace$_{opt}$ && whitespace$_{opt}$ pp-equality-expression*
>
> *pp-equality-expression:*
>> *pp-unary-expression*
>> *pp-equality-expression   whitespace$_{opt}$ == whitespace$_{opt}$ pp-unary-expression*
>> *pp-equality-expression   whitespace$_{opt}$!= whitespace$_{opt}$ pp-unary-expression*
>
> *pp-unary-expression:*
>> *pp-primary-expression*
>> *!   whitespace$_{opt}$ pp-unary-expression*
>
> *pp-primary-expression:*
>> `true`
>> `false`
>> *conditional-symbol*
>> *(whitespace$_{opt}$ pp-expression   whitespace$_{opt}$)*

When referenced in a preprocessing expression, a defined conditional compilation symbol has the boolean value `true`, and an undefined conditional compilation symbol has the boolean value `false`.

Evaluation of a preprocessing expression always yields a boolean value. The rules of evaluation for a preprocessing expression are the same as those for a constant expression (§7.15), except that the only user-defined entities that can be referenced are conditional compilation symbols.

2.5.3 Declaration Directives

The declaration directives define or undefine conditional compilation symbols.

> *pp-declaration:*
>> *whitespace$_{opt}$ #   whitespace$_{opt}$ define whitespace conditional-symbol pp-new-line*
>> *whitespace$_{opt}$ #   whitespace$_{opt}$ undef whitespace conditional-symbol pp-new-line*

pp-new-line:
>   *whitespace*_{opt}   *single-line-comment*_{opt}   *new-line*

The processing of a `#define` directive causes the given conditional compilation symbol to become defined, starting with the source line that follows the directive. Likewise, the processing of an `#undef` directive causes the given conditional compilation symbol to become undefined, starting with the source line that follows the directive.

Any `#define` and `#undef` directives in a source file must occur before the first *token* (§2.4) in the source file; otherwise, a compile-time error occurs. In intuitive terms, `#define` and `#undef` directives must precede any "real code" in the source file.

The following example is valid because the `#define` directives precede the first token (the `namespace` keyword) in the source file.

```
#define Enterprise

#if Professional || Enterprise
    #define Advanced
#endif

namespace Megacorp.Data
{
    #if Advanced
    class PivotTable {...}
    #endif
}
```

The following example results in a compile-time error because a `#define` directive follows real code.

```
#define A
namespace N
{
    #define B
    #if B
    class Class1 {}
    #endif
}
```

A `#define` directive may define a conditional compilation symbol that is already defined without there being any intervening `#undef` for that symbol. The following example defines a conditional compilation symbol A and then defines it again.

```
#define A
#define A
```

A `#undef` may "undefine" a conditional compilation symbol that is not defined. The following example defines a conditional compilation symbol A and then undefines it twice; although the second `#undef` has no effect, it is still valid.

```
#define A
#undef A
#undef A
```

2.5.4 Conditional Compilation Directives

The conditional compilation directives conditionally include or exclude portions of a source file.

pp-conditional:
    pp-if-section pp-elif-sections_{opt} *pp-else-section_{opt}* *pp-endif*

pp-if-section:
    whitespace_{opt} # *whitespace_{opt}* `if` *whitespace pp-expression pp-new-line*
        conditional-section_{opt}

pp-elif-sections:
    pp-elif-section
    pp-elif-sections pp-elif-section

pp-elif-section:
    whitespace_{opt} # *whitespace_{opt}* `elif` *whitespace pp-expression pp-new-line*
        conditional-section_{opt}

pp-else-section:
    whitespace_{opt} # *whitespace_{opt}* `else` *pp-new-line conditional-section_{opt}*

pp-endif:
    whitespace_{opt} # *whitespace_{opt}* `endif` *pp-new-line*

conditional-section:
    input-section
    skipped-section

skipped-section:
    skipped-section-part
    skipped-section skipped-section-part

skipped-section-part:
    skipped-characters_{opt} *new-line*
    pp-directive

skipped-characters:
    whitespace_{opt} *not-number-sign input-characters_{opt}*

not-number-sign:
    Any *input-character* except #

As indicated by the syntax, conditional compilation directives must be written as sets consisting of, in order, an `#if` directive, zero or more `#elif` directives, zero or one `#else` directive, and an #endif directive. Between the directives are conditional sections of source code. Each section is controlled by the immediately preceding directive. A conditional section may itself contain nested conditional compilation directives provided these directives form complete sets.

A *pp-conditional* selects at most one of the contained *conditional-section*s for normal lexical processing.

- The *pp-expression*s of the #if and #elif directives are evaluated in order until one yields true. If an expression yields true, the *conditional-section* of the corresponding directive is selected.

- If all *pp-expression*s yield false, and if an #else directive is present, the *conditional-section* of the #else directive is selected.

- Otherwise, no *conditional-section* is selected.

The selected *conditional-section*, if any, is processed as a normal *input-section*. In other words, the source code contained in the section must adhere to the lexical grammar, tokens are generated from the source code in the section, and preprocessing directives in the section have the prescribed effects.

The remaining *conditional-section*s, if any, are processed as *skipped-section*s. In other words, except for preprocessing directives, the source code in the section does not need to adhere to the lexical grammar, no tokens are generated from the source code in the section, and preprocessing directives in the section must be lexically correct but are not otherwise processed. Within a *conditional-section* that is being processed as a *skipped-section*, any nested *conditional-section*s (contained in nested #if...#endif and #region...#endregion constructs) are also processed as *skipped-section*s.

The following example illustrates how conditional compilation directives can nest.

```
#define Debug   // Debugging on
#undef Trace    // Tracing off

class PurchaseTransaction
{
    void Commit() {
        #if Debug
            CheckConsistency();
            #if Trace
                WriteToLog(this.ToString());
            #endif
        #endif
        CommitHelper();
    }
}
```

Except for preprocessing directives, skipped source code is not subject to lexical analysis. For example, the following is valid despite the unterminated comment in the #else section.

```
#define Debug   // Debugging on

class PurchaseTransaction
{
    void Commit() {
        #if Debug
            CheckConsistency();
        #else
            /* Do something else
        #endif
    }
}
```

Note, however, that preprocessing directives are required to be lexically correct even in skipped sections of source code.

Preprocessing directives are not processed when they appear inside multiline input elements. For example, the following program

```
class Hello
{
    static void Main() {
        System.Console.WriteLine(@"hello,
#if Debug
        world
#else
        Nebraska
#endif
        ");
    }
}
```

results in the following output.

```
hello,
#if Debug
        world
#else
        Nebraska
#endif
```

In peculiar cases, the set of preprocessing directives that is processed might depend on the evaluation of the *pp-expression*. The following example always produces the same token stream (class Q { }), regardless of whether X is defined.

```
#if X
    /*
#else
    /* */ class Q { }
#endif
```

If X is defined, the only processed directives are #if and #endif because of the multiline comment. If X is undefined, then three directives (#if, #else, #endif) are part of the directive set.

2.5.5 Diagnostic Directives

The diagnostic directives explicitly generate error and warning messages that are reported in the same way as other compile-time errors and warnings.

pp-diagnostic:
> *whitespace*$_{opt}$ #   *whitespace*$_{opt}$ error   *pp-message*
> *whitespace*$_{opt}$ #   *whitespace*$_{opt}$ warning   *pp-message*

pp-message:
> *new-line*
> *whitespace   input-characters*$_{opt}$ *new-line*

The following example always produces a warning ("Code review needed before check-in") and produces a compile-time error ("A build can't be both debug and retail") if the conditional symbols Debug and Retail are both defined.

```
#warning Code review needed before check-in

#if Debug && Retail
    #error A build can't be both debug and retail
#endif

class Test {...}
```

Note that a *pp-message* can contain arbitrary text; specifically, it does not need to contain well-formed tokens, as shown by the single quote in the word can't.

2.5.6 Region Directives

The region directives explicitly mark regions of source code.

pp-region:
> *pp-start-region   conditional-section*$_{opt}$ *pp-end-region*

pp-start-region:
> *whitespace*$_{opt}$ #   *whitespace*$_{opt}$ region   *pp-message*

pp-end-region:
> *whitespace*$_{opt}$ #   *whitespace*$_{opt}$ endregion   *pp-message*

No semantic meaning is attached to a region; regions are intended for use by the programmer or by automated tools to mark a section of source code. The message specified in a `#region` or `#endregion` directive likewise has no semantic meaning; it merely serves to identify the region. Matching `#region` and `#endregion` directives may have different *pp-message*s.

The lexical processing of a region

```
#region
...
#endregion
```

corresponds exactly to the lexical processing of a conditional compilation directive of the following form.

```
#if true
...
#endif
```

2.5.7 Line Directives

Line directives can alter the line numbers and source filenames that are reported by the compiler in output such as warnings and errors.

Line directives are most commonly used in meta-programming tools that generate C# source code from some other text input.

pp-line:
    whitespace$_{opt}$ `#` *whitespace$_{opt}$* `line` *whitespace line-indicator pp-new-line*

line-indicator:
    decimal-digits whitespace file-name
    decimal-digits
    `default`
    `hidden`

file-name:
    `"` *file-name-characters* `"`

file-name-characters:
    file-name-character
    file-name-characters file-name-character

file-name-character:
    Any *input-character* except `"`

When no `#line` directives are present, the compiler reports true line numbers and source filenames in its output. The `#line` directive is most commonly used in meta-programming tools that generate C# source code from some other text input. When processing a `#line` directive that includes a *line-indicator* that is not `default`, the compiler treats the line *after* the directive as having the given line number (and filename, if specified).

A `#line default` directive reverses the effect of all preceding `#line` directives. The compiler reports true line information for subsequent lines, precisely as if no `#line` directives had been processed.

A `#line hidden` directive has no effect on the file and line numbers reported in error messages, but it does affect source-level debugging. When debugging, all lines between a `#line hidden` directive and the subsequent `#line` directive (which is not `#line hidden`) have no line number information. When stepping through code in the debugger, these lines will be skipped entirely.

Note that a *file-name* differs from a regular string literal in that escape characters are not processed; the \ character simply designates an ordinary backslash character within a *file-name*.

3. Basic Concepts

3.1 Application Startup

An assembly that has an *entry point* is called an *application*. When an application runs, a new *application domain* is created. Several different instantiations of an application may exist on the same machine at the same time, and each has its own application domain.

An application domain enables application isolation by acting as a container for application state. An application domain acts as a container and boundary for the types defined in the application and the class libraries it uses. Types loaded into one application domain are distinct from the same type loaded into another application domain, and instances of objects are not directly shared between application domains. For instance, each application domain has its own copy of static variables for these types, and a static constructor for a type runs at most once per application domain. Implementations are free to provide implementation-specific policy or mechanisms for creating and destroying application domains.

Application startup occurs when the execution environment calls a designated method, which is the application's entry point. This entry point method is always named Main, and it can have one of the following signatures.

```
static void Main() {...}
static void Main(string[] args) {...}
static int Main() {...}
static int Main(string[] args) {...}
```

As shown, the entry point may optionally return an int value. This return value is used in application termination (§3.2).

The entry point may optionally have one formal parameter. The parameter may have any name, but the type of the parameter must be string[]. If the formal parameter is present, the execution environment creates and passes a string[] argument containing the command-line arguments specified when the application started. The string[] argument is never null, but it may have a length of zero if no command-line arguments were specified.

Because C# supports method overloading, a class or struct can contain multiple definitions of some method, provided each has a different signature. However, within a single program, no class or struct can contain more than one method called `Main` whose definition qualifies it to be used as an application entry point. Other overloaded versions of `Main` are permitted, however, provided they have more than one parameter or their only parameter is other than type `string[]`.

An application can consist of multiple classes or structs. It is possible for more than one of these classes or structs to contain a method called `Main` whose definition qualifies it to be used as an application entry point. In such cases, an external mechanism (such as a command-line compiler option) must be used to select one of these `Main` methods as the entry point.

In C#, every method must be defined as a member of a class or struct. Ordinarily, the declared accessibility (§3.5.1) of a method is determined by the access modifiers (§10.2.3) specified in its declaration, and similarly the declared accessibility of a type is determined by the access modifiers specified in its declaration. For a given method of a given type to be callable, both the type and the member must be accessible. However, the application entry point is a special case. Specifically, the execution environment can access the application's entry point regardless of its declared accessibility and regardless of the declared accessibility of its enclosing type declarations.

In all other respects, entry point methods behave like those that are not entry points.

3.2 Application Termination

Application termination returns control to the execution environment.

If the return type of the application's *entry point* method is `int`, the value returned serves as the application's *termination status code*. The purpose of this code is to communicate success or failure to the execution environment.

If the return type of the entry point method is `void`, reaching the right brace (`}`) that terminates that method or executing a `return` statement that has no expression results in a termination status code of `0`.

Prior to an application's termination, destructors for all of its objects that have not yet been garbage collected are called, unless such cleanup has been suppressed (by a call to the library method `GC.SuppressFinalize`, for example).

3.3 Declarations

Declarations in a C# program define the constituent elements of the program. C# programs are organized using namespaces (§9), which can contain type declarations and nested namespace declarations. Type declarations (§9.5) define classes (§10), structs (§11), interfaces (§13), enums (§14), and delegates (§15). The kinds of members permitted in a type declaration depend on the form of the type declaration. For instance, class declarations can contain declarations for constants (§10.3), fields (§10.4), methods (§10.5), properties (§10.6), events (§10.7), indexers (§10.8), operators (§10.9), instance constructors (§10.10), static constructors (§10.11), destructors (§10.12), and nested types (§10.2.6).

A declaration defines a name in the *declaration space* to which the declaration belongs. Except for overloaded members (§3.6), it is a compile-time error to have two or more declarations that introduce members with the same name in a declaration space. It is never possible for a declaration space to contain different kinds of members with the same name. For example, a declaration space can never contain a field and a method by the same name.

There are several different types of declaration spaces, as described in the following.

- Within all source files of a program, *namespace-member-declaration*s with no enclosing *namespace-declaration* are members of a single combined declaration space called the **global declaration space**.

- Within all source files of a program, *namespace-member-declaration*s within *namespace-declaration*s that have the same fully qualified namespace name are members of a single combined declaration space.

- Each class, struct, or interface declaration creates a new declaration space. Names are introduced into this declaration space through *class-member-declaration*s, *struct-member-declaration*s, or *interface-member-declaration*s. Except for overloaded instance constructor declarations and static constructor declarations, a class or struct member declaration cannot introduce a member by the same name as the class or struct. A class, struct, or interface permits the declaration of overloaded methods and indexers. Furthermore, a class or struct permits the declaration of overloaded instance constructors and operators. For example, a class, struct, or interface may contain multiple method declarations with the same name, provided these method declarations differ in their signature (§3.6). Note that base classes do not contribute to the declaration space of a class, and base interfaces do not contribute to the declaration space of an interface. Thus, a derived class or interface is allowed to declare a member with the same name as an inherited member. Such a member is said to *hide* the inherited member.

- Each enumeration declaration creates a new declaration space. Names are introduced into this declaration space through *enum-member-declaration*s.

3. Basic Concepts

- Each *block* or *switch-block* creates a different declaration space for local variables and constants. Names are introduced into this declaration space through *local-variable-declarations* and *local-constant-declarations*. If a block is the body of an instance constructor, method, or operator declaration, or it is a get or set accessor for an indexer declaration, then the parameters declared in such a declaration are members of the block's **local variable declaration space**. The local variable declaration space of a block includes any nested blocks. Thus, within a nested block it is not possible to declare a local variable with the same name as a local variable in an enclosing block.

- Each *block* or *switch-block* creates a separate declaration space for labels. Names are introduced into this declaration space through *labeled-statements*, and the names are referenced through *goto-statements*. The **label declaration space** of a block includes any nested blocks. Thus, within a nested block it is not possible to declare a label with the same name as a label in an enclosing block.

The textual order in which names are declared is generally of no significance. In particular, textual order is not significant for the declaration and use of namespaces, constants, methods, properties, events, indexers, operators, instance constructors, destructors, static constructors, and types. Declaration order is significant in the following ways.

- Declaration order for field declarations and local variable declarations determines the order in which their initializers (if any) are executed.

- Local variables must be defined before they are used (§3.7).

- Declaration order for enum member declarations (§14.3) is significant when *constant-expression* values are omitted.

The declaration space of a namespace is "open ended," and two namespace declarations with the same fully qualified name contribute to the same declaration space.

```
namespace Megacorp.Data
{
    class Customer
    {
        . . .
    }
}

namespace Megacorp.Data
{
    class Order
    {
        . . .
    }
}
```

These two namespace declarations contribute to the same declaration space, in this case declaring two classes with the fully qualified names `Megacorp.Data.Customer` and

Megacorp.Data.Order. Because the two declarations contribute to the same declaration space, it would cause a compile-time error if each contained a declaration of a class with the same name.

As specified, the declaration space of a block includes any nested blocks. Thus, in the following example, the F and G methods result in a compile-time error because the name i is declared in the outer block and cannot be redeclared in the inner block. However, the H and I methods are valid because the two i's are declared in separate non-nested blocks.

```
class A
{
    void F() {
        int i = 0;
        if (true) {
            int i = 1;
        }
    }

    void G() {
        if (true) {
            int i = 0;
        }
        int i = 1;
    }

    void H() {
        if (true) {
            int i = 0;
        }
        if (true) {
            int i = 1;
        }
    }

    void I() {
        for (int i = 0; i < 10; i++)
            H();
        for (int i = 0; i < 10; i++)
            H();
    }
}
```

3.4 Members

Namespaces and types have *members*. The members of an entity are generally available by using a qualified name that starts with a reference to the entity, followed by a ".". token, followed by the name of the member.

Members of a type are either declared in the type or *inherited* from the base class of the type. When a type inherits from a base class, all members of the base class (except instance constructors, destructors, and static constructors) become members of the derived type.

77

The declared accessibility of a base class member does not control whether the member is inherited—inheritance extends to any member that is not an instance constructor, static constructor, or destructor. However, an inherited member may not be accessible in a derived type either because of its declared accessibility (§3.5.1) or because it is hidden by a declaration in the type itself (§3.7.1.2).

3.4.1 Namespace Members

Namespaces and types that have no enclosing namespace are members of the *global namespace*. This corresponds directly to the names declared in the global declaration space.

Namespaces and types declared within a namespace are members of that namespace. This corresponds directly to the names declared in the declaration space of the namespace.

Namespaces have no access restrictions. It is not possible to declare private, protected, or internal namespaces, and namespace names are always publicly accessible.

3.4.2 Struct Members

The members of a struct are the members declared in the struct and the members inherited from the class `object`.

The members of a simple type correspond directly to the members of the struct type aliased by the simple type.

- The members of `sbyte` are the members of the `System.SByte` struct.
- The members of `byte` are the members of the `System.Byte` struct.
- The members of `short` are the members of the `System.Int16` struct.
- The members of `ushort` are the members of the `System.UInt16` struct.
- The members of `int` are the members of the `System.Int32` struct.
- The members of `uint` are the members of the `System.UInt32` struct.
- The members of `long` are the members of the `System.Int64` struct.
- The members of `ulong` are the members of the `System.UInt64` struct.
- The members of `char` are the members of the `System.Char` struct.
- The members of `float` are the members of the `System.Single` struct.
- The members of `double` are the members of the `System.Double` struct.
- The members of `decimal` are the members of the `System.Decimal` struct.
- The members of `bool` are the members of the `System.Boolean` struct.

3.4.3 **Enumeration Members**

The members of an enumeration are the constants declared in the enumeration and the members inherited from class System.Enum.

3.4.4 **Class Members**

The members of a class are the members declared in the class and the members inherited from the base class (except for the class object, which has no base class). The members inherited from the base class include the constants, fields, methods, properties, events, indexers, operators, and types of the base class, but not the instance constructors, destructors, and static constructors of the base class. Base class members are inherited without regard to their accessibility.

A class declaration may contain declarations of constants, fields, methods, properties, events, indexers, operators, instance constructors, destructors, static constructors, and types.

The members of object and string correspond directly to the members of the class types they alias.

* The members of object are the members of the System.Object class.
* The members of string are the members of the System.String class.

3.4.5 **Interface Members**

The members of an interface are the members declared in the interface and in all base interfaces of the interface and the members inherited from the class object.

3.4.6 **Array Members**

The members of an array are the members inherited from the class System.Array.

3.4.7 **Delegate Members**

The members of a delegate are the members inherited from the class System.Delegate.

3.5 **Member Access**

Declarations of members allow control over member access. The accessibility of a member is established by the declared accessibility (§3.5.1) of the member combined with the accessibility of the immediately containing type, if any.

When access to a particular member is allowed, the member is said to be *accessible*. Conversely, when access to a particular member is disallowed, the member is said to be *inaccessible*. Access to a member is permitted when the textual location in which the access takes place is included in the accessibility domain (§3.5.2) of the member.

3.5.1 Declared Accessibility

The *declared accessibility* of a member can be one of the following.

- Public, which is selected by including a `public` modifier in the member declaration. The intuitive meaning of `public` is "access not limited."

- Protected, which is selected by including a `protected` modifier in the member declaration. The intuitive meaning of `protected` is "access limited to the containing class or types derived from the containing class."

- Internal, which is selected by including an `internal` modifier in the member declaration. The intuitive meaning of `internal` is "access limited to this program."

- Protected internal (meaning protected or internal), which is selected by including both a `protected` and an `internal` modifier in the member declaration. The intuitive meaning of `protected internal` is "access limited to this program or types derived from the containing class."

- Private, which is selected by including a `private` modifier in the member declaration. The intuitive meaning of `private` is "access limited to the containing type."

Depending on the context in which a member declaration takes place, only certain types of declared accessibility are permitted. Furthermore, when a member declaration does not include any access modifiers, the context in which the declaration takes place determines the default declared accessibility.

- Namespaces implicitly have `public` declared accessibility. No access modifiers are allowed on namespace declarations.

- Types declared in compilation units or namespaces can have `public` or `internal` declared accessibility and default to `internal` declared accessibility.

- Class members can have any of the five kinds of declared accessibility and default to `private` declared accessibility. (Note that a type declared as a member of a class can have any of the five kinds of declared accessibility, but a type declared as a member of a namespace can have only `public` or `internal` declared accessibility.)

- Struct members can have `public`, `internal`, or `private` declared accessibility and default to `private` declared accessibility because structs are implicitly sealed. Struct members introduced in a struct (that is, not inherited by that struct) cannot have `protected` or `protected internal` declared accessibility. (Note that a type declared as a member of a struct can have `public`, `internal`, or `private` declared accessibility, but a type declared as a member of a namespace can have only `public` or `internal` declared accessibility.)

- Interface members implicitly have `public` declared accessibility. No access modifiers are allowed on interface member declarations.

- Enumeration members implicitly have `public` declared accessibility. No access modifiers are allowed on enumeration member declarations.

3.5.2 Accessibility Domains

The *accessibility domain* of a member consists of the (possibly disjoint) sections of program text in which access to the member is permitted. For purposes of defining the accessibility domain of a member, a member is said to be "top level" if it is not declared within a type, and a member is said to be "nested" if it is declared within another type. Furthermore, the program text of a program is defined as all program text contained in all source files of the program, and the program text of a type is defined as all program text contained between the opening and closing { and } tokens in the *class-body, struct-body, interface-body,* or *enum-body* of the type (including, possibly, types that are nested within the type).

The accessibility domain of a predefined type (such as `object`, `int`, or `double`) is unlimited.

The accessibility domain of a top-level type `T` that is declared in a program `P` is defined as follows.

- If the declared accessibility of `T` is `public`, the accessibility domain of `T` is the program text of `P` and any program that references `P`.

- If the declared accessibility of `T` is `internal`, the accessibility domain of `T` is the program text of `P`.

From these definitions it follows that the accessibility domain of a top-level type is always at least the program text of the program in which that type is declared.

The accessibility domain of a nested member `M` declared in a type `T` within a program `P` is defined as follows (noting that `M` itself may possibly be a type).

- If the declared accessibility of `M` is `public`, the accessibility domain of `M` is the accessibility domain of `T`.

- If the declared accessibility of `M` is `protected internal`, let `D` be the union of the program text of `P` and the program text of any type derived from `T`, which is declared outside `P`. The accessibility domain of `M` is the intersection of the accessibility domain of `T` with `D`.

- If the declared accessibility of M is `protected`, let D be the union of the program text of T and the program text of any type derived from T. The accessibility domain of M is the intersection of the accessibility domain of T with D.

- If the declared accessibility of M is `internal`, the accessibility domain of M is the intersection of the accessibility domain of T with the program text of P.

- If the declared accessibility of M is `private`, the accessibility domain of M is the program text of T.

From these definitions it follows that the accessibility domain of a nested member is always at least the program text of the type in which the member is declared. Furthermore, it follows that the accessibility domain of a member is never more inclusive than the accessibility domain of the type in which the member is declared.

In intuitive terms, when a type or member M is accessed, the following steps are evaluated to ensure that the access is permitted.

- First, if M is declared within a type (as opposed to a compilation unit or a namespace), a compile-time error occurs if that type is not accessible.

- Then, if M is `public`, the access is permitted.

- Otherwise, if M is `protected internal`, the access is permitted if it occurs within the program in which M is declared or if it occurs within a class derived from the class in which M is declared and takes place through the derived class type (§3.5.3).

- Otherwise, if M is `protected`, the access is permitted if it occurs within the class in which M is declared or if it occurs within a class derived from the class in which M is declared and takes place through the derived class type (§3.5.3).

- Otherwise, if M is `internal`, the access is permitted if it occurs within the program in which M is declared.

- Otherwise, if M is `private`, the access is permitted if it occurs within the type in which M is declared.

- Otherwise, the type or member is inaccessible, and a compile-time error occurs.

In the following example

```
public class A
{
    public static int X;
    internal static int Y;
    private static int Z;
}
```

```
internal class B
{
    public static int X;
    internal static int Y;
    private static int Z;

    public class C
    {
        public static int X;
        internal static int Y;
        private static int Z;
    }

    private class D
    {
        public static int X;
        internal static int Y;
        private static int Z;
    }
}
```

the classes and members have the following accessibility domains.

- The accessibility domain of A and A.X is unlimited.

- The accessibility domain of A.Y, B, B.X, B.Y, B.C, B.C.X, and B.C.Y is the program text of the containing program.

- The accessibility domain of A.Z is the program text of A.

- The accessibility domain of B.Z and B.D is the program text of B, including the program text of B.C and B.D.

- The accessibility domain of B.C.Z is the program text of B.C.

- The accessibility domain of B.D.X and B.D.Y is the program text of B, including the program text of B.C and B.D.

- The accessibility domain of B.D.Z is the program text of B.D.

As the example illustrates, the accessibility domain of a member is never larger than that of a containing type. For example, even though all X members have `public` declared accessibility, all but A.X have accessibility domains that are constrained by a containing type.

As described in §3.4, all members of a base class (except for instance constructors, destructors, and static constructors) are inherited by derived types. This includes even private members of a base class. However, the accessibility domain of a private member includes only the program text of the type in which the member is declared. In the following example, the B class inherits the private member x from the A class.

```
class A
{
    int x;
```

```
        static void F(B b) {
            b.x = 1;    // Ok
        }
    }

    class B: A
    {
        static void F(B b) {
            b.x = 1;    // Error, x not accessible
        }
    }
```

Because the member is private, it is only accessible within the *class-body* of A. Thus, the access to b.x succeeds in the A.F method but fails in the B.F method.

3.5.3 Protected Access for Instance Members

When a `protected` instance member is accessed outside the program text of the class in which it is declared, and when a `protected internal` instance member is accessed outside the program text of the program in which it is declared, the access is required to take place *through* an instance of the derived class type in which the access occurs. In other words, let B be a base class that declares a protected instance member M, and let D be a class that derives from B. Within the *class-body* of D, access to M can take one of the following forms:

- An unqualified *type-name* or *primary-expression* of the form M

- A *primary-expression* of the form E.M, provided the type of E is D or a class derived from D

- A *primary-expression* of the form base.M

In addition to these forms of access, a derived class can access a `protected` instance constructor of a base class in a *constructor-initializer* (§10.10.1).

In the following example, within A, it is possible to access x through instances of both A and B because in either case the access takes place *through* an instance of A or a class derived from A.

```
    public class A
    {
        protected int x;

        static void F(A a, B b) {
            a.x = 1;    // Ok
            b.x = 1;    // Ok
        }
    }
```

```
public class B: A
{
    static void F(A a, B b) {
        a.x = 1;    // Error, must access through instance of B
        b.x = 1;    // Ok
    }
}
```

However, within B, it is not possible to access x through an instance of A because A does not derive from B.

3.5.4 Accessibility Constraints

Several constructs in the C# language require a type to be *at least as accessible as* a member or another type. A type T is said to be at least as accessible as a member or type M if the accessibility domain of T is a superset of the accessibility domain of M. In other words, T is at least as accessible as M if T is accessible in all contexts in which M is accessible.

The following accessibility constraints exist.

- The direct base class of a class type must be at least as accessible as the class type itself.

- The explicit base interfaces of an interface type must be at least as accessible as the interface type itself.

- The return type and parameter types of a delegate type must be at least as accessible as the delegate type itself.

- The type of a constant must be at least as accessible as the constant itself.

- The type of a field must be at least as accessible as the field itself.

- The return type and parameter types of a method must be at least as accessible as the method itself.

- The type of a property must be at least as accessible as the property itself.

- The type of an event must be at least as accessible as the event itself.

- The type and parameter types of an indexer must be at least as accessible as the indexer itself.

- The return type and parameter types of an operator must be at least as accessible as the operator itself.

- The parameter types of an instance constructor must be at least as accessible as the instance constructor itself.

3. Basic Concepts

In the following example, the B class results in a compile-time error because A is not at least as accessible as B.

```
class A {...}
public class B: A {...}
```

Likewise, in the following example, the H method in B results in a compile-time error because the return type A is not at least as accessible as the method.

```
class A {...}
public class B
{
    A F() {...}
    internal A G() {...}
    public A H() {...}
}
```

3.6 Signatures and Overloading

Methods, instance constructors, indexers, and operators are characterized by their *signatures*.

- The signature of a method consists of the name of the method and the type and kind (value, reference, or output) of each of its formal parameters, considered in the order left to right. The signature of a method specifically does not include the return type; furthermore, it does not include the params modifier that may be specified for the rightmost parameter.

- The signature of an instance constructor consists of the type and kind (value, reference, or output) of each of its formal parameters, considered in the order left to right. The signature of an instance constructor specifically does not include the params modifier that may be specified for the rightmost parameter.

- The signature of an indexer consists of the type of each of its formal parameters, considered in the order left to right. The signature of an indexer specifically does not include the element type.

- The signature of an operator consists of the name of the operator and the type of each of its formal parameters, considered in the order left to right. The signature of an operator specifically does not include the result type.

Signatures are the enabling mechanism for *overloading* of members in classes, structs, and interfaces.

- Overloading of methods permits a class, struct, or interface to declare multiple methods with the same name, provided their signatures are unique within that class, struct, or interface.

- Overloading of instance constructors permits a class or struct to declare multiple instance constructors, provided their signatures are unique within that class or struct.

- Overloading of indexers permits a class, struct, or interface to declare multiple indexers, provided their signatures are unique within that class, struct, or interface.

- Overloading of operators permits a class or struct to declare multiple operators with the same name, provided their signatures are unique within that class or struct.

The following example shows a set of overloaded method declarations along with their signatures.

```
interface ITest
{
    void F();                      // F()
    void F(int x);                 // F(int)
    void F(ref int x);             // F(ref int)
    void F(int x, int y);          // F(int, int)
    int F(string s);               // F(string)
    int F(int x);                  // F(int)        error
    void F(string[] a);            // F(string[])
    void F(params string[] a);     // F(string[]) error
}
```

Note that any `ref` and `out` parameter modifiers (§10.5.1) are part of a signature. Thus, `F(int)` and `F(ref int)` are unique signatures. Also, note that the return type and the `params` modifier are not part of a signature, so it is not possible to overload solely based on the return type or on the inclusion or exclusion of the `params` modifier. As such, the declarations of the methods `F(int)` and `F(params string[])` identified in the previous example result in a compile-time error.

3.7 Scopes

The *scope* of a name is the region of program text within which it is possible to refer to the entity declared by the name without qualification of the name. Scopes can be *nested*, and an inner scope may redeclare the meaning of a name from an outer scope (this does not, however, remove the restriction imposed by §3.3 that within a nested block it is not possible to declare a local variable with the same name as a local variable in an enclosing block).

3. Basic Concepts

The name from the outer scope is then said to be hidden in the region of program text covered by the inner scope, and access to the outer name is only possible by qualifying the name.

- The scope of a namespace member declared by a *namespace-member-declaration* (§9.4) with no enclosing *namespace-declaration* is the entire program text.

- The scope of a namespace member declared by a *namespace-member-declaration* within a *namespace-declaration* whose fully qualified name is N is the *namespace-body* of every *namespace-declaration* whose fully qualified name is N or starts with N, followed by a period.

- The scope of a name defined or imported by a *using-directive* (§9.3) extends over the *namespace-member-declarations* of the *compilation-unit* or *namespace-body* in which the *using-directive* occurs. A *using-directive* may make zero or more namespace or type names available within a particular *compilation-unit* or *namespace-body*, but it does not contribute any new members to the underlying declaration space. In other words, a *using-directive* is not transitive but rather affects only the *compilation-unit* or *namespace-body* in which it occurs.

- The scope of a member declared by a *class-member-declaration* (§10.2) is the *class-body* in which the declaration occurs. In addition, the scope of a class member extends to the *class-body* of those derived classes that are included in the accessibility domain (§3.5.2) of the member.

- The scope of a member declared by a *struct-member-declaration* (§11.2) is the *struct-body* in which the declaration occurs.

- The scope of a member declared by an *enum-member-declaration* (§14.3) is the *enum-body* in which the declaration occurs.

- The scope of a parameter declared in a *method-declaration* (§10.5) is the *method-body* of that *method-declaration*.

- The scope of a parameter declared in an *indexer-declaration* (§10.8) is the *accessor-declarations* of that *indexer-declaration*.

- The scope of a parameter declared in an *operator-declaration* (§10.9) is the *block* of that *operator-declaration*.

- The scope of a parameter declared in a *constructor-declaration* (§10.10) is the *constructor-initializer* and *block* of that *constructor-declaration*.

- The scope of a label declared in a *labeled-statement* (§8.4) is the *block* in which the declaration occurs.

- The scope of a local variable declared in a *local-variable-declaration* (§8.5.1) is the block in which the declaration occurs.

- The scope of a local variable declared in a *switch-block* of a `switch` statement (§8.7.2) is the *switch-block*.

- The scope of a local variable declared in a *for-initializer* of a `for` statement (§8.8.3) is the *for-initializer*, the *for-condition*, the *for-iterator*, and the contained *statement* of the `for` statement.

- The scope of a local constant declared in a *local-constant-declaration* (§8.5.2) is the block in which the declaration occurs. It is a compile-time error to refer to a local constant in a textual position that precedes its *constant-declarator*.

Within the scope of a namespace, class, struct, or enumeration member, it is possible to refer to the member in a textual position that precedes the declaration of the member. In the following example, it is valid for F to refer to i before it is declared.

```
class A
{
    void F() {
        i = 1;
    }
    int i = 0;
}
```

Within the scope of a local variable, it is a compile-time error to refer to the local variable in a textual position that precedes the *local-variable-declarator* of the local variable. For example, in the F method, the first assignment to i specifically does not refer to the field declared in the outer scope.

```
class A
{
    int i = 0;

    void F() {
        i = 1;                  // Error, use precedes declaration
        int i;
        i = 2;
    }

    void G() {
        int j = (j = 1);        // Valid
    }

    void H() {
        int a = 1, b = ++a;     // Valid
    }
}
```

Rather, it refers to the local variable and results in a compile-time error because it textually precedes the declaration of the variable. In the G method, using j in the initializer for the declaration of j is valid because its use does not precede the *local-variable-declarator*. In the

H method, a subsequent *local-variable-declarator* correctly refers to a local variable declared in an earlier *local-variable-declarator* within the same *local-variable-declaration*.

The scoping rules for local variables are designed to guarantee that the meaning of a name used in an expression context is always the same within a block. If the scope of a local variable were to extend only from its declaration to the end of the block, then in the previous example the first assignment would assign to the instance variable and the second assignment would assign to the local variable, possibly leading to compile-time errors if the statements of the block were later rearranged.

The meaning of a name within a block may differ based on the context in which the name is used. In the following example, the name A is used in an expression context to refer to the local variable A and in a type context to refer to the class A.

```
using System;

class A {}

class Test
{
    static void Main() {
        string A = "hello, world";
        string s = A;                   // expression context
        Type t = typeof(A);             // type context
        Console.WriteLine(s);           // writes "hello, world"
        Console.WriteLine(t);           // writes "A"
    }
}
```

3.7.1 Name Hiding

The scope of an entity typically encompasses more program text than the declaration space of the entity. In particular, the scope of an entity may include declarations that introduce new declaration spaces containing entities of the same name. Such declarations cause the original entity to become **hidden**. Conversely, an entity is said to be *visible* when it is not hidden.

Name hiding occurs when scopes overlap through nesting and when scopes overlap through inheritance. The characteristics of the two types of hiding are described in the following sections.

3.7.1.1 *Hiding through Nesting*

Name hiding through nesting can occur as a result of nesting namespaces or types within namespaces, as a result of nesting types within classes or structs, and as a result of parameter and local variable declarations.

In the example

```
class A
{
    int i = 0;
    void F() {
        int i = 1;
    }
    void G() {
        i = 1;
    }
}
```

within the F method, the instance variable i is hidden by the local variable i, but within the G method, i still refers to the instance variable.

When a name in an inner scope hides a name in an outer scope, it hides all overloaded occurrences of that name. In the example

```
class Outer
{
    static void F(int i) {}
    static void F(string s) {}
    class Inner
    {
        void G() {
            F(1);                   // Invokes Outer.Inner.F
            F("Hello");             // Error
        }
        static void F(long l) {}
    }
}
```

the call F(1) invokes the F declared in Inner because all outer occurrences of F are hidden by the inner declaration. For the same reason, the call F("Hello") results in a compile-time error.

3.7.1.2 *Hiding through Inheritance*
Name hiding through inheritance occurs when classes or structs redeclare names that were inherited from base classes. This type of name hiding takes one of the following forms.

- A constant, field, property, event, or type introduced in a class or struct hides all base class members with the same name.

- A method introduced in a class or struct hides all nonmethod base class members with the same name and all base class methods with the same signature (method name and parameter count, modifiers, and types).

- An indexer introduced in a class or struct hides all base class indexers with the same signature (parameter count and types).

The rules governing operator declarations (§10.9) make it impossible for a derived class to declare an operator with the same signature as an operator in a base class. Thus, operators never hide one another.

Contrary to hiding a name from an outer scope, hiding an accessible name from an inherited scope causes a warning to be reported. In the following example, the declaration of F in Derived causes a warning to be reported.

```
class Base
{
    public void F() {}
}

class Derived: Base
{
    public void F() {}     // Warning, hiding an inherited name
}
```

Hiding an inherited name is specifically not an error because that would preclude separate evolution of base classes. For example, the previous situation might have come about because a later version of Base introduced an F method that was not present in an earlier version of the class. Had the previous situation been an error, then *any* change made to a base class in a separately versioned class library could potentially cause derived classes to become invalid.

The warning caused by hiding an inherited name can be eliminated by using the new modifier.

```
class Base
{
    public void F() {}
}

class Derived: Base
{
    new public void F() {}
}
```

The new modifier indicates that the F in Derived is "new" and that it is indeed intended to hide the inherited member.

A declaration of a new member hides an inherited member only within the scope of the new member. In the following example

```
class Base
{
    public static void F() {}
}
```

```
class Derived: Base
{
    new private static void F() {}    // Hides Base.F in Derived only
}

class MoreDerived: Derived
{
    static void G() { F(); }          // Invokes Base.F
}
```

the declaration of F in Derived hides the F that was inherited from Base, but because the new F in Derived has private access, its scope does not extend to MoreDerived. Thus, the call F() in MoreDerived.G is valid and will invoke Base.F.

3.8 Namespace and Type Names

Several contexts in a C# program require a *namespace-name* or a *type-name* to be specified. Either form of name is written as one or more identifiers separated by "." tokens.

> *namespace-name:*
>   *namespace-or-type-name*
>
> *type-name:*
>   *namespace-or-type-name*
>
> *namespace-or-type-name:*
>   *identifier*
>   *namespace-or-type-name* . *identifier*

A *type-name* is a *namespace-or-type-name* that refers to a type. Following resolution as described shortly, the *namespace-or-type-name* of a *type-name* must refer to a type; otherwise, a compile-time error occurs.

A *namespace-name* is a *namespace-or-type-name* that refers to a namespace. Following resolution as described shortly, the *namespace-or-type-name* of a *namespace-name* must refer to a namespace; otherwise, a compile-time error occurs.

The meaning of a *namespace-or-type-name* is determined as follows.

- If the *namespace-or-type-name* consists of a single identifier, then the following happens.

    - If the *namespace-or-type-name* appears within the body of a class or struct declaration, then starting with that class or struct declaration and continuing with each enclosing class or struct declaration (if any), if a member with the given name exists, is accessible, and denotes a type, then the *namespace-or-type-name* refers to that member. Note that nontype members (constants, fields, methods, properties, indexers, operators, instance constructors, destructors, and static constructors) are ignored when determining the meaning of a *namespace-or-type-name*.

- Otherwise, starting with the namespace in which the *namespace-or-type-name* occurs, continuing with each enclosing namespace (if any), and ending with the global namespace, the following steps are evaluated until an entity is located.

  • If the namespace contains a namespace member with the given name, then the *namespace-or-type-name* refers to that member and, depending on the member, is classified as a namespace or a type.

  • Otherwise, if the namespace has a corresponding namespace declaration enclosing the location where the *namespace-or-type-name* occurs, then the following occurs.

    - If the namespace declaration contains a *using-alias-directive* that associates the given name with an imported namespace or type, then the *namespace-or-type-name* refers to that namespace or type.

    - Otherwise, if the namespaces imported by the *using-namespace-directive*s of the namespace declaration contain exactly one type with the given name, then the *namespace-or-type-name* refers to that type.

    - Otherwise, if the namespaces imported by the *using-namespace-directive*s of the namespace declaration contain more than one type with the given name, then the *namespace-or-type-name* is ambiguous and an error occurs.

  - Otherwise, the *namespace-or-type-name* is undefined and a compile-time error occurs.

• Otherwise, the *namespace-or-type-name* is of the form N.I, where N is a *namespace-or-type-name* consisting of all identifiers but the rightmost one, and I is the rightmost identifier. N is first resolved as a *namespace-or-type-name*. If the resolution of N is not successful, a compile-time error occurs. Otherwise, N.I is resolved as follows.

  - If N is a namespace and I is the name of an accessible member of that namespace, then N.I refers to that member and, depending on the member, is classified as a namespace or a type.

  - If N is a class or struct type and I is the name of an accessible type in N, then N.I refers to that type.

  - Otherwise, N.I is an *invalid namespace-or-type-name*, and a compile-time error occurs.

3.8.1 Fully Qualified Names

Every namespace and type has a ***fully qualified name***, which uniquely identifies the namespace or type amongst all others. The fully qualified name of a namespace or type N is determined as follows.

- If N is a member of the global namespace, its fully qualified name is N.

- Otherwise, its fully qualified name is S.N, where S is the fully qualified name of the namespace or type in which N is declared.

In other words, the fully qualified name of N is the complete hierarchical path of identifiers that lead to N, starting from the global namespace. Because every member of a namespace or type must have a unique name, it follows that the fully qualified name of a namespace or type is always unique.

The following example shows several namespace and type declarations along with their associated fully qualified names.

```
class A {}              // A

namespace X             // X
{
    class B             // X.B
    {
        class C {}      // X.B.C
    }

    namespace Y         // X.Y
    {
        class D {}      // X.Y.D
    }
}

namespace X.Y           // X.Y
{
    class E {}          // X.Y.E
}
```

3.9 Automatic Memory Management

C# employs automatic memory management, which frees developers from manually allocating and freeing the memory occupied by objects. Automatic memory management policies are implemented by a *garbage collector*. The memory management life cycle of an object is as follows.

1. When the object is created, memory is allocated for it, the constructor is run, and the object is considered live.

2. If the object, or any part of it, cannot be accessed by any possible continuation of execution, other than the running of destructors, the object is considered no longer in use, and it becomes eligible for destruction. The C# compiler and the garbage collector may choose to analyze code to determine which references to an object may be used in the

future. For instance, if a local variable that is in scope is the only existing reference to an object, but that local variable is never referred to in any possible continuation of execution from the current execution point in the procedure, the garbage collector may (but is not required to) treat the object as no longer in use.

3. Once the object is eligible for destruction, at some unspecified later time, the destructor (§10.12) (if any) for the object is run. Unless overridden by explicit calls, the destructor for the object is run once only.

4. Once the destructor for an object is run, if that object (or any part of it) cannot be accessed by any possible continuation of execution, including the running of destructors, the object is considered inaccessible and the object becomes eligible for collection.

5. Finally, at some time after the object becomes eligible for collection, the garbage collector frees the memory associated with that object.

The garbage collector maintains information about object usage and uses this information to make memory management decisions, such as where in memory to locate a newly created object, when to relocate an object, and when an object is no longer in use or inaccessible.

Like other languages that assume the existence of a garbage collector, C# is designed so that the garbage collector may implement a wide range of memory management policies. For instance, C# does not require that destructors be run or that objects be collected as soon as they are eligible or that destructors be run in any particular order or on any particular thread.

The behavior of the garbage collector can be controlled, to some degree, via static methods on the class System.GC. This class can be used to request a collection to occur, destructors to be run (or not run), and so forth.

Because the garbage collector is allowed wide latitude in deciding when to collect objects and run destructors, a conforming implementation may produce output that differs from that shown by the following code. The program creates an instance of class A and an instance of class B.

```
using System;
class A
{
    ~A() {
        Console.WriteLine("Destruct instance of A");
    }
}
class B
{
    object Ref;
```

```
        public B(object o) {
            Ref = o;
        }
        ~B() {
            Console.WriteLine("Destruct instance of B");
        }
    }
    class Test
    {
        static void Main() {
            B b = new B(new A());
            b = null;
            GC.Collect();
            GC.WaitForPendingFinalizers();
        }
    }
```

These objects become eligible for garbage collection when the variable b is assigned the value `null` because after this time it is impossible for any user-written code to access them. The output could be either the following

```
Destruct instance of A
Destruct instance of B
```

or the following

```
Destruct instance of B
Destruct instance of A
```

because the language imposes no constraints on the order in which objects are garbage collected.

In subtle cases, the distinction between "eligible for destruction" and "eligible for collection" can be important. For example, in the following code

```
using System;
class A
{
    ~A() {
        Console.WriteLine("Destruct instance of A");
    }
    public void F() {
        Console.WriteLine("A.F");
        Test.RefA = this;
    }
}
class B
{
    public A Ref;
```

```
        ~B() {
            Console.WriteLine("Destruct instance of B");
            Ref.F();
        }
    }
    class Test
    {
        public static A RefA;
        public static B RefB;

        static void Main() {
            RefB = new B();
            RefA = new A();
            RefB.Ref = RefA;
            RefB = null;
            RefA = null;

            // A and B now eligible for destruction
            GC.Collect();
            GC.WaitForPendingFinalizers();

            // B now eligible for collection, but A is not
            if (RefA != null)
                Console.WriteLine("RefA is not null");
        }
    }
```

if the garbage collector chooses to run the destructor of A before the destructor of B, then the output of this program might be as follows.

```
Destruct instance of A
Destruct instance of B
A.F
RefA is not null
```

Note that although the instance of A was not in use and A's destructor was run, it is still possible for methods of A (in this case, F) to be called from another destructor. Also, note that running of a destructor may cause an object to become usable from the mainline program again. In this case, the running of B's destructor caused an instance of A that was previously not in use to become accessible from the live reference Test.RefA. After the call to WaitForPendingFinalizers, the instance of B is eligible for collection, but the instance of A is not because of the reference Test.RefA.

To avoid confusion and unexpected behavior, it is generally a good idea for destructors to only perform cleanup on data stored in their object's own fields and not to perform any actions on referenced objects or static fields.

3.10 Execution Order

Execution of a C# program proceeds such that the side effects of each executing thread are preserved at critical execution points. A *side effect* is defined as a read or write of a volatile field, a write to a nonvolatile variable, a write to an external resource, and the throwing of an exception. The critical execution points at which the order of these side effects must be preserved are references to volatile fields (§10.4.3), lock statements (§8.12), and thread creation and termination. The execution environment is free to change the order of execution of a C# program, subject to the following constraints.

- Data dependence is preserved within a thread of execution. That is, the value of each variable is computed as if all statements in the thread were executed in original program order.

- Initialization ordering rules are preserved (§10.4.4 and §10.4.5).

- The ordering of side effects is preserved with respect to volatile reads and writes (§10.4.3). Additionally, the execution environment need not evaluate part of an expression if it can deduce that that expression's value is not used and that no needed side effects are produced (including any caused by calling a method or accessing a volatile field). When program execution is interrupted by an asynchronous event (such as an exception thrown by another thread), it is not guaranteed that the observable side effects are visible in the original program order.

4. Types

The types of the C# language are divided into two main categories: value types and reference types.

type:
    value-type
    reference-type

A third category of types, pointers, is available only in unsafe code. This is discussed further in §18.2.

Value types differ from reference types in that variables of the value types directly contain their data, whereas variables of the reference types store *references* to their data, the latter being known as objects. With reference types, it is possible for two variables to reference the same object and thus possible for operations on one variable to affect the object referenced by the other variable. With value types, the variables each have their own copy of the data, and it is not possible for operations on one to affect the other.

C#'s type system is unified such that *a value of any type can be treated as an object*. Every type in C# directly or indirectly derives from the `object` class type, and `object` is the ultimate base class of all types. Values of reference types are treated as objects simply by viewing the values as type `object`. Values of value types are treated as objects by performing boxing and unboxing operations (§4.3).

4.1 Value Types

A value type is either a struct type or an enumeration type. C# provides a set of predefined struct types called the **simple types**. The simple types are identified through reserved words.

value-type:
    struct-type
    enum-type

struct-type:
    type-name
    simple-type

simple-type:
    numeric-type
    `bool`

numeric-type:
    integral-type
    floating-point-type
    `decimal`

integral-type:
    `sbyte`
    `byte`
    `short`
    `ushort`
    `int`
    `uint`
    `long`
    `ulong`
    `char`

floating-point-type:
    `float`
    `double`

enum-type:
    type-name

A variable of a value type always contains a value of that type. Unlike reference types, it is not possible for a value of a value type to be `null` or to reference an object of a more derived type.

Assignment to a variable of a value type creates a *copy* of the value being assigned. This differs from assignment to a variable of a reference type, which copies the reference but not the object identified by the reference.

4.1.1 The System.ValueType Type

All value types implicitly inherit from the class `System.ValueType`, which, in turn, inherits from class `object`. It is not possible for any type to derive from a value type, and value types are thus implicitly sealed (§10.1.1.2).

Note that `System.ValueType` is not itself a *value-type*. Rather, it is a *class-type* from which all *value-types* are automatically derived.

4.1.2 Default Constructors

All value types implicitly declare a public parameterless instance constructor called the *default constructor*. The default constructor returns a zero-initialized instance known as the *default value* for the value type.

- For all *simple-types*, the default value is the value produced by a bit pattern of all zeros.

  - For `sbyte`, `byte`, `short`, `ushort`, `int`, `uint`, `long`, and `ulong`, the default value is `0`.

  - For `char`, the default value is `'\x0000'`.

  - For `float`, the default value is `0.0f`.

  - For `double`, the default value is `0.0d`.

  - For `decimal`, the default value is `0.0m`.

  - For `bool`, the default value is `false`.

- For an *enum-type* `E`, the default value is `0`.

- For a *struct-type*, the default value is the value produced by setting all value type fields to their default value and all reference type fields to `null`.

Like any other instance constructor, the default constructor of a value type is invoked using the `new` operator. For efficiency reasons, this requirement is not intended to actually have the implementation generate a constructor call. In the following example, the variables `i` and `j` are both initialized to zero.

```
class A
{
    void F() {
        int i = 0;
        int j = new int();
    }
}
```

Because every value type implicitly has a public parameterless instance constructor, it is not possible for a struct type to contain an explicit declaration of a parameterless constructor. A struct type is however permitted to declare parameterized instance constructors (§11.3.8).

4. Types

4.1.3 **Struct Types**

A struct type is a value type that can declare constants, fields, methods, properties, index-ers, operators, instance constructors, static constructors, and nested types. Struct types are described in §11.

4.1.4 **Simple Types**

C# provides a set of predefined struct types called the simple types. The simple types are identified through reserved words, but these reserved words are simply aliases for pre-defined struct types in the System namespace, as described in the following table.

Reserved Word	Aliased Type
sbyte	System.SByte
byte	System.Byte
short	System.Int16
ushort	System.UInt16
int	System.Int32
uint	System.UInt32
long	System.Int64
ulong	System.UInt64
char	System.Char
float	System.Single
double	System.Double
bool	System.Boolean
decimal	System.Decimal

Because a simple type aliases a struct type, every simple type has members. For example, int has the members declared in System.Int32 and the members inherited from System.Object, and the following statements are permitted.

```
int i = int.MaxValue;          // System.Int32.MaxValue constant
string s = i.ToString();        // System.Int32.ToString() instance method
string t = 123.ToString();      // System.Int32.ToString() instance method
```

The simple types differ from other struct types in that they permit certain additional operations.

- Most simple types permit values to be created by writing *literals* (§2.4.4). For example, 123 is a literal of type int and 'a' is a literal of type char. C# makes no provision for literals of struct types in general, and nondefault values of other struct types are ultimately always created through instance constructors of those struct types.

- When the operands of an expression are all simple type constants, it is possible for the compiler to evaluate the expression at compile time. Such an expression is known as a *constant-expression* (§7.15). Expressions involving operators defined by other struct types are not considered to be constant expressions.

- Through const declarations it is possible to declare constants of the simple types (§10.3). It is not possible to have constants of other struct types, but a similar effect is provided by static readonly fields.

- Conversions involving simple types can participate in evaluation of conversion operators defined by other struct types, but a user-defined conversion operator can never participate in evaluation of another user-defined operator (§6.4.2).

4.1.5 Integral Types

C# supports nine integral types: sbyte, byte, short, ushort, int, uint, long, ulong, and char. The integral types have the following sizes and ranges of values.

- The sbyte type represents signed 8-bit integers with values between –128 and 127.

- The byte type represents unsigned 8-bit integers with values between 0 and 255.

- The short type represents signed 16-bit integers with values between –32768 and 32767.

- The ushort type represents unsigned 16-bit integers with values between 0 and 65535.

- The int type represents signed 32-bit integers with values between –2147483648 and 2147483647.

- The uint type represents unsigned 32-bit integers with values between 0 and 4294967295.

- The long type represents signed 64-bit integers with values between –9223372036854775808 and 9223372036854775807.

4. Types

- The `ulong` type represents unsigned 64-bit integers with values between 0 and 18446744073709551615.

- The `char` type represents unsigned 16-bit integers with values between 0 and 65535. The set of possible values for the `char` type corresponds to the Unicode character set. Although `char` has the same representation as `ushort`, not all operations permitted on one type are permitted on the other.

The integral-type unary and binary operators always operate with signed 32-bit precision, unsigned 32-bit precision, signed 64-bit precision, or unsigned 64-bit precision.

- For the unary + and ~ operators, the operand is converted to type T, where T is the first of `int`, `uint`, `long`, and `ulong` that can fully represent all possible values of the operand. The operation is then performed using the precision of type T, and the type of the result is T.

- For the unary – operator, the operand is converted to type T, where T is the first of `int` and `long` that can fully represent all possible values of the operand. The operation is then performed using the precision of type T, and the type of the result is T. The unary – operator cannot be applied to operands of type `ulong`.

- For the binary +, –, *, /, %, &, ^, |, ==, !=, >, <, >=, and <= operators, the operands are converted to type T, where T is the first of `int`, `uint`, `long`, and `ulong` that can fully represent all possible values of both operands. The operation is then performed using the precision of type T, and the type of the result is T (or `bool` for the relational operators). It is not permitted for one operand to be of type `long` and the other to be of type `ulong` with the binary operators.

- For the binary << and >> operators, the left operand is converted to type T, where T is the first of `int`, `uint`, `long`, and `ulong` that can fully represent all possible values of the operand. The operation is then performed using the precision of type T, and the type of the result is T.

The `char` type is classified as an integral type, but it differs from the other integral types in two ways.

- There are no implicit conversions from other types to the `char` type. In particular, even though the `sbyte`, `byte`, and `ushort` types have ranges of values that are fully representable using the `char` type, implicit conversions from `sbyte`, `byte`, or `ushort` to `char` do not exist.

- Constants of the `char` type must be written as *character-literals* or as *integer-literals* in combination with a cast to type `char`. For example, `(char)10` is the same as `'\x000A'`.

The `checked` and `unchecked` operators and statements control overflow checking for integral-type arithmetic operations and conversions (§7.5.12). In a `checked` context, an overflow produces a compile-time error or causes a `System.OverflowException` to be thrown. In an `unchecked` context, overflows are ignored and any high-order bits that do not fit in the destination type are discarded.

4.1.6 Floating Point Types

C# supports two floating point types: `float` and `double`. The `float` and `double` types are represented using the 32-bit single-precision and 64-bit double-precision IEEE 754 formats, which provide the following sets of values.

- Positive zero and negative zero. In most situations, positive zero and negative zero behave identically as the simple value zero, but certain operations distinguish between the two (§7.7.2).

- Positive infinity and negative infinity. Infinities are produced by such operations as dividing a nonzero number by zero. For example, `1.0 / 0.0` yields positive infinity, and `−1.0 / 0.0` yields negative infinity.

- The *Not-a-Number* value, often abbreviated NaN. NaNs are produced by invalid floating point operations, such as dividing zero by zero.

- The finite set of nonzero values of the form $s \times m \times 2^e$, where s is 1 or −1, and m and e are determined by the particular floating point type: For `float`, $0 < m < 2^{24}$ and $-149 \leq e \leq 104$, and for `double`, $0 < m < 2^{53}$ and $-1075 \leq e \leq 970$. Denormalized floating point numbers are considered valid nonzero values.

The `float` type can represent values ranging from approximately 1.5×10^{-45} to 3.4×10^{38} with a precision of seven digits.

The `double` type can represent values ranging from approximately 5.0×10^{-324} to 1.7×10^{308} with a precision of 15–16 digits.

If one of the operands of a binary operator is of a floating point type, then the other operand must be of an integral type or a floating point type, and the operation is evaluated as follows.

- If one of the operands is of an integral type, then that operand is converted to the floating point type of the other operand.

- Then, if either of the operands is of type `double`, the other operand is converted to `double`, the operation is performed using at least `double` range and precision, and the type of the result is `double` (or `bool` for the relational operators).

- Otherwise, the operation is performed using at least `float` range and precision, and the type of the result is `float` (or `bool` for the relational operators).

4. Types

The floating point operators, including the assignment operators, never produce exceptions. Instead, in exceptional situations, floating point operations produce zero, infinity, or NaN, as described next.

- If the result of a floating point operation is too small for the destination format, the result of the operation becomes positive zero or negative zero.

- If the result of a floating point operation is too large for the destination format, the result of the operation becomes positive infinity or negative infinity.

- If a floating point operation is invalid, the result of the operation becomes NaN.

- If at least one operand of a floating point operation is NaN, the result of the operation becomes NaN.

Floating point operations may be performed with higher precision than the result type of the operation. For example, some hardware architectures support an "extended" or "long double" floating point type with greater range and precision than the double type and implicitly perform all floating point operations using this higher precision type. Only at excessive cost in performance can such hardware architectures be made to perform floating point operations with *less* precision, and rather than require an implementation to forfeit both performance and precision, C# allows a higher precision type to be used for all floating point operations. Other than delivering more precise results, this rarely has any measurable effects. However, in expressions of the form x * y / z, where the multiplication produces a result that is outside the double range but the subsequent division brings the temporary result back into the double range, the fact that the expression is evaluated in a higher range format may cause a finite result to be produced instead of an infinity.

4.1.7 The decimal Type

The decimal type is a 128-bit data type suitable for financial and monetary calculations. The decimal type can represent values ranging from 1.0×10^{-28} to approximately 7.9×10^{28} with 28–29 significant digits.

The finite set of values of type decimal are of the form $(-1)^s \times c \times 10^{-e}$, where the sign s is 0 or 1, the coefficient c is given by $0 \leq c < 2^{96}$, and the scale e is such that $0 \leq e \leq 28$. The decimal type does not support signed zeros, infinities, or NaNs. A decimal is represented as a 96-bit integer scaled by a power of ten. For decimals with an absolute value less than 1.0m, the value is exact to the twenty-eighth decimal place, but no further. For decimals with an absolute value greater than or equal to 1.0m, the value is exact to 28–29 digits. Contrary to the float and double data types, decimal fractional numbers such as 0.1 can be represented exactly in the decimal representation. In the float and double representations, such numbers are often infinite fractions, making those representations more prone to round off errors.

If one of the operands of a binary operator is of type decimal, then the other operand must be of an integral type or of type decimal. If an integral type operand is present, it is converted to decimal before the operation is performed.

The result of an operation on values of type decimal is the same as calculating an exact result (preserving scale, as defined for each operator) and then rounding to fit the representation. Results are rounded to the nearest representable value and, when a result is equally close to two representable values, to the value that has an even number in the least significant digit position (this is known as "banker's rounding"). A zero result always has a sign of 0 and a scale of 0.

If a decimal arithmetic operation produces a value less than or equal to 5×10^{-29} in absolute value, the result of the operation becomes zero. If a decimal arithmetic operation produces a result that is too large for the decimal format, a System.OverflowException is thrown.

The decimal type has greater precision but smaller range than the floating point types. Thus, conversions from the floating point types to decimal might produce overflow exceptions, and conversions from decimal to the floating point types might cause loss of precision. For these reasons, no implicit conversions exist between the floating point types and decimal, and without explicit casts, it is not possible to mix floating point and decimal operands in the same expression.

4.1.8 The bool Type

The bool type represents boolean logical quantities. The possible values of type bool are true and false.

No standard conversions exist between bool and other types. In particular, the bool type is distinct and separate from the integral types, and a bool value cannot be used in place of an integral value, and vice versa.

In the C and C++ languages, a zero integral or floating point value or a null pointer can be converted to the boolean value false, and a nonzero integral or floating point value or a non-null pointer can be converted to the boolean value true. In C#, such conversions are accomplished by explicitly comparing an integral or floating point value to zero or by explicitly comparing an object reference to null.

4.1.9 Enumeration Types

An enumeration type is a distinct type with named constants. Every enumeration type has an underlying type, which must be byte, sbyte, short, ushort, int, uint, long, or ulong. The set of values of the enumeration type is the same as the set of values of the underlying type. Values of the enumeration type are not restricted to the values of the named constants. Enumeration types are defined through enumeration declarations (§14.1).

4. Types

4.2 Reference Types

A reference type is a class type, an interface type, an array type, or a delegate type.

> *reference-type:*
>   *class-type*
>   *interface-type*
>   *array-type*
>   *delegate-type*
>
> *class-type:*
>   *type-name*
>   `object`
>   `string`
>
> *interface-type:*
>   *type-name*
>
> *array-type:*
>   *non-array-type   rank-specifiers*
>
> *non-array-type:*
>   *type*
>
> *rank-specifiers:*
>   *rank-specifier*
>   *rank-specifiers   rank-specifier*
>
> *rank-specifier:*
>   [*dim-separators*_{opt}   ]
>
> *dim-separators:*
>   ,
>   *dim-separators   ,*
>
> *delegate-type:*
>   *type-name*

A reference type value is a reference to an ***instance*** of the type. An instance of a type is also known as an ***object***. The special value `null` is compatible with all reference types and indicates the absence of an instance.

4.2.1 Class Types

A class type defines a data structure that contains data members (constants and fields), function members (methods, properties, events, indexers, operators, instance constructors, destructors, and static constructors), and nested types. Class types support inheritance, a mechanism whereby derived classes can extend and specialize base classes. Instances of class types are created using *object-creation-expressions* (§7.5.10.1).

Class types are described in §10.

Certain predefined class types have special meaning in the C# language, as described in the following table.

Class Type	Description
System.Object	The ultimate base class of all other types. See §4.2.2.
System.String	The string type of the C# language. See §4.2.3.
System.ValueType	The base class of all value types. See §4.1.1.
System.Enum	The base class of all enum types. See §14.
System.Array	The base class of all array types. See §12.
System.Delegate	The base class of all delegate types. See §15.
System.Exception	The base class of all exception types. See §16.

4.2.2 The object Type

The object class type is the ultimate base class of all other types. Every type in C# directly or indirectly derives from the object class type.

The keyword object is simply an alias for the predefined class System.Object.

4.2.3 The string Type

The string type is a sealed class type that inherits directly from object. Instances of the string class represent Unicode character strings.

Values of the string type can be written as string literals (§2.4.4).

The keyword string is simply an alias for the predefined class System.String.

4.2.4 Interface Types

An interface defines a contract. A class or struct that implements an interface must adhere to its contract. An interface may inherit from multiple base interfaces, and a class or struct may implement multiple interfaces.

4. Types

Interface types are described in §13.

4.2.5 Array Types

An array is a data structure that contains zero or more variables that are accessed through computed indices. The variables contained in an array, also called the "elements" of the array, are all of the same type, and this type is called the "element type" of the array.

Array types are described in §12.

4.2.6 Delegate Types

A delegate is a data structure that refers to one or more methods, and for instance methods, it also refers to their corresponding object instances.

The closest equivalent of a delegate in C or C++ is a function pointer, but whereas a function pointer can only reference static functions, a delegate can reference both static and instance methods. In the latter case, the delegate stores not only a reference to the method's entry point but also a reference to the object instance on which to invoke the method.

Delegate types are described in §15.

4.3 Boxing and Unboxing

The concept of boxing and unboxing is central to C#'s type system. It provides a bridge between *value-type*s and *reference-type*s by permitting any value of a *value-type* to be converted to and from type `object`. Boxing and unboxing enables a unified view of the type system wherein a value of any type can ultimately be treated as an object.

4.3.1 Boxing Conversions

A boxing conversion permits a *value-type* to be implicitly converted to a *reference-type*. The following boxing conversions exist:

- From any *value-type* (including any *enum-type*) to the type `object`
- From any *value-type* (including any *enum-type*) to the type `System.ValueType`
- From any *value-type* to any *interface-type* implemented by the *value-type*
- From any *enum-type* to the type `System.Enum`

Boxing a value of a *value-type* consists of allocating an object instance and copying the *value-type* value into that instance.

The actual process of boxing a value of a *value-type* is best explained by imagining the existence of a **boxing class** for that type. For any *value-type* T, the boxing class behaves as if it were declared as follows.

```
sealed class T_Box: System.ValueType
{
    T value;
    public T_Box(T t) {
        value = t;
    }
}
```

Boxing of a value v of type T now consists of executing the expression new T_Box(v), and returning the resulting instance as a value of type object. Thus, the statements

```
int i = 123;
object box = i;
```

conceptually correspond to

```
int i = 123;
object box = new int_Box(i);
```

Boxing classes such as the previous T_Box and int_Box do not actually exist, and the dynamic type of a boxed value is not actually a class type. Instead, a boxed value of type T has the dynamic type T, and a dynamic type check using the is operator can simply reference type T. This example

```
int i = 123;
object box = i;
if (box is int) {
    Console.Write("Box contains an int");
}
```

will output the string Box contains an int on the console.

A boxing conversion implies *making a copy* of the value being boxed. This is different from a conversion of a *reference-type* to type object, in which the value continues to reference the same instance and simply is regarded as the less derived type object. For example, given the declaration

```
struct Point
{
    public int x, y;
    public Point(int x, int y) {
        this.x = x;
        this.y = y;
    }
}
```

the following statements

```
Point p = new Point(10, 10);
object box = p;
p.x = 20;
Console.Write(((Point)box).x);
```

will output the value 10 on the console because the implicit boxing operation that occurs in the assignment of p to box causes the value of p to be copied. Had Point been declared a class instead, the value 20 would be output because p and box would reference the same instance.

4.3.2 Unboxing Conversions

An unboxing conversion permits a *reference-type* to be explicitly converted to a *value-type*. The following unboxing conversions exist:

- From the type object to any *value-type* (including any *enum-type*)

- From the type System.ValueType to any *value-type* (including any *enum-type*)

- From any *interface-type* to any *value-type* that implements the *interface-type*

- From the type System.Enum to any *enum-type*

An unboxing operation consists of first checking that the object instance is a boxed value of the given *value-type* and then copying the value out of the instance.

Referring to the imaginary boxing class described in the previous section, an unboxing conversion of an object box to a *value-type* T consists of executing the expression ((T_Box)box).value. Thus, the statements

```
object box = 123;
int i = (int)box;
```

conceptually correspond to

```
object box = new int_Box(123);
int i = ((int_Box)box).value;
```

For an unboxing conversion to a given *value-type* to succeed at runtime, the value of the source operand must be a reference to an object that was previously created by boxing a value of that *value-type*. If the source operand is null, a System.NullReferenceException is thrown. If the source operand is a reference to an incompatible object, a System.InvalidCastException is thrown.

5. Variables

Variables represent storage locations. Every variable has a type that determines what values can be stored in the variable. C# is a type-safe language, and the C# compiler guarantees that values stored in variables are always of the appropriate type. The value of a variable can be changed through assignment or through the ++ and -- operators.

A variable must be *definitely assigned* (§5.3) before its value can be obtained.

As described in the following sections, variables are either *initially assigned* or *initially unassigned*. An initially assigned variable has a well-defined initial value and is always considered definitely assigned. An initially unassigned variable has no initial value. For an initially unassigned variable to be considered definitely assigned at a certain location, an assignment to the variable must occur in every possible execution path leading to that location.

5.1 Variable Categories

C# defines seven categories of variables: static variables, instance variables, array elements, value parameters, reference parameters, output parameters, and local variables. The sections that follow describe each of these categories.

In the example

```
class A
{
    public static int x;
    int y;
    void F(int[] v, int a, ref int b, out int c) {
        int i = 1;
        c = a + b++;
    }
}
```

x is a static variable, y is an instance variable, v[0] is an array element, a is a value parameter, b is a reference parameter, c is an output parameter, and i is a local variable.

5.1.1 Static Variables

A field declared with the `static` modifier is called a *static variable*. A static variable comes into existence before execution of the static constructor (§10.11) for its containing type and ceases to exist when the associated application domain ceases to exist.

The initial value of a static variable is the default value (§5.2) of the variable's type.

For purposes of definite assignment checking, a static variable is considered initially assigned.

5.1.2 Instance Variables

A field declared without the `static` modifier is called an *instance variable*.

5.1.2.1 *Instance Variables in Classes*

An instance variable of a class comes into existence when a new instance of that class is created and ceases to exist when there are no references to that instance and the instance's destructor (if any) has executed.

The initial value of an instance variable of a class is the default value (§5.2) of the variable's type.

For the purpose of definite assignment checking, an instance variable of a class is considered initially assigned.

5.1.2.2 *Instance Variables in Structs*

An instance variable of a struct has exactly the same lifetime as the struct variable to which it belongs. In other words, when a variable of a struct type comes into existence or ceases to exist, so too do the instance variables of the struct.

The initial assignment state of an instance variable of a struct is the same as that of the containing struct variable. In other words, when a struct variable is considered initially assigned, so too are its instance variables, and when a struct variable is considered initially unassigned, its instance variables are likewise unassigned.

5.1.3 Array Elements

The elements of an array come into existence when an array instance is created and cease to exist when there are no references to that array instance.

The initial value of each of the elements of an array is the default value (§5.2) of the type of the array elements.

For the purpose of definite assignment checking, an array element is considered initially assigned.

5.1.4 **Value Parameters**

A parameter declared without a `ref` or `out` modifier is a *value parameter*.

A value parameter comes into existence upon invocation of the function member (method, instance constructor, accessor, or operator) to which the parameter belongs and is initialized with the value of the argument given in the invocation. A value parameter ceases to exist upon return of the function member.

For the purpose of definite assignment checking, a value parameter is considered initially assigned.

5.1.5 **Reference Parameters**

A parameter declared with a `ref` modifier is a *reference parameter*.

A reference parameter does not create a new storage location. Instead, a reference parameter represents the same storage location as the variable given as the argument in the function member invocation. Thus, the value of a reference parameter is always the same as the underlying variable.

The following definite assignment rules apply to reference parameters. Note the different rules for output parameters described in §5.1.6.

- A variable must be definitely assigned (§5.3) before it can be passed as a reference parameter in a function member invocation.
- Within a function member, a reference parameter is considered initially assigned.

Within an instance method or instance accessor of a struct type, the `this` keyword behaves exactly as a reference parameter of the struct type (§7.5.7).

5.1.6 **Output Parameters**

A parameter declared with an `out` modifier is an *output parameter*.

An output parameter does not create a new storage location. Instead, an output parameter represents the same storage location as the variable given as the argument in the function member invocation. Thus, the value of an output parameter is always the same as the underlying variable.

The following definite assignment rules apply to output parameters. Note the different rules for reference parameters described in §5.1.5.

- A variable need not be definitely assigned before it can be passed as an output parameter in a function member invocation.

- Following the normal completion of a function member invocation, each variable that was passed as an output parameter is considered assigned in that execution path.

- Within a function member, an output parameter is considered initially unassigned.

- Every output parameter of a function member must be definitely assigned (§5.3) before the function member returns normally.

Within an instance constructor of a struct type, the `this` keyword behaves exactly as an output parameter of the struct type (§7.5.7).

5.1.7 Local Variables

A *local variable* is declared by a *local-variable-declaration*, which may occur in a *block*, a *for-statement*, a *switch-statement*, or a *using-statement*.

The lifetime of a local variable is the portion of program execution during which storage is guaranteed to be reserved for it. This lifetime extends from entry into the *block*, *for-statement*, *switch-statement*, or *using-statement* with which it is associated, until execution of that *block*, *for-statement*, *switch-statement*, or *using-statement* ends in any way. (Entering an enclosed *block* or calling a method suspends, but does not end, execution of the current *block*, *for-statement*, *switch-statement*, or *using-statement*.) If the parent *block*, *for-statement*, *switch-statement*, or *using-statement* is entered recursively, a new instance of the local variable is created each time, and its *local-variable-initializer*, if any, is evaluated each time.

A local variable is not automatically initialized and thus has no default value. For the purpose of definite assignment checking, a local variable is considered initially unassigned. A *local-variable-declaration* may include a *local-variable-initializer*, in which case the variable is considered definitely assigned in its entire scope, except within the expression provided in the *local-variable-initializer*.

Within the scope of a local variable, it is a compile-time error to refer to that local variable in a textual position that precedes its *local-variable-declarator*.

The actual lifetime of a local variable is implementation dependent. For example, a compiler might statically determine that a local variable in a block is only used for a small portion of that block. Using this analysis, the compiler could generate code that results in the variable's storage having a shorter lifetime than its containing block.

The storage referred to by a local reference variable is reclaimed independently of the lifetime of that local reference variable (§3.9).

A local variable is also declared by a *foreach-statement* and by a *specific-catch-clause* for a *try-statement*. For a *foreach-statement*, the local variable is an iteration variable (§8.8.4). For a *specific-catch-clause*, the local variable is an exception variable (§8.10). A local variable declared by a *foreach-statement* or *specific-catch-clause* is considered definitely assigned in its entire scope.

5.2 Default Values

The following categories of variables are automatically initialized to their default values:

- Static variables
- Instance variables of class instances
- Array elements

The default value of a variable depends on the type of the variable and is determined as follows.

- For a variable of a *value-type*, the default value is the same as the value computed by the *value-type*'s default constructor (§4.1.1).
- For a variable of a *reference-type*, the default value is `null`.

Initialization to default values is typically done by having the memory manager or garbage collector initialize memory to all-bits-zero before it is allocated for use. For this reason, it is convenient to use all-bits-zero to represent the `null` reference.

5.3 Definite Assignment

At a given location in the executable code of a function member, a variable is said to be **definitely assigned** if the compiler can prove, by static flow analysis, that the variable has been automatically initialized or has been the target of at least one assignment. The rules of definite assignment are

- An initially assigned variable (§5.3.1) is always considered definitely assigned.
- An initially unassigned variable (§5.3.2) is considered definitely assigned at a given location if all possible execution paths leading to that location contain at least one of the following:
    - A simple assignment (§7.13.1) in which the variable is the left operand
    - An invocation expression (§7.5.5) or object creation expression (§7.5.10.1) that passes the variable as an output parameter

- For a local variable, a local variable declaration (§8.5) that includes a variable initializer

The definite assignment states of instance variables of a *struct-type* variable are tracked individually as well as collectively. In additional to the previous rules, the following rules apply to *struct-type* variables and their instance variables.

- An instance variable is considered definitely assigned if its containing *struct-type* variable is considered definitely assigned.

- A *struct-type* variable is considered definitely assigned if each of its instance variables is considered definitely assigned.

Definite assignment is a requirement in the following contexts.

- A variable must be definitely assigned at each location where its value is obtained. This ensures that undefined values never occur. The occurrence of a variable in an expression is considered to obtain the value of the variable, except when one of the following is true.

  - The variable is the left operand of a simple assignment.
  - The variable is passed as an output parameter.
  - The variable is a *struct-type* variable and occurs as the left operand of a member access.

- A variable must be definitely assigned at each location where it is passed as a reference parameter. This ensures that the function member being invoked can consider the reference parameter initially assigned.

- All output parameters of a function member must be definitely assigned at each location where the function member returns (through a `return` statement or through execution reaching the end of the function member body). This ensures that function members do not return undefined values in output parameters, thus enabling the compiler to consider a function member invocation that takes a variable as an output parameter equivalent to an assignment to the variable.

- The `this` variable of a *struct-type* instance constructor must be definitely assigned at each location where that instance constructor returns.

5.3.1 Initially Assigned Variables
The following categories of variables are classified as initially assigned:

- Static variables
- Instance variables of class instances

- Instance variables of initially assigned struct variables
- Array elements
- Value parameters
- Reference parameters
- Variables declared in a `catch` clause or a `foreach` statement

5.3.2 Initially Unassigned Variables

The following categories of variables are classified as initially unassigned:

- Instance variables of initially unassigned struct variables
- Output parameters, including the `this` variable of struct instance constructors
- Local variables, except those declared in a `catch` clause or a `foreach` statement

5.3.3 Precise Rules for Determining Definite Assignment

To determine that each used variable is definitely assigned, the compiler must use a process that is equivalent to the one described in this section.

The compiler processes the body of each function member that has one or more initially unassigned variables. For each initially unassigned variable v, the compiler determines a **definite assignment state** for v at each of the following points in the function member:

- At the beginning of each statement
- At the end point (§8.1) of each statement
- On each arc that transfers control to another statement or to the end point of a statement
- At the beginning of each expression
- At the end of each expression

The definite assignment state of v can be either

- Definitely assigned. This indicates that on all possible control flows to this point, v has been assigned a value.
- Not definitely assigned. For the state of a variable at the end of an expression of type `bool`, the state of a variable that is not definitely assigned may (but does not necessarily) fall into one of the following substates.
    - Definitely assigned after true expression. This state indicates that v is definitely assigned if the boolean expression evaluated as true but is not necessarily assigned if the boolean expression evaluated as false.

- Definitely assigned after false expression. This state indicates that v is definitely assigned if the boolean expression evaluated as false but is not necessarily assigned if the boolean expression evaluated as true.

The following rules govern how the state of a variable v is determined at each location.

5.3.3.1 *General Rules for Statements*
The following general rules apply to statements.

- v is not definitely assigned at the beginning of a function member body.

- v is definitely assigned at the beginning of any unreachable statement.

- The definite assignment state of v at the beginning of any other statement is determined by checking the definite assignment state of v on all control flow transfers that target the beginning of that statement. If (and only if) v is definitely assigned on all such control flow transfers, then v is definitely assigned at the beginning of the statement. The set of possible control flow transfers is determined in the same way as for checking statement reachability (§8.1).

- The definite assignment state of v at the end point of a block, checked, unchecked, if, while, do, for, foreach, lock, using, or switch statement is determined by checking the definite assignment state of v on all control flow transfers that target the end point of that statement. If v is definitely assigned on all such control flow transfers, then v is definitely assigned at the end point of the statement. Otherwise, v is not definitely assigned at the end point of the statement. The set of possible control flow transfers is determined in the same way as for checking statement reachability (§8.1).

5.3.3.2 *Block Statements, checked, and unchecked Statements*
The definite assignment state of v on the control transfer to the first statement of the statement list in the block (or to the end point of the block if the statement list is empty) is the same as the definite assignment statement of v before the block, checked, or unchecked statement.

5.3.3.3 *Expression Statements*
For an expression statement *stmt* that consists of the expression *expr*

- v has the same definite assignment state at the beginning of *expr* as at the beginning of *stmt*.

- If v if definitely assigned at the end of *expr*, it is definitely assigned at the end point of *stmt*; otherwise, it is not definitely assigned at the end point of *stmt*.

5.3.3.4 *Declaration Statements*

- If *stmt* is a declaration statement without initializers, then v has the same definite assignment state at the end point of *stmt* as at the beginning of *stmt*.

- If *stmt* is a declaration statement with initializers, then the definite assignment state for v is determined as if *stmt* were a statement list, with one assignment statement for each declaration with an initializer (in the order of declaration).

5.3.3.5 *If Statements*

For an `if` statement *stmt* of the form

```
if ( expr )  then-stmt else else-stmt
```

- v has the same definite assignment state at the beginning of *expr* as at the beginning of *stmt*.

- If v is definitely assigned at the end of *expr*, then it is definitely assigned on the control flow transfer to *then-stmt* and to either *else-stmt* or to the end point of *stmt* if there is no `else` clause.

- If v has the state "definitely assigned after true expression" at the end of *expr*, then it is definitely assigned on the control flow transfer to *then-stmt* and not definitely assigned on the control flow transfer to either *else-stmt* or to the end point of *stmt* if there is no `else` clause.

- If v has the state "definitely assigned after false expression" at the end of *expr*, then it is definitely assigned on the control flow transfer to *else-stmt* and not definitely assigned on the control flow transfer to *then-stmt*. It is definitely assigned at the end point of *stmt* if and only if it is definitely assigned at the end point of *then-stmt*.

- Otherwise, v is considered not definitely assigned on the control flow transfer to either the *then-stmt* or *else-stmt* or to the end point of *stmt* if there is no `else` clause.

5.3.3.6 *switch Statements*

In a `switch` statement *stmt* with a controlling expression *expr*

- The definite assignment state of v at the beginning of *expr* is the same as the state of v at the beginning of *stmt*.

- The definite assignment state of v on the control flow transfer to a reachable `case` or `default` section is the same as the definite assignment state of v at the end of *expr*.

5.3.3.7 *while Statements*

For a `while` statement *stmt* of the form

> `while` (*expr*) *while-body*

- *v* has the same definite assignment state at the beginning of *expr* as at the beginning of *stmt*.

- If *v* is definitely assigned at the end of *expr*, then it is definitely assigned on the control flow transfer to *while-body* and to the end point of *stmt*.

- If *v* has the state "definitely assigned after true expression" at the end of *expr*, then it is definitely assigned on the control flow transfer to *while-body* but not definitely assigned at the end point of *stmt*.

- If *v* has the state "definitely assigned after false expression" at the end of *expr*, then it is definitely assigned on the control flow transfer to the end point of *stmt* but not definitely assigned on the control flow transfer to *while-body*.

5.3.3.8 *do Statements*

For a `do` statement *stmt* of the form

> `do` *do-body* `while` (*expr*) ;

- *v* has the same definite assignment state on the control flow transfer from the beginning of *stmt* to *do-body* as at the beginning of *stmt*.

- *v* has the same definite assignment state at the beginning of *expr* as at the end point of *do-body*.

- If *v* is definitely assigned at the end of *expr*, then it is definitely assigned on the control flow transfer to the end point of *stmt*.

- If *v* has the state "definitely assigned after false expression" at the end of *expr*, then it is definitely assigned on the control flow transfer to the end point of *stmt*.

5.3.3.9 *for Statements*

Definite assignment checking for a `for` statement of the form

> `for` (*for-initializer* ; *for-condition* ; *for-iterator*) *embedded-statement*

is done as if the statement were written as follows.

```
{
    for-initializer ;
    while ( for-condition ) {
        embedded-statement ;
        for-iterator ;
    }
}
```

If the *for-condition* is omitted from the `for` statement, then evaluation of definite assignment proceeds as if *for-condition* were replaced with `true` in the previous expansion.

5.3.3.10 *break, continue, and goto Statements*

The definite assignment state of v on the control flow transfer caused by a `break`, `continue`, or `goto` statement is the same as the definite assignment state of v at the beginning of the statement.

5.3.3.11 *throw Statements*

For a statement *stmt* of the form

```
throw expr ;
```

the definite assignment state of v at the beginning of *expr* is the same as the definite assignment state of v at the beginning of *stmt*.

5.3.3.12 *return Statements*

For a statement *stmt* of the form

```
return expr ;
```

- The definite assignment state of v at the beginning of *expr* is the same as the definite assignment state of v at the beginning of *stmt*.

- If v is an output parameter, then it must be definitely assigned either

  - After *expr*

  - Or at the end of the `finally` block of a `try-finally` or `try-catch-finally` that encloses the `return` statement

5.3.3.13 *try-catch Statements*

For a statement *stmt* of the form

```
try  try-block
catch(...)  catch-block-1
...
catch(...)  catch-block-n
```

- The definite assignment state of v at the beginning of *try-block* is the same as the definite assignment state of v at the beginning of *stmt*.

- The definite assignment state of v at the beginning of *catch-block-i* (for any *i*) is the same as the definite assignment state of v at the beginning of *stmt*.

- The definite assignment state of v at the end point of *stmt* is definitely assigned if (and only if) v is definitely assigned at the end point of *try-block* and every *catch-block-i* (for every *i* from 1 to *n*).

5. Variables

5.3.3.14 *try-finally Statements*
For a `try` statement *stmt* of the form

    `try` *try-block* `finally` *finally-block*

- The definite assignment state of v at the beginning of *try-block* is the same as the definite assignment state of v at the beginning of *stmt*.

- The definite assignment state of v at the beginning of *finally-block* is the same as the definite assignment state of v at the beginning of *stmt*.

- The definite assignment state of v at the end point of *stmt* is definitely assigned if (and only if) at least one of the following is true.

    - v is definitely assigned at the end point of *try-block*.

    - v is definitely assigned at the end point of *finally-block*.

If a control flow transfer (for example, a `goto` statement) is made that begins within *try-block* and ends outside of *try-block*, then v is also considered definitely assigned on that control flow transfer if v is definitely assigned at the end point of *finally-block*. (This is not an only if—if v is definitely assigned for another reason on this control flow transfer, then it is still considered definitely assigned.)

5.3.3.15 *try-catch-finally Statements*
Definite assignment analysis for a `try-catch-finally` statement of the form

```
try  try-block
catch(...)  catch-block-1

. . .
catch(...)  catch-block-n
finally  finally-block
```

is done as if the statement were a `try-finally` statement enclosing a `try-catch` statement.

```
try {
    try  try-block
    catch(...)  catch-block-1

    . . .
    catch(...)  catch-block-n
}
finally  finally-block
```

The following example demonstrates how the different blocks of a `try` statement (§8.1) affect definite assignment.

```
class A
{
    static void F() {
        int i, j;
        try {
            goto LABEL;
            // neither i nor j definitely assigned
            i = 1;
            // i definitely assigned
        }
        catch {
            // neither i nor j definitely assigned
            i = 3;
            // i definitely assigned
        }
        finally {
            // neither i nor j definitely assigned
            j = 5;
            // j definitely assigned
        }
        // i and j definitely assigned
    LABEL:;
        // j definitely assigned

    }
}
```

5.3.3.16 *foreach Statements*

For a `foreach` statement *stmt* of the form

    `foreach` (*type identifier* `in` *expr*) *embedded-statement*

- The definite assignment state of *v* at the beginning of *expr* is the same as the state of *v* at the beginning of *stmt*.

- The definite assignment state of *v* on the control flow transfer to *embedded-statement* or to the end point of *stmt* is the same as the state of *v* at the end of *expr*.

5.3.3.17 *using Statements*

For a `using` statement *stmt* of the form

    `using` (*resource-acquisition*) *embedded-statement*

- The definite assignment state of *v* at the beginning of *resource-acquisition* is the same as the state of *v* at the beginning of *stmt*.

- The definite assignment state of *v* on the control flow transfer to *embedded-statement* is the same as the state of *v* at the end of *resource-acquisition*.

5.3.3.18 *lock Statements*

For a `lock` statement *stmt* of the form

> `lock  (  ` *expr* `  )` *embedded-statement*

- The definite assignment state of v at the beginning of *expr* is the same as the state of v at the beginning of *stmt*.

- The definite assignment state of v on the control flow transfer to *embedded-statement* is the same as the state of v at the end of *expr*.

5.3.3.19 *General Rules for Simple Expressions*

The following rule applies to these kinds of expressions: literals (§7.5.1), simple names (§7.5.2), member access expressions (§7.5.4), nonindexed base access expressions (§7.5.8), and `typeof` expressions (§7.5.11).

- The definite assignment state of v at the end of such an expression is the same as the definite assignment state of v at the beginning of the expression.

5.3.3.20 *General Rules for Expressions with Embedded Expressions*

The following rules apply to these kinds of expressions: parenthesized expressions (§7.5.3), element access expressions (§7.5.6), base access expressions with indexing (§7.5.8), increment and decrement expressions (§7.5.9, §7.6.5), cast expressions (§7.6.6), unary `+`, `-`, `~`, and `*` expressions, binary `+`, `-`, `*`, `/`, `%`, `<<`, `>>`, `<`, `<=`, `>`, `>=`, `==`, `!=`, `is`, `as`, `&`, `|`, and `^` expressions (§7.7, §7.8, §7.8, §7.10), compound assignment expressions (§7.13.2), `checked` and `unchecked` expressions (§7.5.12), array and delegate creation expressions (§7.5.10).

Each of these expressions has one or more subexpressions that are unconditionally evaluated in a fixed order. For example, the binary `%` operator evaluates the left side of the operator, then the right side. An indexing operation evaluates the indexed expression and then evaluates each of the index expressions, in order from left to right. For an expression *expr*, which has subexpressions $expr_1, expr_2, ..., expr_n$, evaluated in that order

- The definite assignment state of v at the beginning of $expr_1$ is the same as the definite assignment state at the beginning of *expr*.

- The definite assignment state of v at the beginning of $expr_i$ (*i* greater than one) is the same as the definite assignment state at the end of $expr_{i-1}$.

- The definite assignment state of v at the end of *expr* is the same as the definite assignment state at the end of $expr_n$.

5.3.3.21 *Invocation Expressions and Object Creation Expressions*

For an invocation expression *expr* of the form

primary-expression (arg_1 , $arg2$, ... , arg_n)

or an object creation expression of the form

new *type* (arg_1 , arg_2 , ... , arg_n)

- For an invocation expression, the definite assignment state of v before *primary-expression* is the same as the state of v before *expr*.

- For an invocation expression, the definite assignment state of v before arg_1 is the same as the state of v after *primary-expression*.

- For an object creation expression, the definite assignment state of v before arg_1 is the same as the state of v before *expr*.

- For each argument arg_i, the definite assignment state of v after arg_i is determined by the normal expression rules, ignoring any `ref` or `out` modifiers.

- For each argument arg_i for any i greater than one, the definite assignment state of v before arg_i is the same as the state of v after arg_{i-1}.

- If the variable v is passed as an `out` argument (in other words, an argument of the form `out` v) in any of the arguments, then the state of v after *expr* is definitely assigned. Otherwise, the state of v after *expr* is the same as the state of v after arg_n.

5.3.3.22 *Simple Assignment Expressions*

For an expression *expr* of the form w = *expr-rhs*

- The definite assignment state of v before *expr-rhs* is the same as the definite assignment state of v before *expr*.

- If w is the same variable as v, then the definite assignment state of v after *expr* is definitely assigned. Otherwise, the definite assignment state of v after *expr* is the same as the definite assignment state of v after *expr-rhs*.

5.3.3.23 *&& Expressions*

For an expression *expr* of the form *expr-first* `&&` *expr-second*

- The definite assignment state of v before *expr-first* is the same as the definite assignment state of v before *expr*.

- The definite assignment state of v before *expr-second* is definitely assigned if the state of v after *expr-first* is either definitely assigned or "definitely assigned after true expression." Otherwise, it is not definitely assigned.

- The definite assignment state of *v* after *expr* is determined by

    - If the state of *v* after *expr-first* is definitely assigned, then the state of *v* after *expr* is definitely assigned.

    - Otherwise, if the state of *v* after *expr-second* is definitely assigned, and the state of *v* after *expr-first* is "definitely assigned after false expression," then the state of *v* after *expr* is definitely assigned.

    - Otherwise, if the state of *v* after *expr-second* is definitely assigned or "definitely assigned after true expression," then the state of *v* after *expr* is "definitely assigned after true expression."

    - Otherwise, if the state of *v* after *expr-first* is "definitely assigned after false expression," and the state of *v* after *expr-second* is "definitely assigned after false expression," then the state of *v* after *expr* is "definitely assigned after false expression."

    - Otherwise, the state of *v* after *expr* is not definitely assigned.

In the example

```
class A
{
    static void F(int x, int y) {
        int i;
        if (x >= 0 && (i = y) >= 0) {
            // i definitely assigned
        }
        else {
            // i not definitely assigned
        }
        // i not definitely assigned
    }
}
```

the variable i is considered definitely assigned in one of the embedded statements of an if statement but not in the other. In the if statement in method F, the variable i is definitely assigned in the first embedded statement because execution of the expression (i = y) always precedes execution of this embedded statement. In contrast, the variable i is not definitely assigned in the second embedded statement because x >= 0 might have tested false, resulting in the variable i being unassigned.

5.3.3.24 *|| Expressions*
For an expression *expr* of the form *expr-first* || *expr-second*

- The definite assignment state of *v* before *expr-first* is the same as the definite assignment state of *v* before *expr*.

- The definite assignment state of *v* before *expr-second* is definitely assigned if the state of *v* after *expr-first* is either definitely assigned or "definitely assigned after false expression." Otherwise, it is not definitely assigned.

- The definite assignment statement of *v* after *expr* is determined by the following.

  - If the state of *v* after *expr-first* is definitely assigned, then the state of *v* after *expr* is definitely assigned.

  - Otherwise, if the state of *v* after *expr-second* is definitely assigned, and the state of *v* after *expr-first* is "definitely assigned after true expression," then the state of *v* after *expr* is definitely assigned.

  - Otherwise, if the state of *v* after *expr-second* is definitely assigned or "definitely assigned after false expression," then the state of *v* after *expr* is "definitely assigned after false expression."

  - Otherwise, if the state of *v* after *expr-first* is "definitely assigned after true expression," and the state of *v* after *expr-second* is "definitely assigned after true expression," then the state of *v* after *expr* is "definitely assigned after true expression."

  - Otherwise, the state of *v* after *expr* is not definitely assigned.

In the example

```
class A
{
    static void G(int x, int y) {
        int i;
        if (x >= 0 || (i = y) >= 0) {
            // i not definitely assigned
        }
        else {
            // i definitely assigned
        }
        // i not definitely assigned
    }
}
```

the variable i is considered definitely assigned in one of the embedded statements of an if statement but not in the other. In the if statement in method G, the variable i is definitely assigned in the second embedded statement because execution of the expression (i = y) always precedes execution of this embedded statement. In contrast, the variable i is not definitely assigned in the first embedded statement because x >= 0 might have tested true, resulting in the variable i being unassigned.

5.3.3.25 *! Expressions*

For an expression *expr* of the form ! *expr-operand*

- The definite assignment state of v before *expr-operand* is the same as the definite assignment state of v before *expr*.

- The definite assignment state of v after *expr* is determined by

    - If the state of v after *expr-operand* is definitely assigned, then the state of v after *expr* is definitely assigned.

    - If the state of v after *expr-operand* is not definitely assigned, then the state of v after *expr* is not definitely assigned.

    - If the state of v after *expr-operand* is "definitely assigned after false expression," then the state of v after *expr* is "definitely assigned after true expression."

    - If the state of v after *expr-operand* is "definitely assigned after true expression," then the state of v after *expr* is "definitely assigned after false expression."

5.3.3.26 *?: Expressions*

For an expression *expr* of the form *expr-cond* ? *expr-true* : *expr-false*

- The definite assignment state of v before *expr-cond* is the same as the state of v before *expr*.

- The definite assignment state of v before *expr-true* is definitely assigned if and only if the state of v after *expr-cond* is definitely assigned or "definitely assigned after true expression."

- The definite assignment state of v before *expr-false* is definitely assigned if and only if the state of v after *expr-cond* is definitely assigned or "definitely assigned after false expression."

- The definite assignment state of v after *expr* is determined by

    - If *expr-cond* is a constant expression (§7.15) with value `true`, then the state of v after *expr* is the same as the state of v after *expr-true*.

    - Otherwise, if *expr-cond* is a constant expression (§7.15) with value `false`, then the state of v after *expr* is the same as the state of v after *expr-false*.

    - Otherwise, if the state of v after *expr-true* is definitely assigned and the state of v after *expr-false* is definitely assigned, then the state of v after *expr* is definitely assigned.

    - Otherwise, the state of v after *expr* is not definitely assigned.

5.4 Variable References

A *variable-reference* is an *expression* that is classified as a variable. A *variable-reference* denotes a storage location that can be accessed both to fetch the current value and to store a new value.

> *variable-reference:*
>   *expression*

In C and C++, a *variable-reference* is known as an *lvalue*.

5.5 Atomicity of Variable References

Reads and writes of the following data types are atomic: `bool`, `char`, `byte`, `sbyte`, `short`, `ushort`, `uint`, `int`, `float`, and reference types. In addition, reads and writes of enum types with an underlying type in the previous list are also atomic. Reads and writes of other types, including `long`, `ulong`, `double`, and `decimal`, as well as user-defined types, are not guaranteed to be atomic. Aside from the library functions designed for that purpose, there is no guarantee of atomic read-modify-write, such as in the case of increment or decrement.

6. Conversions

A *conversion* enables an expression of one type to be treated as another type. Conversions can be *implicit* or *explicit*, and this determines whether an explicit cast is required. For instance, the conversion from type int to type long is implicit, so expressions of type int can implicitly be treated as type long. The opposite conversion, from type long to type int, is explicit and so an explicit cast is required.

```
int a = 123;
long b = a;        // implicit conversion from int to long
int c = (int) b;   // explicit conversion from long to int
```

Some conversions are defined by the language. Programs may also define their own conversions (§6.4).

6.1 Implicit Conversions

The following conversions are classified as implicit conversions:

- Identity conversions
- Implicit numeric conversions
- Implicit enumeration conversions
- Implicit reference conversions
- Boxing conversions
- Implicit constant expression conversions
- User-defined implicit conversions

Implicit conversions can occur in a variety of situations, including function member invocations (§7.4.3), cast expressions (§7.6.6), and assignments (§7.13).

The predefined implicit conversions always succeed and never cause exceptions to be thrown. Properly designed user-defined implicit conversions should exhibit these characteristics as well.

6.1.1 Identity Conversion

An identity conversion converts from any type to the same type. This conversion exists only such that an entity that already has a required type can be said to be convertible to that type.

6.1.2 Implicit Numeric Conversions

The implicit numeric conversions are

- From `sbyte` to `short`, `int`, `long`, `float`, `double`, or `decimal`
- From `byte` to `short`, `ushort`, `int`, `uint`, `long`, `ulong`, `float`, `double`, or `decimal`
- From `short` to `int`, `long`, `float`, `double`, or `decimal`
- From `ushort` to `int`, `uint`, `long`, `ulong`, `float`, `double`, or `decimal`
- From `int` to `long`, `float`, `double`, or `decimal`
- From `uint` to `long`, `ulong`, `float`, `double`, or `decimal`
- From `long` to `float`, `double`, or `decimal`
- From `ulong` to `float`, `double`, or `decimal`
- From `char` to `ushort`, `int`, `uint`, `long`, `ulong`, `float`, `double`, or `decimal`
- From `float` to `double`

Conversions from `int`, `uint`, `long`, or `ulong` to `float` and from `long` or `ulong` to `double` may cause a loss of precision but will never cause a loss of magnitude. The other implicit numeric conversions never lose any information.

There are no implicit conversions to the `char` type, so values of the other integral types do not automatically convert to the `char` type.

6.1.3 Implicit Enumeration Conversions

An implicit enumeration conversion permits the *decimal-integer-literal* 0 to be converted to any *enum-type*.

6.1.4 Implicit Reference Conversions

The implicit reference conversions are

- From any *reference-type* to `object`
- From any *class-type* S to any *class-type* T, provided S is derived from T
- From any *class-type* S to any *interface-type* T, provided S implements T
- From any *interface-type* S to any *interface-type* T, provided S is derived from T

- From an *array-type* S with an element type S_E to an *array-type* T with an element type T_E, provided all of the following are true.

  - S and T differ only in element type. In other words, S and T have the same number of dimensions.

  - Both S_E and T_E are *reference-type*s.

  - An implicit reference conversion exists from S_E to T_E.

- From any *array-type* to System.Array

- From any *delegate-type* to System.Delegate

- From the null type to any *reference-type*

The implicit reference conversions are those conversions between *reference-type*s that can be proven to always succeed and therefore require no checks at runtime.

Reference conversions, implicit or explicit, never change the referential identity of the object being converted. In other words, although a reference conversion may change the type of the reference, it never changes the type or value of the object to which it is referring.

6.1.5 Boxing Conversions

A boxing conversion permits a *value-type* to be implicitly converted to a *reference-type*. Boxing a value of a *value-type* consists of allocating an object instance and copying the *value-type* value into that instance.

Boxing conversions are described further in §4.3.1.

6.1.6 Implicit Constant Expression Conversions

An implicit constant expression conversion permits the following conversions.

- A *constant-expression* (§7.15) of type int can be converted to type sbyte, byte, short, ushort, uint, or ulong, provided the value of the *constant-expression* is within the range of the destination type.

- A *constant-expression* of type long can be converted to type ulong, provided the value of the *constant-expression* is not negative.

6.1.7 User-Defined Implicit Conversions

A user-defined implicit conversion consists of an optional standard implicit conversion, followed by execution of a user-defined implicit conversion operator, followed by another optional standard implicit conversion. The exact rules for evaluating user-defined conversions are described in §6.4.3.

6.2 Explicit Conversions

The following conversions are classified as explicit conversions:

- All implicit conversions
- Explicit numeric conversions
- Explicit enumeration conversions
- Explicit reference conversions
- Explicit interface conversions
- Unboxing conversions
- User-defined explicit conversions

Explicit conversions can occur in cast expressions (§7.6.6).

The set of explicit conversions includes all implicit conversions. This means that redundant cast expressions are allowed.

The explicit conversions that are not implicit conversions are conversions that cannot be proven to always succeed, conversions that are known to possibly lose information, and conversions across domains of types sufficiently different to merit explicit notation.

6.2.1 Explicit Numeric Conversions

The explicit numeric conversions are the conversions from a *numeric-type* to another *numeric-type* for which an implicit numeric conversion (§6.1.2) does not already exist:

- From `sbyte` to `byte`, `ushort`, `uint`, `ulong`, or `char`
- From `byte` to `sbyte` and `char`
- From `short` to `sbyte`, `byte`, `ushort`, `uint`, `ulong`, or `char`
- From `ushort` to `sbyte`, `byte`, `short`, or `char`
- From `int` to `sbyte`, `byte`, `short`, `ushort`, `uint`, `ulong`, or `char`
- From `uint` to `sbyte`, `byte`, `short`, `ushort`, `int`, or `char`
- From `long` to `sbyte`, `byte`, `short`, `ushort`, `int`, `uint`, `ulong`, or `char`
- From `ulong` to `sbyte`, `byte`, `short`, `ushort`, `int`, `uint`, `long`, or `char`
- From `char` to `sbyte`, `byte`, or `short`

- From `float` to `sbyte`, `byte`, `short`, `ushort`, `int`, `uint`, `long`, `ulong`, `char`, or `decimal`

- From `double` to `sbyte`, `byte`, `short`, `ushort`, `int`, `uint`, `long`, `ulong`, `char`, `float`, or `decimal`

- From `decimal` to `sbyte`, `byte`, `short`, `ushort`, `int`, `uint`, `long`, `ulong`, `char`, `float`, or `double`

Because the explicit conversions include all implicit and explicit numeric conversions, it is always possible to convert from any *numeric-type* to any other *numeric-type* using a cast expression (§7.6.6).

The explicit numeric conversions possibly lose information or possibly cause exceptions to be thrown. An explicit numeric conversion is processed as follows.

- For a conversion from an integral type to another integral type, the processing depends on the overflow checking context (§7.5.12) in which the conversion takes place.

  - In a `checked` context, the conversion succeeds if the value of the source operand is within the range of the destination type but throws a `System.OverflowException` if the value of the source operand is outside the range of the destination type.

  - In an `unchecked` context, the conversion always succeeds and proceeds as follows.

    - If the source type is larger than the destination type, then the source value is truncated by discarding its "extra" most significant bits. The result is then treated as a value of the destination type.

    - If the source type is smaller than the destination type, then the source value is either sign-extended or zero-extended so that it is the same size as the destination type. Sign-extension is used if the source type is signed; zero-extension is used if the source type is unsigned. The result is then treated as a value of the destination type.

    - If the source type is the same size as the destination type, then the source value is treated as a value of the destination type.

- For a conversion from `decimal` to an integral type, the source value is rounded toward zero to the nearest integral value, and this integral value becomes the result of the conversion. If the resulting integral value is outside the range of the destination type, a `System.OverflowException` is thrown.

- For a conversion from `float` or `double` to an integral type, the processing depends on the overflow checking context (§7.5.12) in which the conversion takes place.

6. Conversions

- In a checked context, the conversion proceeds as follows.

  - If the value of the operand is NaN or infinite, a System.OverflowException is thrown.

  - Otherwise, the source operand is rounded toward zero to the nearest integral value. If this integral value is within the range of the destination type, then this value is the result of the conversion.

  - Otherwise, a System.OverflowException is thrown.

- In an unchecked context, the conversion always succeeds and proceeds as follows.

  - If the value of the operand is NaN or infinite, the result of the conversion is an unspecified value of the destination type.

  - Otherwise, the source operand is rounded toward zero to the nearest integral value. If this integral value is within the range of the destination type, then this value is the result of the conversion.

  - Otherwise, the result of the conversion is an unspecified value of the destination type.

- For a conversion from double to float, the double value is rounded to the nearest float value. If the double value is too small to represent as a float, the result becomes positive zero or negative zero. If the double value is too large to represent as a float, the result becomes positive infinity or negative infinity. If the double value is NaN, the result is also NaN.

- For a conversion from float or double to decimal, the source value is converted to decimal representation and rounded to the nearest number after the twenty-eighth decimal place if required (§4.1.7). If the source value is too small to represent as a decimal, the result becomes zero. If the source value is NaN, infinity, or too large to represent as a decimal, a System.OverflowException is thrown.

- For a conversion from decimal to float or double, the decimal value is rounded to the nearest double or float value. Although this conversion may lose precision, it never causes an exception to be thrown.

6.2.2 Explicit Enumeration Conversions

The explicit enumeration conversions are

- From sbyte, byte, short, ushort, int, uint, long, ulong, char, float, double, or decimal to any *enum-type*

- From any *enum-type* to sbyte, byte, short, ushort, int, uint, long, ulong, char, float, double, or decimal

- From any *enum-type* to any other *enum-type*

An explicit enumeration conversion between two types is processed by treating any participating *enum-type* as the underlying type of that *enum-type* and then performing an implicit or explicit numeric conversion between the resulting types. For example, given an *enum-type* E with and underlying type of int, a conversion from E to byte is processed as an explicit numeric conversion (§6.2.1) from int to byte, and a conversion from byte to E is processed as an implicit numeric conversion (§6.1.2) from byte to int.

6.2.3 Explicit Reference Conversions

The explicit reference conversions are

- From object to any other *reference-type*

- From any *class-type* S to any *class-type* T, provided S is a base class of T

- From any *class-type* S to any *interface-type* T, provided S is not sealed and provided S does not implement T

- From any *interface-type* S to any *class-type* T, provided T is not sealed or provided T implements S

- From any *interface-type* S to any *interface-type* T, provided S is not derived from T

- From an *array-type* S with an element type S_E to an *array-type* T with an element type T_E, provided all of the following are true.

    - S and T differ only in element type. In other words, S and T have the same number of dimensions.

    - Both S_E and T_E are *reference-type*s.

    - An explicit reference conversion exists from S_E to T_E.

- From System.Array and the interfaces it implements to any *array-type*

- From System.Delegate and the interfaces it implements to any *delegate-type*

The explicit reference conversions are those conversions between reference types that require runtime checks to ensure they are correct.

For an explicit reference conversion to succeed at runtime, the value of the source operand must be null, or the *actual* type of the object referenced by the source operand must be a type that can be converted to the destination type by an implicit reference conversion (§6.1.4). If an explicit reference conversion fails, a System.InvalidCastException is thrown.

Reference conversions, implicit or explicit, never change the referential identity of the object being converted. In other words, although a reference conversion may change the type of the reference, it never changes the type or value of the object to which it is referring.

6.2.4 Unboxing Conversions

An unboxing conversion permits a *reference-type* to be explicitly converted to a *value-type*. An unboxing operation consists of first checking that the object instance is a boxed value of the given *value-type* and then copying the value out of the instance.

Unboxing conversions are described further in §4.3.2.

6.2.5 User-Defined Explicit Conversions

A user-defined explicit conversion consists of an optional standard explicit conversion, followed by execution of a user-defined implicit or explicit conversion operator, followed by another optional standard explicit conversion. The exact rules for evaluating user-defined conversions are described in §6.4.4.

6.3 Standard Conversions

The standard conversions are those predefined conversions that can occur as part of a user-defined conversion.

6.3.1 Standard Implicit Conversions

The following implicit conversions are classified as standard implicit conversions:

- Identity conversions (§6.1.1)
- Implicit numeric conversions (§6.1.2)
- Implicit reference conversions (§6.1.4)
- Boxing conversions (§6.1.5)
- Implicit constant expression conversions (§6.1.6)

The standard implicit conversions specifically exclude user-defined implicit conversions.

6.3.2 Standard Explicit Conversions

The standard explicit conversions are all standard implicit conversions plus the subset of the explicit conversions for which an opposite standard implicit conversion exists. In other words, if a standard implicit conversion exists from a type A to a type B, then a standard explicit conversion exists from type A to type B and from type B to type A.

6.4 User-Defined Conversions

C# allows the predefined implicit and explicit conversions to be augmented by **user-defined conversions**. User-defined conversions are introduced by declaring conversion operators (§10.9.3) in class and struct types.

6.4.1 Permitted User-Defined Conversions

C# permits only certain user-defined conversions to be declared. In particular, it is not possible to redefine an already existing implicit or explicit conversion. A class or struct is permitted to declare a conversion from a source type S to a target type T only if all of the following are true.

- S and T are different types.
- Either S or T is the class or struct type in which the operator declaration takes place.
- Neither S nor T is object or an *interface-type*.
- T is not a base class of S, and S is not a base class of T.

The restrictions that apply to user-defined conversions are discussed further in §10.9.3.

6.4.2 Evaluation of User-Defined Conversions

A user-defined conversion converts a value from its type, called the **source type**, to another type, called the **target type**. Evaluation of a user-defined conversion centers on finding the **most specific** user-defined conversion operator for the particular source and target types. This determination is broken into several steps.

- Finding the set of classes and structs from which user-defined conversion operators will be considered. This set consists of the source type and its base classes and the target type and its base classes (with the implicit assumptions that only classes and structs can declare user-defined operators and that nonclass types have no base classes).

- From that set of types, determining which user-defined conversion operators are applicable. For a conversion operator to be applicable, it must be possible to perform a standard conversion (§6.3) from the source type to the operand type of the operator, and it must be possible to perform a standard conversion from the result type of the operator to the target type.

- From the set of applicable user-defined operators, determining which operator is unambiguously the most specific. In general terms, the most specific operator is the operator whose operand type is "closest" to the source type and whose result type is "closest" to the target type. The exact rules for establishing the most specific user-defined conversion operator are defined in the following sections.

Once the most specific user-defined conversion operator has been identified, the actual execution of the user-defined conversion involves up to three steps:

- First, if required, performing a standard conversion from the source type to the operand type of the user-defined conversion operator

- Next, invoking the user-defined conversion operator to perform the conversion

- Finally, if required, performing a standard conversion from the result type of the user-defined conversion operator to the target type

Evaluation of a user-defined conversion never involves more than one user-defined conversion operator. In other words, a conversion from type S to type T will never first execute a user-defined conversion from S to X and then execute a user-defined conversion from X to T.

Exact definitions of evaluation of user-defined implicit or explicit conversions are given in the following sections. The definitions make use of the following terms.

- If a standard implicit conversion (§6.3.1) exists from a type A to a type B, and if neither A nor B are *interface-types*, then A is said to be *encompassed by* B, and B is said to be *encompass* A.

- The *most encompassing type* in a set of types is the one type that encompasses all other types in the set. If no single type encompasses all other types, then the set has no most encompassing type. In more intuitive terms, the most encompassing type is the "largest" type in the set—the one type to which each of the other types can be implicitly converted.

- The *most encompassed type* in a set of types is the one type that is encompassed by all other types in the set. If no single type is encompassed by all other types, then the set has no most encompassed type. In more intuitive terms, the most encompassed type is the "smallest" type in the set—the one type that can be implicitly converted to each of the other types.

6.4.3 User-Defined Implicit Conversions

A user-defined implicit conversion from type S to type T is processed as follows.

- Find the set of types, D, from which user-defined conversion operators will be considered. This set consists of S (if S is a class or struct), the base classes of S (if S is a class), and T (if T is a class or struct).

- Find the set of applicable user-defined conversion operators, U. This set consists of the user-defined implicit conversion operators declared by the classes or structs in D that convert from a type encompassing S to a type encompassed by T. If U is empty, the conversion is undefined and a compile-time error occurs.

- Find the most specific source type, S_X, of the operators in U.

    - If any of the operators in U convert from S, then S_X is S.

    - Otherwise, S_X is the most encompassed type in the combined set of source types of the operators in U. If no most encompassed type can be found, then the conversion is ambiguous and a compile-time error occurs.

- Find the most specific target type, T_X, of the operators in U.

    - If any of the operators in U convert to T, then T_X is T.

    - Otherwise, T_X is the most encompassing type in the combined set of target types of the operators in U. If no most encompassing type can be found, then the conversion is ambiguous and a compile-time error occurs.

- If U contains exactly one user-defined conversion operator that converts from S_X to T_X, then this is the most specific conversion operator. If no such operator exists, or if more than one such operator exists, then the conversion is ambiguous and a compile-time error occurs. Otherwise, the user-defined conversion is applied.

    - If S is not S_X, then a standard implicit conversion from S to S_X is performed.

    - The most specific user-defined conversion operator is invoked to convert from S_X to T_X.

    - If T_X is not T, then a standard implicit conversion from T_X to T is performed.

6.4.4 User-Defined Explicit Conversions

A user-defined explicit conversion from type S to type T is processed as follows.

- Find the set of types, D, from which user-defined conversion operators will be considered. This set consists of S (if S is a class or struct), the base classes of S (if S is a class), T (if T is a class or struct), and the base classes of T (if T is a class).

- Find the set of applicable user-defined conversion operators, U. This set consists of the user-defined implicit or explicit conversion operators declared by the classes or structs in D that convert from a type encompassing or encompassed by S to a type encompassing or encompassed by T. If U is empty, the conversion is undefined and a compile-time error occurs.

- Find the most specific source type, S_X, of the operators in U.

    - If any of the operators in U convert from S, then S_X is S.

    - Otherwise, if any of the operators in U convert from types that encompass S, then S_X is the most encompassed type in the combined set of source types of those operators. If no most encompassed type can be found, then the conversion is ambiguous and a compile-time error occurs.

- Otherwise, S_X is the most encompassing type in the combined set of source types of the operators in U. If no most encompassing type can be found, then the conversion is ambiguous and a compile-time error occurs.

- Find the most specific target type, T_X, of the operators in U.

  - If any of the operators in U convert to T, then T_X is T.

  - Otherwise, if any of the operators in U convert to types that are encompassed by T, then T_X is the most encompassing type in the combined set of target types of those operators. If no most encompassing type can be found, then the conversion is ambiguous and a compile-time error occurs.

  - Otherwise, T_X is the most encompassed type in the combined set of target types of the operators in U. If no most encompassed type can be found, then the conversion is ambiguous and a compile-time error occurs.

- If U contains exactly one user-defined conversion operator that converts from S_X to T_X, then this is the most specific conversion operator. If no such operator exists, or if more than one such operator exists, then the conversion is ambiguous and a compile-time error occurs. Otherwise, the user-defined conversion is applied.

  - If S is not S_X, then a standard explicit conversion from S to S_X is performed.

  - The most specific user-defined conversion operator is invoked to convert from S_X to T_X.

  - If T_X is not T, then a standard explicit conversion from T_X to T is performed.

7. Expressions

An expression is a sequence of operators and operands. This chapter defines the syntax, order of evaluation of operands and operators, and the meaning of expressions.

7.1 Expression Classifications

An expression is classified as one of the following.

- A value. Every value has an associated type.

- A variable. Every variable has an associated type, namely the declared type of the variable.

- A namespace. An expression with this classification can only appear as the left-hand side of a *member-access* (§7.5.4). In any other context, an expression classified as a namespace causes a compile-time error.

- A type. An expression with this classification can only appear as the left-hand side of a *member-access* (§7.5.4) or as an operand for the as operator (§7.9.10), the is operator (§7.9.9), or the typeof operator (§7.5.11). In any other context, an expression classified as a type causes a compile-time error.

- A method group, which is a set of overloaded methods resulting from a member lookup (§7.3). A method group may have an associated instance expression. When an instance method is invoked, the result of evaluating the instance expression becomes the instance represented by this (§7.5.7). A method group is only permitted in an *invocation-expression* (§7.5.5) or a *delegate-creation-expression* (§7.5.10.3). In any other context, an expression classified as a method group causes a compile-time error.

- A property access. Every property access has an associated type, namely the type of the property. Furthermore, a property access may have an associated instance expression. When an accessor (the get or set block) of an instance property access is invoked, the result of evaluating the instance expression becomes the instance represented by this (§7.5.7).

- An event access. Every event access has an associated type, namely the type of the event. Furthermore, an event access may have an associated instance expression. An event access may appear as the left-hand operand of the += and -= operators (§7.13.3). In any other context, an expression classified as an event access causes a compile-time error.

- An indexer access. Every indexer access has an associated type, namely the element type of the indexer. Furthermore, an indexer access has an associated instance expression and an associated argument list. When an accessor (the get or set block) of an indexer access is invoked, the result of evaluating the instance expression becomes the instance represented by this (§7.5.7), and the result of evaluating the argument list becomes the parameter list of the invocation.

- Nothing. This occurs when the expression is an invocation of a method with a return type of void. An expression classified as nothing is only valid in the context of a *statement-expression* (§8.6).

The final result of an expression is never a namespace, type, method group, or event access. Rather, as noted previously, these categories of expressions are intermediate constructs that are only permitted in certain contexts.

A property access or indexer access is always reclassified as a value by performing an invocation of the *get-accessor* or the *set-accessor*. The particular accessor is determined by the context of the property or indexer access: If the access is the target of an assignment, the *set-accessor* is invoked to assign a new value (§7.13.1). Otherwise, the *get-accessor* is invoked to obtain the current value (§7.1.1).

7.1.1 Values of Expressions

Most of the constructs that involve an expression ultimately require the expression to denote a *value*. In such cases, if the actual expression denotes a namespace, a type, a method group, or nothing, a compile-time error occurs. However, if the expression denotes a property access, an indexer access, or a variable, the value of the property, indexer, or variable is implicitly substituted.

- The value of a variable is simply the value currently stored in the storage location identified by the variable. A variable must be considered definitely assigned (§5.3) before its value can be obtained, or otherwise a compile-time error occurs.

- The value of a property access expression is obtained by invoking the *get-accessor* of the property. If the property has no *get-accessor*, a compile-time error occurs. Otherwise, a function member invocation (§7.4.3) is performed, and the result of the invocation becomes the value of the property access expression.

- The value of an indexer access expression is obtained by invoking the *get-accessor* of the indexer. If the indexer has no *get-accessor*, a compile-time error occurs. Otherwise, a function member invocation (§7.4.3) is performed with the argument list associated with the indexer access expression, and the result of the invocation becomes the value of the indexer access expression.

7.2 Operators

Expressions are constructed from **operands** and **operators**. The operators of an expression indicate which operations to apply to the operands. Examples of operators include +, -, *, /, and new. Examples of operands include literals, fields, local variables, and expressions.

There are three kinds of operators.

- Unary operators. The unary operators take one operand and use either prefix notation (such as –x) or postfix notation (such as x++).

- Binary operators. The binary operators take two operands, and they all use infix notation (such as x + y).

- Ternary operator. Only one ternary operator, ?:, exists; it takes three operands and uses infix notation (c? x: y).

The order of evaluation of operators in an expression is determined by the **precedence** and **associativity** of the operators (§7.2.1).

Operands in an expression are evaluated from left to right. For example, in F(i) + G(i++) * H(i), the method F is called using the old value of i, then the method G is called with the old value of i, and, finally, the method H is called with the new value of i. This is separate from and unrelated to operator precedence.

Certain operators can be **overloaded**. Operator overloading permits user-defined operator implementations to be specified for operations where one or both of the operands are of a user-defined class or struct type (§7.2.2).

7.2.1 Operator Precedence and Associativity

When an expression contains multiple operators, the **precedence** of the operators controls the order in which the individual operators are evaluated. For example, the expression x + y * z is evaluated as x + (y * z) because the * operator has higher precedence than the binary + operator. The precedence of an operator is established by the definition of its associated grammar production. For example, an *additive-expression* consists of a sequence of *multiplicative-expression*s separated by + or – operators, thus giving the + and – operators lower precedence than the *, /, and % operators.

7. Expressions

The following table summarizes all operators in order of precedence from highest to lowest.

Section	Category	Operators
7.5	Primary	`x.y f(x) a[x] x++ x-- new typeof` `checked unchecked`
7.6	Unary	`+ - ! ~ ++x --x (T)x`
7.7	Multiplicative	`* / %`
7.7	Additive	`+ -`
7.8	Shift	`<< >>`
7.9	Relational and type testing	`< > <= >= is as`
7.9	Equality	`== !=`
7.10	Logical AND	`&`
7.10	Logical XOR	`^`
7.10	Logical OR	`|`
7.11	Conditional AND	`&&`
7.11	Conditional OR	`||`
7.12	Conditional	`?:`
7.13	Assignment	`= *= /= %= += -= <<= >>= &= ^= |=`

When an operand occurs between two operators with the same precedence, the associativity of the operators controls the order in which the operations are performed.

- Except for the assignment operators, all binary operators are *left-associative*, meaning that operations are performed from left to right. For example, `x + y + z` is evaluated as `(x + y) + z`.

- The assignment operators and the conditional operator (?:) are *right-associative*, meaning that operations are performed from right to left. For example, x = y = z is evaluated as x = (y = z).

Precedence and associativity can be controlled using parentheses. For example, x + y * z first multiplies y by z and then adds the result to x, but (x + y) * z first adds x and y and then multiplies the result by z.

7.2.2 Operator Overloading

All unary and binary operators have predefined implementations that are automatically available in any expression. In addition to the predefined implementations, user-defined implementations can be introduced by including `operator` declarations in classes and structs (§10.9). User-defined operator implementations always take precedence over predefined operator implementations. Only when no applicable user-defined operator implementations exist will the predefined operator implementations be considered.

The *overloadable unary operators* are

```
+ - ! ~ ++ -- true false
```

Although `true` and `false` are not used explicitly in expressions, they are considered operators because they are invoked in several expression contexts: boolean expressions (§7.16), expressions involving the conditional (§7.12), and conditional logical operators (§7.11).

The *overloadable binary operators* are

```
+ - * / % & | ^ << >> == != > < >= <=
```

Only the operators listed previously can be overloaded. In particular, it is not possible to overload member access, method invocation, or the =, &&, ||, ?:, `checked`, `unchecked`, `new`, `typeof`, `as`, and `is` operators.

When a binary operator is overloaded, the corresponding assignment operator, if any, is also implicitly overloaded. For example, an overload of operator * is also an overload of operator *=. This is described further in §7.13. Note that the assignment operator itself (=) cannot be overloaded. An assignment always performs a simple bitwise copy of a value into a variable.

Cast operations, such as (T)x, are overloaded by providing user-defined conversions (§6.4).

7. Expressions

Element access, such as a[x], is not considered an overloadable operator. Instead, user-defined indexing is supported through indexers (§10.8).

In expressions, operators are referenced using operator notation, and in declarations, operators are referenced using functional notation. The following table shows the relationship between operator and functional notations for unary and binary operators. In the first entry, *op* denotes any overloadable unary prefix operator. In the second entry, *op* denotes the unary postfix ++ and -- operators. In the third entry, *op* denotes any overloadable binary operator.

Operator Notation	Functional Notation
op x	operator *op* (x)
x *op*	operator *op* (x)
x *op* y	operator *op* (x, y)

User-defined operator declarations always require at least one of the parameters to be of the class or struct type that contains the operator declaration. Thus, it is not possible for a user-defined operator to have the same signature as a predefined operator.

User-defined operator declarations cannot modify the syntax, precedence, or associativity of an operator. For example, the / operator is always a binary operator, always has the precedence level specified in §7.2.1, and is always left-associative.

Although it is possible for a user-defined operator to perform any computation it pleases, implementations that produce results other than those that are intuitively expected are strongly discouraged. For example, an implementation of operator == should compare the two operands for equality and return an appropriate bool result.

The descriptions of individual operators in §7.5 through §7.13 specify the predefined implementations of the operators and any additional rules that apply to each operator. The descriptions make use of the terms *unary operator overload resolution*, *binary operator overload resolution*, and *numeric promotion*, definitions of which are found in the following sections.

7.2.3 Unary Operator Overload Resolution

An operation of the form *op* x or x *op*, where *op* is an overloadable unary operator and x is an expression of type X, is processed as follows.

- The set of candidate user-defined operators provided by X for the operation `operator` *op*`(x)` is determined using the rules of §7.2.5.

- If the set of candidate user-defined operators is not empty, then this becomes the set of candidate operators for the operation. Otherwise, the predefined unary `operator` *op* implementations become the set of candidate operators for the operation. The predefined implementations of a given operator are specified in the description of the operator (§7.5 and §7.6).

- The overload resolution rules of §7.4.2 are applied to the set of candidate operators to select the best operator with respect to the argument list (x), and this operator becomes the result of the overload resolution process. If overload resolution fails to select a single best operator, a compile-time error occurs.

7.2.4 Binary Operator Overload Resolution

An operation of the form x *op* y, where *op* is an overloadable binary operator, x is an expression of type X, and y is an expression of type Y, is processed as follows.

- The set of candidate user-defined operators provided by X and Y for the operation `operator` *op*`(x, y)` is determined. The set consists of the union of the candidate operators provided by X and the candidate operators provided by Y, each determined using the rules of §7.2.5. If X and Y are the same type, or if X and Y are derived from a common base type, then shared candidate operators only occur in the combined set once.

- If the set of candidate user-defined operators is not empty, then this becomes the set of candidate operators for the operation. Otherwise, the predefined binary `operator` *op* implementations become the set of candidate operators for the operation. The predefined implementations of a given operator are specified in the description of the operator (§7.7 through §7.13).

- The overload resolution rules of §7.4.2 are applied to the set of candidate operators to select the best operator with respect to the argument list (x, y), and this operator becomes the result of the overload resolution process. If overload resolution fails to select a single best operator, a compile-time error occurs.

7. Expressions

7.2.5 Candidate User-Defined Operators

Given a type T and an operation operator *op*(A), where *op* is an overloadable operator and A is an argument list, the set of candidate user-defined operators provided by T for operator *op*(A) is determined as follows.

- For all operator *op* declarations in T, if at least one operator is applicable (§7.4.2.1) with respect to the argument list A, then the set of candidate operators consists of all applicable operator *op* declarations in T.

- Otherwise, if T is object, the set of candidate operators is empty.

- Otherwise, the set of candidate operators provided by T is the set of candidate operators provided by the direct base class of T.

7.2.6 Numeric Promotions

Numeric promotion consists of automatically performing certain implicit conversions of the operands of the predefined unary and binary numeric operators. Numeric promotion is not a distinct mechanism but rather an effect of applying overload resolution to the predefined operators. Numeric promotion specifically does not affect evaluation of user-defined operators, but user-defined operators can be implemented to exhibit similar effects.

As an example of numeric promotion, consider the predefined implementations of the binary * operator:

```
int operator *(int x, int y);
uint operator *(uint x, uint y);
long operator *(long x, long y);
ulong operator *(ulong x, ulong y);
float operator *(float x, float y);
double operator *(double x, double y);
decimal operator *(decimal x, decimal y);
```

When overload resolution rules (§7.4.2) are applied to this set of operators, the effect is to select the first of the operators for which implicit conversions exist from the operand types. For example, for the operation b * s, where b is a byte and s is a short, overload resolution selects operator *(int, int) as the best operator. Thus, the effect is that b and s are converted to int, and the type of the result is int. Likewise, for the operation i * d, where i is an int and d is a double, overload resolution selects operator *(double, double) as the best operator.

7.2.6.1 *Unary Numeric Promotions*

Unary numeric promotion occurs for the operands of the predefined +, −, and ~ unary operators. Unary numeric promotion simply consists of converting operands of type sbyte, byte, short, ushort, or char to type int. Additionally, for the unary – operator, unary numeric promotion converts operands of type uint to type long.

7.2.6.2 *Binary Numeric Promotions*

Binary numeric promotion occurs for the operands of the predefined +, –, *, /, %, &, |, ^, ==, !=, >, <, >=, and <= binary operators. Binary numeric promotion implicitly converts both operands to a common type that, in the case of the nonrelational operators, also becomes the result type of the operation. Binary numeric promotion consists of applying the following rules, in the order they appear here.

- If either operand is of type decimal, the other operand is converted to type decimal, or a compile-time error occurs if the other operand is of type float or double.

- Otherwise, if either operand is of type double, the other operand is converted to type double.

- Otherwise, if either operand is of type float, the other operand is converted to type float.

- Otherwise, if either operand is of type ulong, the other operand is converted to type ulong, or a compile-time error occurs if the other operand is of type sbyte, short, int, or long.

- Otherwise, if either operand is of type long, the other operand is converted to type long.

- Otherwise, if either operand is of type uint and the other operand is of type sbyte, short, or int, both operands are converted to type long.

- Otherwise, if either operand is of type uint, the other operand is converted to type uint.

- Otherwise, both operands are converted to type int.

Note that the first rule disallows any operations that mix the decimal type with the double and float types. The rule follows from that there are no implicit conversions between the decimal type and the double and float types.

Also note that it is not possible for an operand to be of type ulong when the other operand is of a signed integral type. The reason is that no integral type exists that can represent the full range of ulong as well as the signed integral types.

In both of the previous cases, a cast expression can be used to explicitly convert one operand to a type that is compatible with the other operand.

7. Expressions

In the example

```
decimal AddPercent(decimal x, double percent) {
    return x * (1.0 + percent / 100.0);
}
```

a compile-time error occurs because a decimal cannot be multiplied by a double. The error is resolved by explicitly converting the second operand to decimal, as follows.

```
decimal AddPercent(decimal x, double percent) {
    return x * (decimal)(1.0 + percent / 100.0);
}
```

7.3 Member Lookup

A member lookup is the process whereby the meaning of a name in the context of a type is determined. A member lookup may occur as part of evaluating a *simple-name* (§7.5.2) or a *member-access* (§7.5.4) in an expression.

A member lookup of a name N in a type T is processed as follows.

- First, the set of all accessible (§3.5) members named N declared in T and the base types (§7.3.1) of T is constructed. Declarations that include an override modifier are excluded from the set. If no members named N exist and are accessible, then the lookup produces no match, and the following steps are not evaluated.

- Next, members that are hidden by other members are removed from the set. For every member S.M in the set, where S is the type in which the member M is declared, the following rules are applied.

  - If M is a constant, field, property, event, type, or enumeration member, then all members declared in a base type of S are removed from the set.

  - If M is a method, then all nonmethod members declared in a base type of S are removed from the set, and all methods with the same signature as M declared in a base type of S are removed from the set.

- Finally, having removed hidden members, the result of the lookup is determined.

  - If the set consists of a single nonmethod member, then this member is the result of the lookup.

  - Otherwise, if the set contains only methods, then this group of methods is the result of the lookup.

  - Otherwise, the lookup is ambiguous, and a compile-time error occurs (this situation can only occur for a member lookup in an interface that has multiple direct base interfaces).

For member lookups in types other than interfaces, and member lookups in interfaces that are strictly single-inheritance (each interface in the inheritance chain has exactly zero or one direct base interface), the effect of the lookup rules is simply that derived members hide base members with the same name or signature. Such single-inheritance lookups are never ambiguous. The ambiguities that can possibly arise from member lookups in multiple-inheritance interfaces are described in §13.2.5.

7.3.1 Base Types

For purposes of member lookup, a type T is considered to have the following base types.

- If T is object, then T has no base type.

- If T is a *value-type*, the base type of T is the class type object.

- If T is a *class-type*, the base types of T are the base classes of T, including the class type object.

- If T is an *interface-type*, the base types of T are the base interfaces of T and the class type object.

- If T is an *array-type*, the base types of T are the class types System.Array and object.

- If T is a *delegate-type*, the base types of T are the class types System.Delegate and object.

7.4 Function Members

Function members are members that contain executable statements. Function members are always members of types and cannot be members of namespaces. C# defines the following categories of function members:

- Methods

- Properties

- Events

- Indexers

- User-defined operators

- Instance constructors

- Static constructors

- Destructors

7. Expressions

157

Except for destructors and static constructors (which cannot be invoked explicitly), the statements contained in function members are executed through function member invocations. The actual syntax for writing a function member invocation depends on the particular function member category.

The argument list (§7.4.1) of a function member invocation provides actual values or variable references for the parameters of the function member.

Invocations of methods, indexers, operators, and instance constructors employ overload resolution to determine which of a candidate set of function members to invoke. This process is described in §7.4.2.

Once a particular function member has been identified at compile time, possibly through overload resolution, the actual runtime process of invoking the function member is described in §7.4.3.

The following table summarizes the processing that takes place in constructs involving the six categories of function members that can be explicitly invoked. In the table, e, x, y, and value indicate expressions classified as variables or values, T indicates an expression classified as a type, F is the simple name of a method, and P is the simple name of a property.

Construct	Example	Description
Method Invocation	`F(x, y)`	Overload resolution is applied to select the best method F in the containing class or struct. The method is invoked with the argument list `(x, y)`. If the method is not `static`, the instance expression is `this`.
	`T.F(x, y)`	Overload resolution is applied to select the best method F in the class or struct T. A compile-time error occurs if the method is not `static`. The method is invoked with the argument list `(x, y)`.
	`e.F(x, y)`	Overload resolution is applied to select the best method F in the class, struct, or interface given by the type of e. A compile-time error occurs if the method is `static`. The method is invoked with the instance expression e and the argument list `(x, y)`.

Construct	Example	Description
Property Access	P	The get accessor of the property P in the containing class or struct is invoked. A compile-time error occurs if P is write-only. If P is not static, the instance expression is this.
	P = value	The set accessor of the property P in the containing class or struct is invoked with the argument list (value). A compile-time error occurs if P is read-only. If P is not static, the instance expression is this.
	T.P	The get accessor of the property P in the class or struct T is invoked. A compile-time error occurs if P is not static or if P is write-only.
	T.P = value	The set accessor of the property P in the class or struct T is invoked with the argument list (value). A compile-time error occurs if P is not static or if P is read-only.
	e.P	The get accessor of the property P in the class, struct, or interface given by the type of e is invoked with the instance expression e. A compile-time error occurs if P is static or if P is write-only.
	e.P = value	The set accessor of the property P in the class, struct, or interface given by the type of e is invoked with the instance expression e and the argument list (value). A compile-time error occurs if P is static or if P is read-only.

continues

7. Expressions

Construct	Example	Description
Event Access	`E += value`	The `add` accessor of the event `E` in the containing class or struct is invoked. If `E` is not static, the instance expression is `this`.
	`E -= value`	The `remove` accessor of the event `E` in the containing class or struct is invoked. If `E` is not static, the instance expression is `this`.
	`T.E += value`	The `add` accessor of the event `E` in the class or struct `T` is invoked. A compile-time error occurs if `E` is not static.
	`T.E -= value`	The `remove` accessor of the event `E` in the class or struct `T` is invoked. A compile-time error occurs if `E` is not static.
	`e.E += value`	The `add` accessor of the event `E` in the class, struct, or interface given by the type of `e` is invoked with the instance expression `e`. A compile-time error occurs if `E` is static.
	`e.E -= value`	The `remove` accessor of the event `E` in the class, struct, or interface given by the type of `e` is invoked with the instance expression `e`. A compile-time error occurs if `E` is static.

Construct	Example	Description
Indexer Access	`e[x, y]`	Overload resolution is applied to select the best indexer in the class, struct, or interface given by the type of `e`. The `get` accessor of the indexer is invoked with the instance expression `e` and the argument list `(x, y)`. A compile-time error occurs if the indexer is write-only.
	`e[x, y] = value`	Overload resolution is applied to select the best indexer in the class, struct, or interface given by the type of `e`. The `set` accessor of the indexer is invoked with the instance expression `e` and the argument list `(x, y, value)`. A compile-time error occurs if the indexer is read-only.
Operator Invocation	`-x`	Overload resolution is applied to select the best unary operator in the class or struct given by the type of `x`. The selected operator is invoked with the argument list `(x)`.
	`x + y`	Overload resolution is applied to select the best binary operator in the classes or structs given by the types of `x` and `y`. The selected operator is invoked with the argument list `(x, y)`.
Instance Constructor Invocation	`new T(x, y)`	Overload resolution is applied to select the best instance constructor in the class or struct `T`. The instance constructor is invoked with the argument list `(x, y)`.

7.4.1 Argument Lists

Every function member invocation includes an argument list that provides actual values or variable references for the parameters of the function member. The syntax for specifying the argument list of a function member invocation depends on the function member category.

- For instance constructors, methods, and delegates, the arguments are specified as an *argument-list*, as described shortly.

- For properties, the argument list is empty when invoking the get accessor and consists of the expression specified as the right operand of the assignment operator when invoking the set accessor.

- For events, the argument list consists of the expression specified as the right operand of the += or -= operator.

- For indexers, the argument list consists of the expressions specified between the square brackets in the indexer access. When invoking the set accessor, the argument list additionally includes the expression specified as the right operand of the assignment operator.

- For user-defined operators, the argument list consists of the single operand of the unary operator or the two operands of the binary operator.

The arguments of properties (§10.6), events (§10.7), indexers (§10.8), and user-defined operators (§10.9) are always passed as value parameters (§10.5.1.1). Reference and output parameters are not supported for these categories of function members.

The arguments of an instance constructor, method, or delegate invocation are specified as an *argument-list*.

> *argument-list:*
>   *argument*
>   *argument-list* , *argument*
>
> *argument:*
>   *expression*
>   ref *variable-reference*
>   out *variable-reference*

An *argument-list* consists of one or more *argument*s, separated by commas. Each argument can take one of the following forms.

- An *expression*, indicating that the argument is passed as a value parameter (§10.5.1.1).

- The keyword `ref` followed by a *variable-reference* (§5.4), indicating that the argument is passed as a reference parameter (§10.5.1.2). A variable must be definitely assigned (§5.3) before it can be passed as a reference parameter. A volatile field (§10.4.3) cannot be passed as a reference parameter.

- The keyword `out` followed by a *variable-reference* (§5.4), indicating that the argument is passed as an output parameter (§10.5.1.3). A variable is considered definitely assigned (§5.3) following a function member invocation in which the variable is passed as an output parameter. A volatile field (§10.4.3) cannot be passed as an output parameter.

During the runtime processing of a function member invocation (§7.4.3), the expressions or variable references of an argument list are evaluated in order, from left to right, as follows.

- For a value parameter, the argument expression is evaluated and an implicit conversion (§6.1) to the corresponding parameter type is performed. The resulting value becomes the initial value of the value parameter in the function member invocation.

- For a reference or output parameter, the variable reference is evaluated, and the resulting storage location becomes the storage location represented by the parameter in the function member invocation. If the variable reference given as a reference or output parameter is an array element of a *reference-type*, a runtime check is performed to ensure that the element type of the array is identical to the type of the parameter. If this check fails, a `System.ArrayTypeMismatchException` is thrown.

Methods, indexers, and instance constructors may declare their right-most parameter to be a parameter array (§10.5.1.4). Such function members are invoked either in their normal form or in their expanded form depending on which is applicable (§7.4.2.1).

- When a function member with a parameter array is invoked in its normal form, the argument given for the parameter array must be a single expression of a type that is implicitly convertible (§6.1) to the parameter array type. In this case, the parameter array acts precisely like a value parameter.

- When a function member with a parameter array is invoked in its expanded form, the invocation must specify zero or more arguments for the parameter array, where each argument is an expression of a type that is implicitly convertible (§6.1) to the element type of the parameter array. In this case, the invocation creates an instance of the parameter array type with a length corresponding to the number of arguments, initializes the elements of the array instance with the given argument values, and uses the newly created array instance as the actual argument.

7. Expressions

The expressions of an argument list are always evaluated in the order they are written. Thus, the following example

```
class Test
{
    static void F(int x, int y, int z) {
        System.Console.WriteLine("x = {0}, y = {1}, z = {2}", x, y, z);
    }

    static void Main() {
        int i = 0;
        F(i++, i++, i++);
    }
}
```

produces the following output.

```
x = 0, y = 1, z = 2
```

The array covariance rules (§12.5) permit a value of an array type A[] to be a reference to an instance of an array type B[], provided an implicit reference conversion exists from B to A. Because of these rules, when an array element of a *reference-type* is passed as a reference or output parameter, a runtime check is required to ensure that the actual element type of the array is *identical* to that of the parameter. In the example

```
class Test
{
    static void F(ref object x) {...}

    static void Main() {
        object[] a = new object[10];
        object[] b = new string[10];
        F(ref a[0]);    // Ok
        F(ref b[1]);    // ArrayTypeMismatchException
    }
}
```

the second invocation of F causes a System.ArrayTypeMismatchException to be thrown because the actual element type of b is string and not object.

When a function member with a parameter array is invoked in its expanded form, the invocation is processed exactly as if an array creation expression with an array initializer (§7.5.10.2) was inserted around the expanded parameters. For example, given this declaration

```
void F(int x, int y, params object[] args);
```

the following invocations of the expanded form of the method

```
F(10, 20);
F(10, 20, 30, 40);
F(10, 20, 1, "hello", 3.0);
```

correspond exactly to the following.

```
F(10, 20, new object[] {});
F(10, 20, new object[] {30, 40});
F(10, 20, new object[] {1, "hello", 3.0});
```

In particular, note that an empty array is created when there are zero arguments given for the parameter array.

7.4.2 Overload Resolution

Overload resolution is a compile-time mechanism for selecting the best function member to invoke given an argument list and a set of candidate function members. Overload resolution selects the function member to invoke in the following distinct contexts within C#:

- Invocation of a method named in an *invocation-expression* (§7.5.5)

- Invocation of an instance constructor named in an *object-creation-expression* (§7.5.10.1)

- Invocation of an indexer accessor through an *element-access* (§7.5.6)

- Invocation of a predefined or user-defined operator referenced in an expression (§7.2.3 and §7.2.4)

Each of these contexts defines the set of candidate function members and the list of arguments in its own unique way, as described in detail in the previous sections. For example, the set of candidates for a method invocation does not include methods marked `override` (§7.3), and methods in a base class are not candidates if any method in a derived class is applicable (§7.5.5.1).

Once the candidate function members and the argument list have been identified, the selection of the best function member is the same in all cases.

Given the set of applicable candidate function members, the best function member in that set is located. If the set contains only one function member, then that function member is the best function member. Otherwise, the best function member is the one function member that is better than all other function members with respect to the given argument list, provided that each function member is compared to all other function members using the rules in §7.4.2.2. If there is not exactly one function member that is better than all other function members, then the function member invocation is ambiguous and a compile-time error occurs.

The following sections define the terms applicable function member and better function member.

7.4.2.1 *Applicable Function Member*

A function member is said to be an ***applicable function member*** with respect to an argument list A when all of the following are true.

- The number of arguments in A is identical to the number of parameters in the function member declaration.

- For each argument in A, the parameter passing mode of the argument (in other words, value, `ref`, or `out`) is identical to the parameter passing mode of the corresponding parameter, and

  - For a value parameter or a parameter array, an implicit conversion (§6.1) exists from the type of the argument to the type of the corresponding parameter, or

  - For a `ref` or `out` parameter, the type of the argument is identical to the type of the corresponding parameter. After all, a `ref` or `out` parameter is an alias for the argument passed.

For a function member that includes a parameter array, if the function member is applicable by these rules, it is said to be applicable in its ***normal form***. If a function member that includes a parameter array is not applicable in its normal form, the function member may instead be applicable in its ***expanded form***.

- The expanded form is constructed by replacing the parameter array in the function member declaration with zero or more value parameters of the element type of the parameter array such that the number of arguments in the argument list A matches the total number of parameters. If A has fewer arguments than the number of fixed parameters in the function member declaration, the expanded form of the function member cannot be constructed and is thus not applicable.

- If the class, struct, or interface in which the function member is declared already contains another applicable function member with the same signature as the expanded form, the expanded form is not applicable.

- Otherwise, the expanded form is applicable if for each argument in A the parameter passing mode of the argument is identical to the parameter passing mode of the corresponding parameter, and

  - For a fixed value parameter or a value parameter created by the expansion, an implicit conversion (§6.1) exists from the type of the argument to the type of the corresponding parameter, or

  - For a `ref` or `out` parameter, the type of the argument is identical to the type of the corresponding parameter.

7.4.2.2 *Better Function Member*

Given an argument list A with a set of argument types { A_1, A_2, ..., A_N } and two applicable function members M_P and M_Q with parameter types { P_1, P_2, ..., P_N } and { Q_1, Q_2, ..., Q_N }, M_P is defined to be a ***better function member*** than M_Q if

- For each argument, the implicit conversion from A_X to P_X is not worse than the implicit conversion from A_X to Q_X, and

- For at least one argument, the conversion from A_X to P_X is better than the conversion from A_X to Q_X.

When performing this evaluation, if M_P or M_Q is applicable in its expanded form, then P_X or Q_X refers to a parameter in the expanded form of the parameter list.

7.4.2.3 *Better Conversion*

Given an implicit conversion C_1 that converts from a type S to a type T_1, and an implicit conversion C_2 that converts from a type S to a type T_2, the ***better conversion*** of the two conversions is determined as follows.

- If T_1 and T_2 are the same type, neither conversion is better.
- If S is T_1, C_1 is the better conversion.
- If S is T_2, C_2 is the better conversion.
- If an implicit conversion from T_1 to T_2 exists, and no implicit conversion from T_2 to T_1 exists, C_1 is the better conversion.
- If an implicit conversion from T_2 to T_1 exists, and no implicit conversion from T_1 to T_2 exists, C_2 is the better conversion.
- If T_1 is sbyte and T_2 is byte, ushort, uint, or ulong, C_1 is the better conversion.
- If T_2 is sbyte and T_1 is byte, ushort, uint, or ulong, C_2 is the better conversion.
- If T_1 is short and T_2 is ushort, uint, or ulong, C_1 is the better conversion.
- If T_2 is short and T_1 is ushort, uint, or ulong, C_2 is the better conversion.
- If T_1 is int and T_2 is uint, or ulong, C_1 is the better conversion.
- If T_2 is int and T_1 is uint, or ulong, C_2 is the better conversion.
- If T_1 is long and T_2 is ulong, C_1 is the better conversion.
- If T_2 is long and T_1 is ulong, C_2 is the better conversion.
- Otherwise, neither conversion is better.

If an implicit conversion C_1 is defined by these rules to be a better conversion than an implicit conversion C_2, then it is also the case that C_2 is a ***worse conversion*** than C_1.

7.4.3 Function Member Invocation

This section describes the process that takes place at runtime to invoke a particular function member. It is assumed that a compile-time process has already determined the particular member to invoke, possibly by applying overload resolution to a set of candidate function members.

For purposes of describing the invocation process, function members are divided into two categories.

- Static function members. These are instance constructors, static methods, static property accessors, and user-defined operators. Static function members are always nonvirtual.

- Instance function members. These are instance methods, instance property accessors, and indexer accessors. Instance function members are either nonvirtual or virtual and are always invoked on a particular instance. The instance is computed by an instance expression, and it becomes accessible within the function member as this (§7.5.7).

The runtime processing of a function member invocation consists of the following steps, where M is the function member and, if M is an instance member, E is the instance expression.

- If M is a static function member

   - The argument list is evaluated as described in §7.4.1.

   - M is invoked.

- If M is an instance function member declared in a *value-type*

   - E is evaluated. If this evaluation causes an exception, then no further steps are executed.

   - If E is not classified as a variable, then a temporary local variable of E's type is created and the value of E is assigned to that variable. E is then reclassified as a reference to that temporary local variable. The temporary variable is accessible as this within M, but not in any other way. Thus, only when E is a true variable is it possible for the caller to observe the changes that M makes to this.

   - The argument list is evaluated as described in §7.4.1.

   - M is invoked. The variable referenced by E becomes the variable referenced by this.

- If M is an instance function member declared in a *reference-type*

   - E is evaluated. If this evaluation causes an exception, then no further steps are executed.

- The argument list is evaluated as described in §7.4.1.

- If the type of E is a *value-type*, a boxing conversion (§4.3.1) is performed to convert E to type object, and E is considered to be of type object in the following steps. In this case, M could only be a member of System.Object.

- The value of E is checked to be valid. If the value of E is null, a System.NullReferenceException is thrown and no further steps are executed.

- The function member implementation to invoke is determined.

  • If the compile-time type of E is an interface, the function member to invoke is the implementation of M provided by the runtime type of the instance referenced by E. This function member is determined by applying the interface mapping rules (§13.4.2) to determine the implementation of M provided by the runtime type of the instance referenced by E.

  • Otherwise, if M is a virtual function member, the function member to invoke is the implementation of M provided by the runtime type of the instance referenced by E. This function member is determined by applying the rules for determining the most derived implementation (§10.5.3) of M with respect to the runtime type of the instance referenced by E.

  • Otherwise, M is a nonvirtual function member, and the function member to invoke is M itself.

- The function member implementation determined in the previous step is invoked. The object referenced by E becomes the object referenced by this.

7.4.3.1 *Invocations on Boxed Instances*

A function member implemented in a *value-type* can be invoked through a boxed instance of that *value-type* in the following situations:

• When the function member is an override of a method inherited from type object and is invoked through an instance expression of type object

• When the function member is an implementation of an interface function member and is invoked through an instance expression of an *interface-type*

• When the function member is invoked through a delegate

In these situations, the boxed instance is considered to contain a variable of the *value-type*, and this variable becomes the variable referenced by this within the function member invocation. In particular, this means that when a function member is invoked on a boxed instance, it is possible for the function member to modify the value contained in the boxed instance.

7. Expressions

7.5 Primary Expressions

Primary expressions include the simplest forms of expressions.

> *primary-expression:*
>   *primary-no-array-creation-expression*
>   *array-creation-expression*
>
> *primary-no-array-creation-expression:*
>   *literal*
>   *simple-name*
>   *parenthesized-expression*
>   *member-access*
>   *invocation-expression*
>   *element-access*
>   *this-access*
>   *base-access*
>   *post-increment-expression*
>   *post-decrement-expression*
>   *object-creation-expression*
>   *delegate-creation-expression*
>   *typeof-expression*
>   *checked-expression*
>   *unchecked-expression*

Primary expressions are divided between *array-creation-expressions* and *primary-no-array-creation-expressions*. Treating *array-creation-expression* in this way, rather than listing it along with the other simple expression forms, enables the grammar to disallow potentially confusing code such as

```
object o = new int[3][1];
```

that would otherwise be interpreted as follows.

```
object o = (new int[3])[1];
```

7.5.1 Literals

A *primary-expression* that consists of a *literal* (§2.4.4) is classified as a value.

7.5.2 **Simple Names**

A *simple-name* consists of a single identifier.

> *simple-name:*
> > *identifier*

A *simple-name* is evaluated and classified as follows.

- If the *simple-name* appears within a *block* and if the *block*'s (or an enclosing block's) local variable declaration space (§3.3) contains a local variable or parameter with the given name, then the *simple-name* refers to that local variable or parameter and is classified as a variable.

- Otherwise, for each type T, starting with the immediately enclosing class, struct, or enumeration declaration and continuing with each enclosing outer class or struct declaration (if any), if a member lookup of the *simple-name* in T produces a match, then the following happens.

  - If T is the immediately enclosing class or struct type and the lookup identifies one or more methods, the result is a method group with an associated instance expression of this.

  - If T is the immediately enclosing class or struct type, if the lookup identifies an instance member, and if the reference occurs within the *block* of an instance constructor, an instance method, or an instance accessor, the result is the same as a member access (§7.5.4) of the form this.E, where E is the *simple-name*.

  - Otherwise, the result is the same as a member access (§7.5.4) of the form T.E, where E is the *simple-name*. In this case, it is a compile-time error for the *simple-name* to refer to an instance member.

- Otherwise, starting with the namespace in which the *simple-name* occurs, continuing with each enclosing namespace (if any), and ending with the global namespace, the following steps are evaluated until an entity is located.

  - If the namespace contains a namespace member with the given name, then the *simple-name* refers to that member and, depending on the member, is classified as a namespace or a type.

  - Otherwise, if the namespace has a corresponding namespace declaration enclosing the location where the *simple-name* occurs, then

    - If the namespace declaration contains a *using-alias-directive* that associates the given name with an imported namespace or type, then the *simple-name* refers to that namespace or type.

- Otherwise, if the namespaces imported by the *using-namespace-directives* of the namespace declaration contain exactly one type with the given name, then the *simple-name* refers to that type.

- Otherwise, if the namespaces imported by the *using-namespace-directives* of the namespace declaration contain more than one type with the given name, then the *simple-name* is ambiguous and a compile-time error occurs.

- Otherwise, the name given by the *simple-name* is undefined, and a compile-time error occurs.

7.5.2.1 *Invariant Meaning in Blocks*

For each occurrence of a given identifier as a *simple-name* in an expression, every other occurrence of the same identifier as a *simple-name* in an expression within the immediately enclosing *block* (§8.2) or *switch-block* (§8.7.2) must refer to the same entity. This rule ensures that the meaning of a name in the context of an expression is always the same within a block.

The example

```
class Test
{
    double x;

    void F(bool b) {
        x = 1.0;
        if (b) {
            int x;
            x = 1;
        }
    }
}
```

results in a compile-time error because x refers to different entities within the outer block (the extent of which includes the nested block in the `if` statement). In contrast, the example

```
class Test
{
    double x;

    void F(bool b) {
        if (b) {
            x = 1.0;
        }
        else {
            int x;
            x = 1;
        }
    }
}
```

is permitted because the name x is never used in the outer block.

Note that the rule of invariant meaning applies only to simple names. It is perfectly valid for the same identifier to have one meaning as a simple name and another meaning as right operand of a member access (§7.5.4). The example

```
struct Point
{
    int x, y;

    public Point(int x, int y) {
        this.x = x;
        this.y = y;
    }
}
```

illustrates a common pattern of using the names of fields as parameter names in an instance constructor. In the example, the simple names x and y refer to the parameters, but that does not prevent the member access expressions this.x and this.y from accessing the fields.

7.5.3 Parenthesized Expressions

A *parenthesized-expression* consists of an *expression* enclosed in parentheses.

> *parenthesized-expression:*
>   (*expression*)

A *parenthesized-expression* is evaluated by evaluating the *expression* within the parentheses. If the *expression* within the parentheses denotes a namespace, type, or method group, a compile-time error occurs. Otherwise, the result of the *parenthesized-expression* is the result of the evaluation of the contained *expression*.

7.5.4 Member Access

A *member-access* consists of a *primary-expression* or a *predefined-type*, followed by a . token, followed by an *identifier*.

> *member-access:*
>   *primary-expression*   .   *identifier*
>   *predefined-type*   .   *identifier*
>
> *predefined-type:* one of
>   bool   byte   char   decimal   double   float   int   long
>   object   sbyte   short   string   uint   ulong   ushort

A *member-access* of the form E.I, where E is a *primary-expression* or a *predefined-type* and I is an *identifier*, is evaluated and classified as follows.

- If E is a namespace and I is the name of an accessible member of that namespace, then the result is that member, depending on the member, is classified as a namespace or a type.

- If E is a *predefined-type* or a *primary-expression* classified as a type, and a member lookup (§7.3) of I in E produces a match, then E.I is evaluated and classified as follows.

    - If I identifies a type, then the result is that type.

    - If I identifies one or more methods, then the result is a method group with no associated instance expression.

    - If I identifies a static property, then the result is a property access with no associated instance expression.

    - If I identifies a static field

        - If the field is readonly and the reference occurs outside the static constructor of the class or struct in which the field is declared, then the result is a value, namely the value of the static field I in E.

        - Otherwise, the result is a variable, namely the static field I in E.

    - If I identifies a static event

        - If the reference occurs within the class or struct in which the event is declared, and the event was declared without *event-accessor-declarations* (§10.7), then E.I is processed exactly as if I was a static field.

        - Otherwise, the result is an event access with no associated instance expression.

    - If I identifies a constant, then the result is a value, namely the value of that constant.

    - If I identifies an enumeration member, then the result is a value, namely the value of that enumeration member.

    - Otherwise, E.I is an invalid member reference, and a compile-time error occurs.

- If E is a property access, indexer access, variable, or value, the type of which is T, and a member lookup (§7.3) of I in T produces a match, then E.I is evaluated and classified as follows.

    - First, if E is a property or indexer access, then the value of the property or indexer access is obtained (§7.1.1) and E is reclassified as a value.

    - If I identifies one or more methods, then the result is a method group with an associated instance expression of E.

- If I identifies an instance property, then the result is a property access with an associated instance expression of E.

- If T is a *class-type* and I identifies an instance field of that *class-type*

    • If the value of E is null, then a System.NullReferenceException is thrown.

    • Otherwise, if the field is readonly and the reference occurs outside an instance constructor of the class in which the field is declared, then the result is a value, namely the value of the field I in the object referenced by E.

    • Otherwise, the result is a variable, namely the field I in the object referenced by E.

- If T is a *struct-type* and I identifies an instance field of that *struct-type*

    • If E is a value, or if the field is readonly and the reference occurs outside an instance constructor of the struct in which the field is declared, then the result is a value, namely the value of the field I in the struct instance given by E.

    • Otherwise, the result is a variable, namely the field I in the struct instance given by E.

- If I identifies an instance event

    • If the reference occurs within the class or struct in which the event is declared, and the event was declared without *event-accessor-declarations* (§10.7), then E.I is processed exactly as if I was an instance field.

    • Otherwise, the result is an event access with an associated instance expression of E.

• Otherwise, E.I is an invalid member reference, and a compile-time error occurs.

7.5.4.1 *Identical Simple Names and Type Names*

In a member access of the form E.I, if E is a single identifier and if the meaning of E as a *simple-name* (§7.5.2) is a constant, field, property, local variable, or parameter with the same type as the meaning of E as a *type-name* (§3.8), then both possible meanings of E are permitted. The two possible meanings of E.I are never ambiguous because I must be a member of the type E in both cases. In other words, the rule simply permits access to the static members and nested types of E where a compile-time error would otherwise have occurred. For example

```
struct Color
{
    public static readonly Color White = new Color(...);
    public static readonly Color Black = new Color(...);

    public Color Complement() {...}
}
```

```
class A
{
    public Color Color;              // Field Color of type Color

    void F() {
        Color = Color.Black;         // References Color.Black static member
        Color = Color.Complement();  // Invokes Complement() on Color field
    }

    static void G() {
        Color c = Color.White;       // References Color.White static member
    }
}
```

Within the A class, those occurrences of the Color identifier that reference the Color type are underlined, and those that reference the Color field are not underlined.

7.5.5 Invocation Expressions

An *invocation-expression* is used to invoke a method.

> *invocation-expression:*
>   *primary-expression*   (*argument-list*$_{opt}$)

The *primary-expression* of an *invocation-expression* must be a method group or a value of a *delegate-type*. If the *primary-expression* is a method group, the *invocation-expression* is a method invocation (§7.5.5.1). If the *primary-expression* is a value of a *delegate-type*, the *invocation-expression* is a delegate invocation (§7.5.5.2). If the *primary-expression* is neither a method group nor a value of a *delegate-type*, a compile-time error occurs.

The optional *argument-list* (§7.4.1) provides values or variable references for the parameters of the method.

The result of evaluating an *invocation-expression* is classified as follows.

- If the *invocation-expression* invokes a method or delegate that returns void, the result is nothing. An expression that is classified as nothing cannot be an operand of any operator and is permitted only in the context of a *statement-expression* (§8.6).

- Otherwise, the result is a value of the type returned by the method or delegate.

7.5.5.1 *Method Invocations*

For a method invocation, the *primary-expression* of the *invocation-expression* must be a method group. The method group identifies the one method to invoke or the set of overloaded methods from which to choose a specific method to invoke. In the latter case, determination of the specific method to invoke is based on the context provided by the types of the arguments in the *argument-list*.

The compile-time processing of a method invocation of the form `M(A)`, where `M` is a method group and `A` is an optional *argument-list*, consists of the following steps.

- The set of candidate methods for the method invocation is constructed. Starting with the set of methods associated with `M`, which were found by a previous member lookup (§7.3), the set is reduced to those methods that are applicable with respect to the argument list `A`. The set reduction consists of applying the following rules to each method `T.N` in the set, where `T` is the type in which the method `N` is declared.
  - If `N` is not applicable with respect to `A` (§7.4.2.1), then `N` is removed from the set.
  - If `N` is applicable with respect to `A` (§7.4.2.1), then all methods declared in a base type of `T` are removed from the set.

- If the resulting set of candidate methods is empty, then no applicable methods exist, and a compile-time error occurs. If the candidate methods are not all declared in the same type, the method invocation is ambiguous, and a compile-time error occurs (this latter situation can only occur for an invocation of a method in an interface that has multiple direct base interfaces, as described in §13.2.5).

- The best method of the set of candidate methods is identified using the overload resolution rules of §7.4.2. If a single best method cannot be identified, the method invocation is ambiguous, and a compile-time error occurs.

- Given a best method, the invocation of the method is validated in the context of the method group: If the best method is a static method, the method group must have resulted from a *simple-name* or a *member-access* through a type. If the best method is an instance method, the method group must have resulted from a *simple-name*, a *member-access* through a variable or value, or a *base-access*. If neither of these requirements is true, a compile-time error occurs.

Once a method has been selected and validated at compile time by the previous steps, the actual runtime invocation is processed according to the rules of function member invocation described in §7.4.3.

The intuitive effect of the resolution rules described previously is as follows: To locate the particular method invoked by a method invocation, start with the type indicated by the method invocation and proceed up the inheritance chain until at least one applicable, accessible, nonoverride method declaration is found. Then perform overload resolution on the set of applicable, accessible, nonoverride methods declared in that type and invoke the method thus selected.

7.5.5.2 *Delegate Invocations*

For a delegate invocation, the *primary-expression* of the *invocation-expression* must be a value of a *delegate-type*. Furthermore, considering the *delegate-type* to be a function member with

7. Expressions

the same parameter list as the *delegate-type*, the *delegate-type* must be applicable (§7.4.2.1) with respect to the *argument-list* of the *invocation-expression*.

The runtime processing of a delegate invocation of the form D(A), where D is a *primary-expression* of a *delegate-type* and A is an optional *argument-list*, consists of the following steps.

- D is evaluated. If this evaluation causes an exception, no further steps are executed.
- The value of D is checked to be valid. If the value of D is null, a System.NullReferenceException is thrown and no further steps are executed.
- Otherwise, D is a reference to a delegate instance. Function member invocations (§7.4.3) are performed on each of the callable entities in the invocation list of the delegate. For callable entities consisting of an instance and instance method, the instance for the invocation is the instance contained in the callable entity.

7.5.6 Element Access

An *element-access* consists of a *primary-no-array-creation-expression*, followed by a [token, followed by an *expression-list*, followed by a] token. The *expression-list* consists of one or more *expressions*, separated by commas.

element-access:
   primary-no-array-creation-expression   [*expression-list*   ]

expression-list:
   expression
   expression-list   ,   *expression*

If the *primary-no-array-creation-expression* of an *element-access* is a value of an *array-type*, the *element-access* is an array access (§7.5.6.1). Otherwise, the *primary-no-array-creation-expression* must be a variable or value of a class, struct, or interface type that has one or more indexer members, in which case the *element-access* is an indexer access (§7.5.6.2).

7.5.6.1 *Array Access*

For an array access, the *primary-no-array-creation-expression* of the *element-access* must be a value of an *array-type*. The number of expressions in the *expression-list* must be the same as the rank of the *array-type*, and each expression must be of type int, uint, long, ulong, or of a type that can be implicitly converted to one or more of these types.

The result of evaluating an array access is a variable of the element type of the array, namely the array element selected by the value(s) of the expression(s) in the *expression-list*.

The runtime processing of an array access of the form P[A], where P is a *primary-no-array-creation-expression* of an *array-type* and A is an *expression-list*, consists of the following steps.

- P is evaluated. If this evaluation causes an exception, no further steps are executed.

- The index expressions of the *expression-list* are evaluated in order, from left to right. Following evaluation of each index expression, an implicit conversion (§6.1) to one of the following types is performed: int, uint, long, or ulong. The first type in this list for which an implicit conversion exists is chosen. For instance, if the index expression is of type short, then an implicit conversion to int is performed because implicit conversions from short to int and from short to long are possible. If evaluation of an index expression or the subsequent implicit conversion causes an exception, then no further index expressions are evaluated and no further steps are executed.

- The value of P is checked to be valid. If the value of P is null, a System.NullReferenceException is thrown and no further steps are executed.

- The value of each expression in the *expression-list* is checked against the actual bounds of each dimension of the array instance referenced by P. If one or more values are out of range, a System.IndexOutOfRangeException is thrown and no further steps are executed.

- The location of the array element given by the index expression(s) is computed, and this location becomes the result of the array access.

7.5.6.2 *Indexer Access*

For an indexer access, the *primary-no-array-creation-expression* of the *element-access* must be a variable or value of a class, struct, or interface type, and this type must implement one or more indexers that are applicable with respect to the *expression-list* of the *element-access*.

The compile-time processing of an indexer access of the form P[A], where P is a *primary-no-array-creation-expression* of a class, struct, or interface type T and A is an *expression-list*, consists of the following steps.

- The set of indexers provided by T is constructed. The set consists of all indexers declared in T or a base type of T that are not override declarations and are accessible in the current context (§3.5).

- The set is reduced to those indexers that are applicable and not hidden by other indexers. The following rules are applied to each indexer S.I in the set, where S is the type in which the indexer I is declared.

  - If I is not applicable with respect to A (§7.4.2.1), then I is removed from the set.

  - If I is applicable with respect to A (§7.4.2.1), then all indexers declared in a base type of S are removed from the set.

- If the resulting set of candidate indexers is empty, then no applicable indexers exist, and a compile-time error occurs. If the candidate indexers are not all declared in the same type, the indexer access is ambiguous, and a compile-time error occurs (this latter situation can only occur for an indexer access on an instance of an interface that has multiple direct base interfaces).

- The best indexer of the set of candidate indexers is identified using the overload resolution rules of §7.4.2. If a single best indexer cannot be identified, the indexer access is ambiguous, and a compile-time error occurs.

- The index expressions of the *expression-list* are evaluated in order, from left to right. The result of processing the indexer access is an expression classified as an indexer access. The indexer access expression references the indexer determined in the previous step and has an associated instance expression of P and an associated argument list of A.

Depending on the context in which it is used, an indexer access causes invocation of either the *get-accessor* or the *set-accessor* of the indexer. If the indexer access is the target of an assignment, the *set-accessor* is invoked to assign a new value (§7.13.1). In all other cases, the *get-accessor* is invoked to obtain the current value (§7.1.1).

7.5.7 This Access

A *this-access* consists of the reserved word this.

> *this-access:*
>   this

A *this-access* is permitted only in the *block* of an instance constructor, an instance method, or an instance accessor. It has one of the following meanings.

- When this is used in a *primary-expression* within an instance constructor of a class, it is classified as a value. The type of the value is the class within which the usage occurs, and the value is a reference to the object being constructed.

- When this is used in a *primary-expression* within an instance method or instance accessor of a class, it is classified as a value. The type of the value is the class within which the usage occurs, and the value is a reference to the object for which the method or accessor was invoked.

- When this is used in a *primary-expression* within an instance constructor of a struct, it is classified as a variable. The type of the variable is the struct within which the usage occurs, and the variable represents the struct being constructed. The this variable of an instance constructor of a struct behaves exactly the same as an out parameter of the struct type—in particular, this means that the variable must be definitely assigned in every execution path of the instance constructor.

- When `this` is used in a *primary-expression* within an instance method or instance accessor of a struct, it is classified as a variable. The type of the variable is the struct within which the usage occurs, and the variable represents the struct for which the method or accessor was invoked. The `this` variable of an instance method of a struct behaves exactly the same as a `ref` parameter of the struct type.

Using `this` in a *primary-expression* in a context other than the ones listed previously is a compile-time error. In particular, it is not possible to refer to `this` in a static method, in a static property accessor, or in a *variable-initializer* of a field declaration.

7.5.8 Base Access

A *base-access* consists of the reserved word `base` followed by either a `.` token and an identifier or an *expression-list* enclosed in square brackets.

> *base-access:*
>   `base` `.` *identifier*
>   `base` `[` *expression-list* `]`

A *base-access* is used to access base class members that are hidden by similarly named members in the current class or struct. A *base-access* is permitted only in the *block* of an instance constructor, an instance method, or an instance accessor. When `base.I` occurs in a class or struct, `I` must denote a member of the base class of that class or struct. Likewise, when `base[E]` occurs in a class, an applicable indexer must exist in the base class.

At compile time, *base-access* expressions of the form `base.I` and `base[E]` are evaluated exactly as if they were written `((B)this).I` and `((B)this)[E]`, where `B` is the base class of the class or struct in which the construct occurs. Thus, `base.I` and `base[E]` correspond to `this.I` and `this[E]`, except `this` is viewed as an instance of the base class.

When a *base-access* references a virtual function member (a method, property, or indexer), the determination of which function member to invoke at runtime (§7.4.3) changes. The function member that is invoked is determined by finding the most derived implementation (§10.5.3) of the function member with respect to `B` (instead of with respect to the runtime type of `this`, as would be usual in a nonbase access). Thus, within an `override` of a `virtual` function member, a *base-access* can be used to invoke the inherited implementation of the function member. If the function member referenced by a *base-access* is abstract, a compile-time error occurs.

7.5.9 Postfix Increment and Decrement Operators

> *post-increment-expression:*
>   *primary-expression* `++`
>
> *post-decrement-expression:*
>   *primary-expression* `--`

The operand of a postfix increment or decrement operation must be an expression classified as a variable, a property access, or an indexer access. The result of the operation is a value of the same type as the operand.

If the operand of a postfix increment or decrement operation is a property or indexer access, the property or indexer must have both a get and a set accessor. If this is not the case, a compile-time error occurs.

Unary operator overload resolution (§7.2.3) is applied to select a specific operator implementation. Predefined ++ and -- operators exist for the following types: sbyte, byte, short, ushort, int, uint, long, ulong, char, float, double, decimal, and any enum type. The predefined ++ operators return the value produced by adding 1 to the operand, and the predefined -- operators return the value produced by subtracting 1 from the operand.

The runtime processing of a postfix increment or decrement operation of the form x++ or x-- consists of the following steps.

- If x is classified as a variable

    - x is evaluated to produce the variable.

    - The value of x is saved.

    - The selected operator is invoked with the saved value of x as its argument.

    - The value returned by the operator is stored in the location given by the evaluation of x.

    - The saved value of x becomes the result of the operation.

- If x is classified as a property or indexer access

    - The instance expression (if x is not static) and the argument list (if x is an indexer access) associated with x are evaluated, and the results are used in the subsequent get and set accessor invocations.

    - The get accessor of x is invoked, and the returned value is saved.

    - The selected operator is invoked with the saved value of x as its argument.

    - The set accessor of x is invoked with the value returned by the operator as its value argument.

    - The saved value of x becomes the result of the operation.

The ++ and -- operators also support prefix notation (§7.6.5). The result of x++ or x-- is the value of x *before* the operation, whereas the result of ++x or --x is the value of x *after* the operation. In either case, x itself has the same value after the operation.

An `operator ++` or `operator --` implementation can be invoked using either postfix or prefix notation. It is not possible to have separate operator implementations for the two notations.

7.5.10 The new Operator

The `new` operator is used to create new instances of types.

There are three forms of `new` expressions.

- Object creation expressions are used to create new instances of class types and value types.
- Array creation expressions are used to create new instances of array types.
- Delegate creation expressions are used to create new instances of delegate types.

The `new` operator implies creation of an instance of a type but does not necessarily imply dynamic allocation of memory. In particular, instances of value types require no additional memory beyond the variables in which they reside, and no dynamic allocations occur when `new` is used to create instances of value types.

7.5.10.1 *Object Creation Expressions*

An *object-creation-expression* is used to create a new instance of a *class-type* or a *value-type*.

> *object-creation-expression:*
>   new *type* (*argument-list*_{opt})

The *type* of an *object-creation-expression* must be a *class-type* or a *value-type*. The *type* cannot be an `abstract` *class-type*.

The optional *argument-list* (§7.4.1) is permitted only if the *type* is a *class-type* or a *struct-type*.

The compile-time processing of an *object-creation-expression* of the form `new T(A)`, where `T` is a *class-type* or a *value-type* and `A` is an optional *argument-list*, consists of the following steps.

- If `T` is a *value-type* and `A` is not present
  - The *object-creation-expression* is a default constructor invocation. The result of the *object-creation-expression* is a value of type `T`, namely the default value for `T` as defined in §4.1.1.
- Otherwise, if `T` is a *class-type* or a *struct-type*
  - If `T` is an `abstract` *class-type*, a compile-time error occurs.

- The instance constructor to invoke is determined using the overload resolution rules of §7.4.2. The set of candidate instance constructors consists of all accessible instance constructors declared in T that are applicable with respect to A (§7.4.2.1). If the set of candidate instance constructors is empty or if a single best instance constructor cannot be identified, a compile-time error occurs.

- The result of the *object-creation-expression* is a value of type T, namely the value produced by invoking the instance constructor determined in the previous step.

• Otherwise, the *object-creation-expression* is invalid, and a compile-time error occurs.

The runtime processing of an *object-creation-expression* of the form new T(A), where T is *class-type* or a *struct-type* and A is an optional *argument-list*, consists of the following steps.

• If T is a *class-type*

- A new instance of class T is allocated. If there is not enough memory available to allocate the new instance, a System.OutOfMemoryException is thrown and no further steps are executed.

- All fields of the new instance are initialized to their default values (§5.2).

- The instance constructor is invoked according to the rules of function member invocation (§7.4.3). A reference to the newly allocated instance is automatically passed to the instance constructor and the instance can be accessed from within that constructor as this.

• If T is a *struct-type*

- An instance of type T is created by allocating a temporary local variable. Because an instance constructor of a *struct-type* is required to definitely assign a value to each field of the instance being created, no initialization of the temporary variable is necessary.

- The instance constructor is invoked according to the rules of function member invocation (§7.4.3). A reference to the newly allocated instance is automatically passed to the instance constructor, and the instance can be accessed from within that constructor as this.

7.5.10.2 *Array Creation Expressions*
An *array-creation-expression* is used to create a new instance of an *array-type*.

array-creation-expression:
    new *non-array-type* [*expression-list*] *rank-specifiers*$_{opt}$ *array-initializer*$_{opt}$
    new *array-type* *array-initializer*

An array creation expression of the first form allocates an array instance of the type that results from deleting each of the individual expressions from the expression list. For example, the array creation expression `new int[10, 20]` produces an array instance of type `int[,]`, and the array creation expression `new int[10][,]` produces an array of type `int[][,]`. Each expression in the expression list must be of type `int`, `uint`, `long`, or `ulong` or of a type that can be implicitly converted to one or more of these types. The value of each expression determines the length of the corresponding dimension in the newly allocated array instance. Because the length of an array dimension must be nonnegative, it is a compile-time error to have a *constant-expression* with a negative value in the expression list.

Except in an unsafe context (§18.1), the layout of arrays is unspecified.

If an array creation expression of the first form includes an array initializer, each expression in the expression list must be a constant, and the rank and dimension lengths specified by the expression list must match those of the array initializer.

In an array creation expression of the second form, the rank of the specified array type must match that of the array initializer. The individual dimension lengths are inferred from the number of elements in each of the corresponding nesting levels of the array initializer. Thus, the expression

```
new int[,] {{0, 1}, {2, 3}, {4, 5}}
```

exactly corresponds to the following.

```
new int[3, 2] {{0, 1}, {2, 3}, {4, 5}}
```

Array initializers are described further in §12.6.

The result of evaluating an array creation expression is classified as a value, namely a reference to the newly allocated array instance. The runtime processing of an array creation expression consists of the following steps.

- The dimension length expressions of the *expression-list* are evaluated in order, from left to right. Following evaluation of each expression, an implicit conversion (§6.1) to one of the following types is performed: `int`, `uint`, `long`, `ulong`. The first type in this list for which an implicit conversion exists is chosen. If evaluation of an expression or the subsequent implicit conversion causes an exception, then no further expressions are evaluated and no further steps are executed.

- The computed values for the dimension lengths are validated as follows. If one or more of the values are less than zero, a `System.OverflowException` is thrown and no further steps are executed.

- An array instance with the given dimension lengths is allocated. If there is not enough memory available to allocate the new instance, a `System.OutOfMemoryException` is thrown and no further steps are executed.

- All elements of the new array instance are initialized to their default values (§5.2).

- If the array creation expression contains an array initializer, then each expression in the array initializer is evaluated and assigned to its corresponding array element. The evaluations and assignments are performed in the order the expressions are written in the array initializer—in other words, elements are initialized in increasing index order, with the rightmost dimension increasing first. If evaluation of a given expression or the subsequent assignment to the corresponding array element causes an exception, then no further elements are initialized (and the remaining elements will thus have their default values).

An array creation expression permits instantiation of an array with elements of an array type, but the elements of such an array must be manually initialized. For example, the statement

```
int[][] a = new int[100][];
```

creates a single-dimensional array with 100 elements of type `int[]`. The initial value of each element is `null`. It is not possible for the same array creation expression to also instantiate the subarrays, and the statement

```
int[][] a = new int[100][5];   // Error
```

results in a compile-time error. Instantiation of the subarrays must instead be performed manually, as in

```
int[][] a = new int[100][];
for (int i = 0; i < 100; i++) a[i] = new int[5];
```

When an array of arrays has a rectangular shape, which is when the subarrays are all of the same length, it is more efficient to use a multi-dimensional array. In the previous example, instantiation of the array of arrays creates 101 objects—one outer array and 100 subarrays. In contrast

```
int[,] = new int[100, 5];
```

creates only a single object and a two-dimensional array and accomplishes the allocation in a single statement.

7.5.10.3 *Delegate Creation Expressions*

A *delegate-creation-expression* is used to create a new instance of a *delegate-type*.

> *delegate-creation-expression:*
>   new *delegate-type* (*expression*)

The argument of a delegate creation expression must be a method group (§7.1) or a value of a *delegate-type*. If the argument is a method group, it identifies the method and, for an instance method, the object for which to create a delegate. If the argument is a value of a *delegate-type*, it identifies a delegate instance of which to create a copy.

The compile-time processing of a *delegate-creation-expression* of the form new D(E), where D is a *delegate-type* and E is an *expression*, consists of the following steps.

* If E is a method group

  - The set of methods identified by E must include exactly one method that is compatible (§15.1) with D, and this method becomes the one to which the newly created delegate refers. If no matching method exists or if more than one matching method exists, a compile-time error occurs. If the selected method is an instance method, the instance expression associated with E determines the target object of the delegate.

  - As in a method invocation, the selected method must be compatible with the context of the method group: If the method is a static method, the method group must have resulted from a *simple-name* or a *member-access* through a type. If the method is an instance method, the method group must have resulted from a *simple-name* or a *member-access* through a variable or value. If the selected method does not match the context of the method group, a compile-time error occurs.

  - The result is a value of type D, namely a newly created delegate that refers to the selected method and target object.

* Otherwise, if E is a value of a *delegate-type*

  - D and E must be compatible (§15.1); otherwise, a compile-time error occurs.

  - The result is a value of type D, namely a newly created delegate that refers to the same invocation list as E.

* Otherwise, the delegate creation expression is invalid, and a compile-time error occurs.

7.   Expressions

The runtime processing of a *delegate-creation-expression* of the form new D (E), where D is a *delegate-type* and E is an *expression*, consists of the following steps.

- If E is a method group
  - If the method selected at compile time is a static method, the target object of the delegate is null. Otherwise, the selected method is an instance method, and the target object of the delegate is determined from the instance expression associated with E.
    - The instance expression is evaluated. If this evaluation causes an exception, no further steps are executed.
    - If the instance expression is of a *reference-type*, the value computed by the instance expression becomes the target object. If the target object is null, a System.NullReferenceException is thrown and no further steps are executed.
    - If the instance expression is of a *value-type*, a boxing operation (§4.3.1) is performed to convert the value to an object, and this object becomes the target object.
  - A new instance of the delegate type D is allocated. If there is not enough memory available to allocate the new instance, a System.OutOfMemoryException is thrown and no further steps are executed.
  - The new delegate instance is initialized with a reference to the method that was determined at compile time and a reference to the target object computed previously.
- If E is a value of a *delegate-type*
  - E is evaluated. If this evaluation causes an exception, no further steps are executed.
  - If the value of E is null, a System.NullReferenceException is thrown and no further steps are executed.
  - A new instance of the delegate type D is allocated. If there is not enough memory available to allocate the new instance, a System.OutOfMemoryException is thrown and no further steps are executed.
  - The new delegate instance is initialized with the same invocation list as the delegate instance given by E.

The invocation list of a delegate is determined when the delegate is instantiated and then remains constant for the entire lifetime of the delegate. In other words, it is not possible to change the target callable entities of a delegate once it has been created. When two delegates are combined or one is removed from another (§15.1), a new delegate results; no existing delegate has its contents changed.

It is not possible to create a delegate that refers to a property, indexer, user-defined operator, instance constructor, destructor, or static constructor.

As described previously, when a delegate is created from a method group, the formal parameter list and return type of the delegate determine which of the overloaded methods to select. In the example

```
delegate double DoubleFunc(double x);

class A
{
    DoubleFunc f = new DoubleFunc(Square);
    static float Square(float x) {
        return x * x;
    }
    static double Square(double x) {
        return x * x;
    }
}
```

the A.f field is initialized with a delegate that refers to the second Square method because that method exactly matches the formal parameter list and return type of DoubleFunc. Had the second Square method not been present, a compile-time error would have occurred.

7.5.11 The typeof Operator

The typeof operator is used to obtain the System.Type object for a type.

typeof-expression:
    typeof (*type*)
    typeof (void)

The first form of *typeof-expression* consists of a typeof keyword followed by a parenthesized *type*. The result of an expression of this form is the System.Type object for the indicated type. There is only one System.Type object for any given type. This means that for type T, typeof(T) == typeof(T) is always true.

The second form of *typeof-expression* consists of a typeof keyword followed by a parenthesized void keyword. The result of an expression of this form is the System.Type object that represents the absence of a type. The type object returned by typeof(void) is distinct from the type object returned for any type. This special type object is useful in class libraries that allow reflection onto methods in the language, where those methods want to have a way to represent the return type of any method, including void methods, with an instance of System.Type.

The following example

```
using System;

class Test
{
    static void Main() {
        Type[] t = {
            typeof(int),
            typeof(System.Int32),
            typeof(string),
            typeof(double[]),
            typeof(void)
        };
        for (int i = 0; i < t.Length; i++) {
            Console.WriteLine(t[i].FullName);
        }
    }
}
```

produces the following output.

```
System.Int32
System.Int32
System.String
System.Double[]
System.Void
```

Note that int and System.Int32 are the same type.

7.5.12 The checked and unchecked Operators
The checked and unchecked operators are used to control the *overflow checking context* for integral-type arithmetic operations and conversions.

checked-expression:
    checked (*expression*)

unchecked-expression:
    unchecked (*expression*)

The checked operator evaluates the contained expression in a checked context, and the unchecked operator evaluates the contained expression in an unchecked context. A *checked-expression* or *unchecked-expression* corresponds exactly to a *parenthesized-expression* (§7.5.3), except that the contained expression is evaluated in the given overflow checking context.

The overflow checking context can also be controlled through the checked and unchecked statements (§8.11).

The following operations are affected by the overflow checking context established by the `checked` and `unchecked` operators and statements:

- The predefined `++` and `--` unary operators (§7.5.9 and §7.6.5), when the operand is of an integral type

- The predefined `-` unary operator (§7.6.2), when the operand is of an integral type

- The predefined `+`, `-`, `*`, and `/` binary operators (§7.7), when both operands are of integral types

- Explicit numeric conversions (§6.2.1) from one integral type to another integral type or from `float` or `double` to an integral type

When one of the previous operations produce a result that is too large to represent in the destination type, the context in which the operation is performed controls the resulting behavior.

- In a `checked` context, if the operation is a constant expression (§7.15), a compile-time error occurs. Otherwise, when the operation is performed at runtime, a `System.OverflowException` is thrown.

- In an `unchecked` context, the result is truncated by discarding any high-order bits that do not fit in the destination type.

For nonconstant expressions (expressions that are evaluated at runtime) that are not enclosed by any `checked` or `unchecked` operators or statements, the default overflow checking context is `unchecked` unless external factors (such as compiler switches and execution environment configuration) call for `checked` evaluation.

For constant expressions (expressions that can be fully evaluated at compile time), the default overflow checking context is always `checked`. Unless a constant expression is explicitly placed in an `unchecked` context, overflows that occur during the compile-time evaluation of the expression always cause compile-time errors.

In the example

```
class Test
{
    static readonly int x = 1000000;
    static readonly int y = 1000000;

    static int F() {
        return checked(x * y);    // Throws OverflowException
    }

    static int G() {
        return unchecked(x * y);  // Returns -727379968
    }
```

```
        static int H() {
            return x * y;                // Depends on default
        }
    }
```

no compile-time errors are reported because neither of the expressions can be evaluated at compile time. At runtime, the F method throws a `System.OverflowException`, and the G method returns –727379968 (the lower 32 bits of the out-of-range result). The behavior of the H method depends on the default overflow checking context for the compilation, but it is either the same as F or the same as G.

In the example

```
    class Test
    {
        const int x = 1000000;
        const int y = 1000000;

        static int F() {
            return checked(x * y);     // Compile error, overflow
        }

        static int G() {
            return unchecked(x * y);   // Returns -727379968
        }

        static int H() {
            return x * y;               // Compile error, overflow
        }
    }
```

the overflows that occur when evaluating the constant expressions in F and H cause compile-time errors to be reported because the expressions are evaluated in a `checked` context. An overflow also occurs when evaluating the constant expression in G, but because the evaluation takes place in an `unchecked` context, the overflow is not reported.

The `checked` and `unchecked` operators only affect the overflow checking context for those operations that are textually contained within the (and) tokens. The operators have no effect on function members that are invoked as a result of evaluating the contained expression. In the example

```
    class Test
    {
        static int Multiply(int x, int y) {
            return x * y;
        }

        static int F() {
            return checked(Multiply(1000000, 1000000));
        }
    }
```

the use of `checked` in `F` does not affect the evaluation of `x * y` in `Multiply`, so `x * y` is evaluated in the default overflow checking context.

The `unchecked` operator is convenient when writing constants of the signed integral types in hexadecimal notation. In the example

```
class Test
{
    public const int AllBits = unchecked((int)0xFFFFFFFF);
    public const int HighBit = unchecked((int)0x80000000);
}
```

both of the hexadecimal constants are of type `uint`. Because the constants are outside the `int` range, without the `unchecked` operator, the casts to `int` would produce compile-time errors.

The `checked` and `unchecked` operators and statements allow programmers to control certain aspects of some numeric calculations. However, the behavior of some numeric operators depends on their operands' data types. For example, multiplying two decimals always results in an exception on overflow *even* within an explicitly `unchecked` construct. Similarly, multiplying two floats never results in an exception on overflow *even* within an explicitly `checked` construct. In addition, other operators are *never* affected by the mode of checking, whether default or explicit.

7.6 Unary Operators

The +, -, !, ~, ++, --, and cast operators are the unary operators.

> *unary-expression:*
>   *primary-expression*
>   + *unary-expression*
>   - *unary-expression*
>   ! *unary-expression*
>   ~ *unary-expression*
>   *pre-increment-expression*
>   *pre-decrement-expression*
>   *cast-expression*

7.6.1 Unary Plus Operator

For an operation of the form +x, unary operator overload resolution (§7.2.3) is applied to select a specific operator implementation. The operand is converted to the parameter type of the selected operator, and the type of the result is the return type of the operator. The predefined unary plus operators are

```
int operator +(int x);
uint operator +(uint x);
long operator +(long x);
ulong operator +(ulong x);
float operator +(float x);
double operator +(double x);
decimal operator +(decimal x);
```

For each of these operators, the result is simply the value of the operand.

7.6.2 Unary Minus Operator

For an operation of the form –x, unary operator overload resolution (§7.2.3) is applied to select a specific operator implementation. The operand is converted to the parameter type of the selected operator, and the type of the result is the return type of the operator. The predefined negation operators are as follows.

* Integer negation

```
int operator -(int x);
long operator -(long x);
```

The result is computed by subtracting x from zero. If the value of of x is the smallest representable value of the operand type ($\times 2^{31}$ for int or $\times 2^{63}$ for long), then the mathematical negation of x is not representable within the operand type. If this occurs within a checked context, a System.OverflowException is thrown; if it occurs within an unchecked context, the result is the value of the operand and the overflow is not reported.

If the operand of the negation operator is of type uint, it is converted to type long, and the type of the result is long. An exception is the rule that permits the int value –2147483648 (-2^{31}) to be written as a decimal integer literal (§2.4.4.2).

If the operand of the negation operator is of type ulong, a compile-time error occurs. An exception is the rule that permits the long value –9223372036854775808 (-2^{63}) to be written as a decimal integer literal (§2.4.4.2).

* Floating point negation

```
float operator -(float x);
double operator -(double x);
```

The result is the value of x with its sign inverted. If x is NaN, the result is also NaN.

- Decimal negation

```
decimal operator -(decimal x);
```

The result is computed by subtracting x from zero. Decimal negation is equivalent to using the unary minus operator of type `System.Decimal`.

7.6.3 Logical Negation Operator

For an operation of the form `!x`, unary operator overload resolution (§7.2.3) is applied to select a specific operator implementation. The operand is converted to the parameter type of the selected operator, and the type of the result is the return type of the operator. Only one predefined logical negation operator exists.

```
bool operator !(bool x);
```

This operator computes the logical negation of the operand: If the operand is `true`, the result is `false`. If the operand is `false`, the result is `true`.

7.6.4 Bitwise Complement Operator

For an operation of the form `~x`, unary operator overload resolution (§7.2.3) is applied to select a specific operator implementation. The operand is converted to the parameter type of the selected operator, and the type of the result is the return type of the operator. The predefined bitwise complement operators are

```
int operator ~(int x);
uint operator ~(uint x);
long operator ~(long x);
ulong operator ~(ulong x);
```

For each of these operators, the result of the operation is the bitwise complement of x.

Every enumeration type E implicitly provides the following bitwise complement operator.

```
E operator ~(E x);
```

The result of evaluating `~x`, where x is an expression of an enumeration type E with an underlying type U, is exactly the same as evaluating `(E)(~(U)x)`.

7.6.5 Prefix Increment and Decrement Operators

pre-increment-expression:
    ++ *unary-expression*

pre-decrement-expression:
    -- *unary-expression*

7. Expressions

The operand of a prefix increment or decrement operation must be an expression classified as a variable, a property access, or an indexer access. The result of the operation is a value of the same type as the operand.

If the operand of a prefix increment or decrement operation is a property or indexer access, the property or indexer must have both a `get` and a `set` accessor. If this is not the case, a compile-time error occurs.

Unary operator overload resolution (§7.2.3) is applied to select a specific operator implementation. Predefined ++ and -- operators exist for the following types: `sbyte`, `byte`, `short`, `ushort`, `int`, `uint`, `long`, `ulong`, `char`, `float`, `double`, `decimal`, and any enum type. The predefined ++ operators return the value produced by adding 1 to the operand, and the predefined -- operators return the value produced by subtracting 1 from the operand.

The runtime processing of a prefix increment or decrement operation of the form ++x or --x consists of the following steps.

- If x is classified as a variable

  - x is evaluated to produce the variable.

  - The selected operator is invoked with the value of x as its argument.

  - The value returned by the operator is stored in the location given by the evaluation of x.

  - The value returned by the operator becomes the result of the operation.

- If x is classified as a property or indexer access

  - The instance expression (if x is not `static`) and the argument list (if x is an indexer access) associated with x are evaluated, and the results are used in the subsequent `get` and `set` accessor invocations.

  - The `get` accessor of x is invoked.

  - The selected operator is invoked with the value returned by the `get` accessor as its argument.

  - The `set` accessor of x is invoked with the value returned by the operator as its `value` argument.

  - The value returned by the operator becomes the result of the operation.

The ++ and -- operators also support postfix notation (§7.5.9). The result of x++ or x-- is the value of x *before* the operation, whereas the result of ++x or --x is the value of x *after* the operation. In either case, x itself has the same value after the operation.

An `operator ++` or `operator --` implementation can be invoked using either postfix or prefix notation. It is not possible to have separate operator implementations for the two notations.

7.6.6 Cast Expressions

A *cast-expression* is used to explicitly convert an expression to a given type.

> *cast-expression:*
>   (*type*) *unary-expression*

A *cast-expression* of the form `(T) E`, where `T` is a *type* and `E` is a *unary-expression*, performs an explicit conversion (§6.2) of the value of `E` to type `T`. If no explicit conversion exists from the type of `E` to `T`, a compile-time error occurs. Otherwise, the result is the value produced by the explicit conversion. The result is always classified as a value, even if `E` denotes a variable.

The grammar for a *cast-expression* leads to certain syntactic ambiguities. For example, the expression `(x) -y` could either be interpreted as a *cast-expression* (a cast of `–y` to type `x`) or as an *additive-expression* combined with a *parenthesized-expression* (which computes the value $x - y$).

To resolve *cast-expression* ambiguities, the following rule exists: A sequence of one or more *token*s (§2.4) enclosed in parentheses is considered the start of a *cast-expression* only if at least one of the following are true.

- The sequence of tokens is correct grammar for a *type* but not for an *expression*.
- The sequence of tokens is correct grammar for a *type*, and the token immediately following the closing parentheses is the token `~`, the token `!`, the token `(`, an *identifier* (§2.4.1), a *literal* (§2.4.4), or any *keyword* (§2.4.3) except `as` and `is`.

The term "correct grammar" means only that the sequence of tokens must conform to the particular grammatical production. It specifically does not consider the actual meaning of any constituent identifiers. For example, if `x` and `y` are identifiers, then `x.y` is correct grammar for a type, even if `x.y` does not actually denote a type.

From the previous disambiguation rule it follows that, if `x` and `y` are identifiers, `(x)y`, `(x)(y)`, and `(x)(-y)` are *cast-expressions*, but `(x)-y` is not, even if `x` identifies a type. However, if `x` is a keyword that identifies a predefined type (such as `int`), then all four forms are *cast-expressions* (because such a keyword could not possibly be an expression by itself).

7.7 **Arithmetic Operators**

The *, /, %, +, and – operators are the arithmetic operators.

> *multiplicative-expression:*
>> *unary-expression*
>> *multiplicative-expression* *   *unary-expression*
>> *multiplicative-expression* /   *unary-expression*
>> *multiplicative-expression* % *unary-expression*
>
> *additive-expression:*
>> *multiplicative-expression*
>> *additive-expression* +   *multiplicative-expression*
>> *additive-expression* –   *multiplicative-expression*

7.7.1 Multiplication Operator

For an operation of the form x * y, binary operator overload resolution (§7.2.4) is applied to select a specific operator implementation. The operands are converted to the parameter types of the selected operator, and the type of the result is the return type of the operator.

The predefined multiplication operators follow. The operators all compute the product of x and y.

- Integer multiplication

```
int operator *(int x, int y);
uint operator *(uint x, uint y);
long operator *(long x, long y);
ulong operator *(ulong x, ulong y);
```

  In a checked context, if the product is outside the range of the result type, a System.OverflowException is thrown. In an unchecked context, overflows are not reported and any significant high-order bits outside the range of the result type are discarded.

- Floating point multiplication

```
float operator *(float x, float y);
double operator *(double x, double y);
```

The product is computed according to the rules of IEEE 754 arithmetic. The following table lists the results of all possible combinations of nonzero finite values, zeros, infinities, and NaNs. In the table, x and y are positive finite values. z is the result of x * y. If the result is too large for the destination type, z is infinity. If the result is too small for the destination type, z is zero.

	+y	−y	+0	−0	+∞	∞	NaN
+x	+z	−z	+0	−0	+∞	∞	NaN
−x	−z	+z	−0	+0	∞	+∞	NaN
+0	+0	−0	+0	−0	NaN	NaN	NaN
−0	−0	+0	−0	+0	NaN	NaN	NaN
+∞	+∞	∞	NaN	NaN	+∞	∞	NaN
∞	∞	+∞	NaN	NaN	∞	+∞	NaN
NaN	NaN	NaN	NaN	NaN	NaN	NaN	NaN

- Decimal multiplication

```
decimal operator *(decimal x, decimal y);
```

If the resulting value is too large to represent in the `decimal` format, a `System.OverflowException` is thrown. If the result value is too small to represent in the `decimal` format, the result is zero. The scale of the result, before any rounding, is the sum of the scales of the two operands.

Decimal multiplication is equivalent to using the multiplication operator of type `System.Decimal`.

7.7.2 Division Operator

For an operation of the form x / y, binary operator overload resolution (§7.2.4) is applied to select a specific operator implementation. The operands are converted to the parameter types of the selected operator, and the type of the result is the return type of the operator.

The predefined division operators are as follows. The operators all compute the quotient of x and y.

- Integer division

```
int operator /(int x, int y);
uint operator /(uint x, uint y);
long operator /(long x, long y);
ulong operator /(ulong x, ulong y);
```

7. Expressions

If the value of the right operand is zero, a `System.DivideByZeroException` is thrown.

The division rounds the result toward zero, and the absolute value of the result is the largest possible integer that is less than the absolute value of the quotient of the two operands. The result is zero or positive when the two operands have the same sign and zero or negative when the two operands have opposite signs.

If the left operand is the smallest representable `int` or `long` value and the right operand is –1, an overflow occurs. A `System.OverflowException` is always thrown in this situation, regardless of whether the operation occurs in a `checked` or an `unchecked` context.

- Floating point division

```
float operator /(float x, float y);
double operator /(double x, double y);
```

The quotient is computed according to the rules of IEEE 754 arithmetic. The following table lists the results of all possible combinations of nonzero finite values, zeros, infinities, and NaNs. In the table, x and y are positive finite values. z is the result of x / y. If the result is too large for the destination type, z is infinity. If the result is too small for the destination type, z is zero.

	+y	−y	+0	−0	+∞	∞	NaN
+x	+z	−z	+∞	∞	+0	−0	NaN
−x	−z	+z	∞	+∞	−0	+0	NaN
+0	+0	−0	NaN	NaN	+0	−0	NaN
−0	−0	+0	NaN	NaN	−0	+0	NaN
+∞	+∞	∞	+∞	∞	NaN	NaN	NaN
∞	∞	+∞	∞	+∞	NaN	NaN	NaN
NaN	NaN	NaN	NaN	NaN	NaN	NaN	NaN

- Decimal division

```
decimal operator /(decimal x, decimal y);
```

If the value of the right operand is zero, a `System.DivideByZeroException` is thrown. If the resulting value is too large to represent in the `decimal` format, a `System.OverflowException` is thrown. If the result value is too small to represent in the `decimal` format, the result is zero. The scale of the result is the smallest scale that will preserve a result equal to the nearest representable decimal value to the true mathematical result.

Decimal division is equivalent to using the division operator of type `System.Decimal`.

7.7.3 Remainder Operator

For an operation of the form x % y, binary operator overload resolution (§7.2.4) is applied to select a specific operator implementation. The operands are converted to the parameter types of the selected operator, and the type of the result is the return type of the operator.

The predefined remainder operators are as follows. The operators all compute the remainder of the division between x and y.

- Integer remainder

```
int operator %(int x, int y);
uint operator %(uint x, uint y);
long operator %(long x, long y);
ulong operator %(ulong x, ulong y);
```

The result of x % y is the value produced by x − (x / y) * y. If y is zero, a `System.DivideByZeroException` is thrown. The remainder operator never causes an overflow.

- Floating point remainder

```
float operator %(float x, float y);
double operator %(double x, double y);
```

The following table lists the results of all possible combinations of nonzero finite values, zeros, infinities, and NaNs. In the table, x and y are positive finite values. z is the result of x % y and is computed as x − n * y, where n is the largest possible integer that is less than or equal to x / y. This method of computing the remainder is analogous to that used for integer operands but differs from the IEEE 754 definition (in which n is the integer closest to x / y).

	+y	−y	+0	−0	+∞	∞	NaN
+x	+z	+z	NaN	NaN	x	x	NaN
−x	−z	−z	NaN	NaN	−x	−x	NaN
+0	+0	+0	NaN	NaN	+0	+0	NaN
−0	−0	−0	NaN	NaN	−0	−0	NaN
+∞	NaN	NaN	NaN	NaN	NaN	NaN	NaN
∞	NaN	NaN	NaN	NaN	NaN	NaN	NaN
NaN	NaN	NaN	NaN	NaN	NaN	NaN	NaN

- Decimal remainder

```
decimal operator %(decimal x, decimal y);
```

If the value of the right operand is zero, a `System.DivideByZeroException` is thrown. The scale of the result, before any rounding, is the larger of the scales of the two operands, and the sign of the result, if nonzero, is the same as that of x.

Decimal remainder is equivalent to using the remainder operator of type `System.Decimal`.

7.7.4 Addition Operator

For an operation of the form x + y, binary operator overload resolution (§7.2.4) is applied to select a specific operator implementation. The operands are converted to the parameter types of the selected operator, and the type of the result is the return type of the operator.

The predefined addition operators are as follows. For numeric and enumeration types, the predefined addition operators compute the sum of the two operands. When one or both operands are of type string, the predefined addition operators concatenate the string representation of the operands.

- Integer addition

```
int operator +(int x, int y);
uint operator +(uint x, uint y);
long operator +(long x, long y);
ulong operator +(ulong x, ulong y);
```

In a checked context, if the sum is outside the range of the result type, a `System.OverflowException` is thrown. In an unchecked context, overflows are not reported and any significant high-order bits outside the range of the result type are discarded.

- Floating point addition

```
float operator +(float x, float y);
double operator +(double x, double y);
```

The sum is computed according to the rules of IEEE 754 arithmetic. The following table lists the results of all possible combinations of nonzero finite values, zeros, infinities, and NaNs. In the table, x and y are nonzero finite values, and z is the result of x + y. If x and y have the same magnitude but opposite signs, z is positive zero. If x + y is too large to represent in the destination type, z is infinity with the same sign as x + y.

	y	+0	−0	+∞	∞	NaN
x	z	x	x	+∞	∞	NaN
+0	y	+0	+0	+∞	∞	NaN
−0	y	+0	−0	+∞	∞	NaN
+∞	+∞	+∞	+∞	+∞	NaN	NaN
∞	∞	∞	∞	NaN	∞	NaN
NaN	NaN	NaN	NaN	NaN	NaN	NaN

- Decimal addition

```
decimal operator +(decimal x, decimal y);
```

If the resulting value is too large to represent in the `decimal` format, a `System.OverflowException` is thrown. The scale of the result, before any rounding, is the larger of the scales of the two operands.

Decimal addition is equivalent to using the addition operator of type `System.Decimal`.

- Enumeration addition

Every enumeration type implicitly provides the following predefined operators, where E is the enum type and U is the underlying type of E.

```
E operator +(E x, U y);
E operator +(U x, E y);
```

The operators are evaluated exactly as `(E)((U)x + (U)y)`.

- String concatenation

```
string operator +(string x, string y);
string operator +(string x, object y);
string operator +(object x, string y);
```

The binary + operator performs string concatenation when one or both operands are of type `string`. If an operand of string concatenation is `null`, an empty string is substituted. Otherwise, any nonstring argument is converted to its string representation by invoking the virtual `ToString` method inherited from type `object`. If `ToString` returns `null`, an empty string is substituted.

```
using System;

class Test
{
    static void Main() {
        string s = null;
        Console.WriteLine("s = >" + s + "<");      // displays s = ><
        int i = 1;
        Console.WriteLine("i = " + i);             // displays i = 1
        float f = 1.2300E+15F;
        Console.WriteLine("f = " + f);             // displays f = 1.23E+15
        decimal d = 2.900m;
        Console.WriteLine("d = " + d);             // displays d = 2.900
    }
}
```

The result of the string concatenation operator is a string that consists of the characters of the left operand followed by the characters of the right operand. The string concatenation operator never returns a `null` value. A `System.OutOfMemoryException` may be thrown if there is not enough memory available to allocate the resulting string.

- Delegate combination

Every delegate type implicitly provides the following predefined operator, where `D` is the delegate type.

```
D operator +(D x, D y);
```

The binary + operator performs delegate combination when both operands are of some delegate type `D`. (If the operands have different delegate types, a compile-time error occurs.) If the first operand is `null`, the result of the operation is the value of the second operand (even if that is also `null`). Otherwise, if the second operand is `null`, then the result of the operation is the value of the first operand. Otherwise, the result of the operation is a new delegate instance that, when invoked, invokes the first operand and then invokes the second operand. For examples of delegate combination, see §7.7.5 and §15.3. Because `System.Delegate` is not a delegate type, `operator +` is not defined for it.

7.7.5 Subtraction Operator

For an operation of the form $x - y$, binary operator overload resolution (§7.2.4) is applied to select a specific operator implementation. The operands are converted to the parameter types of the selected operator, and the type of the result is the return type of the operator.

The predefined subtraction operators are listed as follows. The operators all subtract y from x.

- Integer subtraction

```
int operator -(int x, int y);
uint operator -(uint x, uint y);
long operator -(long x, long y);
ulong operator -(ulong x, ulong y);
```

In a `checked` context, if the difference is outside the range of the result type, a `System.OverflowException` is thrown. In an `unchecked` context, overflows are not reported and any significant high-order bits outside the range of the result type are discarded.

- Floating point subtraction

```
float operator -(float x, float y);
double operator -(double x, double y);
```

The difference is computed according to the rules of IEEE 754 arithmetic. The following table lists the results of all possible combinations of nonzero finite values, zeros, infinities, and NaNs. In the table, x and y are nonzero finite values, and z is the result of $x - y$. If x and y are equal, z is positive zero. If $x - y$ is too large to represent in the destination type, z is infinity with the same sign as $x - y$.

	y	+0	−0	+∞	∞	NaN
x	z	x	x	∞	+∞	NaN
+0	−y	+0	+0	∞	+∞	NaN
−0	−y	−0	+0	∞	+∞	NaN
+∞	+∞	+∞	+∞	NaN	+∞	NaN
∞	∞	∞	∞	∞	NaN	NaN
NaN	NaN	NaN	NaN	NaN	NaN	NaN

- Decimal subtraction

```
decimal operator -(decimal x, decimal y);
```

If the resulting value is too large to represent in the decimal format, a System.OverflowException is thrown. The scale of the result, before any rounding, is the larger of the scales of the two operands.

Decimal subtraction is equivalent to using the subtraction operator of type System.Decimal.

- Enumeration subtraction

Every enumeration type implicitly provides the following predefined operator, where E is the enum type and U is the underlying type of E.

```
U operator -(E x, E y);
```

This operator is evaluated exactly as `(U)((U)x - (U)y)`. In other words, the operator computes the difference between the ordinal values of x and y, and the type of the result is the underlying type of the enumeration.

```
E operator -(E x, U y);
```

This operator is evaluated exactly as `(E)((U)x - y)`. In other words, the operator subtracts a value from the underlying type of the enumeration, yielding a value of the enumeration.

- Delegate removal

Every delegate type implicitly provides the following predefined operator, where D is the delegate type.

```
D operator -(D x, D y);
```

The binary – operator performs delegate removal when both operands are of some delegate type D. If the operands have different delegate types, a compile-time error occurs. If the first operand is null, the result of the operation is null. Otherwise, if the second operand is null, then the result of the operation is the value of the first operand. Otherwise, both operands represent invocation lists (§15.1) having one or more entries, and the result is a new invocation list consisting of the first operand's list with the second operand's entries removed from it, provided the second operand's list is a proper contiguous sublist of the first's. (To determine sublist equality, corresponding entries are compared as for the delegate equality operator, described in §7.9.8.) Otherwise, the result is the value of the left operand. Neither of the operands' lists is changed in the process. If the second operand's list matches multiple sublists of contiguous entries in the first operand's list, the right-most matching sublist of contiguous entries is removed. If removal results in an empty list, the result is `null`. For example

```
delegate void D(int x);

class C
{
    public static void M1(int i) { /* … */ }
    public static void M2(int i) { /* … */ }
}

class Test
{
    static void Main() {
        D cd1 = new D(C.M1);
        D cd2 = new D(C.M2);
        D cd3 = cd1 + cd2 + cd2 + cd1;          // M1 + M2 + M2 + M1
        cd3 -= cd1;                             // => M1 + M2 + M2

        cd3 = cd1 + cd2 + cd2 + cd1;            // M1 + M2 + M2 + M1
        cd3 -= cd1 + cd2;                       // => M2 + M1

        cd3 = cd1 + cd2 + cd2 + cd1;            // M1 + M2 + M2 + M1
        cd3 -= cd2 + cd2;                       // => M1 + M1

        cd3 = cd1 + cd2 + cd2 + cd1;            // M1 + M2 + M2 + M1
        cd3 -= cd2 + cd1;                       // => M1 + M2

        cd3 = cd1 + cd2 + cd2 + cd1;            // M1 + M2 + M2 + M1
        cd3 -= cd1 + cd1;                       // => M1 + M2 + M2 + M1
    }
}
```

7.8 Shift Operators

The << and >> operators are used to perform bit shifting operations.

shift-expression:
    additive-expression
    shift-expression << *additive-expression*
    shift-expression >> *additive-expression*

For an operation of the form x << count or x >> count, binary operator overload resolution (§7.2.4) is applied to select a specific operator implementation. The operands are converted to the parameter types of the selected operator, and the type of the result is the return type of the operator.

When declaring an overloaded shift operator, the type of the first operand must always be the class or struct containing the operator declaration, and the type of the second operand must always be int.

The predefined shift operators are as follows.

- Shift left

```
int operator <<(int x, int count);
uint operator <<(uint x, int count);
long operator <<(long x, int count);
ulong operator <<(ulong x, int count);
```

The << operator shifts x left by a number of bits computed as described next.

The high-order bits outside the range of the result type of x are discarded, the remaining bits are shifted left, and the low-order empty bit positions are set to zero.

- Shift right

```
int operator >>(int x, int count);
uint operator >>(uint x, int count);
long operator >>(long x, int count);
ulong operator >>(ulong x, int count);
```

The >> operator shifts x right by a number of bits computed as described next.

When x is of type int or long, the low-order bits of x are discarded, the remaining bits are shifted right, and the high-order empty bit positions are set to zero if x is non-negative and set to 1 if x is negative.

When x is of type uint or ulong, the low-order bits of x are discarded, the remaining bits are shifted right, and the high-order empty bit positions are set to zero.

For the predefined operators, the number of bits to shift is computed as follows.

- When the type of x is int or uint, the shift count is given by the low-order five bits of count. In other words, the shift count is computed from count & 0x1F.

- When the type of x is long or ulong, the shift count is given by the low-order six bits of count. In other words, the shift count is computed from count & 0x3F.

If the resulting shift count is zero, the shift operators simply return the value of x.

Shift operations never cause overflows and produce the same results in checked and unchecked contexts.

When the left operand of the >> operator is of a signed integral type, the operator performs an *arithmetic* shift right wherein the value of the most significant bit (the sign bit) of the operand is propagated to the high-order empty bit positions. When the left operand of the >> operator is of an unsigned integral type, the operator performs a *logical* shift right wherein high-order empty bit positions are always set to zero. To perform the opposite operation of that inferred from the operand type, explicit casts can be used. For example, if x is a variable of type int, the operation `unchecked((int)((uint)x >> y))` performs a logical shift right of x.

7.9 Relational and Type-Testing Operators

The ==, !=, <, >, <=, >=, is, and as operators are the relational and type-testing operators.

> *relational-expression:*
>   *shift-expression*
>   *relational-expression* < *shift-expression*
>   *relational-expression* > *shift-expression*
>   *relational-expression* <= *shift-expression*
>   *relational-expression* >= *shift-expression*
>   *relational-expression* is *type*
>   *relational-expression* as *type*
>
> *equality-expression:*
>   *relational-expression*
>   *equality-expression* == *relational-expression*
>   *equality-expression* != *relational-expression*

The is operator is described in §7.9.9, and the as operator is described in §7.9.10.

The ==, !=, <, >, <=, and >= operators are *comparison operators*. For an operation of the form x *op* y, where *op* is a comparison operator, overload resolution (§7.2.4) is applied to select a specific operator implementation. The operands are converted to the parameter types of the selected operator, and the type of the result is the return type of the operator.

The predefined comparison operators are described in the following sections. All predefined comparison operators return a result of type bool, as described in the following table.

Operation	Result
x == y	true if x is equal to y, false otherwise
x != y	true if x is not equal to y, false otherwise
x < y	true if x is less than y, false otherwise
x > y	true if x is greater than y, false otherwise
x <= y	true if x is less than or equal to y, false otherwise
x >= y	true if x is greater than or equal to y, false otherwise

7. Expressions

7.9.1 Integer Comparison Operators

The predefined integer comparison operators are

```
bool operator ==(int x, int y);
bool operator ==(uint x, uint y);
bool operator ==(long x, long y);
bool operator ==(ulong x, ulong y);

bool operator !=(int x, int y);
bool operator !=(uint x, uint y);
bool operator !=(long x, long y);
bool operator !=(ulong x, ulong y);

bool operator <(int x, int y);
bool operator <(uint x, uint y);
bool operator <(long x, long y);
bool operator <(ulong x, ulong y);

bool operator >(int x, int y);
bool operator >(uint x, uint y);
bool operator >(long x, long y);
bool operator >(ulong x, ulong y);

bool operator <=(int x, int y);
bool operator <=(uint x, uint y);
bool operator <=(long x, long y);
bool operator <=(ulong x, ulong y);

bool operator >=(int x, int y);
bool operator >=(uint x, uint y);
bool operator >=(long x, long y);
bool operator >=(ulong x, ulong y);
```

Each of these operators compares the numeric values of the two integer operands and returns a `bool` value that indicates whether the particular relation is `true` or `false`.

7.9.2 Floating Point Comparison Operators

The predefined floating point comparison operators are

```
bool operator ==(float x, float y);
bool operator ==(double x, double y);

bool operator !=(float x, float y);
bool operator !=(double x, double y);

bool operator <(float x, float y);
bool operator <(double x, double y);

bool operator >(float x, float y);
bool operator >(double x, double y);
```

```
bool operator <=(float x, float y);
bool operator <=(double x, double y);

bool operator >=(float x, float y);
bool operator >=(double x, double y);
```

The operators compare the operands according to the rules of the IEEE 754 standard.

- If either operand is NaN, the result is `false` for all operators except `!=`, for which the result is `true`. For any two operands, `x != y` always produces the same result as `!(x == y)`. However, when one or both operands are NaN, the `<`, `>`, `<=`, and `>=` operators *do not* produce the same results as the logical negation of the opposite operator. For example, if either of x and y is NaN, then `x < y` is `false`, but `!(x >= y)` is `true`.

- When neither operand is NaN, the operators compare the values of the two floating point operands with respect to the ordering

```
∞ < -max < ... < -min < -0.0 == +0.0 < +min < ... < +max < +∞
```

where `min` and `max` are the smallest and largest positive finite values that can be represented in the given floating point format. Notable effects of this ordering are

- Negative and positive zeros are considered equal.

- A negative infinity is considered less than all other values but equal to another negative infinity.

- A positive infinity is considered greater than all other values but equal to another positive infinity.

7.9.3 Decimal Comparison Operators

The predefined decimal comparison operators are

```
bool operator ==(decimal x, decimal y);

bool operator !=(decimal x, decimal y);

bool operator <(decimal x, decimal y);

bool operator >(decimal x, decimal y);

bool operator <=(decimal x, decimal y);

bool operator >=(decimal x, decimal y);
```

Each of these operators compares the numeric values of the two decimal operands and returns a `bool` value that indicates whether the particular relation is `true` or `false`. Each decimal comparison is equivalent to using the corresponding relational or equality operator of type `System.Decimal`.

7.9.4 Boolean Equality Operators

The predefined boolean equality operators are

```
bool operator ==(bool x, bool y);

bool operator !=(bool x, bool y);
```

The result of == is true if both x and y are true or if both x and y are false. Otherwise, the result is false.

The result of != is false if both x and y are true or if both x and y are false. Otherwise, the result is true. When the operands are of type bool, the != operator produces the same result as the ^ operator.

7.9.5 Enumeration Comparison Operators

Every enumeration type implicitly provides the following predefined comparison operators.

```
bool operator ==(E x, E y);

bool operator !=(E x, E y);

bool operator <(E x, E y);

bool operator >(E x, E y);

bool operator <=(E x, E y);

bool operator >=(E x, E y);
```

The result of evaluating x *op* y, where x and y are expressions of an enumeration type E with an underlying type U and *op* is one of the comparison operators, is exactly the same as evaluating ((U)x) *op* ((U)y). In other words, the enumeration type comparison operators simply compare the underlying integral values of the two operands.

7.9.6 Reference Type Equality Operators

The predefined reference type equality operators are

```
bool operator ==(object x, object y);

bool operator !=(object x, object y);
```

The operators return the result of comparing the two references for equality or nonequality.

Because the predefined reference type equality operators accept operands of type object, they apply to all types that do not declare applicable operator == and operator != members. Conversely, any applicable user-defined equality operators effectively hide the predefined reference type equality operators.

The predefined reference type equality operators require the operands to be *reference-type* values or the value `null`; furthermore, they require that a standard implicit conversion (§6.3.1) exists from the type of either operand to the type of the other operand. Unless both of these conditions are true, a compile-time error occurs. Notable implications of these rules are

- It is a compile-time error to use the predefined reference type equality operators to compare two references that are known to be different at compile time. For example, if the compile-time types of the operands are two class types A and B, and if neither A nor B derives from the other, then it would be impossible for the two operands to reference the same object. Thus, the operation is considered a compile-time error.

- The predefined reference type equality operators do not permit value type operands to be compared. Therefore, unless a struct type declares its own equality operators, it is not possible to compare values of that struct type.

- The predefined reference type equality operators never cause boxing operations to occur for their operands. It would be meaningless to perform such boxing operations because references to the newly allocated boxed instances would necessarily differ from all other references.

For an operation of the form x == y or x != y, if any applicable `operator ==` or `operator !=` exists, the operator overload resolution (§7.2.4) rules will select that operator instead of the predefined reference type equality operator. However, it is always possible to select the predefined reference type equality operator by explicitly casting one or both of the operands to type `object`. The example

```
using System;

class Test
{
    static void Main() {
        string s = "Test";
        string t = string.Copy(s);
        Console.WriteLine(s == t);
        Console.WriteLine((object)s == t);
        Console.WriteLine(s == (object)t);
        Console.WriteLine((object)s == (object)t);
    }
}
```

produces the following output.

```
True
False
False
False
```

The s and t variables refer to two distinct `string` instances containing the same characters. The first comparison outputs `True` because the predefined string equality operator (§7.9.7) is selected when both operands are of type `string`. The remaining comparisons all output `False` because the predefined reference type equality operator is selected when one or both of the operands are of type `object`.

Note that this technique is not meaningful for value types. The example

```
class Test
{
    static void Main() {
        int i = 123;
        int j = 123;
        System.Console.WriteLine((object)i == (object)j);
    }
}
```

outputs `False` because the casts create references to two separate instances of boxed `int` values.

7.9.7 String Equality Operators
The predefined string equality operators are

```
bool operator ==(string x, string y);

bool operator !=(string x, string y);
```

Two `string` values are considered equal when one of the following is true.

- Both values are `null`.
- Both values are non-null references to string instances that have identical lengths and identical characters in each character position.

The string equality operators compare string *values* rather than string *references*. When two separate string instances contain the exact same sequence of characters, the values of the strings are equal, but the references are different. As described in §7.9.6, the reference type equality operators can be used to compare string references instead of string values.

7.9.8 Delegate Equality Operators
Every delegate type implicitly provides the following predefined comparison operators.

```
bool operator ==(System.Delegate x, System.Delegate y);

bool operator !=(System.Delegate x, System.Delegate y);
```

Two delegate instances are considered equal as follows.

- If either of the delegate instances is `null`, they are equal if and only if both are `null`.

- If either of the delegate instances has an invocation list (§15.1) containing one entry, they are equal if and only if the other also has an invocation list containing one entry, and either

  - Both refer to the same static method, or

  - Both refer to the same nonstatic method on the same target object

- If either of the delegate instances has an invocation list containing two or more entries, those instances are equal if and only if their invocation lists are the same length, and each entry in one's invocation list is equal to the corresponding entry, in order, in the other's invocation list.

Note that delegates of different types can be considered equal by the previous definition as long as they have the same return type and parameter types.

7.9.9 The is Operator

The `is` operator is used to dynamically check if the runtime type of an object is compatible with a given type. The result of the operation `e is T`, where `e` is an expression and `T` is a type, is a boolean value indicating whether `e` can successfully be converted to type `T` by a reference conversion, a boxing conversion, or an unboxing conversion. The operation is evaluated as follows.

- If the compile-time type of `e` is the same as `T`, or if an implicit reference conversion (§6.1.4) or boxing conversion (§6.1.5) exists from the compile-time type of `e` to `T`

  - If `e` is of a reference type, the result of the operation is equivalent to evaluating `e != null`.

  - If `e` is of a value type, the result of the operation is `true`.

- Otherwise, if an explicit reference conversion (§6.2.3) or unboxing conversion (§6.2.4) exists from the compile-time type of `e` to `T`, a dynamic type check is performed.

  - If the value of `e` is `null`, the result is `false`.

  - Otherwise, let `R` be the runtime type of the instance referenced by `e`. If `R` and `T` are the same type, if `R` is a reference type and an implicit reference conversion from `R` to `T` exists, or if `R` is a value type and `T` is an interface type that is implemented by `R`, the result is `true`.

  - Otherwise, the result is `false`.

- Otherwise, no reference or boxing conversion of `e` to type `T` is possible, and the result of the operation is `false`.

Note that the is operator only considers reference conversions, boxing conversions, and unboxing conversions. Other conversions, such as user defined conversions, are not considered by the is operator.

7.9.10 The as Operator

The as operator is used to explicitly convert a value to a given reference type using a reference conversion or a boxing conversion. Unlike a cast expression (§7.6.6), the as operator never throws an exception. Instead, if the indicated conversion is not possible, the resulting value is null.

In an operation of the form e as T, e must be an expression and T must be a reference type. The type of the result is T, and the result is always classified as a value. The operation is evaluated as follows.

- If the compile-time type of e is the same as T, the result is simply the value of e.
- Otherwise, if an implicit reference conversion (§6.1.4) or boxing conversion (§6.1.5) exists from the compile-time type of e to T, this conversion is performed and becomes the result of the operation.
- Otherwise, if an explicit reference conversion (§6.2.3) exists from the compile-time type of e to T, a dynamic type check is performed.
  - If the value of e is null, the result is the value null with the compile-time type T.
  - Otherwise, let R be the runtime type of the instance referenced by e. If R and T are the same type, if R is a reference type and an implicit reference conversion from R to T exists, or if R is a value type and T is an interface type that is implemented by R, the result is the reference given by e with the compile-time type T.
  - Otherwise, the result is the value null with the compile-time type T.
- Otherwise, the indicated conversion is never possible, and a compile-time error occurs.

Note that the as operator only performs reference conversions and boxing conversions. Other conversions, such as user-defined conversions, are not possible with the as operator and should instead be performed using cast expressions.

7.10 Logical Operators

The &, ^, and | operators are the logical operators.

> *and-expression:*
>   *equality-expression*
>   *and-expression* & *equality-expression*

exclusive-or-expression:
    and-expression
    exclusive-or-expression   ^   *and-expression*

inclusive-or-expression:
    exclusive-or-expression
    inclusive-or-expression | *exclusive-or-expression*

For an operation of the form x *op* y, where *op* is one of the logical operators, overload resolution (§7.2.4) is applied to select a specific operator implementation. The operands are converted to the parameter types of the selected operator, and the type of the result is the return type of the operator.

The predefined logical operators are described in the following sections.

7.10.1 Integer Logical Operators

The predefined integer logical operators are

```
int operator &(int x, int y);
uint operator &(uint x, uint y);
long operator &(long x, long y);
ulong operator &(ulong x, ulong y);

int operator |(int x, int y);
uint operator |(uint x, uint y);
long operator |(long x, long y);
ulong operator |(ulong x, ulong y);

int operator ^(int x, int y);
uint operator ^(uint x, uint y);
long operator ^(long x, long y);
ulong operator ^(ulong x, ulong y);
```

The & operator computes the bitwise logical AND of the two operands, the | operator computes the bitwise logical OR of the two operands, and the ^ operator computes the bitwise logical exclusive OR of the two operands. No overflows are possible from these operations.

7.10.2 Enumeration Logical Operators

Every enumeration type E implicitly provides the following predefined logical operators.

```
E operator &(E x, E y);
E operator |(E x, E y);
E operator ^(E x, E y);
```

The result of evaluating x *op* y, where x and y are expressions of an enumeration type E with an underlying type U and *op* is one of the logical operators, is exactly the same as evaluating (E) ((U) x *op* (U) y). In other words, the enumeration type logical operators simply perform the logical operation on the underlying type of the two operands.

7.10.3 Boolean Logical Operators

The predefined boolean logical operators are

```
bool operator &(bool x, bool y);

bool operator |(bool x, bool y);

bool operator ^(bool x, bool y);
```

The result of x & y is true if both x and y are true. Otherwise, the result is false.

The result of x | y is true if either x or y is true. Otherwise, the result is false.

The result of x ^ y is true if x is true and y is false or x is false and y is true. Otherwise, the result is false. When the operands are of type bool, the ^ operator computes the same result as the != operator.

7.11 Conditional Logical Operators

The && and || operators are the conditional logical operators. They are also called the "short-circuiting" logical operators.

> *conditional-and-expression:*
>   *inclusive-or-expression*
>   *conditional-and-expression* && *inclusive-or-expression*
>
> *conditional-or-expression:*
>   *conditional-and-expression*
>   *conditional-or-expression* || *conditional-and-expression*

The && and || operators are conditional versions of the & and | operators.

- The operation x && y corresponds to the operation x & y, except that y is evaluated only if x is true.

- The operation x || y corresponds to the operation x | y, except that y is evaluated only if x is false.

An operation of the form x && y or x || y is processed by applying overload resolution (§7.2.4) as if the operation was written x & y or x | y. Then

- If overload resolution fails to find a single best operator, or if overload resolution selects one of the predefined integer logical operators, a compile-time error occurs.

- Otherwise, if the selected operator is one of the predefined boolean logical operators (§7.10.2), the operation is processed as described in §7.11.1.

- Otherwise, the selected operator is a user-defined operator, and the operation is processed as described in §7.11.2.

It is not possible to directly overload the conditional logical operators. However, because the conditional logical operators are evaluated in terms of the regular logical operators, overloads of the regular logical operators are, with certain restrictions, also considered overloads of the conditional logical operators. This is described further in §7.11.2.

7.11.1 Boolean Conditional Logical Operators

When the operands of && or || are of type bool, or when the operands are of types that do not define an applicable operator & or operator | but do define implicit conversions to bool, the operation is processed as follows.

- The operation x && y is evaluated as x ? y : false. In other words, x is first evaluated and converted to type bool. Then, if x is true, y is evaluated and converted to type bool, and this becomes the result of the operation. Otherwise, the result of the operation is false.

- The operation x || y is evaluated as x ? true : y. In other words, x is first evaluated and converted to type bool. Then, if x is true, the result of the operation is true. Otherwise, y is evaluated and converted to type bool, and this becomes the result of the operation.

7.11.2 User-Defined Conditional Logical Operators

When the operands of && or || are of types that declare an applicable user-defined operator & or operator |, both of the following must be true, where T is the type in which the selected operator is declared.

- The return type and the type of each parameter of the selected operator must be T. In other words, the operator must compute the logical AND or the logical OR of two operands of type T and must return a result of type T.

- T must contain declarations of operator true and operator false.

A compile-time error occurs if either of these requirements is not satisfied. Otherwise, the `&&` or `||` operation is evaluated by combining the user-defined `operator true` or `operator false` with the selected user-defined operator.

- The operation `x && y` is evaluated as `T.false(x) ? x : T.&(x, y)`, where `T.false(x)` is an invocation of the `operator false` declared in `T`, and `T.&(x, y)` is an invocation of the selected `operator &`. In other words, `x` is first evaluated and `operator false` is invoked on the result to determine if `x` is definitely false. Then, if `x` is definitely false, the result of the operation is the value previously computed for `x`. Otherwise, `y` is evaluated, and the selected `operator &` is invoked on the value previously computed for `x` and the value computed for `y` to produce the result of the operation.

- The operation `x || y` is evaluated as `T.true(x) ? x : T.|(x, y)`, where `T.true(x)` is an invocation of the `operator true` declared in `T`, and `T.|(x, y)` is an invocation of the selected `operator |`. In other words, `x` is first evaluated and `operator true` is invoked on the result to determine if `x` is definitely true. Then, if `x` is definitely true, the result of the operation is the value previously computed for `x`. Otherwise, `y` is evaluated, and the selected `operator |` is invoked on the value previously computed for `x` and the value computed for `y` to produce the result of the operation.

In either of these operations, the expression given by `x` is only evaluated once, and the expression given by `y` is either not evaluated or evaluated exactly once.

For an example of a type that implements `operator true` and `operator false`, see §11.4.2.

7.12 Conditional Operator

The `?:` operator is the conditional operator. It is at times also called the ternary operator.

> *conditional-expression:*
>   *conditional-or-expression*
>   *conditional-or-expression* ? *expression* : *expression*

A conditional expression of the form `b ? x : y` first evaluates the condition `b`. Then, if `b` is `true`, `x` is evaluated and becomes the result of the operation. Otherwise, `y` is evaluated and becomes the result of the operation. A conditional expression never evaluates both `x` and `y`.

The conditional operator is right-associative, meaning that operations are grouped from right to left. For example, an expression of the form `a ? b : c ? d : e` is evaluated as `a ? b : (c ? d : e)`.

The first operand of the ?: operator must be an expression of a type that can be implicitly converted to bool or an expression of a type that implements operator true. If neither of these requirements is satisfied, a compile-time error occurs.

The second and third operands of the ?: operator control the type of the conditional expression. Let X and Y be the types of the second and third operands. Then

- If X and Y are the same type, then this is the type of the conditional expression.

- Otherwise, if an implicit conversion (§6.1) exists from X to Y, but not from Y to X, then Y is the type of the conditional expression.

- Otherwise, if an implicit conversion (§6.1) exists from Y to X, but not from X to Y, then X is the type of the conditional expression.

- Otherwise, no expression type can be determined, and a compile-time error occurs.

The runtime processing of a conditional expression of the form b ? x : y consists of the following steps.

- First, b is evaluated, and the bool value of b is determined.
  - If an implicit conversion from the type of b to bool exists, then this implicit conversion is performed to produce a bool value.
  - Otherwise, the operator true defined by the type of b is invoked to produce a bool value.
- If the bool value produced by the previous step is true, then x is evaluated and converted to the type of the conditional expression, and this becomes the result of the conditional expression.
- Otherwise, y is evaluated and converted to the type of the conditional expression, and this becomes the result of the conditional expression.

7.13 Assignment Operators

The assignment operators assign a new value to a variable, a property, an event, or an indexer element.

assignment:
    unary-expression assignment-operator expression

assignment-operator: one of
    =   +=   -=   *=   /=   %=   &= |=   ^=   <<=   >>=

The left operand of an assignment must be an expression classified as a variable, a property access, an indexer access, or an event access.

The = operator is called the *simple assignment operator*. It assigns the value of the right operand to the variable, property, or indexer element given by the left operand. The left operand of the simple assignment operator may not be an event access (except as described in §10.7.1). The simple assignment operator is described in §7.13.1.

The assignment operators other than the = operator are called the *compound assignment operators*. These operators perform the indicated operation on the two operands and then assign the resulting value to the variable, property, or indexer element given by the left operand. The compound assignment operators are described in §7.13.2.

The += and -= operators with an event access expression as the left operand are called the *event assignment operators*. No other assignment operator is valid with an event access as the left operand. The event assignment operators are described in §7.13.3.

The assignment operators are right-associative, meaning that operations are grouped from right to left. For example, an expression of the form a = b = c is evaluated as a = (b = c).

7.13.1 Simple Assignment

The = operator is the simple assignment operator. In a simple assignment, the right operand must be an expression of a type that is implicitly convertible to the type of the left operand. The operation assigns the value of the right operand to the variable, property, or indexer element given by the left operand.

The result of a simple assignment expression is the value assigned to the left operand. The result has the same type as the left operand and is always classified as a value.

If the left operand is a property or indexer access, the property or indexer must have a set accessor. If this is not the case, a compile-time error occurs.

The runtime processing of a simple assignment of the form x = y consists of the following steps.

- If x is classified as a variable

  - x is evaluated to produce the variable.

  - y is evaluated and, if required, converted to the type of x through an implicit conversion (§6.1).

  - If the variable given by x is an array element of a *reference-type*, a runtime check is performed to ensure that the value computed for y is compatible with the array instance of which x is an element. The check succeeds if y is null or if an implicit reference conversion (§6.1.4) exists from the actual type of the instance referenced by y to the actual element type of the array instance containing x. Otherwise, a System.ArrayTypeMismatchException is thrown.

- The value resulting from the evaluation and conversion of y is stored into the location given by the evaluation of x.

- If x is classified as a property or indexer access

  - The instance expression (if x is not static) and the argument list (if x is an indexer access) associated with x are evaluated, and the results are used in the subsequent set accessor invocation.

  - y is evaluated and, if required, converted to the type of x through an implicit conversion (§6.1).

  - The set accessor of x is invoked with the value computed for y as its value argument.

The array covariance rules (§12.5) permit a value of an array type A[] to be a reference to an instance of an array type B[], provided an implicit reference conversion exists from B to A. Because of these rules, assignment to an array element of a *reference-type* requires a runtime check to ensure that the value being assigned is compatible with the array instance. In the example

```
string[] sa = new string[10];
object[] oa = sa;

oa[0] = null;              // Ok
oa[1] = "Hello";           // Ok
oa[2] = new ArrayList();   // ArrayTypeMismatchException
```

the last assignment causes a System.ArrayTypeMismatchException to be thrown because an instance of ArrayList cannot be stored in an element of a string[].

When a property or indexer declared in a *struct-type* is the target of an assignment, the instance expression associated with the property or indexer access must be classified as a variable. If the instance expression is classified as a value, a compile-time error occurs. Because of §7.5.4, the same rule also applies to fields.

Given the declarations

```
struct Point
{
    int x, y;
    public Point(int x, int y) {
        this.x = x;
        this.y = y;
    }
    public int X {
        get { return x; }
        set { x = value; }
    }
}
```

7. Expressions

```
        public int Y {
            get { return y; }
            set { y = value; }
        }
    }
    struct Rectangle
    {
        Point a, b;
        public Rectangle(Point a, Point b) {
            this.a = a;
            this.b = b;
        }
        public Point A {
            get { return a; }
            set { a = value; }
        }
        public Point B {
            get { return b; }
            set { b = value; }
        }
    }
```

in the example

```
Point p = new Point();
p.X = 100;
p.Y = 100;
Rectangle r = new Rectangle();
r.A = new Point(10, 10);
r.B = p;
```

the assignments to p.X, p.Y, r.A, and r.B are permitted because p and r are variables. However, in the example

```
Rectangle r = new Rectangle();
r.A.X = 10;
r.A.Y = 10;
r.B.X = 100;
r.B.Y = 100;
```

the assignments are all invalid because r.A and r.B are not variables.

7.13.2 Compound Assignment

An operation of the form x *op*= y is processed by applying binary operator overload resolution (§7.2.4) as if the operation was written x *op* y. Then

- If the return type of the selected operator is *implicitly* convertible to the type of x, the operation is evaluated as x = x *op* y, except that x is evaluated only once.

- Otherwise, if the selected operator is a predefined operator, if the return type of the selected operator is *explicitly* convertible to the type of x, and if y is *implicitly* convertible to the type of x, then the operation is evaluated as x = (T)(x *op* y), where T is the type of x, except that x is evaluated only once.

- Otherwise, the compound assignment is invalid, and a compile-time error occurs.

The term "evaluated only once" means that in the evaluation of x *op* y, the results of any constituent expressions of x are temporarily saved and then reused when performing the assignment to x. For example, in the assignment A()[B()] += C(), where A is a method returning int[] and B and C are methods returning int, the methods are invoked only once, in the order A, B, C.

When the left operand of a compound assignment is a property access or indexer access, the property or indexer must have both a get accessor and a set accessor. If this is not the case, a compile-time error occurs.

The second previous rule permits x *op*= y to be evaluated as x = (T)(x *op* y) in certain contexts. The rule exists such that the predefined operators can be used as compound operators when the left operand is of type sbyte, byte, short, ushort, or char. Even when both arguments are of one of those types, the predefined operators produce a result of type int, as described in §7.2.6.2. Thus, without a cast it would not be possible to assign the result to the left operand.

The intuitive effect of the rule for predefined operators is simply that x *op*= y is permitted if both of x *op* y and x = y are permitted. In the example

```
byte b = 0;
char ch = '\0';
int i = 0;

b += 1;             // Ok
b += 1000;          // Error, b = 1000 not permitted
b += i;             // Error, b = i not permitted
b += (byte)i;       // Ok

ch += 1;            // Error, ch = 1 not permitted
ch += (char)1;      // Ok
```

the intuitive reason for each error is that a corresponding simple assignment would also have been an error.

7. Expressions

7.13.3 Event Assignment

If the left operand of a += or -= operator is classified as an event access, then the expression is evaluated as follows.

- The instance expression, if any, of the event access is evaluated.

- The right operand of the += or -= operator is evaluated and, if required, converted to the type of the left operand through an implicit conversion (§6.1).

- An event accessor of the event is invoked, with argument list consisting of the right operand, after evaluation and, if necessary, conversion. If the operator was +=, the add accessor is invoked; if the operator was -=, the remove accessor is invoked.

An event assignment expression does not yield a value. Thus, an event assignment expression is valid only in the context of a *statement-expression* (§8.6).

7.14 Expression

An *expression* is either a *conditional-expression* or an *assignment*.

> *expression:*
>> *conditional-expression*
>> *assignment*

7.15 Constant Expressions

A *constant-expression* is an expression that can be fully evaluated at compile time.

> *constant-expression:*
>> *expression*

The type of a constant expression can be one of the following: sbyte, byte, short, ushort, int, uint, long, ulong, char, float, double, decimal, bool, string, any enumeration type, or the null type. The following constructs are permitted in constant expressions:

- Literals (including the null literal)

- References to const members of class and struct types

- References to members of enumeration types

- Parenthesized subexpressions, which are themselves constant expressions

- Cast expressions, provided the target type is one of the types listed

- The predefined +, −, !, and ~ unary operators

- The predefined +, −, *, /, %, <<, >>, &, |, ^, &&, ||, ==, !=, <, >, <=, and >= binary operators, provided each operand is of a type listed

- The ?: conditional operator

Whenever an expression is of one of the types listed previously and contains only the constructs listed previously, the expression is evaluated at compile time. This is true even if the expression is a subexpression of a larger expression that contains nonconstant constructs.

The compile-time evaluation of constant expressions uses the same rules as runtime evaluation of nonconstant expressions, except that where runtime evaluation would have thrown an exception, compile-time evaluation causes a compile-time error to occur.

Unless a constant expression is explicitly placed in an unchecked context, overflows that occur in integral-type arithmetic operations and conversions during the compile-time evaluation of the expression always cause compile-time errors (§7.5.12).

Constant expressions occur in the contexts listed next. In these contexts, a compile-time error occurs if an expression cannot be fully evaluated at compile time.

- Constant declarations (§10.3).

- Enumeration member declarations (§14.3)

- case labels of a switch statement (§8.7.2)

- goto case statements (§8.9.3)

- Dimension lengths in an array creation expression (§7.5.10.2) that includes an initializer

- Attributes (§17)

An implicit constant expression conversion (§6.1.6) permits a constant expression of type int to be converted to sbyte, byte, short, ushort, uint, or ulong, provided the value of the constant expression is within the range of the destination type.

7.16 Boolean Expressions

A *boolean-expression* is an expression that yields a result of type bool.

> *boolean-expression:*
>   *expression*

The controlling conditional expression of an *if-statement* (§8.7.1), *while-statement* (§8.8.1), *do-statement* (§8.8.2), or *for-statement* (§8.8.3) is a *boolean-expression* . The controlling conditional expression of the ? : operator (§7.12) follows the same rules as a *boolean-expression* but, for reasons of operator precedence, is classified as a *conditional-or-expression* .

A *boolean-expression* is required to be of a type that can be implicitly converted to bool or of a type that implements operator true. If neither requirement is satisfied, a compile-time error occurs.

When a boolean expression is of a type that cannot be implicitly converted to bool but does implement operator true, then following evaluation of the expression, the operator true implementation provided by that type is invoked to produce a bool value.

The DBBool struct type in §11.4.2 provides an example of a type that implements operator true and operator false.

8. Statements

C# provides a variety of statements. Most of these statements will be familiar to developers who have programmed in C and C++.

statement:
> *labeled-statement*
> *declaration-statement*
> *embedded-statement*

embedded-statement:
> *block*
> *empty-statement*
> *expression-statement*
> *selection-statement*
> *iteration-statement*
> *jump-statement*
> *try-statement*
> *checked-statement*
> *unchecked-statement*
> *lock-statement*
> *using-statement*

The *embedded-statement* nonterminal is used for statements that appear within other statements. The use of *embedded-statement* rather than *statement* excludes the use of declaration statements and labeled statements in these contexts. The example

```
void F(bool b) {
    if (b)
        int i = 44;
}
```

results in a compile-time error because an `if` statement requires an *embedded-statement* rather than a *statement* for its `if` branch. If this code was permitted, then the variable `i` would be declared, but it could never be used. Note, however, that by placing `i`'s declaration in a block, the example is valid.

8.1 End Points and Reachability

Every statement has an *end point*. In intuitive terms, the end point of a statement is the location that immediately follows the statement. The execution rules for composite statements (statements that contain embedded statements) specify the action that is taken when control reaches the end point of an embedded statement. For example, when control reaches the end point of a statement in a block, control is transferred to the next statement in the block.

If a statement can possibly be reached by execution, the statement is said to be *reachable*. Conversely, if there is no possibility that a statement will be executed, the statement is said to be *unreachable*.

In the example

```
void F() {
    Console.WriteLine("reachable");
    goto Label;
    Console.WriteLine("unreachable");
    Label:
    Console.WriteLine("reachable");
}
```

the second invocation of `Console.WriteLine` is unreachable because there is no possibility that the statement will be executed.

A warning is reported if the compiler determines that a statement is unreachable. It is specifically not an error for a statement to be unreachable.

To determine whether a particular statement or end point is reachable, the compiler performs flow analysis according to the reachability rules defined for each statement. The flow analysis takes into account the values of constant expressions (§7.15) that control the behavior of statements, but the possible values of nonconstant expressions are not considered. In other words, for purposes of control flow analysis, a nonconstant expression of a given type is considered to have any possible value of that type.

In the example

```
void F() {
    const int i = 1;
    if (i == 2) Console.WriteLine("unreachable");
}
```

the boolean expression of the `if` statement is a constant expression because both operands of the `==` operator are constants. As the constant expression is evaluated at compile time, producing the value `false`, the `Console.WriteLine` invocation is considered unreachable. However, if `i` is changed to be a local variable

```
void F() {
    int i = 1;
    if (i == 2) Console.WriteLine("reachable");
}
```

the `Console.WriteLine` invocation is considered reachable, even though, in reality, it will never be executed.

The *block* of a function member is always considered reachable. By successively evaluating the reachability rules of each statement in a block, the reachability of any given statement can be determined.

In the example

```
void F(int x) {
    Console.WriteLine("start");
    if (x < 0) Console.WriteLine("negative");
}
```

the reachability of the second `Console.WriteLine` is determined as follows.

- The first `Console.WriteLine` expression statement is reachable because the block of the `F` method is reachable.

- The end point of the first `Console.WriteLine` expression statement is reachable because that statement is reachable.

- The `if` statement is reachable because the end point of the first `Console.WriteLine` expression statement is reachable.

- The second `Console.WriteLine` expression statement is reachable because the boolean expression of the `if` statement does not have the constant value `false`.

There are two situations in which it is a compile-time error for the end point of a statement to be reachable.

- Because the `switch` statement does not permit a switch section to "fall through" to the next switch section, it is a compile-time error for the end point of the statement list of a switch section to be reachable. If this error occurs, it is typically an indication that a `break` statement is missing.

- It is a compile-time error for the end point of the block of a function member that computes a value to be reachable. If this error occurs, it typically is an indication that a `return` statement is missing.

8. Statements

8.2 Blocks

A *block* permits multiple statements to be written in contexts where a single statement is allowed.

> *block:*
> > {   *statement-list*_{opt}   }

A *block* consists of a *statement-list* (§8.2.1), enclosed in braces. If the statement list is omitted, the block is said to be empty.

A block may contain declaration statements (§8.5). The scope of a local variable or constant declared in a block is the block.

Within a block, the meaning of a name used in an expression context must always be the same (§7.5.2.1).

A block is executed as follows.

- If the block is empty, control is transferred to the end point of the block.
- If the block is not empty, control is transferred to the statement list. When and if control reaches the end point of the statement list, control is transferred to the end point of the block.

The statement list of a block is reachable if the block itself is reachable.

The end point of a block is reachable if the block is empty or if the end point of the statement list is reachable.

8.2.1 Statement Lists

A **statement list** consists of one or more statements written in sequence. Statement lists occur in *blocks* (§8.2) and in *switch-blocks* (§8.7.2).

> *statement-list:*
> > *statement*
> > *statement-list   statement*

A statement list is executed by transferring control to the first statement. When and if control reaches the end point of a statement, control is transferred to the next statement. When and if control reaches the end point of the last statement, control is transferred to the end point of the statement list.

A statement in a statement list is reachable if at least one of the following is true.

- The statement is the first statement and the statement list itself is reachable.

- The end point of the preceding statement is reachable.

- The statement is a labeled statement and the label is referenced by a reachable `goto` statement.

The end point of a statement list is reachable if the end point of the last statement in the list is reachable.

8.3 The Empty Statement

An *empty-statement* does nothing.

> *empty-statement:*
>   ;

An empty statement is used when there are no operations to perform in a context where a statement is required.

Execution of an empty statement simply transfers control to the end point of the statement. Thus, the end point of an empty statement is reachable if the empty statement is reachable.

An empty statement can be used when writing a `while` statement with a null body.

```
bool ProcessMessage() {...}
void ProcessMessages() {
    while (ProcessMessage())
        ;
}
```

Also, an empty statement can be used to declare a label just before the closing } of a block.

```
void F() {
    ...
    if (done) goto exit;
    ...
    exit: ;
}
```

8.4 Labeled Statements

A *labeled-statement* permits a statement to be prefixed by a label. Labeled statements are permitted in blocks but are not permitted as embedded statements.

> *labeled-statement:*
>   *identifier* : *statement*

A labeled statement declares a label with the name given by the *identifier*. The scope of a label is the whole block in which the label is declared, including any nested blocks. It is a compile-time error for two labels with the same name to have overlapping scopes.

A label can be referenced from `goto` statements (§8.9.3) within the scope of the label. This means that `goto` statements can transfer control within blocks and out of blocks, but never into blocks.

Labels have their own declaration space and do not interfere with other identifiers. The example

```
int F(int x) {
    if (x >= 0) goto x;
    x = -x;
    x: return x;
}
```

is valid and uses the name x as both a parameter and a label.

Execution of a labeled statement corresponds exactly to execution of the statement following the label.

In addition to the reachability provided by the normal flow of control, a labeled statement is reachable if the label is referenced by a reachable `goto` statement. (One exception is if a `goto` statement is inside a `try` that includes a `finally` block, and the labeled statement is outside the `try`, and the end point of the `finally` block is unreachable, then the labeled statement is not reachable from that `goto` statement.)

8.5 Declaration Statements

A *declaration-statement* declares a local variable or constant. Declaration statements are permitted in blocks but are not permitted as embedded statements.

> *declaration-statement:*
>   *local-variable-declaration*   ;
>   *local-constant-declaration*   ;

8.5.1 Local Variable Declarations

A *local-variable-declaration* declares one or more local variables.

> *local-variable-declaration:*
>   *type local-variable-declarators*

local-variable-declarators:
   local-variable-declarator
   local-variable-declarators , local-variable-declarator

local-variable-declarator:
   identifier
   identifier = local-variable-initializer

local-variable-initializer:
   expression
   array-initializer

The *type* of a *local-variable-declaration* specifies the type of the variables introduced by the declaration. The type is followed by a list of *local-variable-declarators*, each of which introduces a new variable. A *local-variable-declarator* consists of an *identifier* that names the variable, optionally followed by an = token and a *local-variable-initializer* that gives the initial value of the variable.

The value of a local variable is obtained in an expression using a *simple-name* (§7.5.2), and the value of a local variable is modified using an *assignment* (§7.13). A local variable must be definitely assigned (§5.3) at each location where its value is obtained.

The scope of a local variable declared in a *local-variable-declaration* is the block in which the declaration occurs. It is an error to refer to a local variable in a textual position that precedes the *local-variable-declarator* of the local variable. Within the scope of a local variable, it is a compile-time error to declare another local variable or constant with the same name.

A local variable declaration that declares multiple variables is equivalent to multiple declarations of single variables with the same type. Furthermore, a variable initializer in a local variable declaration corresponds exactly to an assignment statement that is inserted immediately after the declaration.

The example

```
void F() {
    int x = 1, y, z = x * 2;
}
```

corresponds exactly to the following.

```
void F() {
    int x; x = 1;
    int y;
    int z; z = x * 2;
}
```

8.5.2 Local Constant Declarations

A *local-constant-declaration* declares one or more local constants.

> *local-constant-declaration:*
>   const *type constant-declarators*

> *constant-declarators:*
>   *constant-declarator*
>   *constant-declarators , constant-declarator*

> *constant-declarator:*
>   *identifier = constant-expression*

The *type* of a *local-constant-declaration* specifies the type of the constants introduced by the declaration. The type is followed by a list of *constant-declarators*, each of which introduces a new constant. A *constant-declarator* consists of an *identifier* that names the constant, followed by an = token, followed by a *constant-expression* (§7.15) that gives the value of the constant.

The *type* and *constant-expression* of a local constant declaration must follow the same rules as those of a constant member declaration (§10.3).

The value of a local constant is obtained in an expression using a *simple-name* (§7.5.2).

The scope of a local constant is the block in which the declaration occurs. It is an error to refer to a local constant in a textual position that precedes its *constant-declarator*. Within the scope of a local constant, it is a compile-time error to declare another local variable or constant with the same name.

A local constant declaration that declares multiple constants is equivalent to multiple declarations of single constants with the same type.

8.6 Expression Statements

An *expression-statement* evaluates a given expression. The value computed by the expression, if any, is discarded.

> *expression-statement:*
>   *statement-expression ;*

statement-expression:
    invocation-expression
    object-creation-expression
    assignment
    post-increment-expression
    post-decrement-expression
    pre-increment-expression
    pre-decrement-expression

Not all expressions are permitted as statements. In particular, expressions such as `x + y` and `x == 1` that merely compute a value (which will be discarded) are not permitted as statements.

Execution of an *expression-statement* evaluates the contained expression and then transfers control to the end point of the *expression-statement*. The end point of an *expression-statement* is reachable if that *expression-statement* is reachable.

8.7 Selection Statements

Selection statements select one of a number of possible statements for execution based on the value of some expression.

selection-statement:
    if-statement
    switch-statement

8.7.1 The if Statement

The `if` statement selects a statement for execution based on the value of a boolean expression.

if-statement:
    `if` `(` *boolean-expression* `)` *embedded-statement*
    `if` `(` *boolean-expression* `)` *embedded-statement* `else` *embedded-statement*

boolean-expression:
    expression

An `else` part is associated with the lexically nearest preceding `if` that is allowed by the syntax. Thus, an `if` statement of the form

```
if (x) if (y) F(); else G();
```

is equivalent to the following.

```
if (x) {
    if (y) {
        F();
    }
    else {
        G();
    }
}
```

An if statement is executed as follows.

- The *boolean-expression* (§7.16) is evaluated.

- If the boolean expression yields true, control is transferred to the first embedded statement. When and if control reaches the end point of that statement, control is transferred to the end point of the if statement.

- If the boolean expression yields false and if an else part is present, control is transferred to the second embedded statement. When and if control reaches the end point of that statement, control is transferred to the end point of the if statement.

- If the boolean expression yields false and if an else part is not present, control is transferred to the end point of the if statement.

The first embedded statement of an if statement is reachable if the if statement is reachable and the boolean expression does not have the constant value false.

The second embedded statement of an if statement, if present, is reachable if the if statement is reachable and the boolean expression does not have the constant value true.

The end point of an if statement is reachable if the end point of at least one of its embedded statements is reachable. In addition, the end point of an if statement with no else part is reachable if the if statement is reachable and the boolean expression does not have the constant value true.

8.7.2 The switch Statement

The switch statement selects for execution a statement list having an associated switch label that corresponds to the value of the switch expression.

switch-statement:
    switch (*expression*) *switch-block*

switch-block:
    { *switch-sections*_{opt} }

switch-sections:
    switch-section
    switch-sections *switch-section*

switch-section:
    switch-labels   statement-list

switch-labels:
    switch-label
    switch-labels   switch-label

switch-label:
    case   *constant-expression*   :
    default   :

A *switch-statement* consists of the keyword `switch`, followed by a parenthesized expression (called the switch expression), followed by a *switch-block*. The *switch-block* consists of zero or more *switch-sections*, enclosed in braces. Each *switch-section* consists of one or more *switch-labels* followed by a *statement-list* (§8.2.1).

The **governing type** of a `switch` statement is established by the switch expression. If the type of the switch expression is `sbyte`, `byte`, `short`, `ushort`, `int`, `uint`, `long`, `ulong`, `char`, `string`, or an *enum-type*, then that is the governing type of the `switch` statement. Otherwise, exactly one user-defined implicit conversion (§6.4) must exist from the type of the switch expression to one of the following possible governing types: `sbyte`, `byte`, `short`, `ushort`, `int`, `uint`, `long`, `ulong`, `char`, or `string`. If no such implicit conversion exists, or if more than one such implicit conversion exists, a compile-time error occurs.

The constant expression of each `case` label must denote a value of a type that is implicitly convertible (§6.1) to the governing type of the `switch` statement. A compile-time error occurs if two or more `case` labels in the same `switch` statement specify the same constant value.

There can be at most one `default` label in a `switch` statement.

A `switch` statement is executed as follows.

- The switch expression is evaluated and converted to the governing type.
- If one of the constants specified in a `case` label in the same `switch` statement is equal to the value of the switch expression, control is transferred to the statement list following the matched `case` label.
- If none of the constants specified in `case` labels in the same `switch` statement is equal to the value of the switch expression, and if a `default` label is present, control is transferred to the statement list following the `default` label.
- If none of the constants specified in `case` labels in the same `switch` statement is equal to the value of the switch expression, and if no `default` label is present, control is transferred to the end point of the `switch` statement.

8. Statements

If the end point of the statement list of a switch section is reachable, a compile-time error occurs. This is known as the "no fall through" rule. The example

```
switch (i) {
case 0:
    CaseZero();
    break;
case 1:
    CaseOne();
    break;
default:
    CaseOthers();
    break;
}
```

is valid because no switch section has a reachable end point. Unlike C and C++, execution of a switch section is not permitted to "fall through" to the next switch section, and the example

```
switch (i) {
case 0:
    CaseZero();
case 1:
    CaseZeroOrOne();
default:
    CaseAny();
}
```

results in a compile-time error. When execution of a switch section is to be followed by execution of another switch section, an explicit `goto case` or `goto default` statement must be used.

```
switch (i) {
case 0:
    CaseZero();
    goto case 1;
case 1:
    CaseZeroOrOne();
    goto default;
default:
    CaseAny();
    break;
}
```

Multiple labels are permitted in a *switch-section*. The example

```
switch (i) {
case 0:
    CaseZero();
    break;
case 1:
    CaseOne();
    break;
case 2:
default:
    CaseTwo();
    break;
}
```

is valid. The example does not violate the "no fall through" rule because the labels `case 2:` and `default:` are part of the same *switch-section*.

The "no fall through" rule prevents a common class of bugs that occur in C and C++ when `break` statements are accidentally omitted. In addition, because of this rule, the switch sections of a `switch` statement can be arbitrarily rearranged without affecting the behavior of the statement. For example, the sections of the previous `switch` statement can be reversed without affecting the behavior of the statement.

```
switch (i) {
default:
    CaseAny();
    break;
case 1:
    CaseZeroOrOne();
    goto default;
case 0:
    CaseZero();
    goto case 1;
}
```

The statement list of a switch section typically ends in a `break`, `goto case`, or `goto default` statement, but any construct that renders the end point of the statement list unreachable is permitted. For example, a `while` statement controlled by the boolean expression `true` is known to never reach its end point. Likewise, a `throw` or `return` statement always transfers control elsewhere and never reaches its end point. Thus, the following example is valid.

```
switch (i) {
case 0:
    while (true) F();
case 1:
    throw new ArgumentException();
case 2:
    return;
}
```

8. Statements

The governing type of a switch statement may be the type string.

```
void DoCommand(string command) {
    switch (command.ToLower()) {
    case "run":
        DoRun();
        break;
    case "save":
        DoSave();
        break;
    case "quit":
        DoQuit();
        break;
    default:
        InvalidCommand(command);
        break;
    }
}
```

Like the string equality operators (§7.9.7), the switch statement is case sensitive and will execute a given switch section only if the switch expression string exactly matches a case label constant.

When the governing type of a switch statement is string, the value null is permitted as a case label constant.

The *statement-lists* of a *switch-block* may contain declaration statements (§8.5). The scope of a local variable or constant declared in a switch block is the switch block.

Within a switch block, the meaning of a name used in an expression context must always be the same (§7.5.2.1).

The statement list of a given switch section is reachable if the switch statement is reachable and at least one of the following is true.

- The switch expression is a nonconstant value.
- The switch expression is a constant value that matches a case label in the switch section.
- The switch expression is a constant value that does not match any case label, and the switch section contains the default label.
- A switch label of the switch section is referenced by a reachable goto case or goto default statement.

The end point of a switch statement is reachable if at least one of the following is true.

- The switch statement contains a reachable break statement that exits the switch statement.

- The switch statement is reachable, the switch expression is a nonconstant value, and no default label is present.

- The switch statement is reachable, the switch expression is a constant value that does not match any case label, and no default label is present.

8.8 Iteration Statements

Iteration statements repeatedly execute an embedded statement.

> *iteration-statement:*
>   *while-statement*
>   *do-statement*
>   *for-statement*
>   *foreach-statement*

8.8.1 The while Statement

The while statement conditionally executes an embedded statement zero or more times.

> *while-statement:*
>   while (*boolean-expression*) *embedded-statement*

A while statement is executed as follows.

- The *boolean-expression* (§7.16) is evaluated.

- If the boolean expression yields true, control is transferred to the embedded statement. When and if control reaches the end point of the embedded statement (possibly from execution of a continue statement), control is transferred to the beginning of the while statement.

- If the boolean expression yields false, control is transferred to the end point of the while statement.

Within the embedded statement of a while statement, a break statement (§8.9.1) may be used to transfer control to the end point of the while statement (thus ending iteration of the embedded statement), and a continue statement (§8.9.2) may be used to transfer control to the end point of the embedded statement (thus performing another iteration of the while statement).

The embedded statement of a while statement is reachable if the while statement is reachable and the boolean expression does not have the constant value false.

The end point of a `while` statement is reachable if at least one of the following is true.

- The `while` statement contains a reachable `break` statement that exits the `while` statement.

- The `while` statement is reachable and the boolean expression does not have the constant value `true`.

8.8.2 The do Statement

The do statement conditionally executes an embedded statement one or more times.

> *do-statement:*
>   do *embedded-statement* `while` (*boolean-expression*) ;

A do statement is executed as follows.

- Control is transferred to the embedded statement.

- When and if control reaches the end point of the embedded statement (possibly from execution of a `continue` statement), the *boolean-expression* (§7.16) is evaluated. If the boolean expression yields `true`, control is transferred to the beginning of the do statement. Otherwise, control is transferred to the end point of the do statement.

Within the embedded statement of a do statement, a `break` statement (§8.9.1) may be used to transfer control to the end point of the do statement (thus ending iteration of the embedded statement), and a `continue` statement (§8.9.2) may be used to transfer control to the end point of the embedded statement.

The embedded statement of a do statement is reachable if the do statement is reachable.

The end point of a do statement is reachable if at least one of the following is true.

- The do statement contains a reachable `break` statement that exits the do statement.

- The end point of the embedded statement is reachable, and the boolean expression does not have the constant value `true`.

8.8.3 The for Statement

The `for` statement evaluates a sequence of initialization expressions and then, while a condition is true, repeatedly executes an embedded statement and evaluates a sequence of iteration expressions.

> *for-statement:*
>   `for` (*for-initializer*$_{opt}$; *for-condition*$_{opt}$; *for-iterator*$_{opt}$) *embedded-statement*

for-initializer:
>   *local-variable-declaration*
>   *statement-expression-list*

for-condition:
>   *boolean-expression*

for-iterator:
>   *statement-expression-list*

statement-expression-list:
>   *statement-expression*
>   *statement-expression-list , statement-expression*

The *for-initializer*, if present, consists of either a *local-variable-declaration* (§8.5.1) or a list of *statement-expressions* (§8.6) separated by commas. The scope of a local variable declared by a *for-initializer* starts at the *local-variable-declarator* for the variable and extends to the end of the embedded statement. The scope includes the *for-condition* and the *for-iterator*.

The *for-condition*, if present, must be a *boolean-expression* (§7.16).

The *for-iterator*, if present, consists of a list of *statement-expressions* (§8.6) separated by commas.

A for statement is executed as follows.

- If a *for-initializer* is present, the variable initializers or statement expressions are executed in the order they are written. This step is only performed once.

- If a *for-condition* is present, it is evaluated.

- If the *for-condition* is not present or if the evaluation yields `true`, control is transferred to the embedded statement. When and if control reaches the end point of the embedded statement (possibly from execution of a `continue` statement), the expressions of the *for-iterator*, if any, are evaluated in sequence, and then another iteration is performed, starting with evaluation of the *for-condition* in the previous step.

- If the *for-condition* is present and the evaluation yields `false`, control is transferred to the end point of the `for` statement.

Within the embedded statement of a `for` statement, a `break` statement (§8.9.1) may be used to transfer control to the end point of the `for` statement (thus ending iteration of the embedded statement), and a `continue` statement (§8.9.2) may be used to transfer control to the end point of the embedded statement (thus executing the *for-iterator* and performing another iteration of the `for` statement, starting with the *for-condition*).

8. Statements

The embedded statement of a `for` statement is reachable if one of the following is true.

- The `for` statement is reachable, and no *for-condition* is present.
- The `for` statement is reachable, and a *for-condition* is present and does not have the constant value `false`.

The end point of a `for` statement is reachable if at least one of the following is true.

- The `for` statement contains a reachable `break` statement that exits the `for` statement.
- The `for` statement is reachable, and a *for-condition* is present and does not have the constant value `true`.

8.8.4 The foreach Statement

The `foreach` statement enumerates the elements of a collection, executing an embedded statement for each element of the collection.

> *foreach-statement:*
>   foreach (*type identifier* in *expression*) *embedded-statement*

The *type* and *identifier* of a `foreach` statement declare the ***iteration variable*** of the statement. The iteration variable corresponds to a read-only local variable with a scope that extends over the embedded statement. During execution of a `foreach` statement, the iteration variable represents the collection element for which an iteration is currently being performed. A compile-time error occurs if the embedded statement attempts to modify the iteration variable (via assignment or the `++` and `--` operators) or pass the iteration variable as a `ref` or `out` parameter.

The type of the *expression* of a `foreach` statement must be a collection type (as defined in the following), and an explicit conversion (§6.2) must exist from the element type of the collection to the type of the iteration variable. If *expression* has the value `null`, a `System.NullReferenceException` is thrown.

A type `C` is said to be a ***collection type*** if it implements the `System.Collections.IEnumerable` interface or implements the ***collection pattern*** by meeting all of the following criteria.

- `C` contains a `public` instance method with the signature `GetEnumerator()` that returns a *struct-type*, *class-type*, or *interface-type*, which is called `E` in the following text.
- `E` contains a `public` instance method with the signature `MoveNext()` and the return type `bool`.

- E contains a `public` instance property named `Current` that permits reading the current value. The type of this property is said to be the *element type* of the collection type.

A type that implements `IEnumerable` is also a collection type, even if it does not satisfy the previous conditions. (This is possible if it implements some of the `IEnumerable` members via explicit interface member implementation, as described in §13.4.1.)

The `System.Array` type (§12.1.1) is a collection type, and because all array types derive from `System.Array`, any array type expression is permitted in a `foreach` statement. The order in which `foreach` traverses the elements of an array is as follows: For single-dimensional arrays, elements are traversed in increasing index order, starting with index 0 and ending with index `Length` − 1. For multi-dimensional arrays, elements are traversed such that the indices of the rightmost dimension are increased first, then the next left dimension, and so on to the left.

A `foreach` statement of the following form

```
foreach (ElementType element in collection) statement
```

corresponds to one of two possible expansions.

- If the `collection` expression is of a type that implements the collection pattern (as defined previously), the expansion of the `foreach` statement is

```
E enumerator = (collection).GetEnumerator();
try {
    while (enumerator.MoveNext()) {
        ElementType element = (ElementType)enumerator.Current;
        statement;
    }
}
finally {
    IDisposable disposable = enumerator as System.IDisposable;
    if (disposable != null) disposable.Dispose();
}
```

Significant optimizations of the previous code are often easily available. If the type `E` implements `System.IDisposable`, then the expression (`enumerator as System.IDisposable`) will always be non-null and the implementation can safely substitute a simple conversion for a possibly more expensive type test. Conversely, if the type `E` is `sealed` and does not implement `System.IDisposable`, then the expression (`enumerator as System.IDisposable`) will always evaluate to `null`. In this case, the implementation can safely optimize away the entire finally clause.

8. Statements

- Otherwise, the collection expression is of a type that implements System.IEnumerable, and the expansion of the foreach statement is

```
IEnumerator enumerator =
                ((System.Collections.IEnumerable)(collection)).GetEnumerator();
try {
    while (enumerator.MoveNext()) {
        ElementType element = (ElementType)enumerator.Current;
        statement;
    }
}
finally {
    IDisposable disposable = enumerator as System.IDisposable;
    if (disposable != null) disposable.Dispose();
}
```

In either expansion, the enumerator variable is a temporary variable that is inaccessible in, and invisible to, the embedded statement, and the element variable is read-only in the embedded statement.

The following example prints each value in a two-dimensional array in element order.

```
using System;

class Test
{
    static void Main() {
        double[,] values = {
            {1.2, 2.3, 3.4, 4.5},
            {5.6, 6.7, 7.8, 8.9}
        };

        foreach (double elementValue in values)
            Console.Write("{0} ", elementValue);

        Console.WriteLine();
    }
}
```

The output produced is as follows.

```
1.2 2.3 3.4 4.5 5.6 6.7 7.8 8.9
```

8.9 Jump Statements

Jump statements unconditionally transfer control.

jump-statement:
    break-statement
    continue-statement
    goto-statement
    return-statement
    throw-statement

The location to which a jump statement transfers control is called the **target** of the jump statement.

When a jump statement occurs within a block and the target of that jump statement is outside that block, the jump statement is said to **exit** the block. Although a jump statement may transfer control out of a block, it can never transfer control into a block.

Execution of jump statements is complicated by the presence of intervening `try` statements. In the absence of such `try` statements, a jump statement unconditionally transfers control from the jump statement to its target. In the presence of such intervening `try` statements, execution is more complex. If the jump statement exits one or more `try` blocks with associated `finally` blocks, control is initially transferred to the `finally` block of the innermost `try` statement. When and if control reaches the end point of a `finally` block, control is transferred to the `finally` block of the next enclosing `try` statement. This process is repeated until the `finally` blocks of all intervening `try` statements have been executed.

In the example

```
using System;

class Test
{
    static void Main() {
        while (true) {
            try {
                try {
                    Console.WriteLine("Before break");
                    break;
                }
                finally {
                    Console.WriteLine("Innermost finally block");
                }
            }
            finally {
                Console.WriteLine("Outermost finally block");
            }
        }
        Console.WriteLine("After break");
    }
}
```

8. Statements

the `finally` blocks associated with two `try` statements are executed before control is transferred to the target of the jump statement.

The output produced is as follows.

```
Before break
Innermost finally block
Outermost finally block
After break
```

8.9.1 The break Statement

The `break` statement exits the nearest enclosing `switch`, `while`, `do`, `for`, or `foreach` statement.

> *break-statement:*
>   break ;

The target of a `break` statement is the end point of the nearest enclosing `switch`, `while`, `do`, `for`, or `foreach` statement. If a `break` statement is not enclosed by a `switch`, `while`, `do`, `for`, or `foreach` statement, a compile-time error occurs.

When multiple `switch`, `while`, `do`, `for`, or `foreach` statements are nested within each other, a `break` statement applies only to the innermost statement. To transfer control across multiple nesting levels, a `goto` statement (§8.9.3) must be used.

A `break` statement cannot exit a `finally` block (§8.10). When a `break` statement occurs within a `finally` block, the target of the `break` statement must be within the same `finally` block; otherwise, a compile-time error occurs.

A `break` statement is executed as follows.

- If the `break` statement exits one or more `try` blocks with associated `finally` blocks, control is initially transferred to the `finally` block of the innermost `try` statement. When and if control reaches the end point of a `finally` block, control is transferred to the `finally` block of the next enclosing `try` statement. This process is repeated until the `finally` blocks of all intervening `try` statements have been executed.

- Control is transferred to the target of the `break` statement.

Because a `break` statement unconditionally transfers control elsewhere, the end point of a `break` statement is never reachable.

8.9.2 **The continue Statement**

The `continue` statement starts a new iteration of the nearest enclosing `while`, `do`, `for`, or `foreach` statement.

> *continue-statement:*
>   continue ;

The target of a `continue` statement is the end point of the embedded statement of the nearest enclosing `while`, `do`, `for`, or `foreach` statement. If a `continue` statement is not enclosed by a `while`, `do`, `for`, or `foreach` statement, a compile-time error occurs.

When multiple `while`, `do`, `for`, or `foreach` statements are nested within each other, a `continue` statement applies only to the innermost statement. To transfer control across multiple nesting levels, a `goto` statement (§8.9.3) must be used.

A `continue` statement cannot exit a `finally` block (§8.10). When a `continue` statement occurs within a `finally` block, the target of the `continue` statement must be within the same `finally` block; otherwise a compile-time error occurs.

A `continue` statement is executed as follows.

- If the `continue` statement exits one or more `try` blocks with associated `finally` blocks, control is initially transferred to the `finally` block of the innermost `try` statement. When and if control reaches the end point of a `finally` block, control is transferred to the `finally` block of the next enclosing `try` statement. This process is repeated until the `finally` blocks of all intervening `try` statements have been executed.

- Control is transferred to the target of the `continue` statement.

Because a `continue` statement unconditionally transfers control elsewhere, the end point of a `continue` statement is never reachable.

8.9.3 **The goto Statement**

The `goto` statement transfers control to a statement that is marked by a label.

> *goto-statement:*
>   goto *identifier* ;
>   goto case *constant-expression* ;
>   goto default ;

The target of a `goto` *identifier* statement is the labeled statement with the given label. If a label with the given name does not exist in the current function member, or if the `goto` statement is not within the scope of the label, a compile-time error occurs. This rule permits using a goto statement to transfer control *out of* a nested scope, but not *into* a nested scope. In the example

```
using System;
class Test
{
    static void Main(string[] args) {
        string[,] table = {
            {"Red", "Blue", "Green"},
            {"Monday", "Wednesday", "Friday"}
        };
        foreach (string str in args) {
            int row, colm;
            for (row = 0; row <= 1; ++row)
                for (colm = 0; colm <= 2; ++colm)
                    if (str == table[row,colm])
                        goto done;
            Console.WriteLine("{0} not found", str);
            continue;
        done:
            Console.WriteLine("Found {0} at [{1}][{2}]", str, row, colm);
        }
    }
}
```

a goto statement is used to transfer control out of a nested scope.

The target of a goto case statement is the statement list in the immediately enclosing switch statement (§8.7.2), which contains a case label with the given constant value. If the goto case statement is not enclosed by a switch statement, if the *constant-expression* is not implicitly convertible (§6.1) to the governing type of the nearest enclosing switch statement, or if the nearest enclosing switch statement does not contain a case label with the given constant value, a compile-time error occurs.

The target of a goto default statement is the statement list in the immediately enclosing switch statement (§8.7.2), which contains a default label. If the goto default statement is not enclosed by a switch statement, or if the nearest enclosing switch statement does not contain a default label, a compile-time error occurs.

A goto statement cannot exit a finally block (§8.10). When a goto statement occurs within a finally block, the target of the goto statement must be within the same finally block, or otherwise a compile-time error occurs.

A goto statement is executed as follows.

- If the `goto` statement exits one or more `try` blocks with associated `finally` blocks, control is initially transferred to the `finally` block of the innermost `try` statement. When and if control reaches the end point of a `finally` block, control is transferred to the `finally` block of the next enclosing `try` statement. This process is repeated until the `finally` blocks of all intervening `try` statements have been executed.

- Control is transferred to the target of the `goto` statement.

Because a `goto` statement unconditionally transfers control elsewhere, the end point of a `goto` statement is never reachable.

8.9.4 The return Statement

The `return` statement returns control to the caller of the function member in which the `return` statement appears.

> *return-statement:*
>   `return` *expression*_{opt}   `;`

A `return` statement with no expression can be used only in a function member that does not compute a value, that is, a method with the return type `void`, the `set` accessor of a property or indexer, the `add` and `remove` accessors of an event, an instance constructor, a static constructor, or a destructor.

A `return` statement with an expression can only be used in a function member that computes a value, that is, a method with a nonvoid return type, the `get` accessor of a property or indexer, or a user-defined operator. An implicit conversion (§6.1) must exist from the type of the expression to the return type of the containing function member.

It is a compile-time error for a `return` statement to appear in a `finally` block (§8.10).

A `return` statement is executed as follows.

- If the `return` statement specifies an expression, the expression is evaluated and the resulting value is converted to the return type of the containing function member by an implicit conversion. The result of the conversion becomes the value returned to the caller.

- If the `return` statement is enclosed by one or more `try` blocks with associated `finally` blocks, control is initially transferred to the `finally` block of the innermost `try` statement. When and if control reaches the end point of a `finally` block, control is transferred to the `finally` block of the next enclosing `try` statement. This process is repeated until the `finally` blocks of all enclosing `try` statements have been executed.

- Control is returned to the caller of the containing function member.

Because a `return` statement unconditionally transfers control elsewhere, the end point of a `return` statement is never reachable.

8.9.5 The throw Statement

The `throw` statement throws an exception.

throw-statement:
> `throw` *expression*_{opt} `;`

A `throw` statement with an expression throws the value produced by evaluating the expression. The expression must denote a value of the class type `System.Exception` or of a class type that derives from `System.Exception`. If evaluation of the expression produces `null`, a `System.NullReferenceException` is thrown instead.

A `throw` statement with no expression can be used only in a `catch` block, in which case that statement rethrows the exception that is currently being handled by that `catch` block.

Because a `throw` statement unconditionally transfers control elsewhere, the end point of a `throw` statement is never reachable.

When an exception is thrown, control is transferred to the first `catch` clause in an enclosing `try` statement that can handle the exception. The process that takes place from the point of the exception being thrown to the point of transferring control to a suitable exception handler is known as *exception propagation*. Propagation of an exception consists of repeatedly evaluating the following steps until a `catch` clause that matches the exception is found. In this description, the *throw point* is initially the location at which the exception is thrown.

- In the current function member, each `try` statement that encloses the throw point is examined. For each statement S, starting with the innermost `try` statement and ending with the outermost `try` statement, the following steps are evaluated.

  - If the `try` block of S encloses the throw point and if S has one or more `catch` clauses, the `catch` clauses are examined in order of appearance to locate a suitable handler for the exception. The first `catch` clause that specifies the exception type or a base type of the exception type is considered a match. A general `catch` clause (§8.10) is considered a match for any exception type. If a matching `catch` clause is located, the exception propagation is completed by transferring control to the block of that `catch` clause.

  - Otherwise, if the `try` block or a `catch` block of S encloses the throw point and if S has a `finally` block, control is transferred to the `finally` block. If the `finally` block throws another exception, processing of the current exception is terminated. Otherwise, when control reaches the end point of the `finally` block, processing of the current exception is continued.

- If an exception handler was not located in the current function member invocation, the function member invocation is terminated. The previous steps are then repeated for the caller of the function member with a throw point corresponding to the statement from which the function member was invoked.

- If the exception processing terminates all function member invocations in the current thread, indicating that the thread has no handler for the exception, then the thread is itself terminated. The impact of such termination is implementation defined.

8.10 The try Statement

The try statement provides a mechanism for catching exceptions that occur during execution of a block. Furthermore, the try statement provides the ability to specify a block of code that is always executed when control leaves the try statement.

> *try-statement:*
>   try   *block*   *catch-clauses*
>   try   *block*   *finally-clause*
>   try   *block*   *catch-clauses*   *finally-clause*
>
> *catch-clauses:*
>   *specific-catch-clauses*   general-catch-clause$_{opt}$
>   *specific-catch-clauses$_{opt}$*   general-catch-clause
>
> *specific-catch-clauses:*
>   *specific-catch-clause*
>   *specific-catch-clauses*   *specific-catch-clause*
>
> *specific-catch-clause:*
>   catch   (*class-type*   identifier$_{opt}$)   *block*
>
> *general-catch-clause:*
>   catch   *block*
>
> *finally-clause:*
>   finally   *block*

There are three possible forms of try statements:

- A try block followed by one or more catch blocks

- A try block followed by a finally block

- A try block followed by one or more catch blocks followed by a finally block

When a catch clause specifies a *class-type*, the type must be System.Exception or a type that derives from System.Exception.

When a `catch` clause specifies both a *class-type* and an *identifier*, an **exception variable** of the given name and type is declared. The exception variable corresponds to a local variable with a scope that extends over the `catch` block. During execution of the `catch` block, the exception variable represents the exception currently being handled. For purposes of definite assignment checking, the exception variable is considered definitely assigned in its entire scope.

Unless a `catch` clause includes an exception variable name, it is impossible to access the exception object in the `catch` block.

A `catch` clause that specifies neither an exception type nor an exception variable name is a general `catch` clause. A `try` statement can only have one general `catch` clause, and if one is present it must be the last `catch` clause.

Some programming languages may support exceptions that are not representable as an object derived from `System.Exception`, but such exceptions could never be generated by C# code. A general `catch` clause may be used to catch such exceptions. Thus, a general `catch` clause is semantically different from one that specifies the type `System.Exception` in that the former may also catch exceptions from other languages.

To locate a handler for an exception, `catch` clauses are examined in lexical order. A compile-time error occurs if a `catch` clause specifies a type that is the same as, or is derived from, a type that was specified in an earlier `catch` clause for the same `try`. Without this restriction, it would be possible to write unreachable `catch` clauses.

Within a `catch` block, a `throw` statement (§8.9.5) with no expression can be used to rethrow the exception that was caught by the `catch` block. Assignments to an exception variable do not alter the exception that is rethrown.

In the example

```
using System;
class Test
{
    static void F() {
        try {
            G();
        }
        catch (Exception e) {
            Console.WriteLine("Exception in F: " + e.Message);
            e = new Exception("F");
            throw;              // re-throw
        }
    }
    static void G() {
        throw new Exception("G");
    }
```

```
static void Main() {
    try {
        F();
    }
    catch (Exception e) {
        Console.WriteLine("Exception in Main: " + e.Message);
    }
}
}
```

the method `F` catches an exception, writes some diagnostic information to the console, alters the exception variable, and rethrows the exception. The exception that is rethrown is the original exception, so the output produced is

```
Exception in F: G
Exception in Main: G
```

If the first catch block had thrown e instead of rethrowing the current exception, the output produced would be as follows.

```
Exception in F: G
Exception in Main: F
```

It is a compile-time error for a `break`, `continue`, or `goto` statement to transfer control out of a `finally` block. When a `break`, `continue`, or `goto` statement occurs in a `finally` block, the target of the statement must be within the same `finally` block, or otherwise a compile-time error occurs.

It is a compile-time error for a `return` statement to occur in a `finally` block.

A `try` statement is executed as follows.

- Control is transferred to the `try` block.
- When and if control reaches the end point of the `try` block
  - If the `try` statement has a `finally` block, the `finally` block is executed.
  - Control is transferred to the end point of the `try` statement.
- If an exception is propagated to the `try` statement during execution of the `try` block
  - The `catch` clauses, if any, are examined in order of appearance to locate a suitable handler for the exception. The first `catch` clause that specifies the exception type or a base type of the exception type is considered a match. A general `catch` clause is considered a match for any exception type. If a matching `catch` clause is located
    - If the matching `catch` clause declares an exception variable, the exception object is assigned to the exception variable.
    - Control is transferred to the matching `catch` block.

8. Statements

257

- When and if control reaches the end point of the catch block
  - If the try statement has a finally block, the finally block is executed.
  - Control is transferred to the end point of the try statement.
- If an exception is propagated to the try statement during execution of the catch block
  - If the try statement has a finally block, the finally block is executed.
  - The exception is propagated to the next enclosing try statement.
- If the try statement has no catch clauses or if no catch clause matches the exception
  - If the try statement has a finally block, the finally block is executed.
  - The exception is propagated to the next enclosing try statement.

The statements of a finally block are always executed when control leaves a try statement. This is true whether the control transfer occurs as a result of normal execution, as a result of executing a break, continue, goto, or return statement, or as a result of propagating an exception out of the try statement.

If an exception is thrown during execution of a finally block, the exception is propagated to the next enclosing try statement. If another exception was in the process of being propagated, that exception is lost. The process of propagating an exception is discussed further in the description of the throw statement (§8.9.5).

The try block of a try statement is reachable if the try statement is reachable.

A catch block of a try statement is reachable if the try statement is reachable.

The finally block of a try statement is reachable if the try statement is reachable.

The end point of a try statement is reachable if both of the following are true.

- The end point of the try block is reachable or the end point of at least one catch block is reachable.
- If a finally block is present, the end point of the finally block is reachable.

8.11 The checked and unchecked Statements

The checked and unchecked statements are used to control the *overflow checking context* for integral-type arithmetic operations and conversions.

checked-statement:
    checked *block*

unchecked-statement:
    unchecked *block*

The checked statement causes all expressions in the *block* to be evaluated in a checked context, and the unchecked statement causes all expressions in the *block* to be evaluated in an unchecked context.

The checked and unchecked statements are precisely equivalent to the checked and unchecked operators (§7.5.12) except that they operate on blocks instead of expressions.

8.12 The lock Statement

The lock statement obtains the mutual-exclusion lock for a given object, executes a statement, and then releases the lock.

lock-statement:
    lock (*expression*) *embedded-statement*

The expression of a lock statement must denote a value of a *reference-type*. No implicit boxing conversion (§6.1.5) is ever performed for the expression of a lock statement, and thus it is a compile-time error for the expression to denote a value of a *value-type*.

A lock statement of the form

```
lock (x) ...
```

where x is an expression of a *reference-type*, is precisely equivalent to

```
System.Threading.Monitor.Enter(x);
try {
    ...
}
finally {
    System.Threading.Monitor.Exit(x);
}
```

except that x is only evaluated once.

While a mutual-exclusion lock is held, code executing in the same execution thread can also obtain and release the lock. However, code executing in other threads is blocked from obtaining the lock until the lock is released.

The `System.Type` object of a class can conveniently be used as the mutual-exclusion lock for static methods of the class. For example

```
class Cache
{
    public static void Add(object x) {
        lock (typeof(Cache)) {
            ...
        }
    }
    public static void Remove(object x) {
        lock (typeof(Cache)) {
            ...
        }
    }
}
```

8.13 The using Statement

The `using` statement obtains one or more resources, executes a statement, and then disposes of the resource.

> *using-statement:*
>   using (*resource-acquisition*)   *embedded-statement*
>
> *resource-acquisition:*
>   *local-variable-declaration*
>   *expression*

A ***resource*** is a class or struct that implements `System.IDisposable`, which includes a single parameterless method named `Dispose`. Code that is using a resource can call `Dispose` to indicate that the resource is no longer needed. If `Dispose` is not called, then automatic disposal eventually occurs as a consequence of garbage collection.

If the form of *resource-acquisition* is *local-variable-declaration*, then the type of the *local-variable-declaration* must be `System.IDisposable` or a type that can be implicitly converted to `System.IDisposable`. If the form of *resource-acquisition* is *expression*, then this expression must be of type `System.IDisposable` or a type that can be implicitly converted to `System.IDisposable`.

Local variables declared in a *resource-acquisition* are read-only and must include an initializer. A compile-time error occurs if the embedded statement attempts to modify these local variables (via assignment or the ++ and -- operators) or pass them as `ref` or `out` parameters.

A using statement is translated into three parts: acquisition, usage, and disposal. Usage of the resource is implicitly enclosed in a try statement that includes a finally clause. This finally clause disposes of the resource. If a null resource is acquired, then no call to Dispose is made, and no exception is thrown.

A using statement of the form

```
using (ResourceType resource = expression) statement
```

corresponds to one of two possible expansions. When ResourceType is a value type, the expansion is

```
{
    ResourceType resource = expression;
    try {
        statement;
    }
    finally {
        ((IDisposable)resource).Dispose();
    }
}
```

Otherwise, when ResourceType is a reference type, the expansion is

```
{
    ResourceType resource = expression;
    try {
        statement;
    }
    finally {
        if (resource != null) ((IDisposable)resource).Dispose();
    }
}
```

In either expansion, the resource variable is read-only in the embedded statement.

A using statement of the form

```
using (expression) statement
```

has the same two possible expansions, but in this case ResourceType is implicitly the compile-time type of the expression, and the resource variable is inaccessible in, and invisible to, the embedded statement.

When a *resource-acquisition* takes the form of a *local-variable-declaration*, it is possible to acquire multiple resources of a given type. A using statement of the form

```
using (ResourceType r1 = e1, r2 = e2, ..., rN = eN) statement
```

is precisely equivalent to a sequence of nested using statements.

8. Statements

```
using (ResourceType r1 = e1)
    using (ResourceType r2 = e2)
        ...
            using (ResourceType rN = eN)
                statement
```

The following example creates a file named `log.txt` and writes two lines of text to the file. The example then opens that same file for reading and copies the contained lines of text to the console.

```
using System;
using System.IO;

class Test
{
    static void Main() {
        using (TextWriter w = File.CreateText("log.txt")) {
            w.WriteLine("This is line one");
            w.WriteLine("This is line two");
        }

        using (TextReader r = File.OpenText("log.txt")) {
            string s;
            while ((s = r.ReadLine()) != null) {
                Console.WriteLine(s);
            }

        }
    }
}
```

Because the `TextWriter` and `TextReader` classes implement the `IDisposable` interface, the example can use `using` statements to ensure that the underlying file is properly closed following the write or read operations.

9. Namespaces

C# programs are organized using namespaces. Namespaces are used both as an "internal" organization system for a program and as an "external" organization system—a way of presenting program elements that are exposed to other programs.

Using directives (§9.3) are provided to facilitate the use of namespaces.

9.1 Compilation Units

A *compilation-unit* defines the overall structure of a source file. A compilation unit consists of zero or more *using-directives* followed by zero or more *global-attributes* followed by zero or more *namespace-member-declarations*.

> *compilation-unit:*
>   *using-directives*_{opt} *global-attributes*_{opt}   *namespace-member-declarations*_{opt}

A C# program consists of one or more compilation units, each contained in a separate source file. When a C# program is compiled, all of the compilation units are processed together. Thus, compilation units can depend on each other, possibly in a circular fashion.

The *using-directives* of a compilation unit affect the *global-attributes* and *namespace-member-declarations* of that compilation unit but have no effect on other compilation units.

The *global-attributes* (§17) of a compilation unit permit the specification of attributes for the target assembly and module. Assemblies and modules act as physical containers for types. An assembly may consist of several physically separate modules.

The *namespace-member-declarations* of each compilation unit of a program contribute members to a single declaration space called the global namespace. For example

File `A.cs`:

```
class A {}
```

File `B.cs`:

```
class B {}
```

the two compilation units contribute to the single global namespace, in this case declaring two classes with the fully qualified names A and B. Because the two compilation units contribute to the same declaration space, it would have been an error if each contained a declaration of a member with the same name.

9.2 Namespace Declarations

A *namespace-declaration* consists of the keyword `namespace`, followed by a namespace name and body, optionally followed by a semicolon.

> *namespace-declaration:*
>   `namespace` *qualified-identifier namespace-body* `;`*opt*
>
> *qualified-identifier:*
>   *identifier*
>   *qualified-identifier* . *identifier*
>
> *namespace-body:*
>   `{` *using-directives*$_{opt}$ *namespace-member-declarations*$_{opt}$ `}`

A *namespace-declaration* may occur as a top-level declaration in a *compilation-unit* or as a member declaration within another *namespace-declaration*. When a *namespace-declaration* occurs as a top-level declaration in a *compilation-unit*, the namespace becomes a member of the global namespace. When a *namespace-declaration* occurs within another *namespace-declaration*, the inner namespace becomes a member of the outer namespace. In either case, the name of a namespace must be unique within the containing namespace.

Namespaces are implicitly `public`, and the declaration of a namespace cannot include any access modifiers.

Within a *namespace-body*, the optional *using-directives* import the names of other namespaces and types, allowing them to be referenced directly instead of through qualified names. The optional *namespace-member-declarations* contribute members to the declaration space of the namespace. Note that all *using-directives* must appear before any member declarations.

The *qualified-identifier* of a *namespace-declaration* may be a single identifier or a sequence of identifiers separated by . tokens. The latter form permits a program to define a nested namespace without lexically nesting several namespace declarations. The example

```
namespace N1.N2
{
    class A {}

    class B {}
}
```

is semantically equivalent to the following.

```
namespace N1
{
    namespace N2
    {
        class A {}

        class B {}
    }
}
```

Namespaces are open ended, and two namespace declarations with the same fully quali-fied name contribute to the same declaration space (§3.3). In the following example

```
namespace N1.N2
{
    class A {}
}

namespace N1.N2
{
    class B {}
}
```

the previous two namespace declarations contribute to the same declaration space, in this case declaring two classes with the fully qualified names N1.N2.A and N1.N2.B. Because the two declarations contribute to the same declaration space, it would have been an error if each contained a declaration of a member with the same name.

9.3 Using Directives

Using directives facilitate using namespaces and types defined in other namespaces. Using directives impact the name resolution process of *namespace-or-type-names* (§3.8) and *simple-names* (§7.5.2), but unlike declarations, using directives do not contribute new members to the underlying declaration spaces of the compilation units or namespaces within which they are used.

> *using-directives:*
>   *using-directive*
>   *using-directives   using-directive*
>
> *using-directive:*
>   *using-alias-directive*
>   *using-namespace-directive*

A *using-alias-directive* (§9.3.1) introduces an alias for a namespace or type.

A *using-namespace-directive* (§9.3.2) imports the type members of a namespace.

The scope of a *using-directive* extends over the *namespace-member-declarations* of its immediately containing compilation unit or namespace body. The scope of a *using-directive* specifically does not include its peer *using-directive*s. Thus, peer *using-directive*s do not affect each other, and the order in which they are written is insignificant.

9.3.1 Using Alias Directives

A *using-alias-directive* introduces an identifier that serves as an alias for a namespace or type within the immediately enclosing compilation unit or namespace body.

> *using-alias-directive:*
>   using *identifier* = *namespace-or-type-name* ;

Within member declarations in a compilation unit or namespace body that contains a *using-alias-directive*, the identifier introduced by the *using-alias-directive* can be used to reference the given namespace or type. In the example

```
namespace N1.N2
{
    class A {}
}

namespace N3
{
    using A = N1.N2.A;

    class B: A {}
}
```

within member declarations in the N3 namespace, A is an alias for N1.N2.A, and thus the class N3.B derives from the class N1.N2.A. The same effect can be obtained by creating an alias R for N1.N2 and then referencing R.A.

```
namespace N3
{
    using R = N1.N2;

    class B: R.A {}
}
```

The *identifier* of a *using-alias-directive* must be unique within the declaration space of the compilation unit or namespace that immediately contains the *using-alias-directive*. In the example

```
namespace N3
{
    class A {}
}
```

```
namespace N3
{
    using A = N1.N2.A;      // Error, A already exists
}
```

N3 already contains a member A, so it is a compile-time error for a *using-alias-directive* to use that identifier. Likewise, it is a compile-time error for two or more *using-alias-directive*s in the same compilation unit or namespace body to declare aliases by the same name.

A *using-alias-directive* makes an alias available within a particular compilation unit or namespace body, but it does not contribute any new members to the underlying declaration space. In other words, a *using-alias-directive* is not transitive but rather affects only the compilation unit or namespace body in which it occurs. In the example

```
namespace N3
{
    using R = N1.N2;
}

namespace N3
{
    class B: R.A {}         // Error, R unknown
}
```

the scope of the *using-alias-directive* that introduces R only extends to member declarations in the namespace body in which it is contained, so R is unknown in the second namespace declaration. However, placing the *using-alias-directive* in the containing compilation unit causes the alias to become available within both namespace declarations.

```
using R = N1.N2;

namespace N3
{
    class B: R.A {}
}

namespace N3
{
    class C: R.A {}
}
```

Just like regular members, names introduced by *using-alias-directive*s are hidden by similarly named members in nested scopes. In the example

```
using R = N1.N2;

namespace N3
{
    class R {}

    class B: R.A {}         // Error, R has no member A
}
```

the reference to R.A in the declaration of B causes a compile-time error because R refers to N3.R, not N1.N2.

The order in which *using-alias-directive*s are written has no significance, and resolution of the *namespace-or-type-name* referenced by a *using-alias-directive* is not affected by the *using-alias-directive* itself or by other *using-directive*s in the immediately containing compilation unit or namespace body. In other words, the *namespace-or-type-name* of a *using-alias-directive* is resolved as if the immediately containing compilation unit or namespace body had no *using-directive*s. In the example

```
namespace N1.N2 {}

namespace N3
{
    using R1 = N1;          // OK

    using R2 = N1.N2;       // OK

    using R3 = R1.N2;       // Error, R1 unknown
}
```

the last *using-alias-directive* results in a compile-time error because it is not affected by the first *using-alias-directive*.

A *using-alias-directive* can create an alias for any namespace or type, including the namespace within which it appears and any namespace or type nested within that namespace.

Accessing a namespace or type through an alias yields exactly the same result as accessing that namespace or type through its declared name. For example, given the following

```
namespace N1.N2
{
    class A {}
}

namespace N3
{
    using R1 = N1;
    using R2 = N1.N2;

    class B
    {
        N1.N2.A a;          // refers to N1.N2.A
        R1.N2.A b;          // refers to N1.N2.A
        R2.A c;             // refers to N1.N2.A
    }
}
```

the names N1.N2.A, R1.N2.A, and R2.A are equivalent and all refer to the class whose fully qualified name is N1.N2.A.

9.3.2 Using Namespace Directives

A *using-namespace-directive* imports the types contained in a namespace into the immediately enclosing compilation unit or namespace body, enabling the identifier of each type to be used without qualification.

> *using-namespace-directive:*
>   using *namespace-name* ;

Within member declarations in a compilation unit or namespace body that contains a *using-namespace-directive*, the types contained in the given namespace can be referenced directly. In the example

```
namespace N1.N2
{
    class A {}
}

namespace N3
{
    using N1.N2;

    class B: A {}
}
```

within member declarations in the N3 namespace, the type members of N1.N2 are directly available, and thus the class N3.B derives from the class N1.N2.A.

A *using-namespace-directive* imports the types contained in the given namespace but specifically does not import nested namespaces. In the example

```
namespace N1.N2
{
    class A {}
}

namespace N3
{
    using N1;

    class B: N2.A {}   // Error, N2 unknown
}
```

the *using-namespace-directive* imports the types contained in N1, but not the namespaces nested in N1. Thus, the reference to N2.A in the declaration of B results in a compile-time error because no members named N2 are in scope.

Unlike a *using-alias-directive*, a *using-namespace-directive* may import types whose identifiers are already defined within the enclosing compilation unit or namespace body. In effect, names imported by a *using-namespace-directive* are hidden by similarly named members in the enclosing compilation unit or namespace body. In the example

```
namespace N1.N2
{
    class A {}
    class B {}
}
namespace N3
{
    using N1.N2;
    class A {}
}
```

within member declarations in the N3 namespace, A refers to N3.A rather than N1.N2.A.

When more than one namespace imported by *using-namespace-directive*s in the same compilation unit or namespace body contain types by the same name, references to that name are considered ambiguous. In the example

```
namespace N1
{
    class A {}
}
namespace N2
{
    class A {}
}
namespace N3
{
    using N1;
    using N2;
    class B: A {}          // Error, A is ambiguous
}
```

both N1 and N2 contain a member A, and because N3 imports both, referencing A in N3 is a compile-time error. In this situation, the conflict can be resolved through qualification of references to A or by introducing a *using-alias-directive* that picks a particular A. For example

```
namespace N3
{
    using N1;
    using N2;
    using A = N1.A;
    class B: A {}          // A means N1.A
}
```

Like a *using-alias-directive*, a *using-namespace-directive* does not contribute any new members to the underlying declaration space of the compilation unit or namespace but rather affects only the compilation unit or namespace body in which it appears.

The *namespace-name* referenced by a *using-namespace-directive* is resolved in the same way as the *namespace-or-type-name* referenced by a *using-alias-directive*. Thus, *using-namespace-directives* in the same compilation unit or namespace body do not affect each other and can be written in any order.

9.4 Namespace Members

A *namespace-member-declaration* is either a *namespace-declaration* (§9.2) or a *type-declaration* (§9.5).

> *namespace-member-declarations:*
>   *namespace-member-declaration*
>   *namespace-member-declarations*   *namespace-member-declaration*
>
> *namespace-member-declaration:*
>   *namespace-declaration*
>   *type-declaration*

A compilation unit or a namespace body can contain *namespace-member-declarations*, and such declarations contribute new members to the underlying declaration space of the containing compilation unit or namespace body.

9.5 Type Declarations

A *type-declaration* is a *class-declaration* (§10.1), a *struct-declaration* (§11.1), an *interface-declaration* (§13.1), an *enum-declaration* (§14.1), or a *delegate-declaration* (§15.1).

> *type-declaration:*
>   *class-declaration*
>   *struct-declaration*
>   *interface-declaration*
>   *enum-declaration*
>   *delegate-declaration*

A *type-declaration* can occur as a top-level declaration in a compilation unit or as a member declaration within a namespace, class, or struct.

When a type declaration for a type T occurs as a top-level declaration in a compilation unit, the fully qualified name of the newly declared type is simply T. When a type declaration for a type T occurs within a namespace, class, or struct, the fully qualified name of the newly declared type is N.T, where N is the fully qualified name of the containing namespace, class, or struct.

A type declared within a class or struct is called a nested type (§10.2.6).

The permitted access modifiers and the default access for a type declaration depend on the context in which the declaration takes place (§3.5.1).

- Types declared in compilation units or namespaces can have public or internal access. The default is internal access.

- Types declared in classes can have public, protected internal, protected, internal, or private access. The default is private access.

- Types declared in structs can have public, internal, or private access. The default is private access.

10. Classes

A class is a data structure that may contain data members (constants and fields), function members (methods, properties, events, indexers, operators, instance constructors, destructors, and static constructors), and nested types. Class types support inheritance, a mechanism whereby a derived class can extend and specialize a base class.

10.1 Class Declarations

A *class-declaration* is a *type-declaration* (§9.5) that declares a new class.

class-declaration:
    *attributes*_{opt} *class-modifiers*_{opt} `class` *identifier class-base*_{opt} *class-body* ;_{opt}

A *class-declaration* consists of an optional set of *attributes* (§17), followed by an optional set of *class-modifiers* (§10.1.1), followed by the keyword `class` and an *identifier* that names the class, followed by an optional *class-base* specification (§10.1.2), followed by a *class-body* (§10.1.3), optionally followed by a semicolon.

10.1.1 Class Modifiers

A *class-declaration* may optionally include a sequence of class modifiers.

class-modifiers:
    class-modifier
    class-modifiers   class-modifier

class-modifier:
   `new`
   `public`
   `protected`
   `internal`
   `private`
   `abstract`
   `sealed`

It is a compile-time error for the same modifier to appear multiple times in a class declaration.

✗ The new modifier is permitted on nested classes. It specifies that the class hides an inherited member by the same name, as described in §10.2.2. It is a compile-time error for the new modifier to appear on a class declaration that is not a nested class declaration.

The public, protected, internal, and private modifiers control the accessibility of the class. Depending on the context in which the class declaration occurs, some of these modifiers may not be permitted (§3.5.1).

The abstract and sealed modifiers are discussed in the following sections.

10.1.1.1 *Abstract Classes*

The abstract modifier is used to indicate that a class is incomplete and that it is intended to be used only as a base class. An abstract class differs from a nonabstract class in the following ways.

- An abstract class cannot be instantiated directly, and it is a compile-time error to use the new operator on an abstract class. Although it is possible to have variables and values whose compile-time types are abstract, such variables and values will necessarily either be null or contain references to instances of nonabstract classes derived from the abstract types.

- An abstract class is permitted (but not required) to contain abstract members.

- An abstract class cannot be sealed.

When a nonabstract class is derived from an abstract class, the nonabstract class must include actual implementations of all inherited abstract members, thereby overriding those abstract members. In the example

```
abstract class A
{
    public abstract void F();
}

abstract class B: A
{
    public void G() {}
}

class C: B
{
    public override void F() {
        // actual implementation of F
    }
}
```

the abstract class A introduces an abstract method F. Class B introduces an additional method G, but because it does not provide an implementation of F, B must also be declared abstract. Class C overrides F and provides an actual implementation. Because there are no abstract members in C, C is permitted (but not required) to be nonabstract.

10.1.1.2 *Sealed Classes*

The sealed modifier is used to prevent derivation from a class. A compile-time error occurs if a sealed class is specified as the base class of another class.

A sealed class cannot also be an abstract class.

The sealed modifier is primarily used to prevent unintended derivation, but it also enables certain run-time optimizations. In particular, because a sealed class is known to never have any derived classes, it is possible to transform virtual function member invocations on sealed class instances into nonvirtual invocations.

10.1.2 Class Base Specification

A class declaration may include a *class-base* specification, which defines the direct base class of the class and the interfaces (§13) implemented by the class.

> *class-base:*
>   :   *class-type*
>   :   *interface-type-list*
>   :   *class-type*   ,   *interface-type-list*
>
> *interface-type-list:*
>   *interface-type*
>   *interface-type-list*   ,   *interface-type*

10.1.2.1 *Base Classes*

When a *class-type* is included in the *class-base*, it specifies the direct base class of the class being declared. If a class declaration has no *class-base* or if the *class-base* lists only interface types, the direct base class is assumed to be object. A class inherits members from its direct base class, as described in §10.2.1.

In the example

```
class A {}
class B: A {}
```

class A is said to be the direct base class of B, and B is said to be derived from A. Because A does not explicitly specify a direct base class, its direct base class is implicitly object.

The direct base class of a class type must be at least as accessible as the class type itself (§3.5.4). For example, it is a compile-time error for a `public` class to derive from a `private` or `internal` class.

The direct base class of a class type must not be any of the following types: `System.Array`, `System.Delegate`, `System.Enum`, or `System.ValueType`.

The base classes of a class are the direct base class and its base classes. In other words, the set of base classes is the transitive closure of the direct base class relationship. Referring to the previous example, the base classes of B are A and `object`.

Except for class `object`, every class has exactly one direct base class. The `object` class has no direct base class and is the ultimate base class of all other classes.

When a class B derives from a class A, it is a compile-time error for A to depend on B. A class *directly depends on* its direct base class (if any) and *directly depends on* the class within which it is immediately nested (if any). Given this definition, the complete set of classes upon which a class depends is the transitive closure of the *directly depends on* relationship.

The example

```
class A: B {}
class B: C {}
class C: A {}
```

is in error because the classes circularly depend on themselves. Likewise, the example

```
class A: B.C {}
class B: A
{
    public class C {}
}
```

results in a compile-time error because A depends on B.C (its direct base class), which depends on B (its immediately enclosing class), which circularly depends on A.

Note that a class does not depend on the classes that are nested within it. In the example

```
class A
{
    class B: A {}
}
```

B depends on A (because A is both its direct base class and its immediately enclosing class), but A does not depend on B (because B is neither a base class nor an enclosing class of A). Thus, the example is valid.

It is not possible to derive from a `sealed` class. In the example

```
sealed class A {}

class B: A {}      // Error, cannot derive from a sealed class
```

class B is in error because it attempts to derive from the `sealed` class A.

10.1.2.2 *Interface Implementations*
A *class-base* specification may include a list of interface types, in which case the class is said to implement the given interface types. Interface implementations are discussed further in §13.4.

10.1.3 Class Body
The *class-body* of a class defines the members of that class.

class-body:
    { *class-member-declarations$_{opt}$*   }

10.2 Class Members

The members of a class consist of the members introduced by its *class-member-declaration*s and the members inherited from the direct base class.

class-member-declarations:
    class-member-declaration
    class-member-declarations   class-member-declaration

class-member-declaration:
    constant-declaration √
    field-declaration
    method-declaration
    property-declaration
    event-declaration
    indexer-declaration
    operator-declaration
    constructor-declaration
    destructor-declaration
    static-constructor-declaration
    type-declaration

The members of a class are divided into the following categories:

- Constants, which represent constant values associated with the class (§10.3)
- Fields, which are the variables of the class (§10.4)
- Methods, which implement the computations and actions that can be performed by the class (§10.5)
- Properties, which define named characteristics and the actions associated with reading and writing those characteristics (§10.6)
- Events, which define notifications that can be generated by the class (§10.7)
- Indexers, which permit instances of the class to be indexed in the same way (syntactically) as arrays (§10.8)
- Operators, which define the expression operators that can be applied to instances of the class (§10.9)
- Instance constructors, which implement the actions required to initialize instances of the class (§10.10)
- Destructors, which implement the actions to be performed before instances of the class are permanently discarded (§10.12)
- Static constructors, which implement the actions required to initialize the class itself (§10.11)
- Types, which represent the types that are local to the class (§9.5)

Members that can contain executable code are collectively known as the *function members* of the class. The function members of a class are the methods, properties, events, indexers, operators, instance constructors, destructors, and static constructors of that class.

A *class-declaration* creates a new declaration space (§3.3), and the *class-member-declarations* immediately contained by the *class-declaration* introduce new members into this declaration space. The following rules apply to *class-member-declarations*.

- Instance constructors, destructors, and static constructors must have the same name as the immediately enclosing class. All other members must have names that differ from the name of the immediately enclosing class.
- The name of a constant, field, property, event, or type must differ from the names of all other members declared in the same class.
- The name of a method must differ from the names of all other nonmethods declared in the same class. In addition, the signature (§3.6) of a method must differ from the signatures of all other methods declared in the same class.

- The signature of an instance constructor must differ from the signatures of all other instance constructors declared in the same class.

- The signature of an indexer must differ from the signatures of all other indexers declared in the same class.

- The signature of an operator must differ from the signatures of all other operators declared in the same class.

The inherited members of a class (§10.2.1) are not part of the declaration space of a class. Thus, a derived class is allowed to declare a member with the same name or signature as an inherited member (which in effect hides the inherited member).

10.2.1 Inheritance

A class *inherits* the members of its direct base class. Inheritance means that a class implicitly contains all members of its direct base class except for the instance constructors, destructors, and static constructors of the base class. Some important aspects of inheritance are as follows.

- Inheritance is transitive. If C is derived from B, and B is derived from A, then C inherits the members declared in B as well as the members declared in A.

- A derived class *extends* its direct base class. A derived class can add new members to those it inherits, but it cannot remove the definition of an inherited member.

- Instance constructors, destructors, and static constructors are not inherited, but all other members are, regardless of their declared accessibility (§3.5). However, depending on their declared accessibility, inherited members might not be accessible in a derived class.

- A derived class can *hide* (§3.7.1.2) inherited members by declaring new members with the same name or signature. Note, however, that hiding an inherited member does not remove that member—it merely makes that member inaccessible directly through the derived class.

- An instance of a class contains a set of all instance fields declared in the class and its base classes, and an implicit conversion (§6.1.4) exists from a derived class type to any of its base class types. Thus, a reference to an instance of some derived class can be treated as a reference to an instance of any of its base classes.

- A class can declare virtual methods, properties, and indexers, and derived classes can override the implementation of these function members. This enables classes to exhibit polymorphic behavior wherein the actions performed by a function member invocation varies depending on the runtime type of the instance through which that function member is invoked.

10. Classes

10.2.2 The new Modifier

A *class-member-declaration* is permitted to declare a member with the same name or signature as an inherited member. When this occurs, the derived class member is said to hide the base class member. Hiding an inherited member is not considered an error, but it does cause the compiler to issue a warning. To suppress the warning, the declaration of the derived class member can include a new modifier to indicate that the derived member is intended to hide the base member. This topic is discussed further in §3.7.1.2.

If a new modifier is included in a declaration that does not hide an inherited member, a warning to that effect is issued. This warning is suppressed by removing the new modifier.

10.2.3 Access Modifiers

A *class-member-declaration* can have any one of the five possible kinds of declared accessibility (§3.5.1): public, protected internal, protected, internal, or private. Except for the protected internal combination, it is a compile-time error to specify more than one access modifier. When a *class-member-declaration* does not include any access modifiers, private is assumed.

10.2.4 Constituent Types

Types that are used in the declaration of a member are called the constituent types of that member. Possible constituent types are the type of a constant, field, property, event, or indexer, the return type of a method or operator, and the parameter types of a method, indexer, operator, or instance constructor. The constituent types of a member must be at least as accessible as that member itself (§3.5.4).

10.2.5 Static and Instance Members

Members of a class are either *static members* or *instance members*. Generally speaking, it is useful to think of static members as belonging to classes and instance members as belonging to objects (instances of classes).

When a field, method, property, event, operator, or constructor declaration includes a static modifier, it declares a static member. In addition, a constant or type declaration implicitly declares a static member. Static members have the following characteristics.

- When a static member M is referenced in a *member-access* (§7.5.4) of the form E.M, E must denote a type containing M. It is a compile-time error for E to denote an instance.

- A static field identifies exactly one storage location. No matter how many instances of a class are created, there is only ever one copy of a static field.

- A static function member (method, property, event, operator, or constructor) does not operate on a specific instance, and it is a compile-time error to refer to this in such a function member.

When a field, method, property, event, indexer, constructor, or destructor declaration does not include a `static` modifier, it declares an instance member. (An instance member is sometimes called a nonstatic member.) Instance members have the following characteristics.

- When an instance member `M` is referenced in a *member-access* (§7.5.4) of the form `E.M`, `E` must denote an instance of a type containing `M`. It is a compile-time error for `E` to denote a type.

- Every instance of a class contains a separate set of all instance fields of the class.

- An instance function member (method, property, indexer, instance constructor, or destructor) operates on a given instance of the class, and this instance can be accessed as `this` (§7.5.7).

The following example illustrates the rules for accessing static and instance members.

```
class Test
{
    int x;
    static int y;

    void F() {
        x = 1;          // Ok, same as this.x = 1
        y = 1;          // Ok, same as Test.y = 1
    }

    static void G() {
        x = 1;          // Error, cannot access this.x
        y = 1;          // Ok, same as Test.y = 1
    }

    static void Main() {
        Test t = new Test();
        t.x = 1;        // Ok
        t.y = 1;        // Error, cannot access static member through instance
        Test.x = 1;     // Error, cannot access instance member through type
        Test.y = 1;     // Ok
    }
}
```

The `F` method shows that in an instance function member, a *simple-name* (§7.5.2) can be used to access both instance members and static members. The `G` method shows that in a static function member, it is a compile-time error to access an instance member through a *simple-name*. The `Main` method shows that in a *member-access* (§7.5.4), instance members must be accessed through instances, and static members must be accessed through types.

10.2.6 Nested Types

A type declared within a class or struct is called a **nested type**. A type that is declared within a compilation unit or namespace is called a **non-nested type**.

In the example

```
using System;
class A
{
    class B
    {
        static void F() {
            Console.WriteLine("A.B.F");
        }
    }
}
```

class B is a nested type because it is declared within class A, and class A is a non-nested type because it is declared within a compilation unit.

10.2.6.1 *Fully Qualified Name*

The fully qualified name (§3.8.1) for a nested type is S.N, where S is the fully qualified name of the type in which type N is declared.

10.2.6.2 *Declared Accessibility*

Non-nested types can have public or internal declared accessibility and have internal declared accessibility by default. Nested types can also have these forms of declared accessibility, plus one or more additional forms of declared accessibility, depending on whether the containing type is a class or struct.

- A nested type that is declared in a class can have any of five forms of declared accessibility (public, protected internal, protected, internal, or private) and, like other class members, defaults to private declared accessibility.

- A nested type that is declared in a struct can have any of three forms of declared accessibility (public, internal, or private) and, like other struct members, defaults to private declared accessibility.

The example

```
public class List
{
    // Private data structure
    private class Node
    {
        public object Data;
        public Node Next;

        public Node(object data, Node next) {
            this.Data = data;
            this.Next = next;
        }
    }
```

```
        private Node first = null;
        private Node last = null;

        // Public interface

        public void AddToFront(object o) {...}

        public void AddToBack(object o) {...}

        public object RemoveFromFront() {...}

        public object RemoveFromBack() {...}

        public int Count { get {...} }
    }
```

declares a private nested class Node.

10.2.6.3 *Hiding*
A nested type may hide (§3.7.1) a base member. The new modifier is permitted on nested type declarations so that hiding can be expressed explicitly. The example

```
using System;
class Base
{
    public static void M() {
        Console.WriteLine("Base.M");
    }
}
class Derived: Base
{
    new public class M
    {
        public static void F() {
            Console.WriteLine("Derived.M.F");
        }
    }
}
class Test
{
    static void Main() {
        Derived.M.F();
    }
}
```

shows a nested class M that hides the method M defined in Base.

10.2.6.4 *This Access*
A nested type and its containing type have a special relationship with regard to *this-access* (§7.5.7). Specifically, this within a nested type cannot be used to refer to instance members of the containing type. In cases where a nested type needs access to the instance members of its containing type, access can be provided by providing the this for the

instance of the containing type as a constructor argument for the nested type. The following example

```
using System;
class C
{
    int i = 123;
    public void F() {
        Nested n = new Nested(this);
        n.G();
    }
    public class Nested {
        C this_c;
        public Nested(C c) {
            this_c = c;
        }
        public void G() {
            Console.WriteLine(this_c.i);
        }
    }
}
class Test {
    static void Main() {
        C c = new C();
        c.F();
    }
}
```

shows this technique. An instance of C creates an instance of Nested and passes its own this to Nested's constructor to provide subsequent access to C's instance members.

10.2.6.5 *Access to Private and Protected Members of the Containing Type*

A nested type has access to all of the members that are accessible to its containing type, including members of the containing type that have private and protected declared accessibility. The example

```
using System;
class C
{
    private static void F() {
        Console.WriteLine("C.F");
    }
```

```
    public class Nested
    {
        public static void G() {
            F();
        }
    }
}

class Test
{
    static void Main() {
        C.Nested.G();
    }
}
```

shows a class C that contains a nested class Nested. Within Nested, the method G calls the static method F defined in C, and F has private declared accessibility.

A nested type also may access protected members defined in a base type of its containing type. In the example

```
using System;

class Base
{
    protected void F() {
        Console.WriteLine("Base.F");
    }
}

class Derived: Base
{
    public class Nested
    {
        public void G() {
            Derived d = new Derived();
            d.F();      // ok
        }
    }
}

class Test
{
    static void Main() {
        Derived.Nested n = new Derived.Nested();
        n.G();
    }
}
```

the nested class Derived.Nested accesses the protected method F defined in Derived's base class, Base, by calling through an instance of Derived.

10.2.7 Reserved Member Names

To facilitate the underlying C# runtime implementation, for each source member declaration that is a property, event, or indexer, the implementation must reserve two method signatures based on the kind of the member declaration, its name, and its type. It is a compile-time error for a program to declare a member whose signature matches one of these reserved signatures, even if the underlying runtime implementation does not use these reservations.

The reserved names do not introduce declarations, thus they do not participate in member lookup. However, a declaration's associated reserved method signatures do participate in inheritance (§10.2.1) and can be hidden with the new modifier (§10.2.2).

The reservation of these names serves three purposes:

- To allow the underlying implementation to use an ordinary identifier as a method name for get or set access to the C# language feature

- To allow other languages to interoperate using an ordinary identifier as a method name for get or set access to the C# language feature

- To help ensure that the source accepted by one conforming compiler is accepted by another by making the specifics of reserved member names consistent across all C# implementations

The declaration of a destructor (§10.12) also causes a signature to be reserved (§10.2.7.4).

10.2.7.1 *Member Names Reserved for Properties*

For a property P (§10.6) of type T, the following signatures are reserved.

```
T get_P();
void set_P(T value);
```

Both signatures are reserved, even if the property is read-only or write-only.

In the example

```
using System;
class A
{
    public int P {
        get { return 123; }
    }
}
class B: A
{
    new public int get_P() {
        return 456;
    }
```

```
        new public void set_P(int value) {
        }
    }
    class Test
    {
        static void Main() {
            B b = new B();
            A a = b;
            Console.WriteLine(a.P);
            Console.WriteLine(b.P);
            Console.WriteLine(b.get_P());
        }
    }
```

a class A defines a read-only property P, thus reserving signatures for `get_P` and `set_P` methods. A class B derives from A and hides both of these reserved signatures. The example produces the following output.

```
123
123
456
```

10.2.7.2 *Member Names Reserved for Events*
For an event E (§10.7) of delegate type T, the following signatures are reserved.

```
void add_E(T handler);
void remove_E(T handler);
```

10.2.7.3 *Member Names Reserved for Indexers*
For an indexer (§10.8) of type T with parameter list L, the following signatures are reserved.

```
T get_Item(L);
void set_Item(L, T value);
```

Both signatures are reserved, even if the indexer is read-only or write-only.

10.2.7.4 *Member Names Reserved for Destructors*
For a class containing a destructor (§10.12), the following signature is reserved.

```
void Finalize();
```

10.3 **Constants**

A *constant* is a class member that represents a constant value (a value that can be computed at compile time). A *constant-declaration* introduces one or more constants of a given type.

constant-declaration:
    attributes$_{opt}$ *constant-modifiers*$_{opt}$ `const` *type* *constant-declarators* `;`

constant-modifiers:
    constant-modifier
    constant-modifiers *constant-modifier*

constant-modifier:
    `new`
    `public`
    `protected`
    `internal`
    `private`

constant-declarators:
    constant-declarator
    constant-declarators `,` *constant-declarator*

constant-declarator:
    identifier `=` *constant-expression*

A *constant-declaration* may include a set of *attributes* (§17), a `new` modifier (§10.2.2), and a valid combination of the four access modifiers (§10.2.3). The attributes and modifiers apply to all of the members declared by the *constant-declaration*. Even though constants are considered static members, a *constant-declaration* neither requires nor allows a `static` modifier. It is an error for the same modifier to appear multiple times in a constant declaration.

The *type* of a *constant-declaration* specifies the type of the members introduced by the declaration. The type is followed by a list of *constant-declarator*s, each of which introduces a new member. A *constant-declarator* consists of an *identifier* that names the member, followed by an = token, followed by a *constant-expression* (§7.15) that gives the value of the member.

The *type* specified in a constant declaration must be `sbyte`, `byte`, `short`, `ushort`, `int`, `uint`, `long`, `ulong`, `char`, `float`, `double`, `decimal`, `bool`, `string`, an *enum-type*, or a *reference-type*. Each *constant-expression* must yield a value of the target type or of a type that can be converted to the target type by an implicit conversion (§6.1).

The *type* of a constant must be at least as accessible as the constant itself (§3.5.4).

The value of a constant is obtained in an expression using a *simple-name* (§7.5.2) or a *member-access* (§7.5.4).

A constant can itself participate in a *constant-expression*. Thus, a constant may be used in any construct that requires a *constant-expression*. Examples of such constructs include `case` labels, `goto case` statements, `enum` member declarations, attributes, and other constant declarations.

As described in §7.15, a *constant-expression* is an expression that can be fully evaluated at compile time. Because the only way to create a non-null value of a *reference-type* other than `string` is to apply the `new` operator, and because the `new` operator is not permitted in a *constant-expression*, the only possible value for constants of *reference-types* other than `string` is `null`.

When a symbolic name for a constant value is desired but when the type of that value is not permitted in a constant declaration or when the value cannot be computed at compile time by a *constant-expression*, a `readonly` field (§10.4.2) may be used instead.

A constant declaration that declares multiple constants is equivalent to multiple declarations of single constants with the same attributes, modifiers, and type. For example

```
class A
{
    public const double X = 1.0, Y = 2.0, Z = 3.0;
}
```

is equivalent to the following.

```
class A
{
    public const double X = 1.0;
    public const double Y = 2.0;
    public const double Z = 3.0;
}
```

Constants are permitted to depend on other constants within the same program as long as the dependencies are not of a circular nature. The compiler automatically arranges to evaluate the constant declarations in the appropriate order. In the example

```
class A
{
    public const int X = B.Z + 1;
    public const int Y = 10;
}
class B
{
    public const int Z = A.Y + 1;
}
```

the compiler first evaluates `A.Y`, then evaluates `B.Z`, and finally evaluates `A.X`, producing the values `10`, `11`, and `12`. Constant declarations may depend on constants from other programs, but such dependencies are only possible in one direction. Referring to the previous example, if `A` and `B` were declared in separate programs, it would be possible for `A.X` to depend on `B.Z`, but `B.Z` could then not simultaneously depend on `A.Y`.

10. Classes

10.4 Fields

A ***field*** is a member that represents a variable associated with an object or class. A *field-declaration* introduces one or more fields of a given type.

field-declaration:
    attributes$_{opt}$ *field-modifiers*$_{opt}$ *type* *variable-declarators* ;

field-modifiers:
    field-modifier
    field-modifiers *field-modifier*

field-modifier:
    `new`
    `public`
    `protected`
    `internal`
    `private`
    `static`
    `readonly`
    `volatile`

variable-declarators:
    variable-declarator
    variable-declarators , *variable-declarator*

variable-declarator:
    identifier
    identifier = *variable-initializer*

variable-initializer:
    expression
    array-initializer

A *field-declaration* may include a set of *attributes* (§17), a `new` modifier (§10.2.2), a valid combination of the four access modifiers (§10.2.3), and a `static` modifier (§10.4.1). In addition, a *field-declaration* may include a `readonly` modifier (§10.4.2) or a `volatile` modifier (§10.4.3) but not both. The attributes and modifiers apply to all of the members declared by the *field-declaration*. It is an error for the same modifier to appear multiple times in a field declaration.

The *type* of a *field-declaration* specifies the type of the members introduced by the declaration. The type is followed by a list of *variable-declarators*, each of which introduces a new member. A *variable-declarator* consists of an *identifier* that names that member, optionally followed by an = token and a *variable-initializer* (§10.4.5) that gives the initial value of that member.

The *type* of a field must be at least as accessible as the field itself (§3.5.4).

The value of a field is obtained in an expression using a *simple-name* (§7.5.2) or a *member-access* (§7.5.4). The value of a non-read-only field is modified using an *assignment* (§7.13). The value of a non-read-only field can be both obtained and modified using postfix increment and decrement operators (§7.5.9) and prefix increment and decrement operators (§7.6.5).

A field declaration that declares multiple fields is equivalent to multiple declarations of single fields with the same attributes, modifiers, and type. For example

```
class A
{
    public static int X = 1, Y, Z = 100;
}
```

is equivalent to the following.

```
class A
{
    public static int X = 1;
    public static int Y;
    public static int Z = 100;
}
```

10.4.1 Static and Instance Fields

When a field declaration includes a `static` modifier, the fields introduced by the declaration are *static fields*. When no `static` modifier is present, the fields introduced by the declaration are *instance fields*. Static fields and instance fields are two of the several kinds of variables (§5) supported by C#, and at times they are referred to as *static variables* and *instance variables*, respectively.

A static field is not part of a specific instance; instead, it identifies exactly one storage location. No matter how many instances of a class are created, there is only ever one copy of a static field for the associated application domain.

An instance field belongs to an instance. Specifically, every instance of a class contains a separate set of all the instance fields of that class.

When a field is referenced in a *member-access* (§7.5.4) of the form E.M, if M is a static field, E must denote a type containing M, and if M is an instance field, E must denote an instance of a type containing M.

The differences between static and instance members are discussed further in §10.2.5.

10.4.2 Read-Only Fields

When a *field-declaration* includes a `readonly` modifier, the fields introduced by the decla-ration are ***read-only fields***. Direct assignments to read-only fields can only occur as part of that declaration or in an instance constructor or static constructor in the same class. (A read-only field can be assigned to multiple times in these contexts.) Specifically, direct assignments to a `readonly` field are permitted only in the following contexts.

- In the *variable-declarator* that introduces the field (by including a *variable-initializer* in the declaration).

- For an instance field, in the instance constructors of the class that contains the field dec-laration; for a static field, in the static constructor of the class that contains the field declaration. These are also the only contexts in which it is valid to pass a `readonly` field as an `out` or `ref` parameter.

Attempting to assign to a `readonly` field or pass it as an `out` or `ref` parameter in any other context is a compile-time error.

10.4.2.1 *Using Static Read-Only Fields for Constants*

A `static readonly` field is useful when a symbolic name for a constant value is desired but when the type of the value is not permitted in a `const` declaration or when the value cannot be computed at compile time. In the example

```
public class Color
{
    public static readonly Color Black = new Color(0, 0, 0);
    public static readonly Color White = new Color(255, 255, 255);
    public static readonly Color Red = new Color(255, 0, 0);
    public static readonly Color Green = new Color(0, 255, 0);
    public static readonly Color Blue = new Color(0, 0, 255);

    private byte red, green, blue;

    public Color(byte r, byte g, byte b) {
        red = r;
        green = g;
        blue = b;
    }
}
```

the `Black`, `White`, `Red`, `Green`, and `Blue` members cannot be declared as `const` mem-bers because their values cannot be computed at compile time. However, declaring them `static readonly` instead has much the same effect.

10.4.2.2 *Versioning of Constants and Static Read-Only Fields*

Constants and read-only fields have different binary versioning semantics. When an expression references a constant, the value of the constant is obtained at compile time, but when an expression references a read-only field, the value of the field is not obtained until runtime. Consider an application that consists of two separate programs.

```
using System;

namespace Program1
{
    public class Utils
    {
        public static readonly int X = 1;
    }
}

namespace Program2
{
    class Test
    {
        static void Main() {
            Console.WriteLine(Program1.Utils.X);
        }
    }
}
```

The `Program1` and `Program2` namespaces denote two programs that are compiled separately. Because `Program1.Utils.X` is declared as a static read-only field, the value output by the `Console.WriteLine` statement is not known at compile time, but rather is obtained at runtime. Thus, if the value of `X` is changed and `Program1` is recompiled, the `Console.WriteLine` statement will output the new value even if `Program2` is not recompiled. However, had `X` been a constant, the value of `X` would have been obtained at the time `Program2` was compiled and would remain unaffected by changes in `Program1` until `Program2` is recompiled.

10.4.3 Volatile Fields

When a *field-declaration* includes a `volatile` modifier, the fields introduced by that declaration are *volatile fields*.

For nonvolatile fields, optimization techniques that reorder instructions can lead to unexpected and unpredictable results in multi-threaded programs that access fields without synchronization such as that provided by the *lock-statement* (§8.12). These optimizations can be performed by the compiler, by the runtime system, or by hardware. For volatile fields, such reordering optimizations are restricted.

- A read of a volatile field is called a *volatile read*. A volatile read has "acquire semantics"; that is, it is guaranteed to occur prior to any references to memory that occur after it in the instruction sequence.

- A write of a volatile field is called a *volatile write*. A volatile write has "release semantics"; that is, it is guaranteed to happen after any memory references prior to the write instruction in the instruction sequence.

These restrictions ensure that all threads will observe volatile writes performed by any other thread in the order in which they were performed. A conforming implementation is not required to provide a single total ordering of volatile writes as seen from all threads of execution. The type of a volatile field must be one of the following:

- A *reference-type*
- The type byte, sbyte, short, ushort, int, uint, char, float, or bool
- An *enum-type* having an enum base type of byte, sbyte, short, ushort, int, or uint

The example

```
using System;
using System.Threading;

class Test
{
    public static int result;
    public static volatile bool finished;

    static void Thread2() {
        result = 143;
        finished = true;
    }

    static void Main() {
        finished = false;
        // Run Thread2() in a new thread
        new Thread(new ThreadStart(Thread2)).Start();

        // Wait for Thread2 to signal that it has a result by setting
        // finished to true.
        for (;;) {
            if (finished) {
                Console.WriteLine("result = {0}", result);
                return;
            }
        }
    }
}
```

produces the following output.

```
result = 143
```

In this example, the method Main starts a new thread that runs the method Thread2. This method stores a value into a nonvolatile field called result and then stores true in the volatile field finished. The main thread waits for the field finished to be set to true and then reads the field result. Because finished has been declared volatile, the main thread must read the value 143 from the field result. If the field finished had not been declared volatile, then it would be permissible for the store to result to be visible to the main thread *after* the store to finished and hence for the main thread to read the value 0 from the field result. Declaring finished as a volatile field prevents any such inconsistency.

10.4.4 Field Initialization

The initial value of a field, whether it be a static field or an instance field, is the default value (§5.2) of the field's type. It is not possible to observe the value of a field before this default initialization has occurred, and a field is thus never "uninitialized." The example

```
using System;
class Test
{
    static bool b;
    int i;

    static void Main() {
        Test t = new Test();
        Console.WriteLine("b = {0}, i = {1}", b, t.i);
    }
}
```

produces the output

```
b = False, i = 0
```

because b and i are both automatically initialized to default values.

10.4.5 Variable Initializers

Field declarations may include *variable-initializers*. For static fields, variable initializers correspond to assignment statements that are executed during class initialization. For instance fields, variable initializers correspond to assignment statements that are executed when an instance of the class is created.

The example

```
using System;
```

```
class Test
{
    static double x = Math.Sqrt(2.0);
    int i = 100;
    string s = "Hello";

    static void Main() {
        Test a = new Test();
        Console.WriteLine("x = {0}, i = {1}, s = {2}", x, a.i, a.s);
    }
}
```

produces the output

```
x = 1.4142135623731, i = 100, s = Hello
```

because an assignment to x occurs when static field initializers execute, and assignments to i and s occur when the instance field initializers execute.

The default value initialization described in §10.4.4 occurs for all fields, including fields that have variable initializers. Thus, when a class is initialized, all static fields in that class are first initialized to their default values, and then the static field initializers are executed in textual order. Likewise, when an instance of a class is created, all instance fields in that instance are first initialized to their default values, and then the instance field initializers are executed in textual order.

It is possible for static fields with variable initializers to be observed in their default value state. However, this is strongly discouraged as a matter of style. The example

```
using System;

class Test
{
    static int a = b + 1;
    static int b = a + 1;

    static void Main() {
        Console.WriteLine("a = {0}, b = {1}", a, b);
    }
}
```

exhibits this behavior. Despite the circular definitions of a and b, the program is valid. It results in the output

```
a = 1, b = 2
```

because the static fields a and b are initialized to 0 (the default value for int) before their initializers are executed. When the initializer for a runs, the value of b is zero, so a is initialized to 1. When the initializer for b runs, the value of a is already 1, so b is initialized to 2.

10.4.5.1 *Static Field Initialization*

The static field variable initializers of a class correspond to a sequence of assignments that are executed in the textual order in which they appear in the class declaration. If a static constructor (§10.11) exists in the class, execution of the static field initializers occurs immediately prior to executing that static constructor. Otherwise, the static field initializers are executed at an implementation-dependent time prior to the first use of a static field of that class. The example

```
using System;

class Test
{
    static void Main() {
        Console.WriteLine("{0} {1}", B.Y, A.X);
    }

    public static int F(string s) {
        Console.WriteLine(s);
        return 1;
    }
}
class A
{
    public static int X = Test.F("Init A");
}
class B
{
    public static int Y = Test.F("Init B");
}
```

might produce either the output

```
Init A
Init B
1 1
```

or the output

```
Init B
Init A
1 1
```

because the execution of X's initializer and Y's initializer could occur in either order; they are only constrained to occur before the references to those fields. However, in the example

```
using System;

class Test
{
    static void Main() {
        Console.WriteLine("{0} {1}", B.Y, A.X);
    }
```

```
        public static int F(string s) {
            Console.WriteLine(s);
            return 1;
        }
    }
    class A
    {
        static A() {}
        public static int X = Test.F("Init A");
    }
    class B
    {
        static B() {}
        public static int Y = Test.F("Init B");
    }
```

the output must be as follows.

```
    Init B
    Init A
    1 1
```

because the rules for when static constructors execute (as defined in §10.11) state that B's static constructor (and hence B's static field initializers) must run before A's static constructor and field initializers.

10.4.5.2 *Instance Field Initialization*

The instance field variable initializers of a class correspond to a sequence of assignments that are executed immediately upon entry to any one of the instance constructors (§10.10.1) of that class. The variable initializers are executed in the textual order in which they appear in the class declaration. The class instance creation and initialization process is described further in §10.10.

A variable initializer for an instance field cannot reference the instance being created. Thus, it is a compile-time error to reference this in a variable initializer, as it is a compile-time error for a variable initializer to reference any instance member through a *simple-name*. In the example

```
    class A
    {
        int x = 1;
        int y = x + 1; // Error, reference to instance member of this
    }
```

the variable initializer for y results in a compile-time error because it references a member of the instance being created.

10.5 Methods

A **method** is a member that implements a computation or action that can be performed by an object or class. Methods are declared using *method-declarations*.

> *method-declaration:*
>   *method-header method-body*
>
> *method-header:*
>   *attributes$_{opt}$ method-modifiers$_{opt}$ return-type member-name*
>   (*formal-parameter-list$_{opt}$*)
>
> *method-modifiers:*
>   *method-modifier*
>   *method-modifiers method-modifier*
>
> *method-modifier:*
>   `new`
>   `public`
>   `protected`
>   `internal`
>   `private`
>   `static`
>   `virtual`
>   `sealed`
>   `override`
>   `abstract`
>   `extern`
>
> *return-type:*
>   *type*
>   `void`
>
> *member-name:*
>   *identifier*
>   *interface-type . identifier*
>
> *method-body:*
>   *block*
>   ;

A *method-declaration* may include a set of *attributes* (§17) and a valid combination of the four access modifiers (§10.2.3), the `new` (§10.2.2), `static` (§10.5.2), `virtual` (§10.5.3), `override` (§10.5.4), `sealed` (§10.5.5), `abstract` (§10.5.6), and `extern` (§10.5.7) modifiers.

A declaration has a valid combination of modifiers if all of the following are true.

- The declaration includes a valid combination of access modifiers (§10.2.3).
- The declaration does not include the same modifier multiple times.
- The declaration includes at most one of the following modifiers: `static`, `virtual`, and `override`.
- The declaration includes at most one of the following modifiers: `new` and `override`.
- If the declaration includes the `abstract` modifier, then the declaration does not include any of the following modifiers: `static`, `virtual`, `sealed` or `extern`.
- If the declaration includes the `private` modifier, then the declaration does not include any of the following modifiers: `virtual`, `override`, or `abstract`.
- If the declaration includes the `sealed` modifier, then the declaration also includes the `override` modifier.

The *return-type* of a method declaration specifies the type of the value computed and returned by the method. The *return-type* is `void` if the method does not return a value.

The *member-name* specifies the name of the method. Unless the method is an explicit interface member implementation (§13.4.1), the *member-name* is simply an *identifier*. For an explicit interface member implementation, the *member-name* consists of an *interface-type* followed by a " . " and an *identifier*.

The optional *formal-parameter-list* specifies the parameters of the method (§10.5.1).

The *return-type* and each of the types referenced in the *formal-parameter-list* of a method must be at least as accessible as the method itself (§3.5.4).

For `abstract` and `extern` methods, the *method-body* consists simply of a semicolon. For all other methods, the *method-body* consists of a *block*, which specifies the statements to execute when the method is invoked.

The name and the formal parameter list of a method define the signature (§3.6) of the method. Specifically, the signature of a method consists of its name and the number, modifiers, and types of its formal parameters. The return type is not part of a method's signature, and the names of the formal parameters are not part of the method's signature.

The name of a method must differ from the names of all other nonmethods declared in the same class. In addition, the signature of a method must differ from the signatures of all other methods declared in the same class.

10.5.1 **Method Parameters**

The parameters of a method, if any, are declared by the method's *formal-parameter-list*.

> *formal-parameter-list:*
>   *fixed-parameters*
>   *fixed-parameters* , *parameter-array*
>   *parameter-array*
>
> *fixed-parameters:*
>   *fixed-parameter*
>   *fixed-parameters* , *fixed-parameter*
>
> *fixed-parameter:*
>   *attributes*$_{opt}$ *parameter-modifier*$_{opt}$ *type* *identifier*
>
> *parameter-modifier:*
>   `ref`
>   `out`
>
> *parameter-array:*
>   *attributes*$_{opt}$ `params` *array-type* *identifier*

The formal parameter list consists of one or more comma-separated parameters of which only the last may be a *parameter-array*.

A *fixed-parameter* consists of an optional set of *attributes* (§17), an optional `ref` or `out` modifier, a *type*, and an *identifier*. Each *fixed-parameter* declares a parameter of the given type with the given name.

A *parameter-array* consists of an optional set of *attributes* (§17), a `params` modifier, an *array-type*, and an *identifier*. A parameter array declares a single parameter of the given array type with the given name. The *array-type* of a parameter array must be a single-dimensional array type (§12.1). In a method invocation, a parameter array permits either a single argument of the given array type to be specified, or it permits zero or more arguments of the array element type to be specified. Parameter arrays are described further in §10.5.1.4.

A method declaration creates a separate declaration space for parameters and local variables. Names are introduced into this declaration space by the formal parameter list of the method and by local variable declarations in the *block* of the method. All names in the declaration space of a method must be unique. Thus, it is a compile-time error for a parameter or local variable to have the same name as another parameter or local variable.

A method invocation (§7.5.5.1) creates a copy, specific to that invocation, of the formal parameters and local variables of the method, and the argument list of the invocation assigns values or variable references to the newly created formal parameters. Within the *block* of a method, formal parameters can be referenced by their identifiers in *simple-name* expressions (§7.5.2).

There are four kinds of formal parameters:

- Value parameters, which are declared without any modifiers
- Reference parameters, which are declared with the `ref` modifier
- Output parameters, which are declared with the `out` modifier
- Parameter arrays, which are declared with the `params` modifier

As described in §3.6, the `ref` and `out` modifiers are part of a method's signature, but the `params` modifier is not.

10.5.1.1 *Value Parameters*

A parameter declared with no modifiers is a value parameter. A value parameter corresponds to a local variable that gets its initial value from the corresponding argument supplied in the method invocation.

When a formal parameter is a value parameter, the corresponding argument in a method invocation must be an expression of a type that is implicitly convertible (§6.1) to the formal parameter type.

A method is permitted to assign new values to a value parameter. Such assignments only affect the local storage location represented by the value parameter—they have no effect on the actual argument given in the method invocation.

10.5.1.2 *Reference Parameters*

A parameter declared with a `ref` modifier is a reference parameter. Unlike a value parameter, a reference parameter does not create a new storage location. Instead, a reference parameter represents the same storage location as the variable given as the argument in the method invocation.

When a formal parameter is a reference parameter, the corresponding argument in a method invocation must consist of the keyword `ref` followed by a *variable-reference* (§5.3.3) of the same type as the formal parameter. A variable must be definitely assigned before it can be passed as a reference parameter.

Within a method, a reference parameter is always considered definitely assigned.

The example

```
using System;
```

```
class Test
{
    static void Swap(ref int x, ref int y) {
        int temp = x;
        x = y;
        y = temp;
    }

    static void Main() {
        int i = 1, j = 2;
        Swap(ref i, ref j);
        Console.WriteLine("i = {0}, j = {1}", i, j);
    }
}
```

produces the output

```
i = 2, j = 1
```

For the invocation of Swap in Main, x represents i and y represents j. Thus, the invocation has the effect of swapping the values of i and j.

In a method that takes reference parameters, it is possible for multiple names to represent the same storage location. In the example

```
class A
{
    string s;

    void F(ref string a, ref string b) {
        s = "One";
        a = "Two";
        b = "Three";
    }

    void G() {
        F(ref s, ref s);
    }
}
```

the invocation of F in G passes a reference to s for both a and b. Thus, for that invocation, the names s, a, and b all refer to the same storage location, and the three assignments all modify the instance field s.

10.5.1.3 *Output Parameters*

A parameter declared with an out modifier is an output parameter. Similar to a reference parameter, an output parameter does not create a new storage location. Instead, an output parameter represents the same storage location as the variable given as the argument in the method invocation.

When a formal parameter is an output parameter, the corresponding argument in a method invocation must consist of the keyword out followed by a *variable-reference* (§5.3.3) of the same type as the formal parameter. A variable need not be definitely assigned before it can be passed as an output parameter, but following an invocation where a variable was passed as an output parameter, the variable is considered definitely assigned.

Within a method, just like a local variable, an output parameter is initially considered unassigned and must be definitely assigned before its value is used.

Every output parameter of a method must be definitely assigned before the method returns.

Output parameters are typically used in methods that produce multiple return values. For example

```
using System;

class Test
{
    static void SplitPath(string path, out string dir, out string name) {
        int i = path.Length;
        while (i > 0) {
            char ch = path[i - 1];
            if (ch == '\\' || ch == '/' || ch == ':') break;
            i--;
        }
        dir = path.Substring(0, i);
        name = path.Substring(i);
    }

    static void Main() {
        string dir, name;
        SplitPath("c:\\Windows\\System\\hello.txt", out dir, out name);
        Console.WriteLine(dir);
        Console.WriteLine(name);
    }
}
```

The example produces the following output.

```
c:\Windows\System\
hello.txt
```

Note that the dir and name variables can be unassigned before they are passed to SplitPath and that they are considered definitely assigned following the call.

10.5.1.4 *Parameter Arrays*
A parameter declared with a params modifier is a parameter array. If a formal parameter list includes a parameter array, it must be the last parameter in the list and it must be of a single-dimensional array type. For example, the types string[] and string[][] can be

used as the type of a parameter array, but the type `string[,]` cannot. It is not possible to combine the `params` modifier with the modifiers `ref` and `out`.

A parameter array permits arguments to be specified in one of two ways in a method invocation.

- The argument given for a parameter array can be a single expression of a type that is implicitly convertible (§6.1) to the parameter array type. In this case, the parameter array acts precisely like a value parameter.

- Alternatively, the invocation can specify zero or more arguments for the parameter array, where each argument is an expression of a type that is implicitly convertible (§6.1) to the element type of the parameter array. In this case, the invocation creates an instance of the parameter array type with a length corresponding to the number of arguments, initializes the elements of the array instance with the given argument values, and uses the newly created array instance as the actual argument.

Except for allowing a variable number of arguments in an invocation, a parameter array is precisely equivalent to a value parameter (§10.5.1.1) of the same type.

The example

```
using System;
class Test
{
    static void F(params int[] args) {
        Console.Write("Array contains {0} elements:", args.Length);
        foreach (int i in args)
            Console.Write(" {0}", i);
        Console.WriteLine();
    }
    static void Main() {
        int[] arr = {1, 2, 3};
        F(arr);
        F(10, 20, 30, 40);
        F();
    }
}
```

produces the following output.

```
Array contains 3 elements: 1 2 3
Array contains 4 elements: 10 20 30 40
Array contains 0 elements:
```

The first invocation of F simply passes the array a as a value parameter. The second invocation of F automatically creates a four-element `int[]` with the given element values and passes that array instance as a value parameter. Likewise, the third invocation of F creates a zero-element int[] and passes that instance as a value parameter. The second and third invocations are precisely equivalent to writing the following.

```
F(new int[] {10, 20, 30, 40});
F(new int[] {});
```

When performing overload resolution, a method with a parameter array may be applicable either in its normal form or in its expanded form (§7.4.2.1). The expanded form of a method is available only if the normal form of the method is not applicable and only if a method with the same signature as the expanded form is not already declared in the same type.

The example

```
using System;

class Test
{
    static void F(params object[] a) {
        Console.WriteLine("F(object[])");
    }

    static void F() {
        Console.WriteLine("F()");
    }

    static void F(object a0, object a1) {
        Console.WriteLine("F(object,object)");
    }

    static void Main() {
        F();
        F(1);
        F(1, 2);
        F(1, 2, 3);
        F(1, 2, 3, 4);
    }
}
```

produces the following output.

```
F();
F(object[]);
F(object,object);
F(object[]);
F(object[]);
```

In the example, two of the possible expanded forms of the method with a parameter array are already included in the class as regular methods. These expanded forms are therefore not considered when performing overload resolution, and the first and third method invocations thus select the regular methods. When a class declares a method with a parameter array, it is not uncommon to also include some of the expanded forms as regular methods.

By doing so it is possible to avoid the allocation of an array instance that occurs when an expanded form of a method with a parameter array is invoked.

When the type of a parameter array is object[], a potential ambiguity arises between the normal form of the method and the expanded form for a single object parameter. The reason for the ambiguity is that an object[] is itself implicitly convertible to type object. The ambiguity presents no problem, however, because it can be resolved by inserting a cast if needed.

The example

```
using System;

class Test
{
    static void F(params object[] args) {
        foreach (object o in args) {
            Console.Write(o.GetType().FullName);
            Console.Write(" ");
        }
        Console.WriteLine();
    }

    static void Main() {
        object[] a = {1, "Hello", 123.456};
        object o = a;
        F(a);
        F((object)a);
        F(o);
        F((object[])o);
    }
}
```

produces the following output.

```
System.Int32 System.String System.Double
System.Object[]
System.Object[]
System.Int32 System.String System.Double
```

In the first and last invocations of F, the normal form of F is applicable because an implicit conversion exists from the argument type to the parameter type (both are of type object[]). Thus, overload resolution selects the normal form of F, and the argument is passed as a regular value parameter. In the second and third invocations, the normal form of F is not applicable because no implicit conversion exists from the argument type to the parameter type (type object cannot be implicitly converted to type object[]). However, the expanded form of F is applicable, so it is selected by overload resolution. As a result, a one-element object[] is created by the invocation, and the single element of the array is initialized with the given argument value (which itself is a reference to an object[]).

10.5.2 **Static and Instance Methods**

When a method declaration includes a `static` modifier, that method is said to be a static method. When no `static` modifier is present, the method is said to be an instance method.

A static method does not operate on a specific instance, and it is a compile-time error to refer to `this` in a static method.

An instance method operates on a given instance of a class, and that instance can be accessed as `this` (§7.5.7).

When a method is referenced in a *member-access* (§7.5.4) of the form `E.M`, if `M` is a static method, `E` must denote a type containing `M`, and if `M` is an instance method, `E` must denote an instance of a type containing `M`.

The differences between static and instance members are discussed further in §10.2.5.

10.5.3 **Virtual Methods**

When an instance method declaration includes a `virtual` modifier, that method is said to be a virtual method. When no `virtual` modifier is present, the method is said to be a non-virtual method.

The implementation of a nonvirtual method is invariant: The implementation is the same whether the method is invoked on an instance of the class in which it is declared or an instance of a derived class. In contrast, the implementation of a virtual method can be superseded by derived classes. The process of superseding the implementation of an inherited virtual method is known as *overriding* that method (§10.5.4).

In a virtual method invocation, the ***runtime type*** of the instance for which that invocation takes place determines the actual method implementation to invoke. In a nonvirtual method invocation, the ***compile-time type*** of the instance is the determining factor. In precise terms, when a method named `N` is invoked with an argument list `A` on an instance with a compile-time type `C` and a runtime type `R` (where `R` is either `C` or a class derived from `C`), the invocation is processed as follows.

- First, overload resolution is applied to `C`, `N`, and `A` to select a specific method `M` from the set of methods declared in and inherited by `C`. This is described in §7.5.5.1.

- Then, if `M` is a nonvirtual method, `M` is invoked.

- Otherwise, `M` is a virtual method, and the most derived implementation of `M` with respect to `R` is invoked.

For every virtual method declared in or inherited by a class, there exists a *most derived implementation* of the method with respect to that class. The most derived implementation of a virtual method M with respect to a class R is determined as follows.

- If R contains the introducing `virtual` declaration of M, then this is the most derived implementation of M.

- Otherwise, if R contains an `override` of M, then this is the most derived implementation of M.

- Otherwise, the most derived implementation of M with respect to R is the same as the most derived implementation of M with respect to the direct base class of R.

The following example illustrates the differences between virtual and nonvirtual methods.

```
using System;
class A
{
    public void F() { Console.WriteLine("A.F"); }
    public virtual void G() { Console.WriteLine("A.G"); }
}
class B: A
{
    new public void F() { Console.WriteLine("B.F"); }
    public override void G() { Console.WriteLine("B.G"); }
}
class Test
{
    static void Main() {
        B b = new B();
        A a = b;
        a.F();
        b.F();
        a.G();
        b.G();
    }
}
```

In the example, A introduces a nonvirtual method F and a virtual method G. The class B introduces a *new* nonvirtual method F, thus *hiding* the inherited F, and also *overrides* the inherited method G. The example produces the following output.

```
A.F
B.F
B.G
B.G
```

Notice that the statement a.G() invokes B.G, not A.G. This is because the runtime type of the instance (which is B), not the compile-time type of the instance (which is A), determines the actual method implementation to invoke.

Because methods are allowed to hide inherited methods, it is possible for a class to contain several virtual methods with the same signature. This does not present an ambiguity problem because all but the most derived method are hidden. In the example

```csharp
using System;

class A
{
    public virtual void F() { Console.WriteLine("A.F"); }
}

class B: A
{
    public override void F() { Console.WriteLine("B.F"); }
}

class C: B
{
    new public virtual void F() { Console.WriteLine("C.F"); }
}

class D: C
{
    public override void F() { Console.WriteLine("D.F"); }
}

class Test
{
    static void Main() {
        D d = new D();
        A a = d;
        B b = d;
        C c = d;
        a.F();
        b.F();
        c.F();
        d.F();
    }
}
```

the C and D classes contain two virtual methods with the same signature: the one introduced by A and the one introduced by C. The method introduced by C hides the method inherited from A. Thus, the override declaration in D overrides the method introduced by C, and it is not possible for D to override the method introduced by A. The example produces the following output.

```
B.F
B.F
D.F
D.F
```

Note that it is possible to invoke the hidden virtual method by accessing an instance of D through a less derived type in which the method is not hidden.

10.5.4 Override Methods

When an instance method declaration includes an `override` modifier, the method is said to be an *override method*. An override method overrides an inherited virtual method with the same signature. Whereas a virtual method declaration *introduces* a new method, an override method declaration *specializes* an existing inherited virtual method by providing a new implementation of that method.

The method overridden by an `override` declaration is known as the *overridden base method*. For an override method M declared in a class C, the overridden base method is determined by examining each base class of C, starting with the direct base class of C and continuing with each successive direct base class until an accessible method with the same signature as M is located. For the purposes of locating the overridden base method, a method is considered accessible if it is `public`, if it is `protected`, if it is `protected internal`, or if it is `internal` and declared in the same program as C.

A compile-time error occurs unless all of the following are true for an override declaration.

- An overridden base method can be located as described previously.

- The overridden base method is a virtual, abstract, or override method. In other words, the overridden base method cannot be static or nonvirtual.

- The overridden base method is not a sealed method.

- The override declaration and the overridden base method have the same return type.

- The override declaration and the overridden base method have the same declared accessibility. In other words, an override declaration cannot change the accessibility of the virtual method.

An override declaration can access the overridden base method using a *base-access* (§7.5.8). In the example

```
class A
{
    int x;
    public virtual void PrintFields() {
        Console.WriteLine("x = {0}", x);
    }
}
class B: A
{
    int y;
```

```
        public override void PrintFields() {
            base.PrintFields();
            Console.WriteLine("y = {0}", y);
        }
    }
```

the `base.PrintFields()` invocation in B invokes the `PrintFields` method declared in A. A *base-access* disables the virtual invocation mechanism and simply treats the base method as a nonvirtual method. Had the invocation in B been written `((A)this).PrintFields()`, it would recursively invoke the `PrintFields` method declared in B, not the one declared in A, because `PrintFields` is virtual and the runtime type of `((A)this)` is B.

Only by including an `override` modifier can a method override another method. In all other cases, a method with the same signature as an inherited method simply hides the inherited method. In the example

```
    class A
    {
        public virtual void F() {}
    }

    class B: A
    {
        public virtual void F() {}     // Warning, hiding inherited F()
    }
```

the F method in B does not include an `override` modifier and therefore does not override the F method in A. Rather, the F method in B hides the method in A, and a warning is reported because the declaration does not include a `new` modifier.

In the example

```
    class A
    {
        public virtual void F() {}
    }

    class B: A
    {
        new private void F() {}         // Hides A.F within B
    }

    class C: B
    {
        public override void F() {}   // Ok, overrides A.F
    }
```

the F method in B hides the virtual F method inherited from A. Because the new F in B has private access, its scope only includes the class body of B and does not extend to C. Therefore, the declaration of F in C is permitted to override the F inherited from A.

10.5.5 Sealed Methods

When an instance method declaration includes a `sealed` modifier, that method is said to be a *sealed method*. If an instance method declaration includes the `sealed` modifier, it must also include the `override` modifier. Using the `sealed` modifier prevents a derived class from further overriding the method.

The example

```
using System;
class A
{
    public virtual void F() {
        Console.WriteLine("A.F");
    }
    public virtual void G() {
        Console.WriteLine("A.G");
    }
}
class B: A
{
    sealed override public void F() {
        Console.WriteLine("B.F");
    }
    override public void G() {
        Console.WriteLine("B.G");
    }
}
class C: B
{
    override public void G() {
        Console.WriteLine("C.G");
    }
}
```

the class B provides two override methods: an F method that has the `sealed` modifier and a G method that does not. B's use of the sealed `modifier` prevents C from further overriding F.

10.5.6 Abstract Methods

When an instance method declaration includes an `abstract` modifier, that method is said to be an *abstract method*. Although an abstract method is implicitly also a virtual method, it cannot have the modifier `virtual`.

An abstract method declaration introduces a new virtual method but does not provide an implementation of that method. Instead, nonabstract derived classes are required to provide their own implementation by overriding that method. Because an abstract method provides no actual implementation, the *method-body* of an abstract method simply consists of a semicolon.

Abstract method declarations are only permitted in abstract classes (§10.1.1.1).

In the example

```
public abstract class Shape
{
    public abstract void Paint(Graphics g, Rectangle r);
}

public class Ellipse: Shape
{
    public override void Paint(Graphics g, Rectangle r) {
        g.DrawEllipse(r);
    }
}

public class Box: Shape
{
    public override void Paint(Graphics g, Rectangle r) {
        g.DrawRect(r);
    }
}
```

the Shape class defines the abstract notion of a geometrical shape object that can paint itself. The Paint method is abstract because there is no meaningful default implementation. The Ellipse and Box classes are concrete Shape implementations. Because these classes are nonabstract, they are required to override the Paint method and provide an actual implementation.

It is a compile-time error for a *base-access* (§7.5.8) to reference an abstract method. In the example

```
abstract class A
{
    public abstract void F();
}

class B: A
{
    public override void F() {
        base.F();                       // Error, base.F is abstract
    }
}
```

a compile-time error is reported for the base.F() invocation because it references an abstract method.

An abstract method declaration is permitted to override a virtual method. This allows an abstract class to force reimplementation of the method in derived classes, and it makes the original implementation of the method unavailable. In the example

```
using System;
class A
{
    public virtual void F() {
        Console.WriteLine("A.F");
    }
}
abstract class B: A
{
    public abstract override void F();
}
class C: B
{
    public override void F() {
        Console.WriteLine("C.F");
    }
}
```

class A declares a virtual method, class B overrides this method with an abstract method, and class C overrides the abstract method to provide its own implementation.

10.5.7 External Methods

When a method declaration includes an `extern` modifier, that method is said to be an *external method*. External methods are implemented externally, typically using a language other than C#. Because an external method declaration provides no actual implementation, the *method-body* of an external method simply consists of a semicolon.

The `extern` modifier is typically used in conjunction with a `DllImport` attribute (§17.5.1), allowing external methods to be implemented by Dynamic Link Libraries (DLLs). The execution environment may support other mechanisms whereby implementations of external methods can be provided.

When an external method includes a `DllImport` attribute, the method declaration must also include a `static` modifier. This example demonstrates the use of the `extern` modifier and the `DllImport` attribute.

```
using System.Text;
using System.Security.Permissions;
using System.Runtime.InteropServices;
class Path
{
    [DllImport("kernel32", SetLastError=true)]
    static extern bool CreateDirectory(string name, SecurityAttribute sa);
```

```
[DllImport("kernel32", SetLastError=true)]
static extern bool RemoveDirectory(string name);

[DllImport("kernel32", SetLastError=true)]
static extern int GetCurrentDirectory(int bufSize, StringBuilder buf);

[DllImport("kernel32", SetLastError=true)]
static extern bool SetCurrentDirectory(string name);
}
```

10.5.8 Method Body

The *method-body* of a method declaration consists of either a *block* or a semicolon.

Abstract and external method declarations do not provide a method implementation, so their method bodies simply consist of a semicolon. For any other method, the method body is a block (§8.2) that contains the statements to execute when that method is invoked.

When the return type of a method is void, return statements (§8.9.4) in that method's body are not permitted to specify an expression. If execution of the method body of a void method completes normally (that is, control flows off the end of the method body), that method simply returns to its caller.

When the return type of a method is not void, each return statement in that method's body must specify an expression of a type that is implicitly convertible to the return type. The endpoint of the method body of a value-returning method must not be reachable. In other words, in a value-returning method, control is not permitted to flow off the end of the method body.

In the example

```
class A
{
    public int F() {}       // Error, return value required
    public int G() {
        return 1;
    }

    public int H(bool b) {
        if (b) {
            return 1;
        }
        else {
            return 0;
        }
    }
}
```

the value-returning F method results in a compile-time error because control can flow off the end of the method body. The G and H methods are correct because all possible execution paths end in a return statement that specifies a return value.

10.5.9 Method Overloading

The method overload resolution rules are described in §7.4.2.

10.6 Properties

A *property* is a member that provides access to a characteristic of an object or a class. Examples of properties include the length of a string, the size of a font, the caption of a window, the name of a customer, and so on. Properties are a natural extension of fields—both are named members with associated types, and the syntax for accessing fields and properties is the same. However, unlike fields, properties do not denote storage locations. Instead, properties have *accessors* that specify the statements to be executed when their values are read or written. Properties thus provide a mechanism for associating actions with the reading and writing of an object's attributes; furthermore, they permit such attributes to be computed.

Properties are declared using *property-declaration*s.

> *property-declaration:*
>   *attributes$_{opt}$* *property-modifiers$_{opt}$* *type* *member-name* { *accessor-declarations* }
>
> *property-modifiers:*
>   *property-modifier*
>   *property-modifiers* *property-modifier*
>
> *property-modifier:*
>   new
>   public
>   protected
>   internal
>   private
>   static
>   virtual
>   sealed
>   override
>   abstract
>   extern
>
> *member-name:*
>   *identifier*
>   *interface-type* . *identifier*

A *property-declaration* may include a set of *attributes* (§17) and a valid combination of the four access modifiers (§10.2.3), the new (§10.2.2), static (§10.5.2), virtual (§10.5.3), override (§10.5.4), sealed (§10.5.5), abstract (§10.5.6), and extern (§10.5.7) modifiers.

Property declarations are subject to the same rules as method declarations (§10.5) with regard to valid combinations of modifiers.

The *type* of a property declaration specifies the type of the property introduced by the declaration, and the *member-name* specifies the name of the property. Unless the property is an explicit interface member implementation, the *member-name* is simply an *identifier*. For an explicit interface member implementation (§13.4.1), the *member-name* consists of an *interface-type* followed by a " . " and an *identifier*.

The *type* of a property must be at least as accessible as the property itself (§3.5.4).

The *accessor-declarations*, which must be enclosed in { and } tokens, declare the accessors (§10.6.2) of the property. The accessors specify the executable statements associated with reading and writing the property.

Even though the syntax for accessing a property is the same as that for a field, a property is not classified as a variable. Thus, it is not possible to pass a property as a `ref` or `out` argument.

When a property declaration includes an `extern` modifier, the property is said to be an *external property*. Because an external property declaration provides no actual implementation, each of its *accessor-declarations* consists of a semicolon.

10.6.1 Static and Instance Properties

When a property declaration includes a `static` modifier, the property is said to be a *static property*. When no `static` modifier is present, the property is said to be an *instance property*.

A static property is not associated with a specific instance, and it is a compile-time error to refer to `this` in the accessors of a static property.

An instance property is associated with a given instance of a class, and that instance can be accessed as `this` (§7.5.7) in the accessors of that property.

When a property is referenced in a *member-access* (§7.5.4) of the form E.M, if M is a static property, E must denote a type containing M, and if M is an instance property, E must denote an instance of a type containing M.

The differences between static and instance members are discussed further in §10.2.5.

10.6.2 **Accessors**

The *accessor-declarations* of a property specify the executable statements associated with reading and writing that property.

accessor-declarations:
    get-accessor-declaration *set-accessor-declaration$_{opt}$*
    set-accessor-declaration *get-accessor-declaration$_{opt}$*

get-accessor-declaration:
    attributes$_{opt}$ get *accessor-body*

set-accessor-declaration:
    attributes$_{opt}$ set *accessor-body*

accessor-body:
    block
    ;

The accessor declarations consist of a *get-accessor-declaration*, a *set-accessor-declaration*, or both. Each accessor declaration consists of the token get or set followed by an *accessor-body*. For abstract and extern properties, the *accessor-body* for each accessor specified is simply a semicolon. For the accessors of any nonabstract, nonextern property, the *accessor-body* is a *block* that specifies the statements to be executed when the corresponding accessor is invoked.

A get accessor corresponds to a parameterless method with a return value of the property type. Except as the target of an assignment, when a property is referenced in an expression, the get accessor of the property is invoked to compute the value of the property (§7.1.1). The body of a get accessor must conform to the rules for value-returning methods described in §10.5.8. In particular, all return statements in the body of a get accessor must specify an expression that is implicitly convertible to the property type. Furthermore, the endpoint of a get accessor must not be reachable.

A set accessor corresponds to a method with a single value parameter of the property type and a void return type. The implicit parameter of a set accessor is always named value. When a property is referenced as the target of an assignment (§7.13) or as the operand of ++ or -- (§7.5.9, §7.6.5), the set accessor is invoked with an argument (whose value is that of the right-hand side of the assignment or the operand of the ++ or -- operator) that provides the new value (§7.13.1). The body of a set accessor must conform to the rules for void methods described in §10.5.8. In particular, return statements in the set accessor body are not permitted to specify an expression. Because a set accessor implicitly has a parameter named value, it is a compile-time error for a local variable or constant declaration in a set accessor to have that name.

Based on the presence or absence of the get and set accessors, a property is classified as follows.

- A property that includes both a get accessor and a set accessor is said to be a *read-write* property.

- A property that has only a get accessor is said to be a *read-only* property. It is a compile-time error for a read-only property to be the target of an assignment.

- A property that has only a set accessor is said to be a *write-only* property. Except as the target of an assignment, it is a compile-time error to reference a write-only property in an expression.

In the example

```
public class Button: Control
{
    private string caption;
    public string Caption {
        get {
            return caption;
        }
        set {
            if (caption != value) {
                caption = value;
                Repaint();
            }
        }
    }
    public override void Paint(Graphics g, Rectangle r) {
        // Painting code goes here
    }
}
```

the Button control declares a public Caption property. The get accessor of the Caption property returns the string stored in the private caption field. The set accessor checks if the new value is different from the current value, and if so, it stores the new value and repaints the control. Properties often follow the pattern shown previously: The get accessor simply returns a value stored in a private field, and the set accessor modifies that private field and then performs any additional actions required to fully update the state of the object.

Given the previous Button class, the following is an example of using the Caption property.

```
Button okButton = new Button();
okButton.Caption = "OK";        // Invokes set accessor
string s = okButton.Caption;    // Invokes get accessor
```

Here, the set accessor is invoked by assigning a value to the property, and the get accessor is invoked by referencing the property in an expression.

The get and set accessors of a property are not distinct members, and it is not possible to declare the accessors of a property separately. As such, it is not possible for the two accessors of a read-write property to have different accessibility. The example

```
class A
{
    private string name;

    public string Name {           // Error, duplicate member name
        get { return name; }
    }
    public string Name {           // Error, duplicate member name
        set { name = value; }
    }
}
```

does not declare a single read-write property. Rather, it declares two properties with the same name, one read-only and one write-only. Because two members declared in the same class cannot have the same name, the example causes a compile-time error to occur.

When a derived class declares a property by the same name as an inherited property, the derived property hides the inherited property with respect to both reading and writing. In the example

```
class A
{
    public int P {
        set {...}
    }
}
class B: A
{
    new public int P {
        get {...}
    }
}
```

the P property in B hides the P property in A with respect to both reading and writing. Thus, in the statements

```
B b = new B();
b.P = 1;           // Error, B.P is read-only
((A)b).P = 1;      // Ok, reference to A.P
```

the assignment to b.P causes a compile-time error to be reported because the read-only P property in B hides the write-only P property in A. Note, however, that a cast can be used to access the hidden P property.

Unlike public fields, properties provide a separation between an object's internal state and its public interface. Consider the example

```
class Label
{
    private int x, y;
    private string caption;

    public Label(int x, int y, string caption) {
        this.x = x;
        this.y = y;
        this.caption = caption;
    }

    public int X {
        get { return x; }
    }

    public int Y {
        get { return y; }
    }

    public Point Location {
        get { return new Point(x, y); }
    }

    public string Caption {
        get { return caption; }
    }
}
```

Here, the Label class uses two int fields, x and y, to store its location. The location is publicly exposed both as an X and a Y property and as a Location property of type Point. If, in a future version of Label, it becomes more convenient to store the location as a Point internally, the change can be made without affecting the public interface of the class.

```
class Label
{
    private Point location;
    private string caption;

    public Label(int x, int y, string caption) {
        this.location = new Point(x, y);
        this.caption = caption;
    }

    public int X {
        get { return location.x; }
    }
```

```
    public int Y {
        get { return location.y; }
    }
    public Point Location {
        get { return location; }
    }
    public string Caption {
        get { return caption; }
    }
}
```

Had x and y instead been `public readonly` fields, it would have been impossible to make such a change to the Label class.

Exposing state through properties is not necessarily any less efficient than exposing fields directly. In particular, when a property is nonvirtual and contains only a small amount of code, the execution environment may replace calls to accessors with the actual code of the accessors. This process is known as *inlining*, and it makes property access as efficient as field access yet preserves the increased flexibility of properties.

Because invoking a get accessor is conceptually equivalent to reading the value of a field, it is considered bad programming style for get accessors to have observable side effects. In the example

```
class Counter
{
    private int next;
    public int Next {
        get { return next++; }
    }
}
```

the value of the Next property depends on the number of times the property has previously been accessed. Thus, accessing the property produces an observable side effect, and the property should be implemented as a method instead.

The "no side effects" convention for get accessors does not mean that get accessors should always be written to simply return values stored in fields. Indeed, get accessors often compute the value of a property by accessing multiple fields or invoking methods. However, a properly designed get accessor performs no actions that cause observable changes in the state of the object.

Properties can be used to delay initialization of a resource until the moment it is first referenced. For example

```
using System.IO;

public class Console
{
    private static TextReader reader;
    private static TextWriter writer;
    private static TextWriter error;

    public static TextReader In {
        get {
            if (reader == null) {
                reader = new StreamReader(Console.OpenStandardInput());
            }
            return reader;
        }
    }

    public static TextWriter Out {
        get {
            if (writer == null) {
                writer = new StreamWriter(Console.OpenStandardOutput());
            }
            return writer;
        }
    }

    public static TextWriter Error {
        get {
            if (error == null) {
                error = new StreamWriter(Console.OpenStandardError());
            }
            return error;
        }
    }
}
```

The `Console` class contains three properties, `In`, `Out`, and `Error`, that represent the standard input, output, and error devices, respectively. By exposing these members as properties, the `Console` class can delay their initialization until they are actually used. For example, upon first referencing the `Out` property, as in

```
Console.Out.WriteLine("hello, world");
```

the underlying `TextWriter` for the output device is created. But if the application makes no reference to the `In` and `Error` properties, then no objects are created for those devices.

10.6.3 **Virtual, Sealed, Override, and Abstract Accessors**

A `virtual` property declaration specifies that the accessors of the property are virtual. The `virtual` modifier applies to both accessors of a read-write property—it is not possible for only one accessor of a read-write property to be virtual.

An `abstract` property declaration specifies that the accessors of the property are virtual but does not provide an actual implementation of the accessors. Instead, nonabstract derived classes are required to provide their own implementation for the accessors by overriding the property. Because an accessor for an abstract property declaration provides no actual implementation, its *accessor-body* simply consists of a semicolon.

A property declaration that includes both the `abstract` and `override` modifiers specifies that the property is abstract and overrides a base property. The accessors of such a property are also abstract.

Abstract property declarations are only permitted in abstract classes (§10.1.1.1).The accessors of an inherited virtual property can be overridden in a derived class by including a property declaration that specifies an `override` directive. This is known as an ***overriding property declaration***. An overriding property declaration does not declare a new property. Instead, it simply specializes the implementations of the accessors of an existing virtual property.

An overriding property declaration must specify the exact same accessibility modifiers, type, and name as the inherited property. If the inherited property has only a single accessor (in other words, if the inherited property is read-only or write-only), the overriding property must include only that accessor. If the inherited property includes both accessors (in other words, if the inherited property is read-write), the overriding property can include either a single accessor or both accessors.

An overriding property declaration may include the `sealed` modifier. Using this modifier prevents a derived class from further overriding the property. The accessors of a sealed property are also sealed.

Except for differences in declaration and invocation syntax, virtual, sealed, override, and abstract accessors behave exactly like virtual, sealed, override and abstract methods. Specifically, the rules described in §10.5.3, §10.5.4, §10.5.5, and §10.5.6 apply as if accessors were methods of a corresponding form.

* A `get` accessor corresponds to a parameterless method with a return value of the property type and the same modifiers as the containing property.

* A `set` accessor corresponds to a method with a single value parameter of the property type, a `void` return type, and the same modifiers as the containing property.

In the example

```
abstract class A
{
    int y;
    public virtual int X {
        get { return 0; }
    }
    public virtual int Y {
        get { return y; }
        set { y = value; }
    }
    public abstract int Z { get; set; }
}
```

X is a virtual read-only property, Y is a virtual read-write property, and Z is an abstract read-write property. Because Z is abstract, the containing class A must also be declared abstract.

A class that derives from A is as follows.

```
class B: A
{
    int z;
    public override int X {
        get { return base.X + 1; }
    }
    public override int Y {
        set { base.Y = value < 0? 0: value; }
    }
    public override int Z {
        get { return z; }
        set { z = value; }
    }
}
```

Here, the declarations of X, Y, and Z are overriding property declarations. Each property declaration exactly matches the accessibility modifiers, type, and name of the corresponding inherited property. The get accessor of X and the set accessor of Y use the base keyword to access the inherited accessors. The declaration of Z overrides both abstract accessors—thus, there are no outstanding abstract function members in B, and B is permitted to be a nonabstract class.

10.7 Events

An *event* is a member that enables an object or class to provide notifications. Clients can attach executable code for events by supplying *event handlers*.

Events are declared using *event-declarations*.

> *event-declaration:*
>> *attributes*_{opt} *event-modifiers*_{opt} event *type variable-declarators* ;
>> *attributes*_{opt} *event-modifiers*_{opt} event *type member-name*
>>> { *event-accessor-declarations* }
>
> *event-modifiers:*
>> *event-modifier*
>> *event-modifiers event-modifier*
>
> *event-modifier:*
>> new
>> public
>> protected
>> internal
>> private
>> static
>> virtual
>> sealed
>> override
>> abstract
>> extern
>
> *event-accessor-declarations:*
>> *add-accessor-declaration remove-accessor-declaration*
>> *remove-accessor-declaration add-accessor-declaration*
>
> *add-accessor-declaration:*
>> *attributes*_{opt} add *block*
>
> *remove-accessor-declaration:*
>> *attributes*_{opt} remove *block*

An *event-declaration* may include a set of *attributes* (§17) and a valid combination of the four access modifiers (§10.2.3), the new (§10.2.2), static (§10.5.2), virtual (§10.5.3), override (§10.5.4), sealed (§10.5.5), abstract (§10.5.6), and extern (§10.5.7) modifiers.

Event declarations are subject to the same rules as method declarations (§10.5) with regard to valid combinations of modifiers.

The *type* of an event declaration must be a *delegate-type* (§4.2), and that *delegate-type* must be at least as accessible as the event itself (§3.5.4).

An event declaration may include *event-accessor-declaration*s. However, if it does not, for non-extern, nonabstract events, the compiler supplies them automatically (§10.7.1); for extern events, the accessors are provided externally.

An event declaration that omits *event-accessor-declaration*s defines one or more events—one for each of the *variable-declarator*s. The attributes and modifiers apply to all of the members declared by such an *event-declaration*.

It is a compile-time error for an *event-declaration* to include both the abstract modifier and brace-delimited *event-accessor-declaration*s.

When an event declaration includes an extern modifier, the event is said to be an **external event**. Because an external event declaration provides no actual implementation, it is an error for it to include both the extern modifier and *event-accessor-declaration*s.

An event can be used as the left-hand operand of the += and -= operators (§7.13.3). These operators are used, respectively, to attach event handlers to or to remove event handlers from an event, and the access modifiers of the event control the contexts in which such operations are permitted.

Because += and -= are the only operations that are permitted on an event outside the type that declares the event, external code can add and remove handlers for an event but cannot in any other way obtain or modify the underlying list of event handlers.

In an operation of the form x += y or x -= y, when x is an event and the reference takes place outside the type that contains the declaration of x, the result of the operation has type void (as opposed to having the type of x, with the value of x after the assignment). This rule prohibits external code from indirectly examining the underlying delegate of an event.

The following example shows how event handlers are attached to instances of the Button class.

```
public delegate void EventHandler(object sender, EventArgs e);

public class Button: Control
{
    public event EventHandler Click;
}

public class LoginDialog: Form
{
    Button OkButton;
    Button CancelButton;
```

```
        public LoginDialog() {
            OkButton = new Button(...);
            OkButton.Click += new EventHandler(OkButtonClick);
            CancelButton = new Button(...);
            CancelButton.Click += new EventHandler(CancelButtonClick);
        }
        void OkButtonClick(object sender, EventArgs e) {
            // Handle OkButton.Click event
        }
        void CancelButtonClick(object sender, EventArgs e) {
            // Handle CancelButton.Click event
        }
    }
```

Here, the `LoginDialog` instance constructor creates two `Button` instances and attaches event handlers to the `Click` events.

10.7.1 Field-Like Events

Within the program text of the class or struct that contains the declaration of an event, certain events can be used like fields. To be used in this way, an event must not be `abstract` or `extern` and must not explicitly include *event-accessor-declaration*s. Such an event can be used in any context that permits a field. The field contains a delegate (§15) that refers to the list of event handlers that have been added to the event. If no event handlers have been added, the field contains `null`.

In the example

```
    public delegate void EventHandler(object sender, EventArgs e);
    public class Button: Control
    {
        public event EventHandler Click;
        protected void OnClick(EventArgs e) {
            if (Click != null) Click(this, e);
        }
        public void Reset() {
            Click = null;
        }
    }
```

`Click` is used as a field within the `Button` class. As the example demonstrates, the field can be examined, modified, and used in delegate invocation expressions. The `OnClick` method in the `Button` class "raises" the `Click` event. The notion of raising an event is precisely equivalent to invoking the delegate represented by the event—thus, there are no special language constructs for raising events. Note that the delegate invocation is preceded by a check that ensures the delegate is non-null.

Outside the declaration of the Button class, the Click member can only be used on the left-hand side of the += and −= operators, as in

```
b.Click += new EventHandler(...);
```

which appends a delegate to the invocation list of the Click event, and as in

```
b.Click -= new EventHandler(...);
```

which removes a delegate from the invocation list of the Click event.

When compiling a field-like event, the compiler automatically creates storage to hold the delegate and creates accessors for the event that add or remove event handlers to the delegate field. To be thread-safe, the addition or removal operations are done while holding the lock (§8.12) on the containing object for an instance event or the type object (§7.5.11) for a static event.

Thus, an instance event declaration of the form

```
class X {
    public event D Ev;
}
```

could be compiled to something equivalent to the following.

```
class X {
    private D __Ev;   // field to hold the delegate
    public event D Ev {
        add {
            lock(this) { __Ev = __Ev + value; }
        }
        remove {
            lock(this) { __Ev = __Ev - value; }
        }
    }
}
```

Within the class X, references to Ev are compiled to reference the hidden field __Ev instead. The name __Ev is arbitrary; the hidden field could have any name or no name at all.

Similarly, a static event declaration of the form

```
class X {
    public static event D Ev;
}
```

could be compiled to something equivalent to the following.

```
class X {
    private static D __Ev;   // field to hold the delegate
```

```
        public static event D Ev {
            add {
                lock(typeof(X)) { __Ev = __Ev + value; }
            }
            remove {
                lock(typeof(X)) { __Ev = __Ev - value; }
            }
        }
    }
```

10.7.2 Event Accessors

Event declarations typically omit *event-accessor-declaration*s, as in the `Button` example previously. One situation for doing so involves the case in which the storage cost of one field per event is not acceptable. In such cases, a class can include *event-accessor-declaration*s and use a private mechanism for storing the list of event handlers.

The *event-accessor-declarations* of an event specify the executable statements associated with adding and removing event handlers.

The accessor declarations consist of an *add-accessor-declaration* and a *remove-accessor-declaration*. Each accessor declaration consists of the token `add` or `remove` followed by a *block*. The *block* associated with an *add-accessor-declaration* specifies the statements to execute when an event handler is added, and the *block* associated with a *remove-accessor-declaration* specifies the statements to execute when an event handler is removed.

Each *add-accessor-declaration* and *remove-accessor-declaration* corresponds to a method with a single value parameter of the event type and a `void` return type. The implicit parameter of an event accessor is named `value`. When an event is used in an event assignment, the appropriate event accessor is used. Specifically, if the assignment operator is +=, then the add accessor is used, and if the assignment operator is -=, then the remove accessor is used. In either case, the right-hand operand of the assignment operator is used as the argument to the event accessor. The block of an *add-accessor-declaration* or a *remove-accessor-declaration* must conform to the rules for `void` methods described in §10.5.8. In particular, `return` statements in such a block are not permitted to specify an expression.

Because an event accessor implicitly has a parameter named `value`, it is a compile-time error for a local variable or constant declared in an event accessor to have that name.

In the example

```
    class Control: Component
    {
        // Unique keys for events
        static readonly object mouseDownEventKey = new object();
        static readonly object mouseUpEventKey = new object();

        // Return event handler associated with key
        protected Delegate GetEventHandler(object key) {...}
```

```
        // Add event handler associated with key
        protected void AddEventHandler(object key, Delegate handler) {...}

        // Remove event handler associated with key
        protected void RemoveEventHandler(object key, Delegate handler) {...}

        // MouseDown event
        public event MouseEventHandler MouseDown {
            add { AddEventHandler(mouseDownEventKey, value); }
            remove { RemoveEventHandler(mouseDownEventKey, value); }
        }

        // MouseUp event
        public event MouseEventHandler MouseUp {
            add { AddEventHandler(mouseUpEventKey, value); }
            remove { RemoveEventHandler(mouseUpEventKey, value); }
        }

        // Invoke the MouseUp event
        protected void OnMouseUp(MouseEventArgs args) {
            MouseEventHandler handler;
            handler = (MouseEventHandler)GetEventHandler(mouseUpEventKey);
            if (handler != null)
                handler(this, args);
        }
    }
```

the `Control` class implements an internal storage mechanism for events. The `AddEventHandler` method associates a delegate value with a key, the `GetEventHandler` method returns the delegate currently associated with a key, and the `RemoveEventHandler` method removes a delegate as an event handler for the specified event. Presumably, the underlying storage mechanism is designed such that there is no cost for associating a `null` delegate value with a key, and thus unhandled events consume no storage.

10.7.3 Static and Instance Events

When an event declaration includes a `static` modifier, the event is said to be a *static event*. When no `static` modifier is present, the event is said to be an *instance event*.

A static event is not associated with a specific instance, and it is a compile-time error to refer to `this` in the accessors of a static event.

An instance event is associated with a given instance of a class, and this instance can be accessed as `this` (§7.5.7) in the accessors of that event.

When an event is referenced in a *member-access* (§7.5.4) of the form E . M, if M is a static event, E must denote a type containing M, and if M is an instance event, E must denote an instance of a type containing M.

The differences between static and instance members are discussed further in §10.2.5.

10.7.4 **Virtual, Sealed, Override, and Abstract Accessors**

A `virtual` event declaration specifies that the accessors of that event are virtual. The `virtual` modifier applies to both accessors of an event.

An `abstract` event declaration specifies that the accessors of the event are virtual but does not provide an actual implementation of the accessors. Instead, nonabstract derived classes are required to provide their own implementation for the accessors by overriding the event. Because an accessor for an abstract event declaration provides no actual implementation, its *accessor-body* simply consists of a semicolon.

An event declaration that includes both the `abstract` and `override` modifiers specifies that the event is abstract and overrides a base event. The accessors of such an event are also abstract.

Abstract event declarations are only permitted in abstract classes (§10.1.1.1).

The accessors of an inherited virtual event can be overridden in a derived class by including an event declaration that specifies an `override` modifier. This is known as an *overriding event declaration*. An overriding event declaration does not declare a new event. Instead, it simply specializes the implementations of the accessors of an existing virtual event.

An overriding event declaration must specify the exact same accessibility modifiers, type, and name as the overridden event.

An overriding event declaration may include the `sealed` modifier. Using this modifier prevents a derived class from further overriding the event. The accessors of a sealed event are also sealed.

It is a compile-time error for an overriding event declaration to include a `new` modifier.

Except for differences in declaration and invocation syntax, virtual, sealed, override, and abstract accessors behave exactly like virtual, sealed, override, and abstract methods. Specifically, the rules described in §10.5.3, §10.5.4, §10.5.5, and §10.5.6 apply as if accessors were methods of a corresponding form. Each accessor corresponds to a method with a single value parameter of the event type, a `void` return type, and the same modifiers as the containing event.

10.8 **Indexers**

An *indexer* is a member that enables an object to be indexed in the same way as an array. Indexers are declared using *indexer-declarations*.

indexer-declaration:
> *attributes*_{opt} *indexer-modifiers*_{opt} *indexer-declarator* { *accessor-declarations* }

indexer-modifiers:
> *indexer-modifier*
> *indexer-modifiers indexer-modifier*

indexer-modifier:
> new
> public
> protected
> internal
> private
> virtual
> sealed
> override
> abstract
> extern

indexer-declarator:
> *type* this [*formal-parameter-list*]
> *type interface-type* . this [*formal-parameter-list*]

An *indexer-declaration* may include a set of *attributes* (§17) and a valid combination of the four access modifiers (§10.2.3), the new (§10.2.2), virtual (§10.5.3), override (§10.5.4), sealed (§10.5.5), abstract (§10.5.6), and extern (§10.5.7) modifiers.

Indexer declarations are subject to the same rules as method declarations (§10.5) with regard to valid combinations of modifiers, with the one exception being that the static modifier is not permitted on an indexer declaration.

The modifiers virtual, override, and abstract are mutually exclusive except in one case. The abstract and override modifiers may be used together so that an abstract indexer can override a virtual one.

The *type* of an indexer declaration specifies the element type of the indexer introduced by the declaration. Unless the indexer is an explicit interface member implementation, the *type* is followed by the keyword this. For an explicit interface member implementation, the *type* is followed by an *interface-type*, a " . ", and the keyword this. Unlike other members, indexers do not have user-defined names.

The *formal-parameter-list* specifies the parameters of the indexer. The formal parameter list of an indexer corresponds to that of a method (§10.5.1) except that at least one parameter must be specified and that the ref and out parameter modifiers are not permitted.

The *type* of an indexer and each of the types referenced in the *formal-parameter-list* must be at least as accessible as the indexer itself (§3.5.4).

The *accessor-declarations* (§10.6.2), which must be enclosed in { and } tokens, declare the accessors of the indexer. The accessors specify the executable statements associated with reading and writing indexer elements.

Even though the syntax for accessing an indexer element is the same as that for an array element, an indexer element is not classified as a variable. Thus, it is not possible to pass an indexer element as a `ref` or `out` argument.

The formal parameter list of an indexer defines the signature (§3.6) of the indexer. Specifically, the signature of an indexer consists of the number and types of its formal parameters. The element type and names of the formal parameters are not part of an indexer's signature.

The signature of an indexer must differ from the signatures of all other indexers declared in the same class.

Indexers and properties are similar in concept but differ in the following ways.

- A property is identified by its name, whereas an indexer is identified by its signature.

- A property is accessed through a *simple-name* (§7.5.2) or a *member-access* (§7.5.4), whereas an indexer element is accessed through an *element-access* (§7.5.6.2).

- A property can be a `static` member, whereas an indexer is always an instance member.

- A `get` accessor of a property corresponds to a method with no parameters, whereas a `get` accessor of an indexer corresponds to a method with the same formal parameter list as the indexer.

- A `set` accessor of a property corresponds to a method with a single parameter named `value`, whereas a `set` accessor of an indexer corresponds to a method with the same formal parameter list as the indexer, plus an additional parameter named `value`.

- It is a compile-time error for an indexer accessor to declare a local variable with the same name as an indexer parameter.

- In an overriding property declaration, the inherited property is accessed using the syntax `base.P`, where `P` is the property name. In an overriding indexer declaration, the inherited indexer is accessed using the syntax `base[E]`, where `E` is a comma-separated list of expressions.

Aside from these differences, all rules defined in §10.6.2 and §10.6.3 apply to indexer accessors as well as to property accessors.

When an indexer declaration includes an `extern` modifier, the indexer is said to be an *external indexer*. Because an external indexer declaration provides no actual implementation, each of its *accessor-declarations* consists of a semicolon.

The following example declares a `BitArray` class that implements an indexer for accessing the individual bits in the bit array.

```
using System;

class BitArray
{
    int[] bits;
    int length;

    public BitArray(int length) {
        if (length < 0) throw new ArgumentException();
        bits = new int[((length - 1) >> 5) + 1];
        this.length = length;
    }

    public int Length {
        get { return length; }
    }

    public bool this[int index] {
        get {
            if (index < 0 || index >= length) {
                throw new IndexOutOfRangeException();
            }
            return (bits[index >> 5] & 1 << index) != 0;
        }
        set {
            if (index < 0 || index >= length) {
                throw new IndexOutOfRangeException();
            }
            if (value) {
                bits[index >> 5] |= 1 << index;
            }
            else {
                bits[index >> 5] &= ~(1 << index);
            }
        }
    }
}
```

An instance of the `BitArray` class consumes substantially less memory than a corresponding `bool[]` (because each value of the former occupies only one bit instead of the latter's one byte), but it permits the same operations as a `bool[]`.

The following `CountPrimes` class uses a `BitArray` and the classical "sieve" algorithm to compute the number of primes between 1 and a given maximum.

```
class CountPrimes
{
    static int Count(int max) {
        BitArray flags = new BitArray(max + 1);
        int count = 1;
        for (int i = 2; i <= max; i++) {
            if (!flags[i]) {
                for (int j = i * 2; j <= max; j += i) flags[j] = true;
                count++;
            }
        }
        return count;
    }

    static void Main(string[] args) {
        int max = int.Parse(args[0]);
        int count = Count(max);
        Console.WriteLine("Found {0} primes between 1 and {1}", count, max);
    }
}
```

Note that the syntax for accessing elements of the BitArray is precisely the same as for a bool[].

The following example shows a 26 × 10 grid class that has an indexer with two parameters. The first parameter is required to be an uppercase or lowercase letter in the range A–Z, and the second is required to be an integer in the range 0–9.

```
using System;

class Grid
{
    const int NumRows = 26;
    const int NumCols = 10;

    int[,] cells = new int[NumRows, NumCols];

    public int this[char c, int col] {
        get {
            c = Char.ToUpper(c);
            if (c < 'A' || c > 'Z') {
                throw new ArgumentException();
            }
            if (col < 0 || col >= NumCols) {
                throw new IndexOutOfRangeException();
            }
            return cells[c - 'A', col];
        }
```

```
        set {
            c = Char.ToUpper(c);
            if (c < 'A' || c > 'Z') {
                throw new ArgumentException();
            }
            if (col < 0 || col >= NumCols) {
                throw new IndexOutOfRangeException();
            }
            cells[c - 'A', col] = value;
        }
    }
}
```

10.8.1 Indexer Overloading

The indexer overload resolution rules are described in §7.4.2.

10.9 Operators

An *operator* is a member that defines the meaning of an expression operator that can be applied to instances of the class. Operators are declared using *operator-declarations*.

operator-declaration:
    attributes$_{opt}$ *operator-modifiers*   *operator-declarator*   *operator-body*

operator-modifiers:
    operator-modifier
    operator-modifiers   *operator-modifier*

operator-modifier:
    `public`
    `static`
    `extern`

operator-declarator:
    unary-operator-declarator
    binary-operator-declarator
    conversion-operator-declarator

unary-operator-declarator:
    type `operator` *overloadable-unary-operator* `(` *type identifier* `)`

overloadable-unary-operator: one of
    `+`   `-`   `!`   `~`   `++`   `--`   `true`   `false`

binary-operator-declarator:
    type `operator` *overloadable-binary-operator* `(` *type identifier* `,` *type identifier* `)`

overloadable-binary-operator: one of
```
+    -    *    /    %    &    |    ^    <<    >>    ==    !=    >    <    >=    <=
```

conversion-operator-declarator:
```
implicit operator type ( type identifier )
explicit operator type ( type identifier )
```

operator-body:
    block

    ;

There are three categories of overloadable operators: unary operators (§10.9.1), binary operators (§10.9.2), and conversion operators (§10.9.3).

When an operator declaration includes an `extern` modifier, the operator is said to be an ***external operator.*** Because an external operator provides no actual implementation, its *operator-body* consists of a semicolon. For all other operators, the *operator-body* consists of a *block*, which specifies the statements to execute when the operator is invoked. The *block* of an operator must conform to the rules for value-returning methods described in §10.5.8.

The following rules apply to all operator declarations.

* An operator declaration must include both a `public` and a `static` modifier.

* The parameter(s) of an operator must be value parameters. It is a compile-time error for an operator declaration to specify `ref` or `out` parameters.

* The signature of an operator (§10.9.1, §10.9.2, §10.9.3) must differ from the signatures of all other operators declared in the same class.

* All types referenced in an operator declaration must be at least as accessible as the operator itself (§3.5.4).

* It is an error for the same modifier to appear multiple times in an operator declaration.

Each operator category imposes additional restrictions, as described in the following sections.

Like other members, operators declared in a base class are inherited by derived classes. Because operator declarations always require the class or struct in which the operator is declared to participate in the signature of the operator, it is not possible for an operator declared in a derived class to hide an operator declared in a base class. Thus, the `new` modifier is never required, and therefore never permitted, in an operator declaration.

Additional information on unary and binary operators can be found in §7.2.

Additional information on conversion operators can be found in §6.4.

10.9.1 Unary Operators

The following rules apply to unary operator declarations, where T denotes the class or struct type that contains the operator declaration.

- A unary +, -, !, or ~ operator must take a single parameter of type T and can return any type.

- A unary ++ or -- operator must take a single parameter of type T and must return type T.

- A unary true or false operator must take a single parameter of type T and must return type bool.

The signature of a unary operator consists of the operator token (+, -, !, ~, ++, --, true, or false) and the type of the single formal parameter. The return type is not part of a unary operator's signature, and it is not the name of the formal parameter.

The true and false unary operators require pair-wise declaration. A compile-time error occurs if a class declares one of these operators without also declaring the other. The true and false operators are described further in §7.11.2 and §7.16.

The following example shows an implementation and subsequent usage of operator ++ for an integer vector class.

```
public class IntVector
{
    public IntVector(int length) {...}

    public int Length {...}              // read-only property

    public int this[int index] {...}     // read-write indexer

    public static IntVector operator ++(IntVector iv) {
        IntVector temp = new IntVector(iv.Length);
        for (int i = 0; i < iv.Length; i++)
            temp[i] = iv[i] + 1;
        return temp;
    }
}

class Test
{
    static void Main() {
        IntVector iv1 = new IntVector(4); // vector of 4 x 0
        IntVector iv2;

        iv2 = iv1++;    // iv2 contains 4 x 0, iv1 contains 4 x 1
        iv2 = ++iv1;    // iv2 contains 4 x 2, iv1 contains 4 x 2
    }
}
```

Note how the operator method returns the value produced by adding 1 to the operand, just like the postfix increment and decrement operators (§7.5.9) and the prefix increment and decrement operators (§7.6.5). Unlike in C++, this method need not modify the value of its operand directly. In fact, modifying the operand value would violate the standard semantics of the postfix increment operator.

10.9.2 Binary Operators

A binary operator must take two parameters, and at least one of which must have the class or struct type in which the operator is declared. Parameters of the shift operators (§7.8) are further constrained. A binary operator can return any type.

The signature of a binary operator consists of the operator token (+, -, *, /, %, &, |, ^, <<, >>, ==, !=, >, <, >=, or <=) and the types of the two formal parameters. The return type and the names of the formal parameters are not part of a binary operator's signature.

Certain binary operators require pair-wise declaration. For every declaration of either operator of a pair, there must be a matching declaration of the other operator of the pair. Two operator declarations match when they have the same return type and the same type for each parameter. The following operators require pair-wise declaration:

- `operator ==` and `operator !=`
- `operator >` and `operator <`
- `operator >=` and `operator <=`

10.9.3 Conversion Operators

A conversion operator declaration introduces a ***user-defined conversion*** (§6.4), which augments the predefined implicit and explicit conversions.

A conversion operator declaration that includes the `implicit` keyword introduces a user-defined implicit conversion. Implicit conversions can occur in a variety of situations, including function member invocations, cast expressions, and assignments. This is described further in §6.1.

A conversion operator declaration that includes the `explicit` keyword introduces a user-defined explicit conversion. Explicit conversions can occur in cast expressions and are described further in §6.2.

A conversion operator converts from a source type, indicated by the parameter type of the conversion operator, to a target type, indicated by the return type of the conversion operator. A class or struct is permitted to declare a conversion from a source type S to a target type T provided all of the following are true.

- S and T are different types.
- Either S or T is the class or struct type in which the operator declaration takes place.
- Neither S nor T is object or an *interface-type*.
- T is not a base class of S, and S is not a base class of T.

From the second rule it follows that a conversion operator must convert either to or from the class or struct type in which the operator is declared. For example, it is possible for a class or struct type C to define a conversion from C to int and from int to C, but not from int to bool.

It is not possible to redefine a predefined conversion. Thus, conversion operators are not allowed to convert from or to object because implicit and explicit conversions already exist between object and all other types. Likewise, neither the source nor the target types of a conversion can be a base type of the other because a conversion would then already exist.

User-defined conversions are not allowed to convert from or to *interface-type*s. In particular, this restriction ensures that no user-defined transformations occur when converting to an *interface-type* and that a conversion to an *interface-type* succeeds only if the object being converted actually implements the specified *interface-type*.

The signature of a conversion operator consists of the source type and the target type. (Note that this is the only form of member for which the return type participates in the signature.) The implicit or explicit classification of a conversion operator is not part of the operator's signature. Thus, a class or struct cannot declare both an implicit and an explicit conversion operator with the same source and target types.

In general, user-defined implicit conversions should be designed to never throw exceptions and never lose information. If a user-defined conversion can give rise to exceptions (for example, because the source argument is out of range) or loss of information (such as discarding high-order bits), then that conversion should be defined as an explicit conversion.

In the example

```
using System;

public struct Digit
{
    byte value;
```

```
    public Digit(byte value) {
        if (value < 0 || value > 9) throw new ArgumentException();
        this.value = value;
    }

    public static implicit operator byte(Digit d) {
        return d.value;
    }

    public static explicit operator Digit(byte b) {
        return new Digit(b);
    }
}
```

the conversion from `Digit` to `byte` is implicit because it never throws exceptions or loses information, but the conversion from `byte` to `Digit` is explicit because `Digit` can only represent a subset of the possible values of a `byte`.

10.10 Instance Constructors

An *instance constructor* is a member that implements the actions required to initialize an instance of a class. Instance constructors are declared using *constructor-declarations*.

constructor-declaration:
    attributes_{opt}   *constructor-modifiers_{opt}*   *constructor-declarator*   *constructor-body*

constructor-modifiers:
    constructor-modifier
    constructor-modifiers   *constructor-modifier*

constructor-modifier:
    `public`
    `protected`
    `internal`
    `private`
    `extern`

constructor-declarator:
    identifier   (*formal-parameter-list_{opt}*   )   *constructor-initializer_{opt}*

constructor-initializer:
    :   `base`   (*argument-list_{opt}*   )
    :   `this`   (*argument-list_{opt}*   )

constructor-body:
    block
    ;

A *constructor-declaration* may include a set of *attributes* (§17), a valid combination of the four access modifiers (§10.2.3), and an `extern` (§10.5.7) modifier. A constructor declaration is not permitted to include the same modifier multiple times.

The *identifier* of a *constructor-declarator* must name the class in which the instance constructor is declared. If any other name is specified, a compile-time error occurs.

The optional *formal-parameter-list* of an instance constructor is subject to the same rules as the *formal-parameter-list* of a method (§10.5). The formal parameter list defines the signature (§3.6) of an instance constructor and governs the process whereby overload resolution (§7.4.2) selects a particular instance constructor in an invocation.

Each of the types referenced in the *formal-parameter-list* of an instance constructor must be at least as accessible as the constructor itself (§3.5.4).

The optional *constructor-initializer* specifies another instance constructor to invoke before executing the statements given in the *constructor-body* of this instance constructor. This is described further in §10.10.1.

When a constructor declaration includes an `extern` modifier, the constructor is said to be an ***external constructor***. Because an external constructor declaration provides no actual implementation, its *constructor-body* consists of a semicolon. For all other constructors, the *constructor-body* consists of a *block* that specifies the statements to initialize a new instance of the class. This corresponds exactly to the *block* of an instance method with a `void` return type (§10.5.8).

Instance constructors are not inherited. Thus, a class has no instance constructors other than those actually declared in the class. If a class contains no instance constructor declarations, a default instance constructor is automatically provided (§10.10.4).

Instance constructors are invoked by *object-creation-expression*s (§7.5.10.1) and through *constructor-initializer*s.

10.10.1 Constructor Initializers

All instance constructors (except those for class `object`) implicitly include an invocation of another instance constructor immediately before the *constructor-body*. The constructor to implicitly invoke is determined by the *constructor-initializer*.

- An instance constructor initializer of the form `base` (*argument-list*$_{opt}$) causes an instance constructor from the direct base class to be invoked. That constructor is selected using *argument-list* and the overload resolution rules of §7.4.2. The set of candidate instance constructors consists of all accessible instance constructors contained in the direct base class (including any default constructor, as defined in §10.10.4). If this set is empty or if a single best instance constructor cannot be identified, a compile-time error occurs.

- An instance constructor initializer of the form this (*argument-list*$_{opt}$) causes an instance constructor from the class itself to be invoked. The constructor is selected using *argument-list* and the overload resolution rules of §7.4.2. The set of candidate instance constructors consists of all accessible instance constructors declared in the class itself. If this set is empty or if a single best instance constructor cannot be identified, a compile-time error occurs. If an instance constructor declaration includes a constructor initializer that invokes the constructor itself, a compile-time error occurs.

If an instance constructor has no constructor initializer, a constructor initializer of the form base() is implicitly provided. Thus, an instance constructor declaration of the form

```
C(...) {...}
```

is exactly equivalent to the following.

```
C(...): base() {...}
```

The scope of the parameters given by the *formal-parameter-list* of an instance constructor declaration includes the constructor initializer of that declaration. Thus, a constructor initializer is permitted to access the parameters of the constructor. For example

```
class A
{
    public A(int x, int y) {}
}
class B: A
{
    public B(int x, int y): base(x + y, x - y) {}
}
```

An instance constructor initializer cannot access the instance being created. Therefore, it is a compile-time error to reference this in an argument expression of the constructor initializer just like it is a compile-time error for an argument expression to reference any instance member through a *simple-name*.

10.10.2 Instance Variable Initializers

When an instance constructor has no constructor initializer or it has a constructor initializer of the form base(...), that constructor implicitly performs the initializations specified by the *variable-initializer*s of the instance fields declared in its class. This corresponds to a sequence of assignments that are executed immediately upon entry to the constructor and before the implicit invocation of the direct base class constructor. The variable initializers are executed in the textual order in which they appear in the class declaration.

10.10.3 Constructor Execution

Variable initializers are transformed into assignment statements, and these assignment statements are executed before the invocation of the base class instance constructor. This ordering ensures that all instance fields are initialized by their variable initializers before any statements that have access to that instance are executed.

Given the example

```
using System;
class A
{
    public A() {
        PrintFields();
    }
    public virtual void PrintFields() {}
}
class B: A
{
    int x = 1;
    int y;
    public B() {
        y = -1;
    }
    public override void PrintFields() {
        Console.WriteLine("x = {0}, y = {1}", x, y);
    }
}
```

when new B() is used to create an instance of B, the following output is produced.

```
x = 1, y = 0
```

The value of x is 1 because the variable initializer is executed before the base class instance constructor is invoked. However, the value of y is 0 (the default value of an int) because the assignment to y is not executed until after the base class constructor returns.

It is useful to think of instance variable initializers and constructor initializers as statements that are automatically inserted before the *constructor-body*. The example

```
using System;
using System.Collections;

class A
{
    int x = 1, y = -1, count;

    public A() {
        count = 0;
    }
```

```
    public A(int n) {
        count = n;
    }
}
class B: A
{
    double sqrt2 = Math.Sqrt(2.0);
    ArrayList items = new ArrayList(100);
    int max;

    public B(): this(100) {
        items.Add("default");
    }

    public B(int n): base(n - 1) {
        max = n;
    }
}
```

contains several variable initializers; it also contains constructor initializers of both forms (base and this). The example corresponds to the following code, where each comment indicates an automatically inserted statement (the syntax used for the automatically inserted constructor invocations is not valid but merely serves to illustrate the mechanism).

```
using System.Collections;

class A
{
    int x, y, count;

    public A() {
        x = 1;          // Variable initializer
        y = -1;         // Variable initializer
        object();       // Invoke object() constructor
        count = 0;
    }

    public A(int n) {
        x = 1;          // Variable initializer
        y = -1;         // Variable initializer
        object();       // Invoke object() constructor
        count = n;
    }
}
class B: A
{
    double sqrt2;
    ArrayList items;
    int max;

    public B(): this(100) {
        B(100);         // Invoke B(int) constructor
        items.Add("default");
    }
```

```
    public B(int n): base(n - 1) {
        sqrt2 = Math.Sqrt(2.0);        // Variable initializer
        items = new ArrayList(100);    // Variable initializer
        A(n - 1);                      // Invoke A(int) constructor
        max = n;
    }
}
```

10.10.4 Default Constructors

If a class contains no instance constructor declarations, a default instance constructor is automatically provided. That default constructor simply invokes the parameterless constructor of the direct base class. If the direct base class does not have an accessible parameterless instance constructor, a compile-time error occurs. If the class is abstract, then the declared accessibility for the default constructor is protected. Otherwise, the declared accessibility for the default constructor is public. Thus, the default constructor is always of the form

```
protected C(): base() {}
```

or of the form

```
public C(): base() {}
```

where C is the name of the class.

In the example

```
class Message
{
    object sender;
    string text;
}
```

a default constructor is provided because the class contains no instance constructor declarations. Thus, the example is precisely equivalent to the following.

```
class Message
{
    object sender;
    string text;

    public Message(): base() {}
}
```

10.10.5 Private Constructors

When a class T declares only private instance constructors, it is not possible for classes outside the program text of T to derive from T or to directly create instances of T. Thus, if a class contains only static members and is not intended to be instantiated, adding an empty private instance constructor will prevent instantiation. For example

```
public class Trig
{
    private Trig() {}  // Prevent instantiation
    public const double PI = 3.14159265358979323846;
    public static double Sin(double x) {...}
    public static double Cos(double x) {...}
    public static double Tan(double x) {...}
}
```

The `Trig` class groups related methods and constants but is not intended to be instantiated. Therefore, it declares a single empty private instance constructor. At least one instance constructor must be declared to suppress the automatic generation of a default constructor.

10.10.6 Optional Instance Constructor Parameters

The `this(...)` form of constructor initializer is commonly used in conjunction with overloading to implement optional instance constructor parameters. In the example

```
class Text
{
    public Text(): this(0, 0, null) {}
    public Text(int x, int y): this(x, y, null) {}
    public Text(int x, int y, string s) {
        // Actual constructor implementation
    }
}
```

the first two instance constructors merely provide the default values for the missing arguments. Both use a `this(...)` constructor initializer to invoke the third instance constructor, which actually does the work of initializing the new instance. The effect is that of optional constructor parameters.

```
Text t1 = new Text();            // Same as Text(0, 0, null)
Text t2 = new Text(5, 10);       // Same as Text(5, 10, null)
Text t3 = new Text(5, 20, "Hello");
```

10.11 Static Constructors

A *static constructor* is a member that implements the actions required to initialize a class. Static constructors are declared using *static-constructor-declaration*s.

static-constructor-declaration:
    attributes$_{opt}$ *static-constructor-modifiers identifier* ( ) *static-constructor-body*

static-constructor-modifiers:
    extern_{opt} static
    static extern_{opt}

static-constructor-body:
    block

    ;

A *static-constructor-declaration* may include a set of *attributes* (§17) and an `extern` modifier (§10.5.7).

The *identifier* of a *static-constructor-declaration* must name the class in which the static constructor is declared. If any other name is specified, a compile-time error occurs.

When a static constructor declaration includes an `extern` modifier, the static constructor is said to be an ***external static constructor***. Because an external static constructor declaration provides no actual implementation, its *static-constructor-body* consists of a semicolon. For all other static constructor declarations, the *static-constructor-body* consists of a *block* that specifies the statements to execute in order to initialize the class. This corresponds exactly to the *method-body* of a static method with a `void` return type (§10.5.8).

Static constructors are not inherited and cannot be called directly.

The static constructor for a class executes at most once in a given application domain. The execution of a static constructor is triggered by the first of the following events to occur within an application domain.

- An instance of the class is created.

- Any of the static members of the class are referenced.

If a class contains the `Main` method (§3.1) in which execution begins, the static constructor for that class executes before the `Main` method is called. If a class contains any static fields with initializers, those initializers are executed in textual order immediately prior to executing the static constructor.

The example

```
using System;

class Test
{
    static void Main() {
        A.F();
        B.F();
    }
}
```

```
class A
{
    static A() {
        Console.WriteLine("Init A");
    }
    public static void F() {
        Console.WriteLine("A.F");
    }
}
class B
{
    static B() {
        Console.WriteLine("Init B");
    }
    public static void F() {
        Console.WriteLine("B.F");
    }
}
```

must produce the following output.

```
Init A
A.F
Init B
B.F
```

because the execution of A's static constructor is triggered by the call to A.F, and the execution of B's static constructor is triggered by the call to B.F.

It is possible to construct circular dependencies that allow static fields with variable initializers to be observed in their default value state.

The example

```
using System;
class A
{
    public static int X;
    static A() {
        X = B.Y + 1;
    }
}
class B
{
    public static int Y = A.X + 1;
    static B() {}
    static void Main() {
        Console.WriteLine("X = {0}, Y = {1}", A.X, B.Y);
    }
}
```

produces the following output.

```
X = 1, Y = 2
```

To execute the `Main` method, the system first runs the initializer for `B.Y`, prior to class B's static constructor. `Y`'s initializer causes A's static constructor to be run because the value of `A.X` is referenced. The static constructor of A in turn proceeds to compute the value of X and in doing so fetches the default value of Y, which is zero. `A.X` is thus initialized to 1. The process of running A's static field initializers and static constructor then completes, returning to the calculation of the initial value of Y, the result of which becomes 2.

10.12 Destructors

A *destructor* is a member that implements the actions required to destruct an instance of a class. A destructor is declared using a *destructor-declaration*.

> *destructor-declaration:*
>   *attributes*_{opt} `extern`_{opt} ~ *identifier* ( ) *destructor-body*
>
> *destructor-body:*
>   *block*
>   ;

A *destructor-declaration* may include a set of *attributes* (§17).

The *identifier* of a *destructor-declarator* must name the class in which the destructor is declared. If any other name is specified, a compile-time error occurs.

When a destructor declaration includes an `extern` modifier, the destructor is said to be an *external destructor*. Because an external destructor declaration provides no actual implementation, its *destructor-body* consists of a semicolon. For all other destructors, the *destructor-body* consists of a *block* that specifies the statements to execute in order to destruct an instance of the class. A *destructor-body* corresponds exactly to the *method-body* of an instance method with a `void` return type (§10.5.8).

Destructors are not inherited. Thus, a class has no destructors other than the one that may be declared in that class.

Because a destructor is required to have no parameters, it cannot be overloaded, so a class can have, at most, one destructor.

Destructors are invoked automatically and cannot be invoked explicitly. An instance becomes eligible for destruction when it is no longer possible for any code to use that instance. Execution of the destructor for the instance may occur at any time after the instance becomes eligible for destruction. When an instance is destructed, the destructors in that instance's inheritance chain are called, in order, from most derived to least derived. A destructor may be executed on any thread. For further discussion of the rules that govern when and how a destructor is executed, see §3.9.

The output of the example

```
using System;
class A
{
    ~A() {
        Console.WriteLine("A's destructor");
    }
}
class B: A
{
    ~B() {
        Console.WriteLine("B's destructor");
    }
}
class Test
{
    static void Main() {
        B b = new B();
        b = null;
        GC.Collect();
        GC.WaitForPendingFinalizers();
    }
}
```

is as follows

```
B's destructor
A's destructor
```

because destructors in an inheritance chain are called in order, from most derived to least derived.

Destructors are implemented by overriding the virtual method `Finalize` on `System.Object`. C# programs are not permitted to override this method or call it (or overrides of it) directly. For instance, the program

```
class A
{
    override protected void Finalize() {}    // error
    public void F() {
        this.Finalize();                     // error
    }
}
```

contains two errors.

The compiler behaves as if this method, and overrides of it, do not exist at all. Thus, this program

```
class A
{
    void Finalize() {}      // permitted
}
```

is valid, and the method shown hides `System.Object`'s `Finalize` method.

For a discussion of the behavior when an exception is thrown from a destructor, see §16.3.

11. Structs

Structs are similar to classes in that they represent data structures that can contain data members and function members. However, unlike classes, structs are value types and do not require heap allocation. A variable of a struct type directly contains the data of the struct, whereas a variable of a class type contains a reference to the data, the latter known as an object.

Structs are particularly useful for small data structures that have value semantics. Complex numbers, points in a coordinate system, or key-value pairs in a dictionary are all good examples of structs. Key to these data structures is that they have few data members, they do not require use of inheritance or referential identity, and they can be conveniently implemented using value semantics where assignment copies the value instead of the reference.

As described in §4.1.4, the simple types provided by C#, such as `int`, `double`, and `bool`, are in fact all struct types. Just as these predefined types are structs, it is also possible to use structs and operator overloading to implement new "primitive" types in the C# language. Two examples of such types are given at the end of this chapter (§11.4).

11.1 Struct Declarations

A *struct-declaration* is a *type-declaration* (§9.5) that declares a new struct.

> *struct-declaration:*
>   *attributes*$_{opt}$ *struct-modifiers*$_{opt}$ struct *identifier* *struct-interfaces*$_{opt}$
>   *struct-body* ;$_{opt}$

A *struct-declaration* consists of an optional set of *attributes* (§17), followed by an optional set of *struct-modifiers* (§11.1.1), followed by the keyword `struct` and an *identifier* that names the struct, followed by an optional *struct-interfaces* specification (§11.1.2), followed by a *struct-body* (§11.1.3), optionally followed by a semicolon.

11.1.1 **Struct Modifiers**

A *struct-declaration* may optionally include a sequence of struct modifiers.

> *struct-modifiers:*
>   *struct-modifier*
>   *struct-modifiers   struct-modifier*
>
> *struct-modifier:*
>   new
>   public
>   protected
>   internal
>   private

It is a compile-time error for the same modifier to appear multiple times in a struct declaration.

The modifiers of a struct declaration have the same meaning as those of a class declaration (§10.1.1).

11.1.2 **Struct Interfaces**

A struct declaration may include a *struct-interfaces* specification, in which case the struct is said to implement the given interface types.

> *struct-interfaces:*
>   :   *interface-type-list*

Interface implementations are discussed further in §13.4.

11.1.3 **Struct Body**

The *struct-body* of a struct defines the members of the struct.

> *struct-body:*
>   {   *struct-member-declarations*$_{opt}$ }

11.2 **Struct Members**

The members of a struct consist of the members introduced by its *struct-member-declaration*s and the members inherited from the type System.ValueType.

> *struct-member-declarations:*
>   *struct-member-declaration*
>   *struct-member-declarations   struct-member-declaration*

struct-member-declaration:
    constant-declaration
    field-declaration
    method-declaration
    property-declaration
    event-declaration
    indexer-declaration
    operator-declaration
    constructor-declaration
    static-constructor-declaration
    type-declaration

Except for the differences noted in §11.3, the descriptions of class members provided in §10.2 through §10.11 also apply to struct members.

11.3 Class and Struct Differences

Structs differ from classes in several important ways.

- Structs are value types (§11.3.1).
- All struct types implicitly inherit from the class `System.ValueType` (§11.3.2).
- Assignment to a variable of a struct type creates a *copy* of the value being assigned (§11.3.3).
- The default value of a struct is the value produced by setting all value type fields to their default value and all reference type fields to `null` (§11.3.4).
- Boxing and unboxing operations are used to convert between a struct type and `object` (§11.3.5).
- The meaning of `this` is different for structs (§11.3.6).
- Instance field declarations for a struct are not permitted to include variable initializers (§11.3.7).
- A struct is not permitted to declare a parameterless instance constructor (§11.3.8).
- A struct is not permitted to declare a destructor (§11.3.9).

11.3.1 Value Semantics

Structs are value types (§4.1) and are said to have value semantics. Classes, on the other hand, are reference types (§4.2) and are said to have reference semantics.

A variable of a struct type directly contains the data of the struct, whereas a variable of a class type contains a reference to the data, which is known as an object.

With classes, it is possible for two variables to reference the same object and thus possible for operations on one variable to affect the object referenced by the other variable. With structs, the variables each have their own copy of the data (except in the case of `ref` and `out` parameter variables), and it is not possible for operations on one to affect the other. Furthermore, because structs are not reference types, it is not possible for values of a struct type to be `null`.

Given the following declaration

```
struct Point
{
    public int x, y;
    public Point(int x, int y) {
        this.x = x;
        this.y = y;
    }
}
```

the following code fragment outputs the value 10.

```
Point a = new Point(10, 10);
Point b = a;
a.x = 100;
System.Console.WriteLine(b.x);
```

The assignment of a to b creates a copy of the value, and b is thus unaffected by the assignment to a.x. Had `Point` instead been declared as a class, the output would be `100` because a and b would reference the same object.

11.3.2 Inheritance

All struct types implicitly inherit from the class `System.ValueType`, which, in turn, inherits from class `object`. A struct declaration may specify a list of implemented interfaces, but it is not possible for a struct declaration to specify a base class.

Struct types are never abstract and are always implicitly sealed. The `abstract` and `sealed` modifiers are therefore not permitted in a struct declaration.

Because inheritance is not supported for structs, the declared accessibility of a struct member cannot be `protected` or `protected internal`.

Function members in a struct cannot be `abstract` or `virtual`, and the `override` modifier is allowed only to override methods inherited from `System.ValueType`.

11.3.3 **Assignment**

Assignment to a variable of a struct type creates a *copy* of the value being assigned. This differs from assignment to a variable of a class type, which copies the reference but not the object identified by the reference.

Similar to an assignment, when a struct is passed as a value parameter or returned as the result of a function member, a copy of the struct is created. A struct may be passed by reference to a function member using a `ref` or `out` parameter.

When a property or indexer of a struct is the target of an assignment, the instance expression associated with the property or indexer access must be classified as a variable. If the instance expression is classified as a value, a compile-time error occurs. This is described in further detail in §7.13.1.

11.3.4 **Default Values**

As described in §5.2, several kinds of variables are automatically initialized to their default value when they are created. For variables of class types and other reference types, this default value is `null`. However, because structs are value types that cannot be `null`, the default value of a struct is the value produced by setting all value type fields to their default value and all reference type fields to `null`.

Referring to the `Point` struct declared previously, the example

```
Point[] a = new Point[100];
```

initializes each `Point` in the array to the value produced by setting the x and y fields to zero.

The default value of a struct corresponds to the value returned by the default constructor of the struct (§4.1.1). Unlike a class, a struct is not permitted to declare a parameterless instance constructor. Instead, every struct implicitly has a parameterless instance constructor that always returns the value that results from setting all value type fields to their default value and all reference type fields to `null`.

Structs should be designed to consider the default initialization state a valid state. In the example

```
using System;

struct KeyValuePair
{
    string key;
    string value;
```

11. Structs

```
public KeyValuePair(string key, string value) {
    if (key == null || value == null) throw new ArgumentException();
    this.key = key;
    this.value = value;
}
```
}

the user-defined instance constructor protects against null values only where it is explicitly called. In cases where a KeyValuePair variable is subject to default value initialization, the key and value fields will be null, and the struct must be prepared to handle this state.

11.3.5 Boxing and Unboxing

A value of a class type can be converted to type object or to an interface type that is implemented by the class simply by treating the reference as another type at compile time. Likewise, a value of type object or a value of an interface type can be converted back to a class type without changing the reference (but of course a runtime type check is required in this case).

Because structs are not reference types, these operations are implemented differently for struct types. When a value of a struct type is converted to type object or to an interface type that is implemented by the struct, a boxing operation takes place. Likewise, when a value of type object or a value of an interface type is converted back to a struct type, an unboxing operation takes place. A key difference from the same operations on class types is that boxing and unboxing *copies* the struct value either into or out of the boxed instance. Thus, following a boxing or unboxing operation, changes made to the unboxed struct are not reflected in the boxed struct.

For further details on boxing and unboxing, see §4.3.

11.3.6 Meaning of this

Within an instance constructor or instance function member of a class, this is classified as a value. Thus, although this can be used to refer to the instance for which the function member was invoked, it is not possible to assign to this in a function member of a class.

Within an instance constructor of a struct, this corresponds to an out parameter of the struct type, and within an instance function member of a struct, this corresponds to a ref parameter of the struct type. In both cases, this is classified as a variable, and it is possible to modify the entire struct for which the function member was invoked by assigning to this or by passing this as a ref or out parameter.

11.3.7 Field Initializers

As described in §11.3.4, the default value of a struct consists of the value that results from setting all value type fields to their default value and all reference type fields to null. For this reason, a struct does not permit instance field declarations to include variable initializers. This restriction applies only to instance fields. Static fields of a struct are permitted to include variable initializers.

The example

```
struct Point
{
    public int x = 1;   // Error, initializer not permitted
    public int y = 1;   // Error, initializer not permitted
}
```

is in error because the instance field declarations include variable initializers.

11.3.8 Constructors

Unlike a class, a struct is not permitted to declare a parameterless instance constructor. Instead, every struct implicitly has a parameterless instance constructor that always returns the value that results from setting all value type fields to their default value and all reference type fields to null (§4.1.2). A struct can declare instance constructors having parameters. For example

```
struct Point
{
    int x, y;

    public Point(int x, int y) {
        this.x = x;
        this.y = y;
    }
}
```

Given the previous declaration, the statements

```
Point p1 = new Point();

Point p2 = new Point(0, 0);
```

both create a `Point` with x and y initialized to zero.

A struct instance constructor is not permitted to include a constructor initializer of the form base(...).

If the struct instance constructor does not specify a constructor initializer, the this variable corresponds to an out parameter of the struct type, and similar to an out parameter, this must be definitely assigned (§5.3) at every location where the constructor returns. If the struct instance constructor specifies a constructor initializer, the this variable corresponds to a ref parameter of the struct type, and similar to a ref parameter, this is

11. Structs

361

considered definitely assigned on entry to the constructor body. In the following instance constructor implementation

```
struct Point
{
    int x, y;
    public int X {
        set { x = value; }
    }
    public int Y {
        set { y = value; }
    }
    public Point(int x, int y) {
        X = x;       // error, this is not yet definitely assigned
        Y = y;       // error, this is not yet definitely assigned
    }
}
```

no instance member function (including the set accessors for the properties X and Y) can be called until all fields of the struct being constructed have been definitely assigned. Note, however, that if Point were a class instead of a struct, the instance constructor implementation would be permitted.

11.3.9 Destructors
A struct is not permitted to declare a destructor.

11.4 Struct Examples

The following sections show two significant examples of using struct types to create types that can be used similarly to the built-in types of the language but with modified semantics.

11.4.1 Database Integer Type
The following DBInt struct implements an integer type that can represent the complete set of values of the int type, plus an additional state that indicates an unknown value. A type with these characteristics is commonly used in databases.

```
using System;

public struct DBInt
{
    // The Null member represents an unknown DBInt value.

    public static readonly DBInt Null = new DBInt();
```

```
// When the defined field is true, this DBInt represents a known value
// which is stored in the value field. When the defined field is false,
// this DBInt represents an unknown value, and the value field is 0.

int value;
bool defined;

// Private instance constructor. Creates a DBInt with a known value.

DBInt(int value) {
    this.value = value;
    this.defined = true;
}

// The IsNull property is true if this DBInt represents an unknown value.

public bool IsNull { get { return !defined; } }

// The Value property is the known value of this DBInt, or 0 if this
// DBInt represents an unknown value.

public int Value { get { return value; } }

// Implicit conversion from int to DBInt.

public static implicit operator DBInt(int x) {
    return new DBInt(x);
}

// Explicit conversion from DBInt to int. Throws an exception if the
// given DBInt represents an unknown value.

public static explicit operator int(DBInt x) {
    if (!x.defined) throw new InvalidOperationException();
    return x.value;
}

public static DBInt operator +(DBInt x) {
    return x;
}

public static DBInt operator -(DBInt x) {
    return x.defined ? -x.value : Null;
}

public static DBInt operator +(DBInt x, DBInt y) {
    return x.defined && y.defined? x.value + y.value: Null;
}

public static DBInt operator -(DBInt x, DBInt y) {
    return x.defined && y.defined? x.value - y.value: Null;
}

public static DBInt operator *(DBInt x, DBInt y) {
    return x.defined && y.defined? x.value * y.value: Null;
}

public static DBInt operator /(DBInt x, DBInt y) {
    return x.defined && y.defined? x.value / y.value: Null;
}
```

```
        public static DBInt operator %(DBInt x, DBInt y) {
            return x.defined && y.defined? x.value % y.value: Null;
        }

        public static DBBool operator ==(DBInt x, DBInt y) {
            return x.defined && y.defined? x.value == y.value: DBBool.Null;
        }

        public static DBBool operator !=(DBInt x, DBInt y) {
            return x.defined && y.defined? x.value != y.value: DBBool.Null;
        }

        public static DBBool operator >(DBInt x, DBInt y) {
            return x.defined && y.defined? x.value > y.value: DBBool.Null;
        }

        public static DBBool operator <(DBInt x, DBInt y) {
            return x.defined && y.defined? x.value < y.value: DBBool.Null;
        }

        public static DBBool operator >=(DBInt x, DBInt y) {
            return x.defined && y.defined? x.value >= y.value: DBBool.Null;
        }

        public static DBBool operator <=(DBInt x, DBInt y) {
            return x.defined && y.defined? x.value <= y.value: DBBool.Null;
        }

        public override bool Equals(object obj) {
            if (!(obj is DBInt)) return false;
            DBInt x = (DBInt)obj;
            return value == x.value && defined == x.defined;
        }

        public override int GetHashCode() {
            return value;
        }

        public override string ToString() {
            return defined? value.ToString(): "DBInt.Null";
        }
    }
```

11.4.2 Database Boolean Type

The following DBBool struct implements a three-valued logical type. The possible values of this type are DBBool.True, DBBool.False, and DBBool.Null, where the Null member indicates an unknown value. Such three-valued logical types are commonly used in databases.

```
using System;

public struct DBBool
{
    // The three possible DBBool values.

    public static readonly DBBool Null = new DBBool(0);
    public static readonly DBBool False = new DBBool(-1);
    public static readonly DBBool True = new DBBool(1);
```

```
// Private field that stores -1, 0, 1 for False, Null, True.

sbyte value;

// Private instance constructor. The value parameter must be -1, 0, or 1.

DBBool(int value) {
    this.value = (sbyte)value;
}

// Properties to examine the value of a DBBool. Return true if this
// DBBool has the given value, false otherwise.

public bool IsNull { get { return value == 0; } }

public bool IsFalse { get { return value < 0; } }

public bool IsTrue { get { return value > 0; } }

// Implicit conversion from bool to DBBool. Maps true to DBBool.True and
// false to DBBool.False.

public static implicit operator DBBool(bool x) {
    return x? True: False;
}

// Explicit conversion from DBBool to bool. Throws an exception if the
// given DBBool is Null, otherwise returns true or false.

public static explicit operator bool(DBBool x) {
    if (x.value == 0) throw new InvalidOperationException();
    return x.value > 0;
}

// Equality operator. Returns Null if either operand is Null, otherwise
// returns True or False.

public static DBBool operator ==(DBBool x, DBBool y) {
    if (x.value == 0 || y.value == 0) return Null;
    return x.value == y.value? True: False;
}

// Inequality operator. Returns Null if either operand is Null, otherwise
// returns True or False.

public static DBBool operator !=(DBBool x, DBBool y) {
    if (x.value == 0 || y.value == 0) return Null;
    return x.value != y.value? True: False;
}

// Logical negation operator. Returns True if the operand is False, Null
// if the operand is Null, or False if the operand is True.

public static DBBool operator !(DBBool x) {
    return new DBBool(-x.value);
}

// Logical AND operator. Returns False if either operand is False,
// otherwise Null if either operand is Null, otherwise True.

public static DBBool operator &(DBBool x, DBBool y) {
    return new DBBool(x.value < y.value? x.value: y.value);
}
```

11. Structs

365

```
// Logical OR operator. Returns True if either operand is True, otherwise
// Null if either operand is Null, otherwise False.
public static DBBool operator |(DBBool x, DBBool y) {
    return new DBBool(x.value > y.value? x.value: y.value);
}

// Definitely true operator. Returns true if the operand is True, false
// otherwise.
public static bool operator true(DBBool x) {
    return x.value > 0;
}

// Definitely false operator. Returns true if the operand is False, false
// otherwise.
public static bool operator false(DBBool x) {
    return x.value < 0;
}

public override bool Equals(object obj) {
    if (!(obj is DBBool)) return false;
    return value == ((DBBool)obj).value;
}

public override int GetHashCode() {
    return value;
}

public override string ToString() {
    if (value > 0) return "DBBool.True";
    if (value < 0) return "DBBool.False";
    return "DBBool.Null";
}
}
```

12. Arrays

An array is a data structure that contains a number of variables that are accessed through computed indices. The variables contained in an array, also called the elements of the array, are all of the same type, and this type is called the element type of the array.

An array has a rank that determines the number of indices associated with each array element. The rank of an array is also referred to as the dimensions of the array. An array with a rank of one is called a *single-dimensional array*. An array with a rank greater than one is called a *multi-dimensional array*. Specific-sized multi-dimensional arrays are often referred to as two-dimensional arrays, three-dimensional arrays, and so on.

Each dimension of an array has an associated length that is an integral number greater than or equal to zero. The dimension lengths are not part of the type of the array but rather are established when an instance of the array type is created at runtime. The length of a dimension determines the valid range of indices for that dimension: For a dimension of length N, indices can range from 0 to N − 1 inclusive. The total number of elements in an array is the product of the lengths of each dimension in the array. If one or more of the dimensions of an array have a length of zero, the array is said to be empty.

The element type of an array can be any type, including an array type.

12.1 Array Types

An array type is written as a *non-array-type* followed by one or more *rank-specifiers*.

array-type:
    non-array-type   rank-specifiers

non-array-type:
    type

rank-specifiers:
    rank-specifier
    rank-specifiers   rank-specifier

rank-specifier:
     [*dim-separators*~opt~   ]

dim-separators:

     ,
     dim-separators   ,

A *non-array-type* is any *type* that is not itself an *array-type*.

The rank of an array type is given by the leftmost *rank-specifier* in the *array-type*: A *rank-specifier* indicates that the array is an array with a rank of one plus the number of , tokens in the *rank-specifier*.

The element type of an array type is the type that results from deleting the leftmost *rank-specifier*.

- An array type of the form `T[R]` is an array with rank `R` and a non-array element type `T`.

- An array type of the form `T[R][R1]...[RN]` is an array with rank `R` and an element type `T[R1]...[RN]`.

In effect, the *rank-specifiers* are read from left to right *before* the final non-array element type. The type `int[][,,][,]` is a single-dimensional array of three-dimensional arrays of two-dimensional arrays of `int`.

At runtime, a value of an array type can be `null` or a reference to an instance of that array type.

12.1.1 The System.Array Type

The type `System.Array` is the abstract base type of all array types. An implicit reference conversion (§6.1.4) exists from any array type to `System.Array`, and an explicit reference conversion (§6.2.3) exists from `System.Array` to any array type. Note that `System.Array` is not itself an *array-type*. Rather, it is a *class-type* from which all *array-types* are derived.

At runtime, a value of type `System.Array` can be `null` or a reference to an instance of any array type.

12.2 Array Creation

Array instances are created by *array-creation-expressions* (§7.5.10.2) or by field or local variable declarations that include an *array-initializer* (§12.6).

When an array instance is created, the rank and length of each dimension are established and then remain constant for the entire lifetime of the instance. In other words, it is not possible to change the rank of an existing array instance, and it is not possible to resize its dimensions.

An array instance is always of an array type. The `System.Array` type is an abstract type that cannot be instantiated.

Elements of arrays created by *array-creation-expressions* are always initialized to their default value (§5.2).

12.3 Array Element Access

Array elements are accessed using *element-access* expressions (§7.5.6.1) of the form `A[I1, I2, ..., IN]`, where `A` is an expression of an array type and each `IX` is an expression of type `int`, `uint`, `long`, `ulong`, or of a type that can be implicitly converted to one or more of these types. The result of an array element access is a variable, namely the array element selected by the indices.

The elements of an array can be enumerated using a `foreach` statement (§8.8.4).

12.4 Array Members

Every array type inherits the members declared by the `System.Array` type.

12.5 Array Covariance

For any two *reference-type*s `A` and `B`, if an implicit reference conversion (§6.1.4) or explicit reference conversion (§6.2.3) exists from `A` to `B`, then the same reference conversion also exists from the array type `A[R]` to the array type `B[R]`, where `R` is any given *rank-specifier* (but the same for both array types). This relationship is known as **array covariance**. Array covariance in particular means that a value of an array type `A[R]` may actually be a reference to an instance of an array type `B[R]`, provided an implicit reference conversion exists from `B` to `A`.

Because of array covariance, assignments to elements of reference type arrays include a runtime check, which ensures that the value being assigned to the array element is actually of a permitted type (§7.13.1). For example

```
class Test
{
    static void Fill(object[] array, int index, int count, object value) {
        for (int i = index; i < index + count; i++) array[i] = value;
    }

    static void Main() {
        string[] strings = new string[100];
        Fill(strings, 0, 100, "Undefined");
        Fill(strings, 0, 10, null);
        Fill(strings, 90, 10, 0);
    }
}
```

The assignment to array[i] in the Fill method implicitly includes a runtime check, which ensures that the object referenced by value is either null or an instance of a type that is compatible with the actual element type of array. In Main, the first two invocations of Fill succeed, but the third invocation causes a System.ArrayTypeMismatchException to be thrown upon executing the first assignment to array[i]. The exception occurs because a boxed int cannot be stored in a string array.

Array covariance specifically does not extend to arrays of *value-types*. For example, no conversion exists that permits an int[] to be treated as an object[].

12.6 Array Initializers

Array initializers may be specified in field declarations (§10.4), local variable declarations (§8.5.1), and array creation expressions (§7.5.10.2).

array-initializer:
    { *variable-initializer-list$_{opt}$* }
    { *variable-initializer-list* , }

variable-initializer-list:
    variable-initializer
    variable-initializer-list , *variable-initializer*

variable-initializer:
    expression
    array-initializer

An array initializer consists of a sequence of variable initializers, enclosed by { and } tokens and separated by , tokens. Each variable initializer is an expression or, in the case of a multi-dimensional array, a nested array initializer.

The context in which an array initializer is used determines the type of the array being initialized. In an array creation expression, the array type immediately precedes the initializer. In a field or variable declaration, the array type is the type of the field or variable being declared. When an array initializer is used in a field or variable declaration, such as

```
int[] a = {0, 2, 4, 6, 8};
```

it is simply shorthand for an equivalent array creation expression.

```
int[] a = new int[] {0, 2, 4, 6, 8};
```

For a single-dimensional array, the array initializer must consist of a sequence of expressions that are assignment compatible with the element type of the array. The expressions initialize array elements in increasing order, starting with the element at index zero. The number of expressions in the array initializer determines the length of the array instance being created. For example, the previous array initializer creates an int[] instance of length 5 and then initializes the instance with the following values.

```
a[0] = 0; a[1] = 2; a[2] = 4; a[3] = 6; a[4] = 8;
```

For a multi-dimensional array, the array initializer must have as many levels of nesting as there are dimensions in the array. The outermost nesting level corresponds to the leftmost dimension and the innermost nesting level corresponds to the rightmost dimension. The length of each dimension of the array is determined by the number of elements at the corresponding nesting level in the array initializer. For each nested array initializer, the number of elements must be the same as the other array initializers at the same level. The example

```
int[,] b = {{0, 1}, {2, 3}, {4, 5}, {6, 7}, {8, 9}};
```

creates a two-dimensional array with a length of five for the leftmost dimension and a length of two for the rightmost dimension.

```
int[,] b = new int[5, 2];
```

Then it initializes the array instance with the following values.

```
b[0, 0] = 0; b[0, 1] = 1;
b[1, 0] = 2; b[1, 1] = 3;
b[2, 0] = 4; b[2, 1] = 5;
b[3, 0] = 6; b[3, 1] = 7;
b[4, 0] = 8; b[4, 1] = 9;
```

12. Arrays

When an array creation expression includes both explicit dimension lengths and an array initializer, the lengths must be constant expressions and the number of elements at each nesting level must match the corresponding dimension length. The following are some examples.

```
int i = 3;
int[] x = new int[3] {0, 1, 2};        // OK
int[] y = new int[i] {0, 1, 2};        // Error, i not a constant
int[] z = new int[3] {0, 1, 2, 3};     // Error, length/initializer mismatch
```

Here, the initializer for y results in a compile-time error because the dimension length expression is not a constant, and the initializer for z results in a compile-time error because the length and the number of elements in the initializer do not agree.

13. Interfaces

An interface defines a contract. A class or struct that implements an interface must adhere to its contract. An interface may inherit from multiple base interfaces, and a class or struct may implement multiple interfaces.

Interfaces can contain methods, properties, events, and indexers. The interface itself does not provide implementations for the members that it defines. The interface merely specifies the members that must be supplied by classes or structs that implement the interface.

13.1 Interface Declarations

An *interface-declaration* is a *type-declaration* (§9.5) that declares a new interface type.

> *interface-declaration:*
>   *attributes*$_{opt}$ *interface-modifiers*$_{opt}$ interface *identifier* *interface-base*$_{opt}$
>   *interface-body* ;$_{opt}$

An *interface-declaration* consists of an optional set of *attributes* (§17), followed by an optional set of *interface-modifiers* (§13.1.1), followed by the keyword interface and an *identifier* that names the interface, optionally followed by an optional *interface-base* specification (§13.1.2), followed by a *interface-body* (§13.1.3), optionally followed by a semicolon.

13.1.1 Interface Modifiers

An *interface-declaration* may optionally include a sequence of interface modifiers.

> *interface-modifiers:*
>   *interface-modifier*
>   *interface-modifiers* *interface-modifier*
>
> *interface-modifier:*
>   new
>   public
>   protected
>   internal
>   private

It is a compile-time error for the same modifier to appear multiple times in an interface declaration.

The new modifier is only permitted on interfaces defined within a class. It specifies that the interface hides an inherited member by the same name, as described in §10.2.2.

The `public`, `protected`, `internal`, and `private` modifiers control the accessibility of the interface. Depending on the context in which the interface declaration occurs, only some of these modifiers may be permitted (§3.5.1).

13.1.2 Base Interfaces

An interface can inherit from zero or more interfaces, which are called the *explicit base interfaces* of the interface. When an interface has one or more explicit base interfaces, then in the declaration of that interface, the interface identifier is followed by a colon and a comma separated list of base interface identifiers.

> *interface-base:*
> : *interface-type-list*

The explicit base interfaces of an interface must be at least as accessible as the interface itself (§3.5.4). For example, it is a compile-time error to specify a `private` or `internal` interface in the *interface-base* of a `public` interface.

It is a compile-time error for an interface to directly or indirectly inherit from itself.

The *base interfaces* of an interface are the explicit base interfaces and their base interfaces. In other words, the set of base interfaces is the complete transitive closure of the explicit base interfaces, their explicit base interfaces, and so on. An interface inherits all members of its base interfaces. In the example

```
interface IControl
{
    void Paint();
}
interface ITextBox: IControl
{
    void SetText(string text);
}
interface IListBox: IControl
{
    void SetItems(string[] items);
}
interface IComboBox: ITextBox, IListBox {}
```

the base interfaces of `IComboBox` are `IControl`, `ITextBox`, and `IListBox`.

In other words, the previous `IComboBox` interface inherits members `SetText` and `SetItems` as well as `Paint`.

A class or struct that implements an interface also implicitly implements all of the interface's base interfaces.

13.1.3 Interface Body

The *interface-body* of an interface defines the members of the interface.

> *interface-body:*
> { *interface-member-declarations*$_{opt}$ }

13.2 Interface Members

The members of an interface are the members inherited from the base interfaces and the members declared by the interface itself.

> *interface-member-declarations:*
> *interface-member-declaration*
> *interface-member-declarations interface-member-declaration*
>
> *interface-member-declaration:*
> *interface-method-declaration*
> *interface-property-declaration*
> *interface-event-declaration*
> *interface-indexer-declaration*

An interface declaration may declare zero or more members. The members of an interface must be methods, properties, events, or indexers. An interface cannot contain constants, fields, operators, instance constructors, destructors, or types, nor can an interface contain static members of any kind.

All interface members implicitly have public access. It is a compile-time error for interface member declarations to include any modifiers. In particular, interfaces members cannot be declared with the modifiers `abstract`, `public`, `protected`, `internal`, `private`, `virtual`, `override`, or `static`.

The example

```
public delegate void StringListEvent(IStringList sender);

public interface IStringList
{
    void Add(string s);

    int Count { get; }
```

```
            event StringListEvent Changed;
            string this[int index] { get; set; }
        }
```

declares an interface that contains one each of the possible kinds of members: a method, a property, an event, and an indexer.

An *interface-declaration* creates a new declaration space (§3.3), and the *interface-member-declarations* immediately contained by the *interface-declaration* introduce new members into this declaration space. The following rules apply to *interface-member-declaration*s.

- The name of a method must differ from the names of all properties and events declared in the same interface. In addition, the signature (§3.6) of a method must differ from the signatures of all other methods declared in the same interface.

- The name of a property or event must differ from the names of all other members declared in the same interface.

- The signature of an indexer must differ from the signatures of all other indexers declared in the same interface.

The inherited members of an interface are specifically not part of the declaration space of the interface. Thus, an interface is allowed to declare a member with the same name or signature as an inherited member. When this occurs, the derived interface member is said to *hide* the base interface member. Hiding an inherited member is not considered an error, but it does cause the compiler to issue a warning. To suppress the warning, the declaration of the derived interface member must include a new modifier to indicate that the derived member is intended to hide the base member. This topic is discussed further in §3.7.1.2.

If a new modifier is included in a declaration that does not hide an inherited member, a warning is issued to that effect. This warning is suppressed by removing the new modifier.

13.2.1 Interface Methods

Interface methods are declared using *interface-method-declaration*s.

> *interface-method-declaration:*
>   *attributes*$_{opt}$ new$_{opt}$ *return-type identifier* (*formal-parameter-list*$_{opt}$) ;

The *attributes*, *return-type*, *identifier*, and *formal-parameter-list* of an interface method declaration have the same meaning as those of a method declaration in a class (§10.5). An interface method declaration is not permitted to specify a method body, and the declaration therefore always ends with a semicolon.

13.2.2 Interface Properties
Interface properties are declared using *interface-property-declaration*s.

> *interface-property-declaration:*
>   *attributes*$_{opt}$ new$_{opt}$ *type identifier* { *interface-accessors* }

> *interface-accessors:*
>   *attributes*$_{opt}$ get ;
>   *attributes*$_{opt}$ set ;
>   *attributes*$_{opt}$ get ; *attributes*$_{opt}$ set ;
>   *attributes*$_{opt}$ set ; *attributes*$_{opt}$ get ;

The *attributes*, *type*, and *identifier* of an interface property declaration have the same meaning as those of a property declaration in a class (§10.6).

The accessors of an interface property declaration correspond to the accessors of a class property declaration (§10.6.2), except that the accessor body must always be a semicolon. Thus, the accessors simply indicate whether the property is read-write, read-only, or write-only.

13.2.3 Interface Events
Interface events are declared using *interface-event-declaration*s.

> *interface-event-declaration:*
>   *attributes*$_{opt}$ new$_{opt}$ event *type identifier* ;

The *attributes*, *type*, and *identifier* of an interface event declaration have the same meaning as those of an event declaration in a class (§10.7).

13.2.4 Interface Indexers
Interface indexers are declared using *interface-indexer-declaration*s.

> *interface-indexer-declaration:*
>   *attributes*$_{opt}$ new$_{opt}$ *type* this [*formal-parameter-list*] { *interface-accessors* }

The *attributes*, *type*, and *formal-parameter-list* of an interface indexer declaration have the same meaning as those of an indexer declaration in a class (§10.8).

The accessors of an interface indexer declaration correspond to the accessors of a class indexer declaration (§10.8), except that the accessor body must always be a semicolon. Thus, the accessors simply indicate whether the indexer is read-write, read-only, or write-only.

13.2.5 Interface Member Access

Interface members are accessed through member access (§7.5.4) and indexer access (§7.5.6.2) expressions of the form `I.M` and `I[A]`, where `I` is an interface type, `M` is a method, property, or event of that interface type, and `A` is an indexer argument list.

For interfaces that are strictly single inheritance (each interface in the inheritance chain has exactly zero or one direct base interface), the effects of the member lookup (§7.3), method invocation (§7.5.5.1), and indexer access (§7.5.6.2) rules are the same as for classes and structs: More derived members hide less derived members with the same name or signature. However, for multiple-inheritance interfaces, ambiguities can occur when two or more unrelated base interfaces declare members with the same name or signature. This section shows several examples of such situations. In all cases, explicit casts can be used to resolve the ambiguities.

In the example

```
interface IList
{
    int Count { get; set; }
}

interface ICounter
{
    void Count(int i);
}

interface IListCounter: IList, ICounter {}

class C
{
    void Test(IListCounter x) {
        x.Count(1);                 // Error
        x.Count = 1;                // Error
        ((IList)x).Count = 1;       // Ok, invokes IList.Count.set
        ((ICounter)x).Count(1);     // Ok, invokes ICounter.Count
    }
}
```

the first two statements cause compile-time errors because the member lookup (§7.3) of `Count` in `IListCounter` is ambiguous. As illustrated by the example, the ambiguity is resolved by casting `x` to the appropriate base interface type. Such casts have no runtime costs—they merely consist of viewing the instance as a less derived type at compile time.

In the example

```
interface IInteger
{
    void Add(int i);
}
```

```
interface IDouble
{
    void Add(double d);
}

interface INumber: IInteger, IDouble {}

class C
{
    void Test(INumber n) {
        n.Add(1);                   // Error, both Add methods are applicable
        n.Add(1.0);                 // Ok, only IDouble.Add is applicable
        ((IInteger)n).Add(1);       // Ok, only IInteger.Add is a candidate
        ((IDouble)n).Add(1);        // Ok, only IDouble.Add is a candidate
    }
}
```

the invocation n.Add(1) is ambiguous because a method invocation (§7.5.5.1) requires all overloaded candidate methods to be declared in the same type. However, the invocation n.Add(1.0) is permitted because only IDouble.Add is applicable. When explicit casts are inserted, there is only one candidate method and thus no ambiguity.

In the example

```
interface IBase
{
    void F(int i);
}

interface ILeft: IBase
{
    new void F(int i);
}

interface IRight: IBase
{
    void G();
}

interface IDerived: ILeft, IRight {}

class A
{
    void Test(IDerived d) {
        d.F(1);                 // Invokes ILeft.F
        ((IBase)d).F(1);        // Invokes IBase.F
        ((ILeft)d).F(1);        // Invokes ILeft.F
        ((IRight)d).F(1);       // Invokes IBase.F
    }
}
```

the IBase.F member is hidden by the ILeft.F member. The invocation d.F(1) thus selects ILeft.F, even though IBase.F appears to not be hidden in the access path that leads through IRight.

The intuitive rule for hiding in multiple-inheritance interfaces is simply this: If a member is hidden in any access path, it is hidden in all access paths. Because the access path from IDerived to ILeft to IBase hides IBase.F, the member is also hidden in the access path from IDerived to IRight to IBase.

13.3 Fully Qualified Interface Member Names

An interface member is sometimes referred to by its *fully qualified name*. The fully qualified name of an interface member consists of the name of the interface in which the member is declared, followed by a dot, followed by the name of the member. The fully qualified name of a member references the interface in which the member is declared. For example, given the declarations

```
interface IControl
{
    void Paint();
}
interface ITextBox: IControl
{
    void SetText(string text);
}
```

the fully qualified name of Paint is IControl.Paint, and the fully qualified name of SetText is ITextBox.SetText.

In the previous example, it is not possible to refer to Paint as ITextBox.Paint.

When an interface is part of a namespace, the fully qualified name of an interface member includes the namespace name. For example

```
namespace System
{
    public interface ICloneable
    {
        object Clone();
    }
}
```

Here, the fully qualified name of the Clone method is System.ICloneable.Clone.

13.4 Interface Implementations

Interfaces may be implemented by classes and structs. To indicate that a class or struct implements an interface, the interface identifier is included in the base class list of the class or struct. For example

```
interface ICloneable
{
    object Clone();
}
interface IComparable
{
    int CompareTo(object other);
}
class ListEntry: ICloneable, IComparable
{
    public object Clone() {...}
    public int CompareTo(object other) {...}
}
```

A class or struct that implements an interface also implicitly implements all of the interface's base interfaces. This is true even if the class or struct does not explicitly list all base interfaces in the base class list. For example

```
interface IControl
{
    void Paint();
}
interface ITextBox: IControl
{
    void SetText(string text);
}
class TextBox: ITextBox
{
    public void Paint() {...}
    public void SetText(string text) {...}
}
```

Here, class `TextBox` implements both `IControl` and `ITextBox`.

13.4.1 Explicit Interface Member Implementations

For the purpose of implementing interfaces, a class or struct may declare *explicit interface member implementations*. An explicit interface member implementation is a method, property, event, or indexer declaration that references a fully qualified interface member name. For example

```
interface ICloneable
{
    object Clone();
}

interface IComparable
{
    int CompareTo(object other);
}
```

```
class ListEntry: ICloneable, IComparable
{
    object ICloneable.Clone() {...}
    int IComparable.CompareTo(object other) {...}
}
```

Here, `ICloneable.Clone` and `IComparable.CompareTo` are explicit interface member implementations.

In some cases, the name of an interface member may not be appropriate for the implementing class, in which case the interface member may be implemented using explicit interface member implementation. A class implementing a file abstraction, for example, would likely implement a `Close` member function that has the effect of releasing the file resource and implement the `Dispose` method of the `IDisposable` interface using explicit interface member implementation.

```
interface IDisposable
{
    void Dispose();
}
class MyFile: IDisposable
{
    void IDisposable.Dispose() {
        Close();
    }
    public void Close() {
        // Do what's necessary to close the file
        System.GC.SuppressFinalize(this);
    }
}
```

It is not possible to access an explicit interface member implementation through its fully qualified name in a method invocation, property access, or indexer access. An explicit interface member implementation can only be accessed through an interface instance and is in that case referenced simply by its member name.

It is a compile-time error for an explicit interface member implementation to include access modifiers, and it is a compile-time error to include the modifiers `abstract`, `virtual`, `override`, or `static`.

Explicit interface member implementations have different accessibility characteristics than other members. Because explicit interface member implementations are never accessible through their fully qualified name in a method invocation or a property access, they are in a sense private. However, because they can be accessed through an interface instance, they are in a sense also public.

Explicit interface member implementations serve two primary purposes.

- Because explicit interface member implementations are not accessible through class or struct instances, they allow interface implementations to be excluded from the public interface of a class or struct. This is particularly useful when a class or struct implements an internal interface that is of no interest to a consumer of that class or struct.
- Explicit interface member implementations allow disambiguation of interface members with the same signature. Without explicit interface member implementations, it would be impossible for a class or struct to have different implementations of interface members with the same signature and return type, as would it be impossible for a class or struct to have any implementation at all of interface members with the same signature but with different return types.

For an explicit interface member implementation to be valid, the class or struct must name an interface in its base class list that contains a member whose fully qualified name, type, and parameter types exactly match those of the explicit interface member implementation. Thus, in the following class

```
class Shape: ICloneable
{
    object ICloneable.Clone() {...}
    int IComparable.CompareTo(object other) {...}    // invalid
}
```

the declaration of `IComparable.CompareTo` results in a compile-time error because `IComparable` is not listed in the base class list of `Shape` and is not a base interface of `ICloneable`. Likewise, in the declarations

```
class Shape: ICloneable
{
    object ICloneable.Clone() {...}
}
class Ellipse: Shape
{
    object ICloneable.Clone() {...}   // invalid
}
```

the declaration of `ICloneable.Clone` in `Ellipse` results in a compile-time error because `ICloneable` is not explicitly listed in the base class list of `Ellipse`.

The fully qualified name of an interface member must reference the interface in which the member was declared. Thus, in the declarations

```
interface IControl
{
    void Paint();
}
```

```
interface ITextBox: IControl
{
    void SetText(string text);
}
class TextBox: ITextBox
{
    void IControl.Paint() {...}
    void ITextBox.SetText(string text) {...}
}
```

the explicit interface member implementation of `Paint` must be written as `IControl.Paint`.

13.4.2 Interface Mapping

A class or struct must provide implementations of all members of the interfaces that are listed in the base class list of the class or struct. The process of locating implementations of interface members in an implementing class or struct is known as *interface mapping*.

Interface mapping for a class or struct C locates an implementation for each member of each interface specified in the base class list of C. The implementation of a particular interface member I.M, where I is the interface in which the member M is declared, is determined by examining each class or struct S, starting with C and repeating for each successive base class of C, until a match is located.

- If S contains a declaration of an explicit interface member implementation that matches I and M, then this member is the implementation of I.M.

- Otherwise, if S contains a declaration of a nonstatic public member that matches M, then this member is the implementation of I.M.

A compile-time error occurs if implementations cannot be located for all members of all interfaces specified in the base class list of C. Note that the members of an interface include those members that are inherited from base interfaces.

For purposes of interface mapping, a class member A matches an interface member B when

- A and B are methods, and the name, type, and formal parameter lists of A and B are identical.

- A and B are properties, the name and type of A and B are identical, and A has the same accessors as B (A is permitted to have additional accessors if it is not an explicit interface member implementation).

- A and B are events, and the name and type of A and B are identical.

- A and B are indexers, the type and formal parameter lists of A and B are identical, and A has the same accessors as B (A is permitted to have additional accessors if it is not an explicit interface member implementation).

Notable implications of the interface mapping algorithm are

- Explicit interface member implementations take precedence over other members in the same class or struct when determining the class or struct member that implements an interface member.
- Neither nonpublic nor static members participate in interface mapping.

In the example

```
interface ICloneable
{
    object Clone();
}
class C: ICloneable
{
    object ICloneable.Clone() {...}
    public object Clone() {...}
}
```

the ICloneable.Clone member of C becomes the implementation of Clone in ICloneable because explicit interface member implementations take precedence over other members.

If a class or struct implements two or more interfaces containing a member with the same name, type, and parameter types, it is possible to map each of those interface members onto a single class or struct member. For example

```
interface IControl
{
    void Paint();
}
interface IForm
{
    void Paint();
}
class Page: IControl, IForm
{
    public void Paint() {...}
}
```

Here, the Paint methods of both IControl and IForm are mapped onto the Paint method in Page. It is of course also possible to have separate explicit interface member implementations for the two methods.

If a class or struct implements an interface that contains hidden members, then some members must necessarily be implemented through explicit interface member implementations. For example

```
interface IBase
{
    int P { get; }
}

interface IDerived: IBase
{
    new int P();
}
```

An implementation of this interface would require at least one explicit interface member implementation and would take one of the following forms.

```
class C: IDerived
{
    int IBase.P { get {...} }
    int IDerived.P() {...}
}

class C: IDerived
{
    public int P { get {...} }
    int IDerived.P() {...}
}

class C: IDerived
{
    int IBase.P { get {...} }
    public int P() {...}
}
```

When a class implements multiple interfaces that have the same base interface, there can be only one implementation of the base interface. In the example

```
interface IControl
{
    void Paint();
}

interface ITextBox: IControl
{
    void SetText(string text);
}

interface IListBox: IControl
{
    void SetItems(string[] items);
}
```

```
class ComboBox: IControl, ITextBox, IListBox
{
    void IControl.Paint() {...}
    void ITextBox.SetText(string text) {...}
    void IListBox.SetItems(string[] items) {...}
}
```

it is not possible to have separate implementations for the IControl named in the base class list, the IControl inherited by ITextBox, and the IControl inherited by IListBox. Indeed, there is no notion of a separate identity for these interfaces. Rather, the implementations of ITextBox and IListBox share the same implementation of IControl, and ComboBox is simply considered to implement three interfaces: IControl, ITextBox, and IListBox.

The members of a base class participate in interface mapping. In the example

```
interface Interface1
{
    void F();
}
class Class1
{
    public void F() {}
    public void G() {}
}
class Class2: Class1, Interface1
{
    new public void G() {}
}
```

the method F in Class1 is used in Class2's implementation of Interface1.

13.4.3 Interface Implementation Inheritance

A class inherits all interface implementations provided by its base classes.

Without explicitly *reimplementing* an interface, a derived class cannot in any way alter the interface mappings it inherits from its base classes. For example, in the declarations

```
interface IControl
{
    void Paint();
}
class Control: IControl
{
    public void Paint() {...}
}
```

```
class TextBox: Control
{
    new public void Paint() {...}
}
```

the Paint method in TextBox hides the Paint method in Control, but it does not alter the mapping of Control.Paint onto IControl.Paint and calls to Paint through class instances and interface instances will have the following effects.

```
Control c = new Control();
TextBox t = new TextBox();
IControl ic = c;
IControl it = t;
c.Paint();        // invokes Control.Paint();
t.Paint();        // invokes TextBox.Paint();
ic.Paint();       // invokes Control.Paint();
it.Paint();       // invokes Control.Paint();
```

However, when an interface method is mapped onto a virtual method in a class, it is possible for derived classes to override the virtual method and alter the implementation of the interface. For example, rewriting the previous declarations to

```
interface IControl
{
    void Paint();
}

class Control: IControl
{
    public virtual void Paint() {...}
}

class TextBox: Control
{
    public override void Paint() {...}
}
```

the following effects will now be observed.

```
Control c = new Control();
TextBox t = new TextBox();
IControl ic = c;
IControl it = t;
c.Paint();        // invokes Control.Paint();
t.Paint();        // invokes TextBox.Paint();
ic.Paint();       // invokes Control.Paint();
it.Paint();       // invokes TextBox.Paint();
```

Because explicit interface member implementations cannot be declared virtual, it is not possible to override an explicit interface member implementation. However, it is perfectly valid for an explicit interface member implementation to call another method, and that other method can be declared virtual to allow derived classes to override it. For example

```
interface IControl
{
    void Paint();
}
class Control: IControl
{
    void IControl.Paint() { PaintControl(); }
    protected virtual void PaintControl() {...}
}
class TextBox: Control
{
    protected override void PaintControl() {...}
}
```

Here, classes derived from `Control` can specialize the implementation of `IControl.Paint` by overriding the `PaintControl` method.

13.4.4 Interface Reimplementation

A class that inherits an interface implementation is permitted to *reimplement* the interface by including it in the base class list.

A reimplementation of an interface follows exactly the same interface mapping rules as an initial implementation of an interface. Thus, the inherited interface mapping has no effect whatsoever on the interface mapping established for the reimplementation of the interface. For example, in the declarations

```
interface IControl
{
    void Paint();
}
class Control: IControl
{
    void IControl.Paint() {...}
}
class MyControl: Control, IControl
{
    public void Paint() {}
}
```

the fact that `Control` maps `IControl.Paint` onto `Control.IControl.Paint` does not affect the reimplementation in `MyControl`, which maps `IControl.Paint` onto `MyControl.Paint`.

Inherited public member declarations and inherited explicit interface member declarations participate in the interface mapping process for reimplemented interfaces. For example

```
interface IMethods
{
    void F();
    void G();
    void H();
    void I();
}

class Base: IMethods
{
    void IMethods.F() {}
    void IMethods.G() {}
    public void H() {}
    public void I() {}
}

class Derived: Base, IMethods
{
    public void F() {}
    void IMethods.H() {}
}
```

Here, the implementation of `IMethods` in `Derived` maps the interface methods onto `Derived.F`, `Base.IMethods.G`, `Derived.IMethods.H`, and `Base.I`.

When a class implements an interface, it implicitly also implements all of that interface's base interfaces. Likewise, a reimplementation of an interface is also implicitly a reimplementation of all of the interface's base interfaces. For example

```
interface IBase
{
    void F();
}

interface IDerived: IBase
{
    void G();
}

class C: IDerived
{
    void IBase.F() {...}

    void IDerived.G() {...}
}

class D: C, IDerived
{
    public void F() {...}

    public void G() {...}
}
```

Here, the reimplementation of `IDerived` also reimplements `IBase`, mapping `IBase.F` onto `D.F`.

13.4.5 Abstract Classes and Interfaces

Like a nonabstract class, an abstract class must provide implementations of all members of the interfaces that are listed in the base class list of the class. However, an abstract class is permitted to map interface methods onto abstract methods. For example

```
interface IMethods
{
    void F();
    void G();
}

abstract class C: IMethods
{
    public abstract void F();
    public abstract void G();
}
```

Here, the implementation of `IMethods` maps `F` and `G` onto abstract methods, which must be overridden in nonabstract classes that derive from `C`.

Note that explicit interface member implementations cannot be abstract, but explicit interface member implementations are of course permitted to call abstract methods. For example

```
interface IMethods
{
    void F();
    void G();
}

abstract class C: IMethods
{
    void IMethods.F() { FF(); }

    void IMethods.G() { GG(); }

    protected abstract void FF();

    protected abstract void GG();
}
```

Here, nonabstract classes that derive from `C` would be required to override `FF` and `GG`, thus providing the actual implementation of `IMethods`.

14. Enums

An *enum type* is a distinct value type (§4.1) that declares a set of named constants.

The example

```
enum Color
{
    Red,
    Green,
    Blue
}
```

declares an enum type named `Color` with members `Red`, `Green`, and `Blue`.

14.1 Enum Declarations

An enum declaration declares a new enum type. An enum declaration begins with the keyword `enum` and defines the name, accessibility, underlying type, and members of the enum.

> *enum-declaration:*
>   *attributes*_{opt} *enum-modifiers*_{opt} enum *identifier* *enum-base*_{opt} *enum-body* *;*_{opt}
>
> *enum-base:*
>   : *integral-type*
>
> *enum-body:*
>   { *enum-member-declarations*_{opt} }
>   { *enum-member-declarations* , }

Each enum type has a corresponding integral type called the *underlying type* of the enum type. This underlying type must be able to represent all the enumerator values defined in the enumeration. An enum declaration may explicitly declare an underlying type of `byte`, `sbyte`, `short`, `ushort`, `int`, `uint`, `long` or `ulong`. Note that `char` cannot be used as an underlying type. An enum declaration that does not explicitly declare an underlying type has an underlying type of `int`.

The example

```
enum Color: long
{
    Red,
    Green,
    Blue
}
```

declares an enum with an underlying type of `long`. A developer might choose to use an underlying type of `long`, as in the example, to enable the use of values that are in the range of `long` but not in the range of `int` or to preserve this option for the future.

14.2 Enum Modifiers

An *enum-declaration* may optionally include a sequence of enum modifiers.

enum-modifiers:
    enum-modifier
    enum-modifiers *enum-modifier*

enum-modifier:
    new
    public
    protected
    internal
    private

It is a compile-time error for the same modifier to appear multiple times in an enum declaration.

The modifiers of an enum declaration have the same meaning as those of a class declaration (§10.1.1). Note, however, that the `abstract` and `sealed` modifiers are not permitted in an enum declaration. Enums cannot be abstract and do not permit derivation.

14.3 Enum Members

The body of an enum type declaration defines zero or more enum members, which are the named constants of the enum type. No two enum members can have the same name.

enum-member-declarations:
    enum-member-declaration
    enum-member-declarations , *enum-member-declaration*

enum-member-declaration:
    attributes$_{opt}$ *identifier*
    attributes$_{opt}$ *identifier* = *constant-expression*

Each enum member has an associated constant value. The type of this value is the underlying type for the containing enum. The constant value for each enum member must be in the range of the underlying type for the enum. The example

```
enum Color: uint
{
    Red = -1,
    Green = -2,
    Blue = -3
}
```

results in a compile-time error because the constant values –1, –2, and –3 are not in the range of the underlying integral type `uint`.

Multiple enum members may share the same associated value. The example

```
enum Color
{
    Red,
    Green,
    Blue,

    Max = Blue
}
```

shows an enum in which two enum members—`Blue` and `Max`—have the same associated value.

The associated value of an enum member is assigned either implicitly or explicitly. If the declaration of the enum member has a *constant-expression* initializer, the value of that constant expression, implicitly converted to the underlying type of the enum, is the associated value of the enum member. If the declaration of the enum member has no initializer, its associated value is set implicitly, as follows.

- If the enum member is the first enum member declared in the enum type, its associated value is zero.

- Otherwise, the associated value of the enum member is obtained by increasing the associated value of the textually preceding enum member by one. This increased value must be within the range of values that can be represented by the underlying type; otherwise, a compile-time error occurs.

14. Enums

The example

```
using System;

enum Color
{
    Red,
    Green = 10,
    Blue
}

class Test
{
    static void Main() {
        Console.WriteLine(StringFromColor(Color.Red));
        Console.WriteLine(StringFromColor(Color.Green));
        Console.WriteLine(StringFromColor(Color.Blue));
    }

    static string StringFromColor(Color c) {
        switch (c) {
        case Color.Red:
            return String.Format("Red = {0}", (int) c);

        case Color.Green:
            return String.Format("Green = {0}", (int) c);

        case Color.Blue:
            return String.Format("Blue = {0}", (int) c);

        default:
            return "Invalid color";
        }
    }
}
```

prints the enum member names and their associated values. The output is

```
Red = 0
Green = 10
Blue = 11
```

for the following reasons.

- The enum member Red is automatically assigned the value zero (because it has no initializer and is the first enum member).

- The enum member Green is explicitly given the value 10.

- The enum member Blue is automatically assigned the value one greater than the member that textually precedes it.

The associated value of an enum member may not, directly or indirectly, use the value of its own associated enum member. Other than this circularity restriction, enum member initializers may freely refer to other enum member initializers, regardless of their textual position. Within an enum member initializer, values of other enum members are always treated as having the type of their underlying type, so that casts are not necessary when referring to other enum members.

The example

```
enum Circular
{
    A = B,
    B
}
```

results in a compile-time error because the declarations of A and B are circular. A depends on B explicitly, and B depends on A implicitly.

Enum members are named and scoped in a manner exactly analogous to fields within classes. The scope of an enum member is the body of its containing enum type. Within that scope, enum members can be referred to by their simple name. From all other code, the name of an enum member must be qualified with the name of its enum type. Enum members do not have any declared accessibility—an enum member is accessible if its containing enum type is accessible.

14.4 The System.Enum Type

The type System.Enum is the abstract base class of all enum types (this is distinct and different from the underlying type of the enum type), and the members inherited from System.Enum are available in any enum type. A boxing conversion (§4.3.1) exists from any enum type to System.Enum, and an unboxing conversion (§4.3.2) exists from System.Enum to any enum type.

Note that System.Enum is not itself an *enum-type*. Rather, it is a *class-type* from which all *enum-types* are derived. The type System.Enum inherits from the type System.ValueType (§4.1.1), which, in turn, inherits from type object. At runtime, a value of type System.Enum can be null or a reference to a boxed value of any enum type.

14.5 Enum Values and Operations

Each enum type defines a distinct type; an explicit enumeration conversion (§6.2.2) is required to convert between an enum type and an integral type or between two enum types. The set of values that an enum type can take on is not limited by its enum members. In particular, any value of the underlying type of an enum can be cast to the enum type and is a distinct valid value of that enum type.

Enum members have the type of their containing enum type (except within other enum member initializers, as described in §14.3). The value of an enum member declared in enum type E with associated value v is (E)v.

The following operators can be used on values of enum types: ==, !=, <, >, <=, >= (§7.9.5), binary + (§7.7.4), binary - (§7.7.5), ^, &, | (§7.10.2), ~ (§7.6.4), ++, -- (§7.5.9 and §7.6.5), and sizeof (§18.5.4).

15. Delegates

Delegates enable scenarios that other languages—such as C++, Pascal, and Modula—have addressed with function pointers. Unlike C++ function pointers, however, delegates are fully object oriented, and unlike C++ pointers to member functions, delegates encapsulate both an object instance and a method.

A delegate declaration defines a class that is derived from the class `System.Delegate`. A delegate instance encapsulates an invocation list, which is a list of one or more methods, each of which is referred to as a callable entity. For instance methods, a callable entity consists of an instance and a method on that instance. For static methods, a callable entity consists of just a method. Invoking a delegate instance with an appropriate set of arguments causes each of the delegate's callable entities to be invoked with the given set of arguments.

An interesting and useful property of a delegate instance is that it does not know or care about the classes of the methods it encapsulates; all that matters is that those methods be compatible (§15.1) with the delegate's type. This makes delegates perfectly suited for "anonymous" invocation.

15.1 Delegate Declarations

A *delegate-declaration* is a *type-declaration* (§9.5) that declares a new delegate type.

> *delegate-declaration:*
>   *attributes$_{opt}$ delegate-modifiers$_{opt}$*   delegate   *return-type   identifier*
>   (*formal-parameter-list$_{opt}$*   )   ;
>
> *delegate-modifiers:*
>   *delegate-modifier*
>   *delegate-modifiers   delegate-modifier*

delegate-modifier:
```
new
public
protected
internal
private
```

It is a compile-time error for the same modifier to appear multiple times in a delegate declaration.

The `new` modifier is only permitted on delegates declared within another type, in which case it specifies that such a delegate hides an inherited member by the same name, as described in §10.2.2.

The `public`, `protected`, `internal`, and `private` modifiers control the accessibility of the delegate type. Depending on the context in which the delegate declaration occurs, some of these modifiers may not be permitted (§3.5.1).

The delegate's type name is *identifier*.

The optional *formal-parameter-list* specifies the parameters of the delegate, and *return-type* indicates the return type of the delegate. A method and a delegate type are **compatible** if both of the following are true.

- They have the same number or parameters, with the same types, in the same order, with the same parameter modifiers.

- Their return types are the same.

Delegate types in C# are name equivalent, not structurally equivalent. Specifically, two different delegate types that have the same parameter lists and return type are considered different delegate types. However, instances of two distinct but structurally equivalent delegate types may compare as equal (§7.9.8).

For example

```
delegate int D1(int i, double d);

class A
{
    public static int M1(int a, double b) {...}
}

class B
{
    delegate int D2(int c, double d);
```

```
    public static int M1(int f, double g) {...}

    public static void M2(int k, double l) {...}

    public static int M3(int g) {...}

    public static void M4(int g) {...}
}
```

The delegate types `D1` and `D2` are both compatible with the methods `A.M1` and `B.M1` because they have the same return type and parameter list; however, these delegate types are two different types, so they are not interchangeable. The delegate types `D1` and `D2` are incompatible with the methods `B.M2`, `B.M3`, and `B.M4` because they have different return types or parameter lists.

The only way to declare a delegate type is via a *delegate-declaration*. A delegate type is a class type that is derived from `System.Delegate`. Delegate types are implicitly `sealed`, so it is not permissible to derive any type from a delegate type. It is also not permissible to derive a nondelegate class type from `System.Delegate`. Note that `System.Delegate` is not itself a delegate type; it is a class type from which all delegate types are derived.

C# provides special syntax for delegate instantiation and invocation. Except for instantiation, any operation that can be applied to a class or class instance can also be applied to a delegate class or instance, respectively. In particular, it is possible to access members of the `System.Delegate` type via the usual member access syntax.

The set of methods encapsulated by a delegate instance is called an invocation list. When a delegate instance is created (§15.2) from a single method, it encapsulates that method, and its invocation list contains only one entry. However, when two non-null delegate instances are combined, their invocation lists are concatenated—in the order of left operand then right operand—to form a new invocation list, which contains two or more entries.

Delegates are combined using the binary + (§7.7.4) and += operators (§7.13.2). A delegate can be removed from a combination of delegates using the binary - (§7.7.5) and -= operators (§7.13.2). Delegates can be compared for equality (§7.9.8).

The following example shows the instantiation of a number of delegates and their corresponding invocation lists.

```
delegate void D(int x);

class C
{
    public static void M1(int i) {...}

    public static void M2(int i) {...}
}
```

15. Delegates

```
class Test
{
    static void Main() {
        D cd1 = new D(C.M1);    // M1
        D cd2 = new D(C.M2);    // M2
        D cd3 = cd1 + cd2;      // M1 + M2
        D cd4 = cd3 + cd1;      // M1 + M2 + M1
        D cd5 = cd4 + cd3;      // M1 + M2 + M1 + M1 + M2
    }

}
```

When cd1 and cd2 are instantiated, they each encapsulate one method. When cd3 is instantiated, it has an invocation list of two methods, M1 and M2, in that order. cd4's invocation list contains M1, M2, and M1, in that order. Finally, cd5's invocation list contains M1, M2, M1, M1, and M2, in that order. For more examples of combining (as well as removing) delegates, see §15.3.

15.2 Delegate Instantiation

An instance of a delegate is created by a *delegate-creation-expression* (§7.5.10.3). The newly created delegate instance then refers to one of the following:

- The static method referenced in the *delegate-creation-expression*

- The target object (which cannot be null) and instance method referenced in the *delegate-creation-expression*

- Another delegate.

For example

```
delegate void D(int x);

class C
{
    public static void M1(int i) {...}
    public void M2(int i) {...}
}

class Test
{
    static void Main() {
        D cd1 = new D(C.M1);    // static method
        Test t = new C();
        D cd2 = new D(t.M2);    // instance method
        D cd3 = new D(cd2);     // another delegate
    }
}
```

Once instantiated, delegate instances always refer to the same target object and method. Remember, when two delegates are combined or one is removed from another, a new delegate results with its own invocation list; the invocation lists of the delegates combined or removed remain unchanged.

15.3 Delegate Invocation

C# provides special syntax for invoking a delegate. When a non-null delegate instance whose invocation list contains one entry is invoked, it invokes the one method with the same arguments it was given and returns the same value as the referred to method. (See §7.5.5.2 for detailed information on delegate invocation.) If an exception occurs during the invocation of such a delegate, and that exception is not caught within the method that was invoked, the search for an exception catch clause continues in the method that called the delegate as if that method had directly called the method to which that delegate referred.

Invocation of a delegate instance whose invocation list contains multiple entries proceeds by invoking each of the methods in the invocation list, synchronously, in order. Each method so called is passed the same set of arguments as was given to the delegate instance. If such a delegate invocation includes reference parameters (§10.5.1.2), each method invocation will occur with a reference to the same variable; changes to that variable by one method in the invocation list will be visible to methods further down the invocation list. If the delegate invocation includes output parameters or a return value, their final value will come from the invocation of the last delegate in the list.

If an exception occurs during the processing of the invocation of such a delegate, and that exception is not caught within the method that was invoked, the search for an exception catch clause continues in the method that called the delegate, and any methods further down the invocation list are not invoked.

Attempting to invoke a delegate instance whose value is `null` results in an exception of type `System.NullReferenceException`.

The following example shows how to instantiate, combine, remove, and invoke delegates.

```
using System;
delegate void D(int x);
class C
{
    public static void M1(int i) {
        Console.WriteLine("C.M1: " + i);
    }
```

```
        public static void M2(int i) {
            Console.WriteLine("C.M2: " + i);
        }

        public void M3(int i) {
            Console.WriteLine("C.M3: " + i);
        }
    }

    class Test
    {
        static void Main() {
            D cd1 = new D(C.M1);
            cd1(-1);                // call M1

            D cd2 = new D(C.M2);
            cd2(-2);                // call M2

            D cd3 = cd1 + cd2;
            cd3(10);                // call M1 then M2

            cd3 += cd1;
            cd3(20);                // call M1, M2, then M1

            C c = new C();
            D cd4 = new D(c.M3);
            cd3 += cd4;
            cd3(30);                // call M1, M2, M1, then M3

            cd3 -= cd1;             // remove last M1
            cd3(40);                // call M1, M2, then M3

            cd3 -= cd4;
            cd3(50);                // call M1 then M2

            cd3 -= cd2;
            cd3(60);                // call M1

            cd3 -= cd2;             // impossible removal is benign
            cd3(60);                // call M1

            cd3 -= cd1;             // invocation list is empty so cd3 is null

            //      cd3(70);        // System.NullReferenceException thrown

            cd3 -= cd1;             // impossible removal is benign
        }
    }
```

As shown in the statement cd3 += cd1;, a delegate can be present in an invocation list multiple times. In this case, it is simply invoked once per occurrence. In an invocation list such as this, when that delegate is removed, the last occurrence in the invocation list is the one actually removed.

Immediately prior to the execution of the final statement, cd3 -= cd1;, the delegate cd3 refers to an empty invocation list. Attempting to remove a delegate from an empty list (or to remove a nonexistent delegate from a nonempty list) is not an error.

The output produced is

```
C.M1: -1
C.M2: -2
C.M1: 10
C.M2: 10
C.M1: 20
C.M2: 20
C.M1: 20
C.M1: 30
C.M2: 30
C.M1: 30
C.M3: 30
C.M1: 40
C.M2: 40
C.M3: 40
C.M1: 50
C.M2: 50
C.M1: 60
C.M1: 60
```

16. Exceptions

Exceptions in C# provide a structured, uniform, and type-safe way of handling both system-level and application-level error conditions. The exception mechanism in C# is quite similar to that of C++ with a few important differences.

- In C#, all exceptions must be represented by an instance of a class type derived from System.Exception. In C++, any value of any type can be used to represent an exception.

- In C#, a finally block (§8.10) can be used to write termination code that executes in both normal execution and exceptional conditions. Such code is difficult to write in C++ without duplicating code.

- In C#, system-level exceptions such as overflow, divide-by-zero, and null dereferences have well-defined exception classes and are on a par with application-level error conditions.

16.1 Causes of Exceptions

An exception can be thrown in two different ways.

- A throw statement (§8.9.5) throws an exception immediately and unconditionally. Control never reaches the statement immediately following the throw.

- Certain exceptional conditions that arise during the processing of C# statements and expressions cause an exception in certain circumstances when the operation cannot be completed normally. For example, an integer division operation (§7.7.2) throws a System.DivideByZeroException if the denominator is zero. See §16.4 for a list of the various exceptions that can occur in this way.

16.2 The System.Exception Class

The System.Exception class is the base type of all exceptions. This class has a few notable properties that all exceptions share.

- Message is a read-only property of type string that contains a human-readable description of the reason for the exception.

- InnerException is a read-only property of type Exception. If its value is non-null, it refers to the exception that caused the current exception—that is, the current exception was raised in a catch block handling the InnerException. Otherwise, its value is null, indicating that this exception was not caused by another exception. The number of exception objects chained together in this manner can be arbitrary.

The value of these properties can be specified in calls to the instance constructor for System.Exception.

16.3 How Exceptions Are Handled

Exceptions are handled by a try statement (§8.10).

When an exception occurs, the system searches for the nearest catch clause that can handle the exception, as determined by the runtime type of the exception. First, the current method is searched for a lexically enclosing try statement, and the associated catch clauses of the try statement are considered in order. If that fails, the method that called the current method is searched for a lexically enclosing try statement that encloses the point of the call to the current method. This search continues until a catch clause is found that can handle the current exception by naming an exception class that is of the same class, or a base class, of the runtime type of the exception being thrown. A catch clause that does not name an exception class can handle any exception.

Once a matching catch clause is found, the system prepares to transfer control to the first statement of the catch clause. Before execution of the catch clause begins, the system first executes, in order, any finally clauses that were associated with try statements that are more nested than the one that caught the exception.

If no matching catch clause is found, one of two things occurs.

- If the search for a matching catch clause reaches a static constructor (§10.11) or static field initializer, then a System.TypeInitializationException is thrown at the point that triggered the invocation of the static constructor. The inner exception of the System.TypeInitializationException contains the exception that was originally thrown.

- If the search for matching catch clauses reaches the code that initially started the thread, then execution of the thread is terminated. The impact of such termination is implementation defined.

Exceptions that occur during destructor execution are worth special mention. If an exception occurs during destructor execution, and that exception is not caught, then the execution of that destructor is terminated and the destructor of the base class (if any) is called. If there is no base class (as in the case of the object type) or if there is no base class destructor, then the exception is discarded.

16.4 Common Exception Classes

The following exceptions are thrown by certain C# operations.

Exception	Description
System.ArithmeticException	A base class for exceptions that occur during arithmetic operations, such as System.DivideByZeroException and System.OverflowException
System.ArrayTypeMismatchException	Thrown when a store into an array fails because the actual type of the stored element is incompatible with the actual type of the array
System.DivideByZeroException	Thrown when an attempt to divide an integral value by zero occurs
System.IndexOutOfRangeException	Thrown when an attempt to index an array via an index that is less than zero or outside the bounds of the array
System.InvalidCastException	Thrown when an explicit conversion from a base type or interface to a derived type fails at runtime
System.NullReferenceException	Thrown when a null reference is used in a way that causes the referenced object to be required
System.OutOfMemoryException	Thrown when an attempt to allocate memory (via new) fails

continues

16. Exceptions

Exception	Description
`System.OverflowException`	Thrown when an arithmetic operation in a `checked` context overflows
`System.StackOverflowException`	Thrown when the execution stack is exhausted by having too many pending method calls; typically indicative of very deep or unbounded recursion
`System.TypeInitializationException`	Thrown when a static constructor throws an exception and no `catch` clause exists to catch it

17. Attributes

Much of the C# language enables the programmer to specify declarative information about the entities defined in the program. For example, the accessibility of a method in a class is specified by decorating it with the *method-modifiers* `public`, `protected`, `internal`, and `private`.

C# enables programmers to invent new kinds of declarative information, called **attributes**. Programmers can then attach attributes to various program entities and retrieve attribute information in a runtime environment. For instance, a framework might define a `HelpAttribute` attribute that can be placed on certain program elements (such as classes and methods) to provide a mapping from those program elements to their documentation.

Attributes are defined through the declaration of attribute classes (§17.1), which may have positional and named parameters (§17.1.2). Attributes are attached to entities in a C# program using attribute specifications (§17.2) and can be retrieved at runtime as attribute instances (§17.3).

17.1 Attribute Classes

A class that derives from the abstract class `System.Attribute`, whether directly or indirectly, is an **attribute class**. The declaration of an attribute class defines a new kind of attribute that can be placed on a declaration. By convention, attribute classes are named with a suffix of `Attribute`. Uses of an attribute may either include or omit this suffix.

17.1.1 Attribute Usage
The attribute `AttributeUsage` (§17.4.1) is used to describe how an attribute class can be used.

`AttributeUsage` has a positional parameter (§17.1.2) that enables an attribute class to specify the kinds of declarations on which it can be used. The example

```
using System;

[AttributeUsage(AttributeTargets.Class | AttributeTargets.Interface)]
public class SimpleAttribute: Attribute
{
    ...
}
```

defines an attribute class named `SimpleAttribute` that can be placed on *class-declarations* and *interface-declarations* only. The example

```
[Simple] class Class1 {...}

[Simple] interface Interface1 {...}
```

shows several uses of the `Simple` attribute. Although this attribute is defined with the name `SimpleAttribute`, when this attribute is used, the `Attribute` suffix may be omitted, resulting in the short name `Simple`. Thus, the previous example is semantically equivalent to the following.

```
[SimpleAttribute] class Class1 {...}

[SimpleAttribute] interface Interface1 {...}
```

`AttributeUsage` has a named parameter (§17.1.2) called `AllowMultiple`, which indicates whether the attribute can be specified more than once for a given entity. If `AllowMultiple` for an attribute class is true, then that attribute class is a ***multi-use attribute class*** and can be specified more than once on an entity. If `AllowMultiple` for an attribute class is false or it is unspecified, then that attribute class is a ***single-use attribute class*** and can be specified at most once on an entity.

The example

```
using System;

[AttributeUsage(AttributeTargets.Class, AllowMultiple = true)]
public class AuthorAttribute: Attribute
{
    private string name;

    public AuthorAttribute(string name) {
        this.name = name;
    }

    public string Name {
        get { return name; }
    }
}
```

defines a multi-use attribute class named `AuthorAttribute`. The example

```
[Author("Brian Kernighan"), Author("Dennis Ritchie")]
class Class1
{
    ...
}
```

shows a class declaration with two uses of the `Author` attribute.

`AttributeUsage` has another named parameter called `Inherited`, which indicates whether the attribute, when specified on a base class, is also inherited by classes that derive from that base class. If `Inherited` for an attribute class is true, then that attribute is inherited. If `Inherited` for an attribute class is false or it is unspecified, then that attribute is not inherited.

An attribute class X not having an `AttributeUsage` attribute attached to it, as in

```
using System;

class X: Attribute {...}
```

is equivalent to the following.

```
using System;

[AttributeUsage(
    AttributeTargets.All,
    AllowMultiple = false,
    Inherited = true)
]
class X: Attribute {...}
```

17.1.2 Positional and Named Parameters

Attribute classes can have *positional parameters* and *named parameters*. Each public instance constructor for an attribute class defines a valid sequence of positional parameters for that attribute class. Each nonstatic public read-write field and property for an attribute class defines a named parameter for the attribute class.

The example

```
using System;

[AttributeUsage(AttributeTargets.Class)]
public class HelpAttribute: Attribute
{
    public HelpAttribute(string url) {    // Positional parameter
        ...
    }

    public string Topic {                 // Named parameter
        get {...}
        set {...}
    }
```

```
        public string Url {
            get {...}
        }
    }
```

defines an attribute class named `HelpAttribute` that has one positional parameter, `url`, and one named parameter, `Topic`. Although it is nonstatic and public, the property `Url` does not define a named parameter because it is not read-write.

This attribute class might be used as follows.

```
[Help("http://www.mycompany.com/.../Class1.htm")]
class Class1
{
    ...
}

[Help("http://www.mycompany.com/.../Misc.htm", Topic = "Class2")]
class Class2
{
    ...
}
```

17.1.3 Attribute Parameter Types

The types of positional and named parameters for an attribute class are limited to the *attribute parameter types*, which are

- One of the following types: `bool`, `byte`, `char`, `double`, `float`, `int`, `long`, `sbyte`, `short`, `string`, `uint`, `ulong`, `ushort`

- The type `object`

- The type `System.Type`

- An enum type, provided it has public accessibility and the types in which it is nested (if any) also have public accessibility (§17.2)

- Single-dimensional arrays of the previous types

17.2 Attribute Specification

Attribute specification is the application of a previously defined attribute to a declaration. An attribute is a piece of additional declarative information that is specified for a declaration. Attributes can be specified at global scope (to specify attributes on the containing assembly or module) and for *type-declaration* s (§9.5), *class-member-declaration* s (§10.2), *interface-member-declaration* s(§13.2), *struct-member-declaration* s(§11.2), *enum-member-declaration* s(§14.3), *accessor-declarations* (§10.6.2), *event-accessor-declarations* (§10.7.1), and *formal-parameter-lists* (§10.5.1).

Attributes are specified in ***attribute sections***. An attribute section consists of a pair of square brackets, which surround a comma-separated list of one or more attributes. The order in which attributes are specified in such a list, and the order in which sections attached to the same program entity are arranged, is not significant. For instance, the attribute specifications [A][B], [B][A], [A, B], and [B, A] are equivalent.

global-attributes:
> *global-attribute-sections*

global-attribute-sections:
> *global-attribute-section*
> *global-attribute-sections   global-attribute-section*

global-attribute-section:
> [*global-attribute-target-specifier   attribute-list*]
> [*global-attribute-target-specifier   attribute-list* ,]

global-attribute-target-specifier:
> *global-attribute-target* :

global-attribute-target:
> `assembly`
> `module`

attributes:
> *attribute-sections*

attribute-sections:
> *attribute-section*
> *attribute-sections   attribute-section*

attribute-section:
> [*attribute-target-specifier*~opt~ *attribute-list*]
> [*attribute-target-specifier*~opt~ *attribute-list* ,]

attribute-target-specifier:
> *attribute-target* :

attribute-target:
> `field`
> `event`
> `method`
> `param`
> `property`
> `return`
> `type`

attribute-list:
    attribute
    attribute-list , attribute

attribute:
    attribute-name attribute-arguments$_{opt}$

attribute-name:
    type-name

attribute-arguments:
    (*positional-argument-list*$_{opt}$)
    (*positional-argument-list , named-argument-list*)
    (*named-argument-list*)

positional-argument-list:
    positional-argument
    positional-argument-list , positional-argument

positional-argument:
    attribute-argument-expression

named-argument-list:
    named-argument
    named-argument-list , named-argument

named-argument:
    identifier = attribute-argument-expression

attribute-argument-expression:
    expression

An attribute consists of an *attribute-name* and an optional list of positional and named arguments. The positional arguments (if any) precede the named arguments. A positional argument consists of an *attribute-argument-expression*; a named argument consists of a name, followed by an equal sign, followed by an *attribute-argument-expression*, which, together, are constrained by the same rules as simple assignment. The order of named arguments is not significant.

The *attribute-name* identifies an attribute class. If the form of *attribute-name* is *type-name*, then this name must refer to an attribute class. Otherwise, a compile-time error occurs. The example

```
class Class1 {}
[Class1] class Class2 {}// Error
```

results in a compile-time error because it attempts to use Class1 as an attribute class when Class1 is not an attribute class.

Certain contexts permit the specification of an attribute on more than one target. A program can explicitly specify the target by including an *attribute-target-specifier*. When an attribute is placed at the global level, a *global-attribute-target-specifier* is required. In all other locations, a reasonable default is applied, but an *attribute-target-specifier* can be used to affirm or override the default in certain ambiguous cases (or to just affirm the default in unambiguous cases). Thus, typically, *attribute-target-specifier*s can be omitted except at the global level. The potentially ambiguous contexts are resolved as follows.

- An attribute specified at global scope can apply either to the target assembly or the target module. No default exists for this context, so an *attribute-target-specifier* is always required in this context. The presence of the `assembly` *attribute-target-specifier* indicates that the attribute applies to the target assembly; the presence of the `module` *attribute-target-specifier* indicates that the attribute applies to the target module.

- An attribute specified on a delegate declaration can apply either to the delegate being declared or to its return value. In the absence of an *attribute-target-specifier*, the attribute applies to the delegate. The presence of the `type` *attribute-target-specifier* indicates that the attribute applies to the delegate; the presence of the `return` *attribute-target-specifier* indicates that the attribute applies to the return value.

- An attribute specified on a method declaration can apply either to the method being declared or to its return value. In the absence of an *attribute-target-specifier*, the attribute applies to the method. The presence of the `method` *attribute-target-specifier* indicates that the attribute applies to the method; the presence of the `return` *attribute-target-specifier* indicates that the attribute applies to the return value.

- An attribute specified on an operator declaration can apply either to the operator being declared or to its return value. In the absence of an *attribute-target-specifier*, the attribute applies to the operator. The presence of the `method` *attribute-target-specifier* indicates that the attribute applies to the operator; the presence of the `return` *attribute-target-specifier* indicates that the attribute applies to the return value.

- An attribute specified on an event declaration that omits event accessors can apply to the event being declared, to the associated field (if the event is not abstract), or to the associated add and remove methods. In the absence of an *attribute-target-specifier*, the attribute applies to the event. The presence of the `event` *attribute-target-specifier* indicates that the attribute applies to the event; the presence of the `field` *attribute-target-specifier* indicates that the attribute applies to the field; and the presence of the `method` *attribute-target-specifier* indicates that the attribute applies to the methods.

- An attribute specified on a get accessor declaration for a property or indexer declaration can apply either to the associated method or to its return value. In the absence of an *attribute-target-specifier*, the attribute applies to the method. The presence of the `method` *attribute-target-specifier* indicates that the attribute applies to the method; the presence of the `return` *attribute-target-specifier* indicates that the attribute applies to the return value.

- An attribute specified on a set accessor for a property or indexer declaration can apply either to the associated method or to its lone implicit parameter. In the absence of an *attribute-target-specifier*, the attribute applies to the method. The presence of the method *attribute-target-specifier* indicates that the attribute applies to the method; the presence of the param *attribute-target-specifier* indicates that the attribute applies to the parameter.

- An attribute specified on an add or remove accessor declaration for an event declaration can apply either to the associated method or to its lone parameter. In the absence of an *attribute-target-specifier*, the attribute applies to the method. The presence of the method *attribute-target-specifier* indicates that the attribute applies to the method; the presence of the param *attribute-target-specifier* indicates that the attribute applies to the parameter.

In other contexts, inclusion of an *attribute-target-specifier* is permitted but unnecessary. For instance, a class declaration may either include or omit the specifier type.

```
[type: Author("Brian Kernighan")]
class Class1 {}

[Author("Dennis Ritchie")]
class Class2 {}
```

It is an error to specify an invalid *attribute-target-specifier*. For instance, the specifier param cannot be used on a class declaration.

```
[param: Author("Brian Kernighan")]    // Error
class Class1 {}
```

By convention, attribute classes are named with a suffix of Attribute. An *attribute-name* of the form *type-name* may either include or omit this suffix. If an attribute class is found both with and without this suffix, an ambiguity is present, and a compile-time error results. If the *attribute-name* is spelled such that its right-most identifier is a verbatim identifier (§2.4.2), then only an attribute without a suffix is matched, thus enabling such an ambiguity to be resolved. The example

```
using System;

[AttributeUsage(AttributeTargets.All)]
public class X: Attribute
{}

[AttributeUsage(AttributeTargets.All)]
public class XAttribute: Attribute
{}

[X]                     // Error: ambiguity
class Class1 {}

[XAttribute]            // Refers to XAttribute
class Class2 {}
```

```
[@X]                        // Refers to X
class Class3 {}

[@XAttribute]               // Refers to XAttribute
class Class4 {}
```

shows two attribute classes named X and XAttribute. The attribute [X] is ambiguous because it could refer to either X or XAttribute. Using a verbatim identifier allows the exact intent to be specified in such rare cases. The attribute [XAttribute] is not ambiguous (although it would be if there was an attribute class named XAttributeAttribute!). If the declaration for class X is removed, then both attributes refer to the attribute class named XAttribute, as follows.

```
using System;

[AttributeUsage(AttributeTargets.All)]
public class XAttribute: Attribute
{}

[X]                         // Refers to XAttribute
class Class1 {}

[XAttribute]                // Refers to XAttribute
class Class2 {}

[@X]                        // Error: no attribute named "X"
class Class3 {}
```

It is a compile-time error to use a single-use attribute class more than once on the same entity. The example

```
using System;

[AttributeUsage(AttributeTargets.Class)]
public class HelpStringAttribute: Attribute
{
    string value;

    public HelpStringAttribute(string value) {
        this.value = value;
    }

    public string Value {
        get {...}
    }
}

[HelpString("Description of Class1")]
[HelpString("Another description of Class1")]
public class Class1 {}
```

results in a compile-time error because it attempts to use HelpString, which is a single-use attribute class, more than once on the declaration of Class1.

An expression E is an *attribute-argument-expression* if all of the following statements are true.

- The type of E is an attribute parameter type (§17.1.3).
- At compile time, the value of E can be resolved to one of the following:
  - A constant value
  - A System.Type object
  - A one-dimensional array of *attribute-argument-expressions*

For example

```
using System;

[AttributeUsage(AttributeTargets.Class)]
public class TestAttribute: Attribute
{
    public int P1 {
        get {...}
        set {...}
    }

    public Type P2 {
        get {...}
        set {...}
    }

    public object P3 {
        get {...}
        set {...}
    }
}
[Test(P1 = 1234, P3 = new int[] {1, 3, 5}, P2 = typeof(float))]
class MyClass {}
```

17.3 Attribute Instances

An *attribute instance* is an instance that represents an attribute at runtime. An attribute is defined with an attribute class, positional arguments, and named arguments. An attribute instance is an instance of the attribute class that is initialized with the positional and named arguments.

Retrieval of an attribute instance involves both compile-time and runtime processing, as described in the following sections.

17.3.1 Compilation of an Attribute

The compilation of an *attribute* with attribute class T, *positional-argument-list* P, and *named-argument-list* N, consists of the following steps.

- Follow the compile-time processing steps for compiling an *object-creation-expression* of the form new T(P). These steps either result in a compile-time error or determine an instance constructor C on T that can be invoked at runtime.

- If C does not have public accessibility, then a compile-time error occurs.

- For each *named-argument* Arg in N

  - Let Name be the *identifier* of the *named-argument* Arg.

  - Name must identify a nonstatic read-write public field or property on T. If T has no such field or property, then a compile-time error occurs.

- Keep the following information for runtime instantiation of the attribute: the attribute class T, the instance constructor C on T, the *positional-argument-list* P, and the *named-argument-list* N.

17.3.2 Runtime Retrieval of an Attribute Instance

Compilation of an *attribute* yields an attribute class T, an instance constructor C on T, a *positional-argument-list* P, and a *named-argument-list* N. Given this information, an attribute instance can be retrieved at runtime using the following steps.

- Follow the runtime processing steps for executing an *object-creation-expression* of the form new T(P) using the instance constructor C as determined at compile time. These steps either result in an exception or produce an instance O of T.

- For each *named-argument* Arg in N, in order

  - Let Name be the *identifier* of the *named-argument* Arg. If Name does not identify a non-static public read-write field or property on O, then an exception is thrown.

  - Let Value be the result of evaluating the *attribute-argument-expression* of Arg.

  - If Name identifies a field on O, then set this field to Value.

  - Otherwise, Name identifies a property on O. Set this property to Value.

  - The result is O, an instance of the attribute class T that has been initialized with the *positional-argument-list* P and the *named-argument-list* N.

17.4 Reserved Attributes

A small number of attributes affect the language in some way. These attributes include

- `System.AttributeUsageAttribute` (§17.4.1), which describes the ways in which an attribute class can be used

- `System.Diagnostics.ConditionalAttribute` (§17.4.2), which defines conditional methods

- `System.ObsoleteAttribute` (§17.4.3), which marks a member as obsolete

17.4.1 The AttributeUsage Attribute

The attribute `AttributeUsage` is used to describe the manner in which the attribute class can be used.

A class that is decorated with the `AttributeUsage` attribute must derive from `System.Attribute`, either directly or indirectly. Otherwise, a compile-time error occurs.

```
namespace System
{
    [AttributeUsage(AttributeTargets.Class)]
    public class AttributeUsageAttribute: Attribute
    {
        public AttributeUsageAttribute(AttributeTargets validOn) {...}

        public virtual bool AllowMultiple { get {...} set {...} }

        public virtual bool Inherited { get {...} set {...} }

        public virtual AttributeTargets ValidOn { get {...} }
    }
    public enum AttributeTargets
    {
        Assembly     = 0x0001,
        Module       = 0x0002,
        Class        = 0x0004,
        Struct       = 0x0008,
        Enum         = 0x0010,
        Constructor  = 0x0020,
        Method       = 0x0040,
        Property     = 0x0080,
        Field        = 0x0100,
        Event        = 0x0200,
        Interface    = 0x0400,
        Parameter    = 0x0800,
        Delegate     = 0x1000,
        ReturnValue  = 0x2000,
```

```
      All = Assembly | Module | Class | Struct | Enum | Constructor |
          Method | Property | Field | Event | Interface | Parameter |
          Delegate | ReturnValue
  }
}
```

17.4.2 The Conditional Attribute

The attribute `Conditional` enables the definition of *conditional methods*. The `Conditional` attribute indicates a condition by testing a conditional compilation symbol. Calls to a conditional method are either included or omitted depending on whether this symbol is defined at the point of the call. If the symbol is defined, the call is included; otherwise, the call (including evaluation of the parameters of the call) is omitted.

```
namespace System.Diagnostics
{
    [AttributeUsage(AttributeTargets.Method, AllowMultiple = true)]
    public class ConditionalAttribute: Attribute
    {
        public ConditionalAttribute(string conditionString) {...}

        public string ConditionString { get {...} }
    }
}
```

A conditional method is subject to the following restrictions.

- The conditional method must be a method in a class or struct declaration. A compile-time error occurs if the `Conditional` attribute is specified on a method in an interface declaration.

- The conditional method must have a return type of `void`.

- The conditional method must not be marked with the `override` modifier. A conditional method may be marked with the `virtual` modifier, however. Overrides of such a method are implicitly conditional and must not be explicitly marked with a `Conditional` attribute.

- The conditional method must not be an implementation of an interface method. Otherwise, a compile-time error occurs.

In addition, a compile-time error occurs if a conditional method is used in a *delegate-creation-expression*. The example

```
#define DEBUG

using System;
using System.Diagnostics;
```

```
class Class1
{
    [Conditional("DEBUG")]
    public static void M() {
        Console.WriteLine("Executed Class1.M");
    }
}
class Class2
{
    public static void Test() {
        Class1.M();
    }
}
```

declares Class1.M as a conditional method. Class2's Test method calls this method. Because the conditional compilation symbol DEBUG is defined, if Class2.Test is called, it will call M. If the symbol DEBUG had not been defined, then Class2.Test would not call Class1.M.

It is important to note that the inclusion or exclusion of a call to a conditional method is controlled by the conditional compilation symbols at the point of the call. In the example, the classes Class2 and Class3 each contain calls to the conditional method Class1.F, which is conditional based on whether DEBUG is defined.

File class1.cs:

```
using System.Diagnostics;
class Class1
{
    [Conditional("DEBUG")]
    public static void F() {
        Console.WriteLine("Executed Class1.F");
    }
}
```

File class2.cs:

```
#define DEBUG
class Class2
{
    public static void G() {
        Class1.F();             // F is called
    }
}
```

File class3.cs:

```
#undef DEBUG
```

```
class Class3
{
    public static void H() {
        Class1.F();                      // F is not called
    }
}
```

Because this symbol is defined in the context of `Class2` but not `Class3`, the call to `F` in `Class2` is included, and the call to `F` in `Class3` is omitted.

Using conditional methods in an inheritance chain can be confusing. Calls made to a conditional method through `base`, of the form `base.M`, are subject to the normal conditional method call rules. In the example, `Class2` includes a call to the `M` defined in its base class.

File `class1.cs`:

```
using System;
using System.Diagnostics;

class Class1
{
    [Conditional("DEBUG")]
    public virtual void M() {
        Console.WriteLine("Class1.M executed");
    }
}
```

File `class2.cs`:

```
using System;

class Class2: Class1
{
    public override void M() {
        Console.WriteLine("Class2.M executed");
        base.M();                        // base.M is not called!
    }
}
```

File `class3.cs`:

```
#define DEBUG

using System;

class Class3
{
    public static void Test() {
        Class2 c = new Class2();
        c.M();                           // M is called
    }
}
```

This call is omitted because the base method is conditional based on the presence of the symbol DEBUG, which is undefined. Thus, the method writes to the console Class2.M executed only. Judicious use of *pp-declarations* can eliminate such problems.

17.4.3 The Obsolete Attribute

The attribute Obsolete is used to mark types and members of types that should no longer be used.

```
namespace System
{
    [AttributeUsage(
        AttributeTargets.Class |
        AttributeTargets.Struct |
        AttributeTargets.Enum |
        AttributeTargets.Interface |
        AttributeTargets.Delegate |
        AttributeTargets.Method |
        AttributeTargets.Constructor |
        AttributeTargets.Property |
        AttributeTargets.Field |
        AttributeTargets.Event,
        Inherited = false)
    ]
    public class ObsoleteAttribute: Attribute
    {
        public ObsoleteAttribute() {...}

        public ObsoleteAttribute(string message) {...}

        public ObsoleteAttribute(string message, bool error) {...}

        public string Message { get {...} }

        public bool IsError { get {...} }
    }
}
```

If a program uses a type or member that is decorated with the Obsolete attribute, the compiler issues a warning or an error. Specifically, the compiler issues a warning if no error parameter is provided or if the error parameter is provided and has the value false. The compiler issues an error if the error parameter is specified and has the value true.

In the example

```
[Obsolete("This class is obsolete; use class B instead")]
class A
{
    public void F() {}
}
```

```
class B
{
    public void F() {}
}
class Test
{
    static void Main() {
        A a = new A();      // Warning
        a.F();
    }
}
```

the class A is decorated with the Obsolete attribute. Each use of A in Main results in a warning that includes the specified message "This class is obsolete; use class B instead."

17.5 Attributes for Interoperation

17.5.1 Interoperation with COM and Win32 Components

The .NET Framework provides a large number of attributes that enable C# programs to interoperate with components written using COM and Win32 DLLs. For example, the DllImport attribute can be used on a static extern method to indicate that the implementation of the method is to be found in a Win32 DLL. These attributes are found in the System.Runtime.InteropServices namespace, and detailed documentation for these attributes is found in the .NET Framework documentation.

17.5.2 Interoperation with Other .NET Languages

17.5.2.1 *The IndexerName Attribute*

Indexers are implemented in .NET using indexed properties and have a name in the .NET metadata. If no IndexerName attribute is present for an indexer, then the name Item is used by default. The IndexerName attribute enables a developer to override this default and specify a different name.

```
namespace System.Runtime.CompilerServices.CSharp
{
    [AttributeUsage(AttributeTargets.Property)]
    public class IndexerNameAttribute: Attribute
    {
        public IndexerNameAttribute(string indexerName) {...}

        public string Value { get {...} }
    }
}
```

18. Unsafe Code

The core C# language, as defined in the preceding chapters, differs notably from C and C++ in its omission of pointers as a data type. Instead, C# provides references and the ability to create objects that are managed by a garbage collector. This design, coupled with other features, makes C# a much safer language than C or C++. In the core C# language it is simply not possible to have an uninitialized variable, a "dangling" pointer, or an expression that indexes an array beyond its bounds. Whole categories of bugs that routinely plague C and C++ programs are thus eliminated.

Although practically every pointer type construct in C or C++ has a reference type counterpart in C#, nonetheless, there are situations where access to pointer types becomes a necessity. For example, interfacing with the underlying operating system, accessing a memory-mapped device, or implementing a time-critical algorithm may not be possible or practical without access to pointers. To address this need, C# provides the ability to write *unsafe code*.

In unsafe code it is possible to declare and operate on pointers, to perform conversions between pointers and integral types, to take the address of variables, and so forth. In a sense, writing unsafe code is much like writing C code within a C# program.

Unsafe code is in fact a "safe" feature from the perspective of both developers and users. Unsafe code must be clearly marked with the modifier `unsafe`, so developers cannot possibly use unsafe features accidentally, and the execution engine works to ensure that unsafe code cannot be executed in an untrusted environment.

18.1 Unsafe Contexts

The unsafe features of C# are available only in *unsafe contexts*. An unsafe context is introduced by including an `unsafe` modifier in the declaration of a type or member or by employing an *unsafe-statement*.

- A declaration of a class, struct, interface, or delegate may include an `unsafe` modifier, in which case the entire textual extent of that type declaration (including the body of the class, struct, or interface) is considered an unsafe context.

- A declaration of a field, method, property, event, indexer, operator, instance constructor, destructor, or static constructor may include an `unsafe` modifier, in which case the entire textual extent of that member declaration is considered an unsafe context.

- An *unsafe-statement* enables the use of an unsafe context within a *block*. The entire textual extent of the associated *block* is considered an unsafe context.

The associated grammar extensions are as follows. For brevity, ellipses (...) represent productions that appear in preceding chapters.

> *class-modifier:*
>
> ...
>
> unsafe
>
> *struct-modifier:*
>
> ...
>
> unsafe
>
> *interface-modifier:*
>
> ...
>
> unsafe
>
> *delegate-modifier:*
>
> ...
>
> unsafe
>
> *field-modifier:*
>
> ...
>
> unsafe
>
> *method-modifier:*
>
> ...
>
> unsafe
>
> *property-modifier:*
>
> ...
>
> unsafe
>
> *event-modifier:*
>
> ...
>
> unsafe

indexer-modifier:
> ...
> unsafe

operator-modifier:
> ...
> unsafe

constructor-modifier:
> ...
> unsafe

destructor-declaration:
> attributes$_{opt}$ extern$_{opt}$ unsafe$_{opt}$ ~ *identifier* ( ) *destructor-body*
> attributes$_{opt}$ unsafe$_{opt}$ extern$_{opt}$ ~ *identifier* ( ) *destructor-body*

static-constructor-modifiers:
> extern$_{opt}$ unsafe$_{opt}$ static
> unsafe$_{opt}$ extern$_{opt}$ static
> extern$_{opt}$ static unsafe$_{opt}$
> unsafe$_{opt}$ static extern$_{opt}$
> static extern$_{opt}$ unsafe$_{opt}$
> static unsafe$_{opt}$ extern$_{opt}$

embedded-statement:
> ...
> *unsafe-statement*

unsafe-statement:
> unsafe *block*

In the example

```
public unsafe struct Node
{
    public int Value;
    public Node* Left;
    public Node* Right;
}
```

the `unsafe` modifier specified in the struct declaration causes the entire textual extent of the struct declaration to become an unsafe context. Thus, it is possible to declare the `Left` and `Right` fields to be of a pointer type. The previous example could also be written as follows.

```
public struct Node
{
    public int Value;
    public unsafe Node* Left;
    public unsafe Node* Right;
}
```

Here, the `unsafe` modifiers in the field declarations cause those declarations to be considered unsafe contexts.

Other than establishing an unsafe context, thus permitting the use of pointer types, the `unsafe` modifier has no effect on a type or a member. In the example

```
public class A
{
    public unsafe virtual void F() {
        char* p;
        . . .
    }
}
public class B: A
{
    public override void F() {
        base.F();
        . . .
    }
}
```

the `unsafe` modifier on the F method in A simply causes the textual extent of F to become an unsafe context in which the unsafe features of the language can be used. In the override of F in B, there is no need to specify the `unsafe` modifier again—unless, of course, the F method in B itself needs access to unsafe features.

The situation is slightly different when a pointer type is part of the method's signature.

```
public unsafe class A
{
    public virtual void F(char* p) {...}
}
public class B: A
{
    public unsafe override void F(char* p) {...}
}
```

Here, because F's signature includes a pointer type, it can only be written in an unsafe context. However, the unsafe context can be introduced by either making the entire class unsafe, as is the case in A, or by including an `unsafe` modifier in the method declaration, as is the case in B.

18.2 Pointer Types

In an unsafe context, a *type* (§4) may be a *pointer-type* as well as a *value-type* or a *reference-type*.

> *type:*
> > *value-type*
> > *reference-type*
> > *pointer-type*

A *pointer-type* is written as an *unmanaged-type* or the keyword `void`, followed by a * token.

> *pointer-type:*
> > *unmanaged-type*   *
> > `void` *
>
> *unmanaged-type:*
> > *type*

The type specified before the * in a pointer type is called the **referent type** of the pointer type. It represents the type of the variable to which a value of the pointer type points.

Unlike references (values of reference types), pointers are not tracked by the garbage collector—the garbage collector has no knowledge of pointers and the data to which they point. For this reason a pointer is not permitted to point to a reference or to a struct that contains references, and the referent type of a pointer must be an *unmanaged-type*.

An *unmanaged-type* is any type that is not a *reference-type* and does not contain *reference-type* fields at any level of nesting. In other words, an *unmanaged-type* is one of the following:

- `sbyte`, `byte`, `short`, `ushort`, `int`, `uint`, `long`, `ulong`, `char`, `float`, `double`, `decimal`, or `bool`
- Any *enum-type*
- Any *pointer-type*
- Any user-defined *struct-type* that contains fields of *unmanaged-type*s only

The intuitive rule for mixing of pointers and references is that referents of references (objects) are permitted to contain pointers, but referents of pointers are not permitted to contain references.

Some examples of pointer types are given in the following table.

Example	Description
byte*	Pointer to byte
char*	Pointer to char
int**	Pointer to pointer to int
int*[]	Single-dimensional array of pointers to int
void*	Pointer to unknown type

For a given implementation, all pointer types must have the same size and representation.

Unlike C and C++, when multiple pointers are declared in the same declaration, in C# the `*` is written along with the underlying type only, not as a prefix punctuator on each pointer name. For example

```
int* pi, pj;   // NOT as int *pi, *pj;
```

The value of a pointer having type T* represents the *address* of a variable of type T. The pointer indirection operator * (§18.5.1) may be used to access this variable. For example, given a variable P of type int*, the expression *P denotes the int variable found at the address contained in P.

Like an object reference, a pointer may be null. Applying the indirection operator to a null pointer results in implementation-defined behavior. A pointer with value null is represented by all-bits-zero.

The void* type represents a pointer to an unknown type. Because the referent type is unknown, the indirection operator cannot be applied to a pointer of type void*, nor can any arithmetic be performed on such a pointer. However, a pointer of type void* can be cast to any other pointer type (and vice versa).

Pointer types are a separate category of types. Unlike reference types and value types, pointer types do not inherit from object, and no conversions exist between pointer types and object. In particular, boxing and unboxing (§4.3) are not supported for pointers. However, conversions are permitted between different pointer types and between pointer types and the integral types. This is described in §18.4.

A *pointer-type* may be used as the type of a volatile field (§10.4.3).

Although pointers can be passed as `ref` or `out` parameters, doing so can cause undefined behavior because the pointer may well be set to point to a local variable that no longer exists when the called method returns or the fixed object to which it used to point is no longer fixed. For example

```
using System;

class Test
{
    static int value = 20;

    unsafe static void F(out int* pi1, ref int* pi2) {
        int i = 10;
        pi1 = &i;

        fixed (int* pj = &value) {
            // ...
            pi2 = pj;
        }
    }

    static void Main() {
        int i = 10;
        unsafe {
            int* px1;
            int* px2 = &i;

            F(out px1, ref px2);

            Console.WriteLine("*px1 = {0}, *px2 = {1}",
                *px1, *px2);   // undefined behavior
        }
    }
}
```

A method can return a value of some type, and that type can be a pointer. For example, when given a pointer to a contiguous sequence of `int`s, that sequence's element count, and some other `int` value, the following method returns the address of that value in that sequence if a match occurs; otherwise, it returns `null`.

```
unsafe static int* Find(int* pi, int size, int value) {
    for (int i = 0; i < size; ++i) {
        if (*pi == value)
            return pi;
        ++pi;
    }
    return null;
}
```

In an unsafe context, several constructs are available for operating on pointers.

- The * operator may be used to perform pointer indirection (§18.5.1).

- The -> operator may be used to access a member of a struct through a pointer (§18.5.2).

- The [] operator may be used to index a pointer (§18.5.3).

- The & operator may be used to obtain the address of a variable (§18.5.4).

- The ++ and -- operators may be used to increment and decrement pointers (§18.5.5).

- The + and - operators may be used to perform pointer arithmetic (§18.5.6).

- The ==, !=, <, >, <=, and => operators may be used to compare pointers (§18.5.7).

- The stackalloc operator may be used to allocate memory from the call stack (§18.7).

- The fixed statement may be used to temporarily fix a variable so its address can be obtained (§18.6).

18.3 Fixed and Moveable Variables

The address-of operator (§18.5.4) and the fixed statement (§18.6) divide variables into two categories: *fixed variables* and *moveable variables*.

Fixed variables reside in storage locations that are unaffected by operation of the garbage collector. (Examples of fixed variables include local variables, value parameters, and variables created by dereferencing pointers.) On the other hand, moveable variables reside in storage locations that are subject to relocation or disposal by the garbage collector. (Examples of moveable variables include fields in objects and elements of arrays.)

The & operator (§18.5.4) permits the address of a fixed variable to be obtained without restrictions. However, because a moveable variable is subject to relocation or disposal by the garbage collector, the address of a moveable variable can only be obtained using a fixed statement (§18.6), and that address remains valid only for the duration of that fixed statement.

In precise terms, a fixed variable is one of the following.

- A variable resulting from a *simple-name* (§7.5.2) that refers to a local variable or a value parameter.

- A variable resulting from a *member-access* (§7.5.4) of the form V.I, where V is a fixed variable of a *struct-type*.

- A variable resulting from a *pointer-indirection-expression* (§18.5.1) of the form *P, a *pointer-member-access* (§18.5.2) of the form P->I, or a *pointer-element-access* (§18.5.3) of the form P[E].

All other variables are classified as moveable variables.

Note that a static field is classified as a moveable variable. Also note that a `ref` or `out` parameter is classified as a moveable variable, even if the argument given for the parameter is a fixed variable. Finally, note that a variable produced by dereferencing a pointer is always classified as a fixed variable.

18.4 Pointer Conversions

In an unsafe context, the set of available implicit conversions (§6.1) is extended to include the following implicit pointer conversions:

- From any *pointer-type* to the type `void*`
- From the `null` type to any *pointer-type*

Additionally, in an unsafe context, the set of available explicit conversions (§6.2) is extended to include the following explicit pointer conversions.

- From any *pointer-type* to any other *pointer-type*
- From `sbyte`, `byte`, `short`, `ushort`, `int`, `uint`, `long`, or `ulong` to any *pointer-type*
- From any *pointer-type* to `sbyte`, `byte`, `short`, `ushort`, `int`, `uint`, `long`, or `ulong`

Finally, in an unsafe context, the set of standard implicit conversions (§6.3.1) includes the following pointer conversion.

- From any *pointer-type* to the type `void*`

Conversions between two pointer types never change the actual pointer value. In other words, a conversion from one pointer type to another has no effect on the underlying address given by the pointer.

When one pointer type is converted to another, if the resulting pointer is not correctly aligned for the pointed-to type, the behavior is undefined if the result is dereferenced. In general, the concept "correctly aligned" is transitive: If a pointer to type A is correctly aligned for a pointer to type B, which, in turn, is correctly aligned for a pointer to type C, then a pointer to type A is correctly aligned for a pointer to type C.

Consider the following case in which a variable having one type is accessed via a pointer to a different type.

```
char c = 'A';
char* pc = &c;
void* pv = pc;
int* pi = (int*)pv;
int i = *pi;        // undefined
*pi = 123456;       // undefined
```

When a pointer type is converted to a pointer to byte, the result points to the lowest addressed byte of the variable. Successive increments of the result, up to the size of the variable, yield pointers to the remaining bytes of that variable. For example, the following method displays each of the eight bytes in a double as a hexadecimal value.

```
using System;

class Test
{
    static void Main() {
        double d = 123.456e23;
        unsafe {
            byte* pb = (byte*)&d;
            for (int i = 0; i < sizeof(double); ++i)
                Console.Write("{0:X2} ", *pb++);
            Console.WriteLine();
        }
    }
}
```

Of course, the output produced depends on endianness.

Mappings between pointers and integers are implementation defined. However, on 32-bit and 64-bit processor architectures with a linear address space, conversions of pointers to or from integral types typically behave like conversions of uint or ulong values, respectively, to or from those integral types.

18.5 Pointers in Expressions

In an unsafe context, an expression may yield a result of a pointer type, but outside an unsafe context it is a compile-time error for an expression to be of a pointer type. In precise terms, outside an unsafe context a compile-time error occurs if any *simple-name* (§7.5.2), *member-access* (§7.5.4), *invocation-expression* (§7.5.5), or *element-access* (§7.5.6) is of a pointer type.

In an unsafe context, the *primary-no-array-creation-expression* (§7.5) and *unary-expression* (§7.6) productions permit the following additional constructs.

primary-no-array-creation-expression:

> ...

> *pointer-member-access*
> *pointer-element-access*
> *sizeof-expression*

unary-expression:

    ...

    pointer-indirection-expression
    addressof-expression

These constructs are described in the following sections. The precedence and associativity of the unsafe operators is implied by the grammar.

18.5.1 Pointer Indirection

A *pointer-indirection-expression* consists of an asterisk (*) followed by a *unary-expression*.

pointer-indirection-expression:
    * *unary-expression*

The unary * operator denotes *pointer indirection* and is used to obtain the variable to which a pointer points. The result of evaluating *P, where P is an expression of a pointer type T*, is a variable of type T. It is a compile-time error to apply the unary * operator to an expression of type void* or to an expression that is not of a pointer type.

The effect of applying the unary * operator to a null pointer is implementation defined. In particular, there is no guarantee that this operation throws a System.NullReferenceException.

If an invalid value has been assigned to the pointer, the behavior of the unary * operator is undefined. Among the invalid values for dereferencing a pointer by the unary * operator are an address inappropriately aligned for the type pointed to (see the example in §18.4) and the address of a variable after the end of its lifetime.

For purposes of definite assignment analysis, a variable produced by evaluating an expression of the form *P is considered initially assigned (§5.3.1).

18.5.2 Pointer Member Access

A *pointer-member-access* consists of a *primary-expression*, followed by a -> token, followed by an *identifier*.

pointer-member-access:
    primary-expression -> *identifier*

In a pointer member access of the form P->I, P must be an expression of a pointer type other than void*, and I must denote an accessible member of the type to which P points.

A pointer member access of the form P->I is evaluated exactly as (*P).I. For a description of the pointer indirection operator (*), see §18.5.1. For a description of the member access operator (.), see §7.5.4.

In the example

```
using System;

struct Point
{
    public int x;
    public int y;

    public override string ToString() {
        return "(" + x + "," + y + ")";
    }
}

class Test
{
    static void Main() {
        Point point;
        unsafe {
            Point* p = &point;
            p->x = 10;
            p->y = 20;
            Console.WriteLine(p->ToString());
        }
    }
}
```

the -> operator is used to access fields and invoke a method of a struct through a pointer. Because the operation P->I is precisely equivalent to (*P).I, the Main method could equally well have been written as follows.

```
class Test
{
    static void Main() {
        Point point;
        unsafe {
            Point* p = &point;
            (*p).x = 10;
            (*p).y = 20;
            Console.WriteLine((*p).ToString());
        }
    }
}
```

18.5.3 Pointer Element Access

A *pointer-element-access* consists of a *primary-no-array-creation-expression* followed by an expression enclosed in [and].

pointer-element-access:
> *primary-no-array-creation-expression* [*expression*]

In a pointer element access of the form P[E], P must be an expression of a pointer type other than void*, and E must be an expression of a type that can be implicitly converted to int, uint, long, or ulong.

A pointer element access of the form P[E] is evaluated exactly as *(P + E). For a description of the pointer indirection operator (*), see §18.5.1. For a description of the pointer addition operator (+), see §18.5.6.

In the example

```
class Test
{
    static void Main() {
        unsafe {
            char* p = stackalloc char[256];
            for (int i = 0; i < 256; i++) p[i] = (char)i;
        }
    }
}
```

a pointer element access is used to initialize the character buffer in a for loop. Because the operation P[E] is precisely equivalent to *(P + E), the example could equally well have been written as follows.

```
class Test
{
    static void Main() {
        unsafe {
            char* p = stackalloc char[256];
            for (int i = 0; i < 256; i++) *(p + i) = (char)i;
        }
    }
}
```

The pointer element access operator does not check for out-of-bounds errors and the behavior when accessing an out-of-bounds element is undefined. This is the same as C and C++.

18.5.4 The address-of Operator

An *addressof-expression* consists of an ampersand (&) followed by a *unary-expression*.

addressof-expression:
    & *unary-expression*

Given an expression E that is of a type T and is classified as a fixed variable (§18.3), the construct &E computes the address of the variable given by E. The type of the result is T* and is classified as a value. A compile-time error occurs if E is not classified as a variable, if E is classified as a volatile field (§10.4.3), or if E denotes a moveable variable. In the last case, a fixed statement (§18.6) can be used to temporarily "fix" the variable before obtaining its address.

The & operator does not require its argument to be definitely assigned, but following an & operation, the variable to which the operator is applied is considered definitely assigned in the execution path in which the operation occurs. It is the responsibility of the programmer to ensure that correct initialization of the variable actually does take place in this situation.

In the example

```
using System;
class Test
{
    static void Main() {
        int i;
        unsafe {
            int* p = &i;
            *p = 123;
        }
        Console.WriteLine(i);
    }
}
```

i is considered definitely assigned following the &i operation used to initialize p. The assignment to *p in effect initializes i, but the inclusion of this initialization is the responsibility of the programmer, and no compile-time error would occur if the assignment was removed.

The rules of definite assignment for the & operator exist such that redundant initialization of local variables can be avoided. For example, many external Application Programming Interfaces (APIs) take a pointer to a structure that is filled in by the API. Calls to such APIs typically pass the address of a local struct variable, and without the rule, redundant initialization of the struct variable would be required.

As stated in §7.5.4, outside an instance constructor or static constructor for a struct or class that defines a readonly field, that field is considered a value, not a variable. As such, its address cannot be taken. Similarly, the address of a constant cannot be taken.

18.5.5 Pointer Increment and Decrement

In an unsafe context, the ++ and -- operators (§7.5.9 and §7.6.5) can be applied to pointer variables of all types except void*. Thus, for every pointer type T*, the following operators are implicitly defined.

```
T* operator ++(T* x);
T* operator --(T* x);
```

The operators produce the same results as x + 1 and x – 1, respectively (§18.5.6). In other words, for a pointer variable of type T*, the ++ operator adds sizeof(T) to the address contained in the variable, and the -- operator subtracts sizeof(T) from the address contained in the variable.

If a pointer increment or decrement operation overflows the domain of the pointer type, the result is implementation defined, but no exceptions are produced.

18.5.6 Pointer Arithmetic

In an unsafe context, the + and – operators (§7.7.4 and §7.7.5) can be applied to values of all pointer types except void*. Thus, for every pointer type T*, the following operators are implicitly defined.

```
T* operator +(T* x, int y);
T* operator +(T* x, uint y);
T* operator +(T* x, long y);
T* operator +(T* x, ulong y);

T* operator +(int x, T* y);
T* operator +(uint x, T* y);
T* operator +(long x, T* y);
T* operator +(ulong x, T* y);

T* operator -(T* x, int y);
T* operator -(T* x, uint y);
T* operator -(T* x, long y);
T* operator -(T* x, ulong y);

long operator -(T* x, T* y);
```

Given an expression P of a pointer type T* and an expression N of type int, uint, long, or ulong, the expressions P + N and N + P compute the pointer value of type T* that results from adding N * sizeof(T) to the address given by P. Likewise, the expression P - N computes the pointer value of type T* that results from subtracting N * sizeof(T) from the address given by P.

Given two expressions, P and Q, of a pointer type T*, the expression P – Q computes the difference between the addresses given by P and Q and then divides that difference by sizeof(T). The type of the result is always long. In effect, P - Q is computed as ((long)(P) - (long)(Q)) / sizeof(T).

The example

```
using System;

class Test
{
```

```
static void Main() {
    unsafe {
        int* values = stackalloc int[20];
        int* p = &values[1];
        int* q = &values[15];
        Console.WriteLine("p - q = {0}", p - q);
        Console.WriteLine("q - p = {0}", q - p);
    }
}
```

produces the following output.

```
p - q = -14
q - p = 14
```

If a pointer arithmetic operation overflows the domain of the pointer type, the result is truncated in an implementation-defined fashion, but no exceptions are produced.

18.5.7 Pointer Comparison

In an unsafe context, the ==, !=, <, >, <=, and => operators (§7.9) can be applied to values of all pointer types. The pointer comparison operators are as follows.

```
bool operator ==(void* x, void* y);

bool operator !=(void* x, void* y);

bool operator <(void* x, void* y);

bool operator >(void* x, void* y);

bool operator <=(void* x, void* y);

bool operator >=(void* x, void* y);
```

Because an implicit conversion exists from any pointer type to the void* type, operands of any pointer type can be compared using these operators. The comparison operators compare the addresses given by the two operands as if they were unsigned integers.

18.5.8 The sizeof Operator

The sizeof operator returns the number of bytes occupied by a variable of a given type. The type specified as an operand to sizeof must be an *unmanaged-type* (§18.2).

sizeof-expression:
    sizeof (*unmanaged-type*)

The result of the `sizeof` operator is a value of type `int`. For certain predefined types, the `sizeof` operator yields a constant value as shown in the following table.

Expression	Result
sizeof(sbyte)	1
sizeof(byte)	1
sizeof(short)	2
sizeof(ushort)	2
sizeof(int)	4
sizeof(uint)	4
sizeof(long)	8
sizeof(ulong)	8
sizeof(char)	2
sizeof(float)	4
sizeof(double)	8
sizeof(bool)	1

For all other types, the result of the `sizeof` operator is implementation defined and is classified as a value, not a constant.

The order in which members are packed into a struct is unspecified.

For alignment purposes, there may be unnamed padding at the beginning of a struct, within a struct, and at the end of the struct. The contents of the bits used as padding are indeterminate.

When applied to an operand that has struct type, the result is the total number of bytes in a variable of that type, including any padding.

18. Unsafe Code

18.6 The fixed Statement

In an unsafe context, the *embedded-statement* (§8) production permits an additional construct, the `fixed` statement, which is used to "fix" a moveable variable such that its address remains constant for the duration of the statement.

> *embedded-statement:*
>
> ...
> *fixed-statement*
>
> *fixed-statement:*
>   `fixed` (*pointer-type fixed-pointer-declarators*) *embedded-statement*
>
> *fixed-pointer-declarators:*
>   *fixed-pointer-declarator*
>   *fixed-pointer-declarators* , *fixed-pointer-declarator*
>
> *fixed-pointer-declarator:*
>   *identifier* = *fixed-pointer-initializer*
>
> *fixed-pointer-initializer:*
>   & *variable-reference*
>   *expression*

Each *fixed-pointer-declarator* declares a local variable of the given *pointer-type* and initializes that local variable with the address computed by the corresponding *fixed-pointer-initializer*. A local variable declared in a `fixed` statement is accessible in any *fixed-pointer-initializers* occurring to the right of that variable's declaration and in the *embedded-statement* of the `fixed` statement. A local variable declared by a `fixed` statement is considered read-only. A compile-time error occurs if the embedded statement attempts to modify this local variable (via assignment or the ++ and -- operators) or pass it as a `ref` or `out` parameter.

A *fixed-pointer-initializer* can be one of the following.

- The token & followed by a *variable-reference* (§5.3.3) to a moveable variable (§18.3) of an unmanaged type T, provided the type T* is implicitly convertible to the pointer type given in the `fixed` statement. In this case, the initializer computes the address of the given variable, and the variable is guaranteed to remain at a fixed address for the duration of the `fixed` statement.

- An expression of an *array-type* with elements of an unmanaged type T, provided the type T* is implicitly convertible to the pointer type given in the `fixed` statement. In this case, the initializer computes the address of the first element in the array, and the entire array is guaranteed to remain at a fixed address for the duration of the `fixed` statement. The behavior of the `fixed` statement is implementation defined if the array expression is `null` or if the array has zero elements.

- An expression of type `string`, provided the type `char*` is implicitly convertible to the pointer type given in the `fixed` statement. In this case, the initializer computes the address of the first character in the string, and the entire string is guaranteed to remain at a fixed address for the duration of the `fixed` statement. The behavior of the `fixed` statement is implementation defined if the string expression is null.

For each address computed by a *fixed-pointer-initializer* the `fixed` statement ensures that the variable referenced by the address is not subject to relocation or disposal by the garbage collector for the duration of the `fixed` statement. For example, if the address computed by a *fixed-pointer-initializer* references a field of an object or an element of an array instance, the `fixed` statement guarantees that the containing object instance is not relocated or disposed of during the lifetime of the statement.

It is the programmer's responsibility to ensure that pointers created by `fixed` statements do not survive beyond execution of those statements. For example, when pointers created by `fixed` statements are passed to external APIs, it is the programmer's responsibility to ensure that the APIs retain no memory of these pointers.

Fixed objects may cause fragmentation of the heap (because they cannot be moved). For that reason, objects should be fixed only when absolutely necessary and then only for the shortest amount of time possible.

The example

```
class Test
{
    static int x;
    int y;

    unsafe static void F(int* p) {
        *p = 1;
    }

    static void Main() {
        Test t = new Test();
        int[] a = new int[10];
        unsafe {
            fixed (int* p = &x) F(p);
            fixed (int* p = &t.y) F(p);
            fixed (int* p = &a[0]) F(p);
            fixed (int* p = a) F(p);
        }
    }
}
```

demonstrates several uses of the `fixed` statement. The first statement fixes and obtains the address of a static field, the second statement fixes and obtains the address of an instance field, and the third statement fixes and obtains the address of an array element. In each case it would have been an error to use the regular & operator because the variables are all classified as moveable variables.

The third and fourth `fixed` statements in the previous example produce identical results. In general, for an array instance a, specifying &a[0] in a `fixed` statement is the same as simply specifying a.

The following is another example of the `fixed` statement, this time using `string`.

```
class Test
{
    static string name = "xx";
    unsafe static void F(char* p) {
        for (int i = 0; p[i] != '\0'; ++i)
            Console.WriteLine(p[i]);
    }
    static void Main() {
        unsafe {
            fixed (char* p = name) F(p);
            fixed (char* p = "xx") F(p);
        }
    }
}
```

In an unsafe context array elements of single-dimensional arrays are stored in increasing index order, starting with index 0 and ending with index Length − 1. For multi-dimensional arrays, array elements are stored such that the indices of the rightmost dimension are increased first, then the next left dimension, and so on to the left. Within a `fixed` statement that obtains a pointer p to an array instance a, the pointer values ranging from p to p + a.Length − 1 represent addresses of the elements in the array. Likewise, the variables ranging from p[0] to p[a.Length − 1] represent the actual array elements. Given the way in which arrays are stored, an array of any dimension can be treated as though it were linear.

For example

```
using System;
class Test
{
    static void Main() {
        int[,,] a = new int[2,3,4];
        unsafe {
            fixed (int* p = a) {
                for (int i = 0; i < a.Length; ++i)// treat as linear
                    p[i] = i;
            }
        }
```

```
                for (int i = 0; i < 2; ++i)
                    for (int j = 0; j < 3; ++j) {
                        for (int k = 0; k < 4; ++k)
                            Console.Write("[{0},{1},{2}] = {3,2} ", i, j, k, a[i,j,k]);
                        Console.WriteLine();
                    }
            }
        }
```

produces the following output.

```
    [0,0,0] =  0 [0,0,1] =  1 [0,0,2] =  2 [0,0,3] =  3
    [0,1,0] =  4 [0,1,1] =  5 [0,1,2] =  6 [0,1,3] =  7
    [0,2,0] =  8 [0,2,1] =  9 [0,2,2] = 10 [0,2,3] = 11
    [1,0,0] = 12 [1,0,1] = 13 [1,0,2] = 14 [1,0,3] = 15
    [1,1,0] = 16 [1,1,1] = 17 [1,1,2] = 18 [1,1,3] = 19
    [1,2,0] = 20 [1,2,1] = 21 [1,2,2] = 22 [1,2,3] = 23
```

In the example

```
class Test
{
    unsafe static void Fill(int* p, int count, int value) {
        for (; count != 0; count--) *p++ = value;
    }
    static void Main() {
        int[] a = new int[100];
        unsafe {
            fixed (int* p = a) Fill(p, 100, -1);
        }
    }
}
```

a fixed statement is used to fix an array so its address can be passed to a method that takes a pointer.

A char* value produced by fixing a string instance always points to a null-terminated string. Within a fixed statement that obtains a pointer p to a string instance s, the pointer values ranging from p to p + s.Length - 1 represent addresses of the characters in the string, and the pointer value p + s.Length always points to a null character (the character with value '\0').

Modifying objects of managed type through fixed pointers can result in undefined behavior. For example, because strings are immutable, it is the programmer's responsibility to ensure that the characters referenced by a pointer to a fixed string are not modified.

The automatic null-termination of strings is particularly convenient when calling external APIs that expect "C-style" strings. Note, however, that a string instance is permitted to contain null characters. If such null characters are present, the string will appear truncated when treated as a null-terminated char*.

18.7 Stack Allocation

In an unsafe context, a local variable declaration (§8.5.1) may include a stack allocation initializer that allocates memory from the call stack.

local-variable-initializer:
   expression
   array-initializer
   stackalloc-initializer

stackalloc-initializer:
   stackalloc *unmanaged-type* [*expression*]

The *unmanaged-type* indicates the type of the items that will be stored in the newly allocated location, and the *expression* indicates the number of these items. Taken together, these specify the required allocation size. Because the size of a stack allocation cannot be negative, it is a compile-time error to specify the number of items as a *constant-expression* that evaluates to a negative value.

A stack allocation initializer of the form stackalloc T[E] requires T to be an unmanaged type (§18.2) and E to be an expression of type int. The construct allocates E * sizeof(T) bytes from the call stack and returns a pointer, of type T*, to the newly allocated block. If E is a negative value, then the behavior is undefined. If E is zero, then no allocation is made, and the pointer returned is implementation defined. If there is not enough memory available to allocate a block of the given size, a System.StackOverflowException is thrown.

The content of the newly allocated memory is undefined.

Stack allocation initializers are not permitted in catch or finally blocks (§8.10).

There is no way to explicitly free memory allocated using stackalloc. All stack allocated memory blocks created during the execution of a function member are automatically discarded when that function member returns. This corresponds to the alloca function, an extension commonly found in C and C++ implementations.

In the example

```
using System;
```

```
class Test
{
    static string IntToString(int value) {
        int n = value >= 0? value: -value;
        unsafe {
            char* buffer = stackalloc char[16];
            char* p = buffer + 16;
            do {
                *--p = (char)(n % 10 + '0');
                n /= 10;
            } while (n != 0);
            if (value < 0) *--p = '-';
            return new string(p, 0, (int)(buffer + 16 - p));
        }
    }

    static void Main() {
        Console.WriteLine(IntToString(12345));
        Console.WriteLine(IntToString(-999));
    }
}
```

a `stackalloc` initializer is used in the `IntToString` method to allocate a buffer of 16 characters on the stack. The buffer is automatically discarded when the method returns.

18.8 Dynamic Memory Allocation

Except for the `stackalloc` operator, C# provides no predefined constructs for managing non-garbage-collected memory. Such services are typically provided by supporting class libraries or imported directly from the underlying operating system. For example, the following `Memory` class illustrates how the heap functions of an underlying operating system might be accessed from C#.

```
using System;
using System.Runtime.InteropServices;

public unsafe class Memory
{
    // Handle for the process heap. This handle is used in all calls to the
    // HeapXXX APIs in the methods below.

    static int ph = GetProcessHeap();

    // Private instance constructor to prevent instantiation.

    private Memory() {}

    // Allocates a memory block of the given size. The allocated memory is
    // automatically initialized to zero.
```

```
public static void* Alloc(int size) {
    void* result = HeapAlloc(ph, HEAP_ZERO_MEMORY, size);
    if (result == null) throw new OutOfMemoryException();
    return result;
}

// Copies count bytes from src to dst. The source and destination
// blocks are permitted to overlap.

public static void Copy(void* src, void* dst, int count) {
    byte* ps = (byte*)src;
    byte* pd = (byte*)dst;
    if (ps > pd) {
        for (; count != 0; count--) *pd++ = *ps++;
    }
    else if (ps < pd) {
        for (ps += count, pd += count; count != 0; count--) *--pd = *--ps;
    }
}

// Frees a memory block.

public static void Free(void* block) {
    if (!HeapFree(ph, 0, block)) throw new InvalidOperationException();
}

// Re-allocates a memory block. If the reallocation request is for a
// larger size, the additional region of memory is automatically
// initialized to zero.

public static void* ReAlloc(void* block, int size) {
    void* result = HeapReAlloc(ph, HEAP_ZERO_MEMORY, block, size);
    if (result == null) throw new OutOfMemoryException();
    return result;
}

// Returns the size of a memory block.

public static int SizeOf(void* block) {
    int result = HeapSize(ph, 0, block);
    if (result == -1) throw new InvalidOperationException();
    return result;
}

// Heap API flags

const int HEAP_ZERO_MEMORY = 0x00000008;

// Heap API functions

[DllImport("kernel32")]
static extern int GetProcessHeap();

[DllImport("kernel32")]
static extern void* HeapAlloc(int hHeap, int flags, int size);

[DllImport("kernel32")]
static extern bool HeapFree(int hHeap, int flags, void* block);
```

```
    [DllImport("kernel32")]
    static extern void* HeapReAlloc(int hHeap, int flags,
        void* block, int size);

    [DllImport("kernel32")]
    static extern int HeapSize(int hHeap, int flags, void* block);
}
```

An example that uses the Memory class is as follows.

```
class Test
{
    static void Main() {
        unsafe {
            byte* buffer = (byte*)Memory.Alloc(256);
            try {
                for (int i = 0; i < 256; i++) buffer[i] = (byte)i;
                byte[] array = new byte[256];
                fixed (byte* p = array) Memory.Copy(buffer, p, 256);
            }
            finally {
                Memory.Free(buffer);
            }
            for (int i = 0; i < 256; i++) Console.WriteLine(array[i]);
        }
    }
}
```

The example allocates 256 bytes of memory through Memory.Alloc and initializes the memory block with values increasing from 0 to 255. It then allocates a 256-element byte array and uses Memory.Copy to copy the contents of the memory block into the byte array. Finally, the memory block is freed using Memory.Free, and the contents of the byte array are output on the console.

18. Unsafe Code

453

Part II

C# 2.0

19. Introduction to C# 2.0

C# 2.0 introduces several language extensions, the most important of which are generics, anonymous methods, iterators, and partial types.

- Generics permit classes, structs, interfaces, delegates, and methods to be parameterized by the types of data they store and manipulate. Generics are useful because they provide stronger compile-time type checking, require fewer explicit conversions between data types, and reduce the need for boxing operations and runtime type checks.

- Anonymous methods allow code blocks to be written "in-line" where delegate values are expected. Anonymous methods are similar to lambda functions in the Lisp programming language. C# 2.0 supports the creation of "closures" where anonymous methods access surrounding local variables and parameters.

- Iterators are methods that incrementally compute and yield a sequence of values. Iterators make it easy for a type to specify how the `foreach` statement will iterate over its elements.

- Partial types allow classes, structs, and interfaces to be broken into multiple pieces stored in different source files for easier development and maintenance. Additionally, partial types allow separation of machine-generated and user-written parts of types so that it is easier to augment code generated by a tool.

This chapter introduces these new features. Following the introduction are four chapters that provide a complete technical specification of the features.

The language extensions in C# 2.0 were designed to ensure maximum compatibility with existing code. For example, even though C# 2.0 gives special meaning to the words `where`, `yield`, and `partial` in certain contexts, these words can still be used as identifiers. Indeed, C# 2.0 adds no new keywords because such keywords could conflict with identifiers in existing code.

19.1 Generics

Generics permit classes, structs, interfaces, delegates, and methods to be parameterized by the types of data they store and manipulate. C# generics will be immediately familiar to users of generics in Eiffel or Ada or to users of C++ templates; however, they do not suffer many of the complications of the latter.

19.1.1 Why Generics?

Without generics, general-purpose data structures can use type `object` to store data of any type. For example, the following simple `Stack` class stores its data in an `object` array, and its two methods, `Push` and `Pop`, use `object` to accept and return data, respectively.

```
public class Stack
{
    object[] items;
    int count;
    public void Push(object item) {...}
    public object Pop() {...}
}
```

Although using type `object` makes the `Stack` class flexible, it is not without drawbacks. For example, it is possible to push a value of any type, such as a `Customer` instance, onto a stack. However, when a value is retrieved, the result of the `Pop` method must explicitly be cast back to the appropriate type, which is tedious to write and carries a performance penalty for runtime type checking.

```
Stack stack = new Stack();
stack.Push(new Customer());
Customer c = (Customer)stack.Pop();
```

If a value of a value type, such as an `int`, is passed to the `Push` method, it is automatically boxed. When the `int` is later retrieved, it must be unboxed with an explicit type cast.

```
Stack stack = new Stack();
stack.Push(3);
int i = (int)stack.Pop();
```

Such boxing and unboxing operations add performance overhead because they involve dynamic memory allocations and runtime type checks.

A further issue with the `Stack` class is that it is not possible to enforce the kind of data placed on a stack. Indeed, a `Customer` instance can be pushed on a stack and then accidentally cast to the wrong type after it is retrieved.

```
Stack stack = new Stack();
stack.Push(new Customer());
string s = (string)stack.Pop();
```

Although the previous code is an improper use of the `Stack` class, the code is technically speaking correct and a compile-time error is not reported. The problem does not become apparent until the code is executed, at which point an `InvalidCastException` is thrown.

The `Stack` class would clearly benefit from the ability to specify its element type. With generics, that becomes possible.

19.1.2 Creating and Using Generics

Generics provide a facility for creating types that have *type parameters*. The following example declares a generic `Stack` class with a type parameter `T`. The type parameter is specified in < and > delimiters after the class name. Rather than forcing conversions to and from `object`, instances of `Stack<T>` accept the type for which they are created and store data of that type without conversion. The type parameter `T` acts as a placeholder until an actual type is specified at use. Note that `T` is used as the element type for the internal items array, the type for the parameter to the `Push` method, and the return type for the `Pop` method.

```
public class Stack<T>
{
    T[] items;
    int count;
    public void Push(T item) {...}
    public T Pop() {...}
}
```

When the generic class `Stack<T>` is used, the actual type to substitute for `T` is specified. In the following example, `int` is given as the *type argument* for `T`.

```
Stack<int> stack = new Stack<int>();
stack.Push(3);
int x = stack.Pop();
```

The `Stack<int>` type is called a *constructed type*. In the `Stack<int>` type, every occurrence of `T` is replaced with the type argument `int`. When an instance of `Stack<int>` is created, the native storage of the `items` array is an `int[]` rather than `object[]`, providing substantial storage efficiency compared to the nongeneric `Stack`. Likewise, the `Push` and `Pop` methods of a `Stack<int>` operate on `int` values, making it a compile-time error to push values of other types onto the stack and eliminating the need to explicitly cast values back to their original type when they are retrieved.

Generics provide strong typing, meaning for example that it is an error to push an `int` onto a stack of `Customer` objects. Just as a `Stack<int>` is restricted to operate only on int values, so is `Stack<Customer>` restricted to `Customer` objects, and the compiler will report errors on the last two lines of the following example.

```
Stack<Customer> stack = new Stack<Customer>();
stack.Push(new Customer());
Customer c = stack.Pop();
stack.Push(3);                  // Type mismatch error
int x = stack.Pop();            // Type mismatch error
```

Generic type declarations may have any number of type parameters. The previous `Stack<T>` example has only one type parameter, but a generic `Dictionary` class might have two type parameters, one for the type of the keys and one for the type of the values.

```
public class Dictionary<K,V>
{
    public void Add(K key, V value) {...}

    public V this[K key] {...}
}
```

When `Dictionary<K,V>` is used, two type arguments would have to be supplied.

```
Dictionary<string,Customer> dict = new Dictionary<string,Customer>();
dict.Add("Peter", new Customer());
Customer c = dict["Peter"];
```

19.1.3 Generic Type Instantiations

Similar to a nongeneric type, the compiled representation of a generic type is Intermediate Language (IL) instructions and metadata. The representation of the generic type of course also encodes the existence and use of type parameters.

The first time an application creates an instance of a constructed generic type, such as `Stack<int>`, the Just-In-Time (JIT) compiler of the .NET Common Language Runtime converts the generic IL and metadata to native code, substituting actual types for type parameters in the process. Subsequent references to that constructed generic type then use the same native code. The process of creating a specific constructed type from a generic type is known as a *generic type instantiation*.

The .NET Common Language Runtime creates a specialized copy of the native code for each generic type instantiation with a value type, but it shares a single copy of the native code for all reference types (because, at the native code level, references are just pointers with the same representation).

19.1.4 Constraints

Commonly, a generic class will do more than just store data based on a type parameter. Often, the generic class will want to invoke methods on objects whose type is given by a type parameter. For example, an `Add` method in a `Dictionary<K,V>` class might need to compare keys using a `CompareTo` method.

```
public class Dictionary<K,V>
{
    public void Add(K key, V value)
    {
        ...
        if (key.CompareTo(x) < 0) {...}   // Error, no CompareTo method
        ...
    }
}
```

Because the type argument specified for K could be any type, the only members that can be assumed to exist on the key parameter are those declared by type object, such as Equals, GetHashCode, and ToString; a compile-time error therefore occurs in the previous example. It is of course possible to cast the key parameter to a type that contains a CompareTo method. For example, the key parameter could be cast to IComparable.

```
public class Dictionary<K,V>
{
    public void Add(K key, V value)
    {
        ...
        if (((IComparable)key).CompareTo(x) < 0) {...}
        ...
    }
}
```

Although this solution works, it requires a dynamic type check at runtime, which adds overhead. It furthermore defers error reporting to runtime, throwing an InvalidCastException if a key does not implement IComparable.

To provide stronger compile-time type checking and reduce type casts, C# permits an optional list of *constraints* to be supplied for each type parameter. A type parameter constraint specifies a requirement that a type must fulfill in order to be used as an argument for that type parameter. Constraints are declared using the word where, followed by the name of a type parameter, followed by a list of class or interface types and optionally the constructor constraint new().

For the Dictionary<K,V> class to ensure that keys always implement IComparable, the class declaration can specify a constraint for the type parameter K.

```
public class Dictionary<K,V> where K: IComparable
{
    public void Add(K key, V value)
    {
        ...
        if (key.CompareTo(x) < 0) {...}
        ...
    }
}
```

Given this declaration, the compiler will ensure that any type argument supplied for K is a type that implements IComparable. Furthermore, it is no longer necessary to explicitly cast the key parameter to IComparable before calling the CompareTo method; all members of a type given as a constraint for a type parameter are directly available on values of that type parameter type.

For a given type parameter, it is possible to specify any number of interfaces as constraints, but no more than one class. Each constrained type parameter has a separate where clause. In the following example, the type parameter K has two interface constraints, and the type parameter E has a class constraint and a constructor constraint.

```
public class EntityTable<K,E>
    where K: IComparable<K>, IPersistable
    where E: Entity, new()
{
    public void Add(K key, E entity)
    {
        ...
        if (key.CompareTo(x) < 0) {...}
        ...
    }
}
```

The constructor constraint, new(), in the previous example ensures that a type used as a type argument for E has a public, parameterless constructor, and it permits the generic class to use new E() to create instances of that type.

Type parameter constrains should be used with care. Although they provide stronger compile-time type checking and in some cases improve performance, they also restrict the possible uses of a generic type. For example, a generic class List<T> might constrain T to implement IComparable such that the list's Sort method can compare items. However, doing so would preclude use of List<T> for types that do not implement IComparable, even if the Sort method is never actually called in those cases.

19.1.5 Generic Methods

In some cases, a type parameter is not needed for an entire class but is needed only inside a particular method. Often, this occurs when creating a method that takes a generic type as a parameter. For example, when using the Stack<T> class described earlier, a common pattern might be to push multiple values in a row, and it might be convenient to write a method that does so in a single call. For a particular constructed type, such as Stack<int>, the method would look like this.

```
void PushMultiple(Stack<int> stack, params int[] values) {
    foreach (int value in values) stack.Push(value);
}
```

This method can be used to push multiple `int` values onto a `Stack<int>`.

```
Stack<int> stack = new Stack<int>();
PushMultiple(stack, 1, 2, 3, 4);
```

However, the previous method only works with the particular constructed type `Stack<int>`. To have it work with any `Stack<T>`, the method must be written as a *generic method*. A generic method has one or more type parameters specified in < and > delimiters after the method name. The type parameters can be used within the parameter list, return type, and body of the method. A generic `PushMultiple` method would look like this.

```
void PushMultiple<T>(Stack<T> stack, params T[] values) {
    foreach (T value in values) stack.Push(value);
}
```

Using this generic method, it is possible to push multiple items onto any `Stack<T>`. When calling a generic method, type arguments are given in angle brackets in the method invocation. For example

```
Stack<int> stack = new Stack<int>();
PushMultiple<int>(stack, 1, 2, 3, 4);
```

This generic `PushMultiple` method is more reusable than the previous version because it works on any `Stack<T>`, but it appears to be less convenient to call because the desired `T` must be supplied as a type argument to the method. In many cases, however, the compiler can deduce the correct type argument from the other arguments passed to the method, using a process called *type inferencing*. In the previous example, because the first regular argument is of type `Stack<int>`, and the subsequent arguments are of type `int`, the compiler can reason that the type parameter must be `int`. Thus, the generic `PushMultiple` method can be called without specifying the type parameter.

```
Stack<int> stack = new Stack<int>();
PushMultiple(stack, 1, 2, 3, 4);
```

19.2 Anonymous Methods

Event handlers and other callbacks are often invoked exclusively through delegates and never directly. Even so, it has thus far been necessary to place the code of event handlers and callbacks in distinct methods to which delegates are explicitly created. In contrast, *anonymous methods* allow the code associated with a delegate to be written "in-line" where the delegate is used, conveniently tying the code directly to the delegate instance. Besides this convenience, anonymous methods have shared access to the local state of the containing function member. To achieve the same state sharing using named methods

19. Introduction to C# 2.0

requires "lifting" local variables into fields in instances of manually authored helper classes.

The following example shows a simple input form that contains a list box, a text box, and a button. When the button is clicked, an item containing the text in the text box is added to the list box.

```
class InputForm: Form
{
    ListBox listBox;
    TextBox textBox;
    Button addButton;

    public MyForm() {
        listBox = new ListBox(...);
        textBox = new TextBox(...);
        addButton = new Button(...);

        addButton.Click += new EventHandler(AddClick);
    }

    void AddClick(object sender, EventArgs e) {
        listBox.Items.Add(textBox.Text);
    }
}
```

Even though only a single statement is executed in response to the button's `Click` event, that statement must be extracted into a separate method with a full parameter list, and an `EventHandler` delegate referencing that method must be manually created. Using an anonymous method, the event handling code becomes significantly more succinct.

```
class InputForm: Form
{
    ListBox listBox;
    TextBox textBox;
    Button addButton;

    public MyForm() {
        listBox = new ListBox(...);
        textBox = new TextBox(...);
        addButton = new Button(...);

        addButton.Click += delegate {
            listBox.Items.Add(textBox.Text);
        };
    }
}
```

An anonymous method consists of the keyword `delegate`, an optional parameter list, and a statement list enclosed in { and } delimiters. The anonymous method in the previous example does not use the parameters supplied by the delegate, and it can therefore omit the parameter list. To gain access to the parameters, the anonymous method can include a parameter list.

```
addButton.Click += delegate(object sender, EventArgs e) {
    MessageBox.Show(((Button)sender).Text);
};
```

In the previous examples, an implicit conversion occurs from the anonymous method to the EventHandler delegate type (the type of the Click event). This implicit conversion is possible because the parameter list and return type of the delegate type are compatible with the anonymous method. The exact rules for compatibility are as follows:

- The parameter list of a delegate is compatible with an anonymous method if one of the following is true.

  - The anonymous method has no parameter list, and the delegate has no out parameters.

  - The anonymous method includes a parameter list that exactly matches the delegate's parameters in number, types, and modifiers.

- The return type of a delegate is compatible with an anonymous method if one of the following is true.

  - The delegate's return type is void, and the anonymous method has no return statements or only return statements with no expression.

  - The delegate's return type is not void, and the expressions associated with all return statements in the anonymous method can be implicitly converted to the return type of the delegate.

Both the parameter list and the return type of a delegate must be compatible with an anonymous method before an implicit conversion to that delegate type can occur.

The following example uses anonymous methods to write functions "in-line." The anonymous methods are passed as parameters of a Function delegate type.

```
using System;

delegate double Function(double x);

class Test
{
    static double[] Apply(double[] a, Function f) {
        double[] result = new double[a.Length];
        for (int i = 0; i < a.Length; i++) result[i] = f(a[i]);
        return result;
    }

    static double[] MultiplyAllBy(double[] a, double factor) {
        return Apply(a, delegate(double x) { return x * factor; });
    }

    static void Main() {
        double[] a = {0.0, 0.5, 1.0};
```

```
        double[] squares = Apply(a, delegate(double x) { return x * x; });
        double[] doubles = MultiplyAllBy(a, 2.0);
    }
}
```

The `Apply` method applies a given `Function` to the elements of a `double[]`, returning a `double[]` with the results. In the `Main` method, the second parameter passed to `Apply` is an anonymous method that is compatible with the `Function` delegate type. The anonymous method simply returns the square of its argument, and thus the result of that `Apply` invocation is a `double[]` containing the squares of the values in a.

The `MultiplyAllBy` method returns a `double[]` created by multiplying each of the values in the argument array a by a given `factor`. To produce its result, `MultiplyAllBy` invokes the `Apply` method, passing an anonymous method that multiplies the argument x by `factor`.

Local variables and parameters whose scope contains an anonymous method are called *outer variables* of the anonymous method. In the `MultiplyAllBy` method, a and `factor` are outer variables of the anonymous method passed to `Apply`, and because the anonymous method references `factor`, `factor` is said to have been *captured* by the anonymous method. Ordinarily, the lifetime of a local variable is limited to execution of the block or statement with which it is associated. However, the lifetime of a captured outer variable is extended at least until the delegate referring to the anonymous method becomes eligible for garbage collection.

19.2.1 Method Group Conversions

As described in the previous section, an anonymous method can be implicitly converted to a compatible delegate type. C# 2.0 permits this same type of conversion for a method group, allowing explicit delegate instantiations to be omitted in almost all cases. For example, the following statements

```
addButton.Click += new EventHandler(AddClick);

Apply(a, new Function(Math.Sin));
```

can instead be written as follows.

```
addButton.Click += AddClick;

Apply(a, Math.Sin);
```

When the shorter form is used, the compiler automatically infers which delegate type to instantiate, but the effects are otherwise the same as the longer form.

19.3 **Iterators**

The C# `foreach` statement is used to iterate over the elements of an *enumerable* collection. In order to be enumerable, a collection must have a parameterless `GetEnumerator` method that returns an *enumerator*. Generally, enumerators are difficult to implement, but the task is significantly simplified with iterators.

An *iterator* is a statement block that *yields* an ordered sequence of values. An iterator is distinguished from a normal statement block by the presence of one or more `yield` statements.

* The `yield return` statement produces the next value of the iteration.

* The `yield break` statement indicates that the iteration is complete.

An iterator may be used as the body of a function member as long as the return type of the function member is one of the *enumerator interfaces* or one of the *enumerable interfaces*.

* The enumerator interfaces are `System.Collections.IEnumerator` and types constructed from `System.Collections.Generic.IEnumerator<T>`.

* The enumerable interfaces are `System.Collections.IEnumerable` and types constructed from `System.Collections.Generic.IEnumerable<T>`.

It is important to understand that an iterator is not a kind of member but is a means of implementing a function member. A member implemented via an iterator may be overridden or overloaded by other members that may or may not be implemented with iterators.

The following `Stack<T>` class implements its `GetEnumerator` method using an iterator. The iterator enumerates the elements of the stack in top to bottom order.

```
using System.Collections.Generic;

public class Stack<T>: IEnumerable<T>
{
    T[] items;
    int count;

    public void Push(T data) {...}

    public T Pop() {...}

    public IEnumerator<T> GetEnumerator() {
        for (int i = count - 1; i >= 0; --i) {
            yield return items[i];
        }
    }
}
```

The presence of the GetEnumerator method makes Stack<T> an enumerable type, allowing instances of Stack<T> to be used in a foreach statement. The following example pushes the values 0 through 9 onto an integer stack and then uses a foreach loop to display the values in top to bottom order.

```
using System;

class Test
{
    static void Main() {
        Stack<int> stack = new Stack<int>();
        for (int i = 0; i < 10; i++) stack.Push(i);
        foreach (int i in stack) Console.Write("{0} ", i);
        Console.WriteLine();
    }
}
```

The output of the example is as follows.

```
9 8 7 6 5 4 3 2 1 0
```

The foreach statement implicitly calls a collection's parameterless GetEnumerator method to obtain an enumerator. There can only be one such parameterless GetEnumerator method defined by a collection, yet it is often appropriate to have multiple ways of enumerating and ways of controlling the enumeration through parameters. In such cases, a collection can use iterators to implement properties or methods that return one of the enumerable interfaces. For example, Stack<T> might introduce two new properties, TopToBottom and BottomToTop, of type IEnumerable<T>.

```
using System.Collections.Generic;

public class Stack<T>: IEnumerable<T>
{
    T[] items;
    int count;

    public void Push(T data) {...}

    public T Pop() {...}

    public IEnumerator<T> GetEnumerator() {
        for (int i = count - 1; i >= 0; --i) {
            yield return items[i];
        }
    }

    public IEnumerable<T> TopToBottom {
        get {
            return this;
        }
    }
```

```
public IEnumerable<T> BottomToTop {
    get {
        for (int i = 0; i < count; i++) {
            yield return items[i];
        }
    }
}
```

The get accessor for the TopToBottom property just returns this because the stack itself is an enumerable. The BottomToTop property returns an enumerable implemented with a C# iterator. The following example shows how the properties can be used to enumerate stack elements in either order.

```
using System;

class Test
{
    static void Main() {
        Stack<int> stack = new Stack<int>();
        for (int i = 0; i < 10; i++) stack.Push(i);

        foreach (int i in stack.TopToBottom) Console.Write("{0} ", i);
        Console.WriteLine();

        foreach (int i in stack.BottomToTop) Console.Write("{0} ", i);
        Console.WriteLine();
    }
}
```

Of course, these properties can be used outside of a foreach statement as well. The following example passes the results of invoking the properties to a separate Print method. The example also shows an iterator used as the body of a FromToBy method that takes parameters.

```
using System;
using System.Collections.Generic;

class Test
{
    static void Print(IEnumerable<int> collection) {
        foreach (int i in collection) Console.Write("{0} ", i);
        Console.WriteLine();
    }

    static IEnumerable<int> FromToBy(int from, int to, int by) {
        for (int i = from; i <= to; i += by) {
            yield return i;
        }
    }
}
```

```
static void Main() {
    Stack<int> stack = new Stack<int>();
    for (int i = 0; i < 10; i++) stack.Push(i);
    Print(stack.TopToBottom);
    Print(stack.BottomToTop);
    Print(FromToBy(10, 20, 2));
    }
}
```

The output of the example is as follows.

```
9 8 7 6 5 4 3 2 1 0
0 1 2 3 4 5 6 7 8 9
10 12 14 16 18 20
```

The generic and nongeneric enumerable interfaces contain a single member, a GetEnumerator method that takes no arguments and returns an enumerator interface. An enumerable acts as an *enumerator factory*. Properly implemented enumerables generate independent enumerators each time their GetEnumerator method is called. Assuming the internal state of the enumerable has not changed between two calls to GetEnumerator, the two enumerators returned should produce the same set of values in the same order. This should hold even if the lifetime of the enumerators overlap as in the following code sample.

```
using System;
using System.Collections.Generic;

class Test
{
    static IEnumerable<int> FromTo(int from, int to) {
        while (from <= to) yield return from++;
    }

    static void Main() {
        IEnumerable<int> e = FromTo(1, 10);
        foreach (int x in e) {
            foreach (int y in e) {
                Console.Write("{0,3} ", x * y);
            }
            Console.WriteLine();
        }
    }
}
```

The previous code prints a simple multiplication table of the integers 1 through 10. Note that the FromTo method is invoked only once to generate the enumerable e. However, e.GetEnumerator() is invoked multiple times (by the foreach statements) to generate multiple equivalent enumerators. These enumerators all encapsulate the iterator code specified in the declaration of FromTo. Note that the iterator code modifies the from parameter.

Nevertheless, the enumerators act independently because each enumerator is given *its own copy* of the `from` and `to` parameters. The sharing of transient state between enumerators is one of several common subtle flaws that should be avoided when implementing enumerables and enumerators. C# iterators are designed to help avoid these problems and to implement robust enumerables and enumerators in a simple, intuitive way.

19.4 Partial Types

Although it is good programming practice to maintain all source code for a type in a single file, sometimes a type becomes large enough that this is an impractical constraint. Furthermore, programmers often use source code generators to produce the initial structure of an application and then modify the resulting code. Unfortunately, when source code is emitted again sometime in the future, existing modifications are overwritten.

Partial types allow classes, structs, and interfaces to be broken into multiple pieces stored in different source files for easier development and maintenance. Additionally, partial types allow separation of machine-generated and user-written parts of types so that it is easier to augment code generated by a tool.

A new type modifier, `partial`, is used when defining a type in multiple parts. The following is an example of a partial class that is implemented in two parts. The two parts may be in different source files, for example, because the first part is machine generated by a database mapping tool and the second part is manually authored.

```
public partial class Customer
{
    private int id;
    private string name;
    private string address;
    private List<Order> orders;

    public Customer() {
        ...
    }
}
public partial class Customer
{
    public void SubmitOrder(Order order) {
        orders.Add(order);
    }

    public bool HasOutstandingOrders() {
        return orders.Count > 0;
    }
}
```

When the previous two parts are compiled together, the resulting code is the same as if the class had been written as a single unit.

```csharp
public class Customer
{
    private int id;
    private string name;
    private string address;
    private List<Order> orders;

    public Customer() {
        ...
    }

    public void SubmitOrder(Order order) {
        orders.Add(order);
    }

    public bool HasOutstandingOrders() {
        return orders.Count > 0;
    }
}
```

All parts of a partial type must be compiled together such that the parts can be merged at compile time. Partial types specifically do not allow already compiled types to be extended.

20. Generics

20.1 Generic Class Declarations

A generic class declaration is a declaration of a class that requires type parameters to be supplied in order to form actual types.

A class declaration may optionally define type parameters.

> *class-declaration:*
>   *attributes*$_{opt}$ *class-modifiers*$_{opt}$ `class`   *identifier*   *type-parameter-list*$_{opt}$ *class-base*$_{opt}$
>   *type-parameter-constraints-clauses*$_{opt}$ *class-body*   `;`$_{opt}$

A class declaration may not supply *type-parameter-constraints-clauses* (§20.7) unless it also supplies a *type-parameter-list*.

A class declaration that supplies a *type-parameter-list* is a generic class declaration. Additionally, any class nested inside a generic class declaration or a generic struct declaration is itself a generic class declaration because type parameters for the containing type must be supplied to create a constructed type.

Generic class declarations follow the same rules as normal class declarations except where noted and particularly with regard to naming, nesting, and the permitted access controls. Generic class declarations may be nested inside nongeneric class declarations.

A generic class is referenced using a **constructed type** (§20.5). Given the generic class declaration

```
class List<T> {}
```

some examples of constructed types are `List<T>`, `List<int>` and `List<List<string>>`. A constructed type that uses one or more type parameters, such as `List<T>`, is called an **open constructed type**. A constructed type that uses no type parameters, such as `List<int>`, is called a **closed constructed type**.

Generic types may not be "overloaded"; that is, the identifier of a generic type must be uniquely named within a scope in the same way as ordinary types.

```
class C {}
class C<V> {}          // Error, C defined twice
class C<U,V> {}         // Error, C defined twice
```

However, the type lookup rules used during unqualified type name lookup (§20.9.3) and member access (§20.9.4) do take the number of type parameters into account.

20.1.1 Type Parameters

Type parameters may be supplied on a class declaration. Each type parameter is a simple identifier that denotes a placeholder for a type argument that is supplied to create a constructed type. A type parameter is a formal placeholder for a type that will be supplied later. By contrast, a type argument (§20.5.1) is the actual type that is substituted for the type parameter when a constructed type is referenced.

> *type-parameter-list:*
>   < *type-parameters* >
>
> *type-parameters:*
>   *type-parameter*
>   *type-parameters* , *type-parameter*
>
> *type-parameter:*
>   *attributes*$_{opt}$ *identifier*

Each type parameter in a class declaration defines a name in the declaration space (§3.3) of that class. Thus, it cannot have the same name as another type parameter or a member declared in that class. A type parameter cannot have the same name as the type itself.

The scope (§3.7) of a type parameter on a class includes the *class-base, type-parameter-constraints-clauses,* and *class-body.* Unlike members of a class, it does not extend to derived classes. Within its scope, a type parameter can be used as a type.

> *type:*
>   *value-type*
>   *reference-type*
>   *type-parameter*

Because a type parameter can be instantiated with many different actual type arguments, type parameters have slightly different operations and restrictions than other types. These include the following.

* A type parameter cannot be used directly to declare a base class or interface (§20.1.3).
* The rules for member lookup on type parameters depend on the constraints, if any, applied to the type parameter. They are detailed in §20.7.2.

- The available conversions for a type parameter depend on the constraints, if any, applied to the type parameter. They are detailed in §20.7.4.

- The literal `null` cannot be converted to a type given by a type parameter, except if the type parameter is constrained by a class constraint (§20.7.4). However, a default value expression (§20.8.1) can be used instead. In addition, a value with a type given by a type parameter *can* be compared with `null` using `==` and `!=` (§20.8.4).

- A `new` expression (§20.8.2) can only be used with a type parameter if the type parameter is constrained by a *constructor-constraint* (§20.7).

- A type parameter cannot be used anywhere within an attribute.

- A type parameter cannot be used in a member access or type name to identify a static member or a nested type (§20.9.1, §20.9.4).

- In unsafe code, a type parameter cannot be used as an *unmanaged-type* (§18.2).

As a type, type parameters are purely a compile-time construct. At runtime, each type parameter is bound to a runtime type that was specified by supplying a type argument to the generic type declaration. Thus, the type of a variable declared with a type parameter will, at runtime, be a closed type (§20.5.2). The runtime execution of all statements and expressions involving type parameters uses the actual type that was supplied as the type argument for that parameter.

20.1.2 The Instance Type

Each class declaration has an associated constructed type, the **instance type**. For a generic class declaration, the instance type is formed by creating a constructed type (§20.4) from the type declaration, with each of the supplied type arguments being the corresponding type parameter. Because the instance type uses the type parameters, it is only valid where the type parameters are in scope: inside the class declaration. The instance type is the type of `this` for code written inside the class declaration. For nongeneric classes, the instance type is simply the declared class. The following shows several class declarations along with their instance types.

```
class A<T>                            // instance type: A<T>
{
    class B {}                        // instance type: A<T>.B

    class C<U> {}                     // instance type: A<T>.C<U>
}
class D {}                            // instance type: D
```

20.1.3 Base Specification

The base class specified in a class declaration may be a constructed class type (§20.5). A base class may not be a type parameter on its own, but it may involve the type parameters that are in scope.

```
class Extend<V>: V {}          // Error, type parameter used as base class
```

A generic class declaration may not use `System.Attribute` as a direct or indirect base class.

The base interfaces specified in a class declaration may be constructed interface types (§20.5). A base interface may not be a type parameter on its own, but it may involve the type parameters that are in scope. The following code illustrates how a class can implement and extend constructed types.

```
class C<U,V> {}

interface I1<V> {}

class D: C<string,int>, I1<string> {}

class E<T>: C<int,T>, I1<T> {}
```

The base interfaces of a generic class declaration must satisfy the uniqueness rule described in §20.3.1.

Methods in a class that override or implement methods from a base class or interface must provide appropriate methods of specialized types. The following code illustrates how methods are overridden and implemented. This is explained further in §20.1.10.

```
class C<U,V>
{
    public virtual void M1(U x, List<V> y) {...}
}

interface I1<V>
{
    V M2(V x);
}

class D: C<string,int>, I1<string>
{
    public override void M1(string x, List<int> y) {...}

    public string M2(string x) {...}
}
```

20.1.4 Members of Generic Classes

All members of a generic class may use type parameters from any enclosing class, either directly or as part of a constructed type. When a particular closed constructed type (§20.5.2) is used at runtime, each use of a type parameter is replaced with the actual type argument supplied to the constructed type. For example

```
class C<V>
{
    public V f1;
    public C<V> f2 = null;
```

```
        public C(V x) {
            this.f1 = x;
            this.f2 = this;
        }
    }

    class Application
    {
        static void Main() {
            C<int> x1 = new C<int>(1);
            Console.WriteLine(x1.f1);              // Prints 1

            C<double> x2 = new C<double>(3.1415);
            Console.WriteLine(x2.f1);              // Prints 3.1415
        }
    }
```

Within instance function members, the type of this is the instance type (§20.1.2) of the declaration.

Apart from using type parameters as types, members in generic class declarations follow the same rules as members of nongeneric classes. Additional rules that apply to particular kinds of members are discussed in the following sections.

20.1.5 Static Fields in Generic Classes

A static variable in a generic class declaration is shared amongst all instances of the same closed constructed type (§20.5.2) but is not shared amongst instances of different closed constructed types. These rules apply regardless of whether the type of the static variable involves any type parameters.

For example

```
    class C<V>
    {
        static int count = 0;

        public C() {
            count++;
        }

        public static int Count {
            get { return count; }
        }
    }


    class Application
    {
        static void Main() {
            C<int> x1 = new C<int>();
            Console.WriteLine(C<int>.Count);       // Prints 1
```

```
        C<double> x2 = new C<double>();
        Console.WriteLine(C<int>.Count);   // Prints 1

        C<int> x3 = new C<int>();
        Console.WriteLine(C<int>.Count);   // Prints 2
    }
}
```

20.1.6 Static Constructors in Generic Classes

Static constructors in generic classes are used to initialize static fields and perform other initialization for each different closed constructed type that is created from a particular generic class declaration. The type parameters of the generic type declaration are in scope and can be used within the body of the static constructor.

A new closed constructed class type is initialized the first time that either:

- An instance of the closed constructed type is created

- Any of the static members of the closed constructed type are referenced

To initialize a new closed constructed class type, first a new set of static fields (§20.1.5) for that particular closed constructed type is created. Each of the static fields is initialized to its default value (§5.2). Next, the static field initializers (§10.4.5.1) are executed for those static fields. Finally, the static constructor is executed.

Because the static constructor is executed exactly once for each closed constructed class type, it is a convenient place to enforce runtime checks on the type parameter that cannot be checked at compile time via constraints (§20.7). For example, the following type uses a static constructor to enforce that the type parameter is a reference type.

```
class Gen<T>
{
    static Gen() {
        if ((object)T.default != null) {
            throw new ArgumentException("T must be a reference type");
        }
    }
}
```

20.1.7 Accessing Protected Members

Within a generic class declaration, access to inherited protected instance members is permitted through an instance of any class type constructed from the generic class. Specifically, the rules for accessing `protected` and `protected internal` instance members specified in §3.5.3 are augmented with the following rule for generics.

- Within a generic class G, access to an inherited protected instance member M using a *primary-expression* of the form E.M is permitted if the type of E is a class type constructed from G or a class type inherited from a class type constructed from G.

In the example

```
class C<T>
{
    protected T x;
}

class D<T>: C<T>
{
    static void F() {
        D<T> dt = new D<T>();
        D<int> di = new D<int>();
        D<string> ds = new D<string>();
        dt.x = T.default;
        di.x = 123;
        ds.x = "test";
    }
}
```

the three assignments to x are permitted because they all take place through instances of class types constructed from the generic type.

20.1.8 Overloading in Generic Classes

Methods, constructors, indexers, and operators within a generic class declaration can be overloaded; however, overloading is constrained so that ambiguities cannot occur within constructed classes. Two function members declared with the same names in the same generic class declaration must have parameter types such that no closed constructed type could have two members with the same name and signature. When considering all possible closed constructed types, this rule includes type arguments that do not currently exist in the current program but could be written. Type constraints on the type parameter are ignored for the purpose of this rule.

The following examples show overloads that are valid and invalid according to this rule.

```
interface I1<T> {...}

interface I2<T> {...}

class G1<U>
{
    long F1(U u);                // Invalid overload, G<int> would have two
    int F1(int i);              // members with the same signature

    void F2(U u1, U u2);        // Valid overload, no type argument for U
    void F2(int i, string s);   // could be int and string simultaneously

    void F3(I1<U> a);           // Valid overload
    void F3(I2<U> a);

    void F4(U a);               // Valid overload
    void F4(U[] a);
}
```

20. Generics

479

```
class G2<U,V>
{
    void F5(U u, V v);          // Invalid overload, G2<int,int> would have
    void F5(V v, U u);          // two members with the same signature

    void F6(U u, I1<V> v);      // Invalid overload, G2<I1<int>,int> would
    void F6(I1<V> v, U u);      // have two members with the same signature

    void F7(U u1, I1<V> v2);    // Valid overload, U cannot be V and I1<V>
    void F7(V v1, U u2);        // simultaneously

    void F8(ref U u);           // Invalid overload
    void F8(out V v);
}

class C1 {...}

class C2 {...}

class G3<U,V> where U: C1 where V: C2
{
    void F9(U u);               // Invalid overload, constraints on U and V
    void F9(V v);               // are ignored when checking overloads
}
```

20.1.9 Parameter Array Methods and Type Parameters

Type parameters may be used in the type of a parameter array. For example, given the declaration

```
class C<V>
{
    static void F(int x, int y, params V[] args);
}
```

the following invocations of the expanded form of the method

```
C<int>.F(10, 20);
C<object>.F(10, 20, 30, 40);
C<string>.F(10, 20, "hello", "goodbye");
```

correspond exactly to the following.

```
C<int>.F(10, 20, new int[] {});
C<object>.F(10, 20, new object[] {30, 40});
C<string>.F(10, 20, new string[] {"hello", "goodbye"} );
```

20.1.10 Overriding and Generic Classes

Function members in generic classes can override function members in base classes, as usual. If the base class is a nongeneric type or a closed constructed type, then any overriding function member cannot have constituent types that involve type parameters. However, if the base class is an open constructed type, then an overriding function member can use type parameters in its declaration. When determining the overridden base member, the members of the base classes must be determined by substituting type arguments, as described in §20.5.4. Once the members of the base classes are determined, the rules for overriding are the same as for nongeneric classes.

The following example demonstrates how the overriding rules work in the presence of generics.

```
abstract class C<T>
{
    public virtual T F() {...}
    public virtual C<T> G() {...}
    public virtual void H(C<T> x) {...}
}
class D: C<string>
{
    public override string F() {...}      // Ok
    public override C<string> G() {...}   // Ok
    public override void H(C<T> x) {...} // Error, should be C<string>
}
class E<T,U>: C<U>
{
    public override U F() {...}           // Ok
    public override C<U> G() {...}        // Ok
    public override void H(C<T> x) {...} // Error, should be C<U>
}
```

20.1.11 Operators in Generic Classes

Generic class declarations may define operators, following the same rules as normal class declarations. The instance type (§20.1.2) of the class declaration must be used in the declaration of operators in a manner analogous to the normal rules for operators, as follows.

- A unary operator must take a single parameter of the instance type. The unary ++ and -- operators must return the instance type.

- At least one of the parameters of a binary operator must be of the instance type.

- Either the parameter type or the return type of a conversion operator must be the instance type.

The following shows some examples of valid operator declarations in a generic class.

```
class X<T>
{
    public static X<T> operator ++(X<T> operand) {...}
    public static int operator *(X<T> op1, int op2) {...}
    public static explicit operator X<T>(T value) {...}
}
```

For a conversion operator that converts from a source type S to a target type T, when the rules specified in §10.9.3 are applied, any type parameters associated with S or T are considered to be unique types that have no inheritance relationship with other types, and any constraints on those type parameters are ignored.

In the example

```
class C<T> {...}
class D<T>: C<T>
{
    public static implicit operator C<int>(D<T> value) {...}    // Ok
    public static implicit operator C<T>(D<T> value) {...}      // Error
}
```

the first operator declaration is permitted because, for the purposes of §10.9.3, T and int are considered unique types with no relationship. However, the second operator is an error because C<T> is the base class of D<T>.

Given the previous example, it is possible to declare operators that, for some type arguments, specify conversions that already exist as predefined conversions. In the example

```
struct Nullable<T>
{
    public static implicit operator Nullable<T>(T value) {...}
    public static explicit operator T(Nullable<T> value) {...}
}
```

when type object is specified as a type argument for T, the second operator declares a conversion that already exists (an implicit, and therefore also an explicit, conversion exists from any type to type object).

In cases where a predefined conversion exists between two types, any user-defined conversions between those types are ignored. Specifically

- If a predefined implicit conversion (§6.1) exists from type S to type T, all user-defined conversions (implicit or explicit) from S to T are ignored.

- If a predefined explicit conversion (§6.2) exists from type S to type T, any user-defined explicit conversions from S to T are ignored. However, user-defined implicit conversions from S to T are still considered.

For all types but object, the operators declared by the Nullable<T> type do not conflict with predefined conversions. For example

```
void F(int i, Nullable<int> n) {
    i = n;                          // Error
    i = (int)n;                     // User-defined explicit conversion
    n = i;                          // User-defined implicit conversion
    n = (Nullable<int>)i;           // User-defined implicit conversion
}
```

However, for type `object`, predefined conversions hide the user-defined conversions in all cases but one:

```
void F(object o, Nullable<object> n) {
    o = n;                          // Pre-defined boxing conversion
    o = (object)n;                  // Pre-defined boxing conversion
    n = o;                          // User-defined implicit conversion
    n = (Nullable<object>)o;        // Pre-defined unboxing conversion
}
```

20.1.12 Nested Types in Generic Classes

A generic class declaration can contain nested type declarations. The type parameters of the enclosing class may be used within the nested types. A nested type declaration may contain additional type parameters that apply only to the nested type.

Every type declaration contained within a generic class declaration is implicitly a generic type declaration. When writing a reference to a type nested within a generic type, the containing constructed type, including its type arguments, must be named. However, from within the outer class, the inner type can be used without qualification; the instance type of the outer class can be implicitly used when constructing the inner type. The following example shows three different correct ways to refer to a constructed type created from `Inner`; the first two are equivalent.

```
class Outer<T>
{
    class Inner<U>
    {
        static void F(T t, U u) {...}
    }

    static void F(T t) {
        Outer<T>.Inner<string>.F(t, "abc");   // These two statements have
        Inner<string>.F(t, "abc");            // the same effect

        Outer<int>.Inner<string>.F(3, "abc"); // This type is different

        Outer.Inner<string>.F(t, "abc");      // Error, Outer needs type arg
    }
}
```

Although it is bad programming style, the type parameters in a nested type can hide a member or type parameter declared in the outer type.

20. Generics

483

```
class Outer<T>
{
    class Inner<T>      // Valid, hides Outer's T
    {
        public T t;     // Refers to Inner's T
    }
}
```

20.1.13 Application Entry Point

The application entry point method (§3.1) may not be in a generic class declaration.

20.2 Generic Struct Declarations

Like a class declaration, a `struct` declaration may optionally define type parameters.

struct-declaration:
   attributes$_{opt}$ *struct-modifiers*$_{opt}$ `struct` *identifier type-parameter-list*$_{opt}$*struct-interfaces*$_{opt}$
      type-parameter-constraints-clauses$_{opt}$ *struct-body* ; $_{opt}$

The rules for generic class declarations apply equally to generic struct declarations, except where the exceptions noted in §11.3 for *struct-declaration*s apply.

20.3 Generic Interface Declarations

Interfaces may also optionally define type parameters.

interface-declaration:
   attributes$_{opt}$ *interface-modifiers*$_{opt}$ `interface`   *identifier   type-parameter-list*$_{opt}$
      interface-base$_{opt}$ *type-parameter-constraints-clauses*$_{opt}$ *interface-body* ; $_{opt}$

An interface that is declared with type parameters is a generic interface declaration. Except where noted, generic interface declarations follow the same rules as normal interface declarations.

Each type parameter in an interface declaration defines a name in the declaration space (§3.3) of that interface. The scope (§3.7) of a type parameter on an interface includes the *interface-base, type-parameter-constraints-clauses,* and *interface-body.* Within its scope, a type parameter can be used as a type. The same restrictions apply to type parameters on interfaces as apply to type parameters on classes (§20.1.1).

Methods within generic interfaces are subject to the same overload rules as methods within generic classes (§20.1.8).

20.3.1 Uniqueness of Implemented Interfaces

The interfaces implemented by a generic type declaration must remain unique for all possible constructed types. Without this rule, it would be impossible to determine the correct method to call for certain constructed types. For example, suppose a generic class declaration were permitted to be written as follows.

```
interface I<T>
{
    void F();
}

class X<U,V>: I<U>, I<V>                    // Error: I<U> and I<V> conflict
{
    void I<U>.F() {...}
    void I<V>.F() {...}
}
```

Were this permitted, it would be impossible to determine which code to execute in the following case.

```
I<int> x = new X<int,int>();
x.F();
```

To determine if the interface list of a generic type declaration is valid, the following steps are performed.

- Let `L` be the list of interfaces directly specified in a generic class, struct, or interface declaration `C`.

- Add to `L` any base interfaces of the interfaces already in `L`.

- Remove any duplicates from `L`.

- If any possible constructed type created from `C` would, after type arguments are substituted into `L`, cause two interfaces in `L` to be identical, then the declaration of `C` is invalid. Constraint declarations are not considered when determining all possible constructed types.

In the class declaration `X` above, the interface list `L` consists of `I<U>` and `I<V>`. The declaration is invalid because any constructed type with `U` and `V` being the same type would cause these two interfaces to be identical types.

20.3.2 Explicit Interface Member Implementations

Explicit interface member implementations work with constructed interface types in essentially the same way as with simple interface types. As usual, an explicit interface member implementation must be qualified by an *interface-type*, indicating which interface is being implemented. This type may be a simple interface or a constructed interface, as in the following example.

```
interface IList<T>
{
    T[] GetElements();
}
interface IDictionary<K,V>
{
    V this[K key];

    void Add(K key, V value);
}
class List<T>: IList<T>, IDictionary<int,T>
{
    T[] IList<T>.GetElements() {...}

    T IDictionary<int,T>.this[int index] {...}

    void IDictionary<int,T>.Add(int index, T value) {...}
}
```

20.4 Generic Delegate Declarations

A delegate declaration may include type parameters.

> *delegate-declaration:*
>   *attributes* ~~opt~~ *delegate-modifiers* ~~opt~~ `delegate` *return-type identifier type-parameter-list* ~~opt~~
>   (*formal-parameter-list*~~opt~~) *type-parameter-constraints-clauses*~~opt~~ ;

A delegate that is declared with type parameters is a generic delegate declaration. A delegate declaration may not supply *type-parameter-constraints-clauses* (§20.7) unless it also supplies a *type-parameter-list*. Generic delegate declarations follow the same rules as normal delegate declarations, except where noted. Each type parameter in a generic delegate declaration defines a name in a special declaration space (§3.3) that is associated with that delegate declaration. The scope (§3.7) of a type parameter on a delegate declaration includes the *return-type, formal-parameter-list*, and *type-parameter-constraints-clauses*.

Like other generic type declarations, type arguments must be given to form a constructed delegate type. The parameter types and return type of a constructed delegate type are formed by substituting, for each type parameter in the delegate declaration, the corresponding type argument of the constructed delegate type. The resulting return type and parameter types are used for determining what methods are compatible (§15.1) with a constructed delegate type. For example

```
delegate bool Predicate<T>(T value);

class X
{
    static bool F(int i) {...}
```

```
        static bool G(string s) {...}
        static void Main() {
            Predicate<int> p1 = F;
            Predicate<string> p2 = G;
        }
    }
```

Note that the two assignments in the previous `Main` method are equivalent to the following longer form.

```
static void Main() {
    Predicate<int> p1 = new Predicate<int>(F);
    Predicate<string> p2 = new Predicate<string>(G);
}
```

The shorter form is permitted because of method group conversions, which are described in §21.9.

20.5 Constructed Types

A generic type declaration, by itself, does not denote a type. Instead, a generic type declaration is used as a "blueprint" to form many different types, by way of applying *type arguments*. The type arguments are written within angle brackets (< and >) immediately following the name of the generic type declaration. A type that is named with at least one type argument is called a ***constructed type***. A constructed type can be used in most places in the language that a type name can appear.

type-name:
    namespace-or-type-name

namespace-or-type-name:
    identifier   type-argument-list$_{opt}$
    namespace-or-type-name . identifier type-argument-list$_{opt}$

Constructed types can also be used in expressions as simple names (§20.9.3) or when accessing a member (§20.9.4).

When a *namespace-or-type-name* is evaluated, only generic types with the correct number of type parameters are considered. Thus, it is possible to use the same identifier to identify different types as long as the types have different numbers of type parameters and are declared in different namespaces. This is useful when mixing generic and nongeneric classes in the same program.

```
namespace System.Collections
{
    class Queue {...}
}
```

```
namespace System.Collections.Generic
{
    class Queue<ElementType> {...}
}

namespace MyApplication
{
    using System.Collections;
    using System.Collections.Generic;

    class X
    {
        Queue q1;            // System.Collections.Queue
        Queue<int> q2;       // System.Collections.Generic.Queue
    }
}
```

The detailed rules for name lookup in these productions is described in §20.9. The resolution of ambiguities in these productions is described in §20.6.5.

A *type-name* might identify a constructed type even though it does not specify type parameters directly. This can occur where a type is nested within a generic class declaration, and the instance type of the containing declaration is implicitly used for name lookup (§20.1.12).

```
class Outer<T>
{
    public class Inner {...}

    public Inner i;        // Type of i is Outer<T>.Inner
}
```

In unsafe code, a constructed type cannot be used as an *unmanaged-type* (§18.2).

20.5.1 Type Arguments

Each argument in a type argument list is simply a *type*.

type-argument-list:
    < *type-arguments* >

type-arguments:
    type-argument
    type-arguments , *type-argument*

type-argument:
    type

Type arguments may in turn be constructed types or type parameters. In unsafe code (§18), a *type-argument* may not be a pointer type. Each type argument must satisfy any constraints on the corresponding type parameter (§20.7.1).

20.5.2 Open and Closed Types

All types can be classified as either *open types* or *closed types*. An open type is a type that involves type parameters. More specifically

- A type parameter defines an open type.

- An array type is an open type if and only if its element type is an open type.

- A constructed type is an open type if and only if one or more of its type arguments is an open type.

A closed type is a type that is not an open type.

At runtime, all of the code within a generic type declaration is executed in the context of a closed constructed type that was created by applying type arguments to the generic declaration. Each type parameter within the generic class is bound to a particular runtime type. The runtime processing of all statements and expressions always occurs with closed types, and open types occur only during compile-time processing.

Each closed constructed type has its own set of static variables, which are not shared with any other closed constructed types. Because an open type does not exist at runtime, there are no static variables associated with an open type. Two closed constructed types are the same type if they are constructed from the same type declaration, and corresponding type arguments are the same type.

20.5.3 Base Classes and Interfaces of a Constructed Type

A constructed class type has a direct base class, just like a simple class type. If the generic class declaration does not specify a base class, the base class is `object`. If a base class is specified in the generic class declaration, the base class of the constructed type is obtained by substituting, for each *type-parameter* in the base class declaration, the corresponding *type-argument* of the constructed type. Given the generic class declarations

```
class B<U,V> {...}
class G<T>: B<string,T[]> {...}
```

the base class of the constructed type `G<int>` would be `B<string, int[]>`.

Similarly, constructed class, struct, and interface types have a set of explicit base interfaces. The explicit base interfaces are formed by taking the explicit base interface declarations on the generic type declaration and substituting, for each *type-parameter* in the base interface declaration, the corresponding *type-argument* of the constructed type.

The set of all base classes and base interfaces for a type is formed, as usual, by recursively getting the base classes and interfaces of the immediate base classes and interfaces. For example, given the generic class declarations

20. Generics

```
class A {...}
class B<T>: A {...}
class C<T>: B<IComparable<T>> {...}
class D<T>: C<T[]> {...}
```

the base classes of D<int> are C<int[]>, B<IComparable<int[]>>, A, and object.

20.5.4 Members of a Constructed Type

The noninherited members of a constructed type are obtained by substituting, for each *type-parameter* in the member declaration, the corresponding *type-argument* of the constructed type.

For example, given the generic class declaration

```
class Gen<T,U>
{
    public T[,] a;
    public void G(int i, T t, Gen<U,T> gt) {...}
    public U Prop { get {...} set {...} }
    public int H(double d) {...}
}
```

the constructed type Gen<int[],IComparable<string>> has the following members.

```
public int[,][] a;
public void G(int i, int[] t, Gen<IComparable<string>,int[]> gt) {...}
public IComparable<string> Prop { get {...} set {...} }
public int H(double d) {...}
```

Note that the substitution process is based on the semantic meaning of type declarations and is not simply textual substitution. The type of the member a in the generic class declaration Gen is "two-dimensional array of T," so the type of the member a in the previous instantiated type is "two-dimensional array of one-dimensional array of int," or int[,][].

The inherited members of a constructed type are obtained in a similar way. First, all the members of the immediate base class are determined. If the base class is itself a constructed type, this may involve a recursive application of the current rule. Then, each of the inherited members is transformed by substituting, for each *type-parameter* in the member declaration, the corresponding *type-argument* of the constructed type.

```
class B<U>
{
    public U F(long index) {...}
}
```

```
class D<T>: B<T[]>
{
    public T G(string s) {...}
}
```

In the previous example, the constructed type D<int> has a noninherited member public int G(string s) obtained by substituting the type argument int for the type parameter T. D<int> also has an inherited member from the class declaration B. This inherited member is determined by first determining the members of the constructed type B<T[]> by substituting T[] for U, yielding public T[] F(long index). Then, the type argument int is substituted for the type parameter T, yielding the inherited member public int[] F(long index).

20.5.5 Accessibility of a Constructed Type

A constructed type $C<T_1, ..., T_N>$ is accessible when all its parts $C, T_1, ..., T_N$ are accessible. For instance, if the generic type name C is public and all of the *type-arguments* $T_1, ..., T_N$ are accessible as public, then the constructed type is accessible as public; but if either the *type-name* or one of the *type-arguments* has accessibility private, then the accessibility of the constructed type is private. If one *type-argument* has accessibility protected, and another has accessibility internal, then the constructed type is accessible only in this class and its subclasses in this assembly.

More precisely, the accessibility domain for a constructed type is the intersection of the accessibility domains of its constituent parts. Thus, if a method has a return type or argument type that is a constructed type where one constituent part is private, then the method must have an accessibility domain that is private; see §3.5.

20.5.6 Conversions

Constructed types follow the same conversion rules (§6) as do nongeneric types. When applying these rules, the base classes and interfaces of constructed types must be determined as described in §20.5.3.

No special conversions exist between constructed reference types other than those described in §6. In particular, unlike array types, constructed reference types do not exhibit "co-variant" conversions. This means that a type List<B> has no conversion (either implicit or explicit) to List<A> even if B is derived from A. Likewise, no conversion exists from List<B> to List<object>.

The rationale for this is simple: If a conversion to List<A> is permitted, then apparently one can store values of type A into the list. But this would break the invariant that every object in a list of type List<B> is always a value of type B, or else unexpected failures may occur when assigning into collection classes.

20. Generics

491

The behavior of conversions and runtime type checks is illustrated as follows.

```
class A {...}

class B: A {...}

class Collection {...}

class List<T>: Collection {...}

class Test
{
    void F() {
        List<A> listA = new List<A>();
        List<B> listB = new List<B>();

        Collection c1 = listA;        // Ok, List<A> is a Collection
        Collection c2 = listB;        // Ok, List<B> is a Collection

        List<A> a1 = listB;           // Error, no implicit conversion
        List<A> a2 = (List<A>)listB;  // Error, no explicit conversion
    }
}
```

20.5.7 The System.Nullable <T> Type

The `System.Nullable<T>` generic struct type defined in the .NET Base Class Library represents a value of type `T` that may be null. The `System.Nullable<T>` type is useful in a variety of situations, such as to denote nullable columns in a database table or optional attributes in an Extensible Markup Language (XML) element.

An implicit conversion exists from the null type to any type constructed from `System.Nullable<T>`. The result of such a conversion is the default value of `System.Nullable<T>`. In other words, writing this

```
Nullable<int> x = null;
Nullable<string> y = null;
```

is the same as writing the following.

```
Nullable<int> x = Nullable<int>.default;
Nullable<string> y = Nullable<string>.default;
```

20.5.8 Using Alias Directives

Using aliases may name a closed constructed type but may not name a generic type declaration without supplying type arguments. For example

```
namespace N1
{
    class A<T>
    {
        class B {}
    }
```

```
        class C {}
    }

    namespace N2
    {
        using W = N1.A;         // Error, cannot name generic type

        using X = N1.A.B;       // Error, cannot name generic type

        using Y = N1.A<int>;    // Ok, can name closed constructed type

        using Z = N1.C;         // Ok
    }
```

20.5.9 Attributes

An open type may not be used anywhere inside an attribute. A closed constructed type can be used as the argument to an attribute but cannot be used as the *attribute-name* because `System.Attribute` cannot be the base type of a generic class declaration.

```
    class A: Attribute
    {
        public A(Type t) {...}
    }

    class B<T>: Attribute {}            // Error, cannot use Attribute as base

    class List<T>
    {
        [A(typeof(T))] T t;             // Error, open type in attribute
    }

    class X
    {
        [A(typeof(List<int>))] int x; // Ok, closed constructed type

        [B<int>] int y;                 // Error, invalid attribute name
    }
```

20.6 Generic Methods

A generic method is a method that is generic with respect to certain types. A generic method declaration names, in addition to normal parameters, a set of type parameters that are provided when using the method. Generic methods may be declared inside class, struct, or interface declarations, which may themselves be either generic or nongeneric. If a generic method is declared inside a generic type declaration, the body of the method can refer to both the type parameters of the method and the type parameters of the containing declaration.

> *class-member-declaration:*
>
>   ...
>   *generic-method-declaration*

20. Generics

493

struct-member-declaration:

   ...

   generic-method-declaration

interface-member-declaration:

   ...

   interface-generic-method-declaration

Generic methods are declared by placing a type parameter list following the name of the method.

generic-method-declaration:
   generic-method-header method-body

generic-method-header:
   attributes$_{opt}$ method-modifiers$_{opt}$ return-type member-name type-parameter-list
     (*formal-parameter-list$_{opt}$*) *type-parameter-constraints-clauses$_{opt}$*

interface-generic-method-declaration:
   attributes$_{opt}$ new$_{opt}$ return-type identifier type-parameter-list
     (*formal-parameter-list$_{opt}$*) *type-parameter-constraints-clauses$_{opt}$* ;

The *type-parameter-list* and *type-parameter-constraints-clauses* have the same syntax and function as in a generic type declaration. The type parameters declared by the *type-parameter-list* are in scope throughout the *generic-method-declaration* and may be used to form types throughout that scope including the *return-type*, the *method-body*, and the *type-parameter-constraints-clauses* but excluding the *attributes*.

The name of a method type parameter cannot be the same as the name of an ordinary parameter to the same method.

The following example finds the first element in an array, if any, that satisfies the given test delegate. Generic delegates are described in §20.4.

```
public delegate bool Test<T>(T item);

public class Finder
{
    public static T Find<T>(T[] items, Test<T> test) {
        foreach (T item in items) {
            if (test(item)) return item;
        }
        throw new InvalidOperationException("Item not found");
    }
}
```

A generic method may not be declared `extern`. All other method modifiers are valid on a generic method.

20.6.1 Generic Method Signatures

For the purposes of signature comparisons, any type parameter constraints are ignored, as are the names of the type parameters, but the number of type parameters is relevant, as are the ordinal positions of type parameters in left-to-right ordering. The following example shows how method signatures are affected by this rule.

```
class A {}

class B {}

interface IX
{
    T F1<T>(T[] a, int i);      // Error, both declarations have the same
    void F1<U>(U[] a, int i);   // signature because return type and type
                                // parameter names are not significant

    void F2<T>(int x);          // Ok, the number of type parameters is part
    void F2(int x);             // of the signature

    void F3<T>(T t) where T: A; // Error, constraints are not
    void F3<T>(T t) where T: B; // considered in signatures
}
```

Overloading of generic methods is further constrained by a rule similar to that which governs overloaded methods in a generic type declaration (20.1.8). Two generic methods declared with the same names and same number of type arguments must have parameter types such that no list of closed type arguments, when applied to both methods in the same order, yield two methods with the same signature. Constraints are not considered for the purposes of this rule. For example

```
class X<T>
{
    void F<U>(T t, U u) {...}   // Error, X<int>.F<int> yields two methods
    void F<U>(U u, T t) {...}   // with the same signature
}
```

20.6.2 Virtual Generic Methods

Generic methods can be declared using the `abstract`, `virtual`, and `override` modifiers. The signature matching rules described in §20.6.1 are used when matching methods for overriding or interface implementation. When a generic method overrides a generic method declared in a base class or implements a method in a base interface, the constraints given for each method type parameter must be the same in both declarations, where method type parameters are identified by ordinal positions, left to right.

```
abstract class Base
{
    public abstract T F<T,U>(T t, U u);

    public abstract T G<T>(T t) where T: IComparable;
}
```

```
class Derived: Base
{
    public override X F<X,Y>(X x, Y y) {...}      // Ok
    public override T G<T>(T t) {...}             // Error
}
```

The override of F is correct because type parameter names are permitted to differ. The override of G is incorrect because the given type parameter constraints (in this case, none) do not match those of the method being overridden.

20.6.3 Calling Generic Methods

A generic method invocation may explicitly specify a type argument list, or it may omit the type argument list and rely on type inference to determine the type arguments. The exact compile-time processing of a method invocation, including a generic method invocation, is described in §20.9.5. When a generic method is invoked without a type argument list, type inference takes place as described in §20.6.4.

The following example shows how overload resolution occurs after type inference and after type arguments are substituted into the parameter list.

```
class Test
{
    static void F<T>(int x, T y) {
        Console.WriteLine("one");
    }

    static void F<T>(T x, long y) {
        Console.WriteLine("two");
    }

    static void Main() {
        F<int>(5, 324);        // Ok, prints "one"
        F<byte>(5, 324);       // Ok, prints "two"
        F<double>(5, 324);     // Error, ambiguous

        F(5, 324);             // Ok, prints "one"
        F(5, 324L);            // Error, ambiguous
    }
}
```

20.6.4 Inference of Type Arguments

When a generic method is called without specifying type arguments, a *type inference* process attempts to infer type arguments for the call. The presence of type inference allows a more convenient syntax to be used for calling a generic method and allows the programmer to avoid specifying redundant type information. For example, given the method declaration

```
class Util
{
    static Random rand = new Random();

    static public T Choose<T>(T first, T second) {
        return (rand.Next(2) == 0)? first: second;
    }
}
```

it is possible to invoke the Choose method without explicitly specifying a type argument.

```
int i = Util.Choose(5, 213);              // Calls Choose<int>

string s = Util.Choose("foo", "bar");     // Calls Choose<string>
```

Through type inference, the type arguments int and string are determined from the arguments to the method.

Type inference occurs as part of the compile-time processing of a method invocation (§20.9.5) and takes place before the overload resolution step of the invocation. When a particular method group is specified in a method invocation, and no type arguments are specified as part of the method invocation, type inference is applied to each generic method in the method group. If type inference succeeds, then the inferred type arguments are used to determine the types of arguments for subsequent overload resolution. If overload resolution chooses a generic method as the one to invoke, then the inferred type arguments are used as the actual type arguments for the invocation. If type inference for a particular method fails, that method does not participate in overload resolution. The failure of type inference, in and of itself, does not cause a compile-time error. However, it often leads to a compile-time error when overload resolution then fails to find any applicable methods.

If the supplied number of arguments is different from the number of parameters in the method, then inference immediately fails. Otherwise, type inference first occurs independently for each regular argument that is supplied to the method. Assume this argument has type A, and the corresponding parameter has type P. Type inferences are produced by relating the types A and P according to the following steps.

- Nothing is inferred from the argument (but type inference succeeds) if any of the following are true.
    - P does not involve any method type parameters.
    - The argument is the null literal.
    - The argument is an anonymous method.
    - The argument is a method group.

- If P is an array type and A is an array type of the same rank, then replace A and P respectively with the element types of A and P and repeat this step.

- If P is an array type and A is not an array type of the same rank, then type inference fails for the generic method.

- If P is a method type parameter, then type inference succeeds for this argument, and A is the type inferred for that type parameter.

- Otherwise, P must be a constructed type. If, for each method type parameter M_X that occurs in P, exactly one type T_X can be determined such that replacing each M_X with each T_X produces a type to which A is convertible by a standard implicit conversion, then inference succeeds for this argument and each T_X is the type inferred for each M_X. Method type parameter constraints, if any, are ignored for the purpose of type inference. If, for a given M_X, no T_X exists or more than one T_X exists, then type inference fails for the generic method (a situation where more than one T_X exists can only occur if P is a generic interface type and A implements multiple constructed versions of that interface).

If all of the method arguments are processed successfully by the previous algorithm, then all inferences that were produced from the arguments are pooled. This pooled set of inferences must have the following properties.

- Each type parameter of the method must have had a type argument inferred for it. In short, the set of inferences must be *complete*.

- If a type parameter occurred more than once, then all of the inferences for that type parameter must infer the same type argument. In short, the set of inferences must be *consistent*.

If a complete and consistent set of inferred type arguments is found, then type inference is said to have succeeded for the given generic method and argument list.

If the generic method was declared with a parameter array (§10.5.1.4), then type inference is first performed against the method in its normal form. If type inference succeeds, and the resultant method is applicable, then the method is eligible for overload resolution in its normal form. Otherwise, type inference is performed against the method in its expanded form (§7.4.2.1).

20.6.5 Grammar Ambiguities

The productions for *simple-name* and *member-access* in §20.9.3 and §20.9.4 can give rise to ambiguities in the grammar for expressions. For example, the statement

```
F(G<A,B>(7));
```

could be interpreted as a call to F with two arguments, G < A and B > (7). Alternatively, it could be interpreted as a call to F with one argument, which is a call to a generic method G with two type arguments and one regular argument.

If an expression could be parsed in two different valid ways, where > can be either interpreted as all or part of an operator or as ending a *type-argument-list*, the token immediately following the > is examined. If it is one of the following

    (   )   ]   >   :   ;   ,   .   ?

then the > is interpreted as the end of a *type-argument-list*. Otherwise, the > is interpreted as an operator.

20.6.6 Using a Generic Method with a Delegate

An instance of a delegate can be created that refers to a generic method declaration. The exact compile-time processing of a delegate creation expression, including a delegate creation expression that refers to a generic method, is described in §20.9.6.

The type arguments used when invoking a generic method through a delegate are determined when the delegate is instantiated. The type arguments can be given explicitly via a *type-argument-list* or determined by type inference (§20.6.4). If type inference is used, the parameter types of the delegate are used as argument types in the inference process. The return type of the delegate is *not* used for inference. The following example shows both ways of supplying a type argument to a delegate instantiation expression.

```
delegate int D(string s, int i);

delegate int E();

class X
{
    public static T F<T>(string s, T t) {...}

    public static T G<T>() {...}

    static void Main() {
        D d1 = new D(F<int>);      // Ok, type argument given explicitly
        D d2 = new D(F);           // Ok, int inferred as type argument

        E e1 = new E(G<int>);      // Ok, type argument given explicitly
        E e2 = new E(G);           // Error, cannot infer from return type
    }
}
```

In the previous example, a nongeneric delegate type was instantiated using a generic method. It is also possible to create an instance of a constructed delegate type (§20.4) using a generic method. In all cases, type arguments are given or inferred when the delegate instance is created, and a *type-argument-list* may not be supplied when a delegate is invoked (§15.3).

20.6.7 No Generic Properties, Events, Indexers, or Operators

Properties, events, indexers, and operators may not themselves have type parameters (although they can occur in generic classes and use the type parameters from an enclosing class). If a property-like construct is required that must itself be generic, a generic method must be used instead.

20.7 Constraints

Generic type and method declarations can optionally specify type parameter constraints by including *type-parameter-constraints-clauses* in the declaration.

> *type-parameter-constraints-clauses:*
>   *type-parameter-constraints-clause*
>   *type-parameter-constraints-clauses* *type-parameter-constraints-clause*
>
> *type-parameter-constraints-clause:*
>   where *type-parameter* : *type-parameter-constraints*
>
> *type-parameter-constraints:*
>   *class-constraint*
>   *interface-constraints*
>   *constructor-constraint*
>   *class-constraint* , *interface-constraints*
>   *class-constraint* , *constructor-constraint*
>   *interface-constraints* , *constructor-constraint*
>   *class-constraint* , *interface-constraints* , *constructor-constraint*
>
> *class-constraint:*
>   *class-type*
>
> *interface-constraints:*
>   *interface-constraint*
>   *interface-constraints* , *interface-constraint*
>
> *interface-constraint:*
>   *interface-type*
>
> *constructor-constraint:*
>   new ( )

Each type parameter constraints clause consists of the token where, followed by the name of a type parameter, followed by a colon and the list of constraints for that type parameter. There can be only one where clause for each type parameter, but the where clauses may be listed in any order. Similar to the get and set tokens in a property accessor, the where token is not a keyword.

The list of constraints given in a `where` clause may include any of the following components in this order: a single class constraint, one or more interface constraints, and the constructor constraint `new()`.

If a constraint is a class type or an interface type, that type specifies a minimal "base type" that every type argument used for that type parameter must support. Whenever a constructed type or generic method is used, the type argument is checked against the constraints on the type parameter at compile time. The type argument supplied must derive from or implement all of the constraints given for that type parameter.

The type specified as a *class-constraint* must satisfy the following rules.

- The type must be a class type.
- The type must not be `sealed`.
- The type must not be one of the following special types: `System.Array`, `System.Delegate`, `System.Enum`, or `System.ValueType`.
- The type must not be `object`. Because all types derive from `object`, such a constraint would have no effect if it were permitted.
- At most, one constraint for a given type parameter can be a class type.

The type specified as an *interface-constraint* must satisfy the following rules.

- The type must be an interface type.
- The same type may not be specified more than once in a given `where` clause.

In either case, the constraint may involve any of the type parameters of the associated type or method declaration as part of a constructed type and may involve the type being declared, but the constraint may not be a type parameter alone.

Any class or interface type specified as a type parameter constraint must be at least as accessible (§10.5.4) as the generic type or method being declared.

If the `where` clause for a type parameter includes a constructor constraint of the form `new()`, it is possible to use the `new` operator to create instances of the type (§20.8.2). Any type argument used for a type parameter with a constructor constraint must have a parameterless constructor (see §20.7.1 for details).

The following are examples of possible constraints.

```
interface IPrintable
{
    void Print();
}
```

```
interface IComparable<T>
{
    int CompareTo(T value);
}

interface IKeyProvider<T>
{
    T GetKey();
}

class Printer<T> where T: IPrintable {...}

class SortedList<T> where T: IComparable<T> {...}

class Dictionary<K,V>
    where K: IComparable<K>
    where V: IPrintable, IKeyProvider<K>, new()
{
    ...
}
```

The following example is in error because it attempts to use a type parameter directly as a constraint.

```
class Extend<T,U> where U: T {...}// Error
```

Values of a constrained type parameter type can be used to access the instance members implied by the constraints. In the example

```
interface IPrintable
{
    void Print();
}

class Printer<T> where T: IPrintable
{
    void PrintOne(T x) {
        x.Print();
    }
}
```

the methods of IPrintable can be invoked directly on x because T is constrained to always implement IPrintable.

20.7.1 Satisfying Constraints

Whenever a constructed type is used or a generic method is referenced, the supplied type arguments are checked against the type parameter constraints declared on the generic type or method. For each where clause, the type argument A that corresponds to the named type parameter is checked against each constraint as follows.

- If the constraint is a class type or an interface type, let C represent that constraint with the supplied type arguments substituted for any type parameters that appear in the constraint. To satisfy the constraint, it must be the case that type A is convertible to type C by one of the following:

  - An identity conversion (§6.1.1)

  - An implicit reference conversion (§6.1.4)

  - A boxing conversion (§6.1.5)

  - An implicit conversion from a type parameter A to C (§20.7.4).

- If the constraint is new(), the type argument A must not be abstract and must have a public parameterless constructor. This is satisfied if one of the following is true.

  - A is a value type (as described in §4.1.2, all value types have a public default constructor).

  - A is a class that is not abstract and A contains a public constructor with no parameters.

  - A is not abstract and has a default constructor (§10.10.4).

A compile-time error occurs if one or more of a type parameter's constraints are not satisfied by the given type arguments.

Because type parameters are not inherited, constraints are never inherited either. In the following example, D must specify a constraint on its type parameter T so that T satisfies the constraint imposed by the base class B<T>. In contrast, class E need not specify a constraint because List<T> implements IEnumerable for any T.

```
class B<T> where T: IEnumerable {...}
class D<T>: B<T> where T: IEnumerable {...}
class E<T>: B<List<T>> {...}
```

20.7.2 Member Lookup on Type Parameters

The results of member lookup in a type given by a type parameter T depends on the constraints, if any, specified for T. If T has no constraints or only the new() constraint, then member lookup on T returns the same set of members as member lookup on object. Otherwise, the first stage of member lookup (§20.9.2) considers all the members in each of the types that are constraints for T. After performing the first stage of member lookup for each of the type constraints of T, the results are combined, and then hidden members are removed from the combined results.

20. Generics

503

Before the advent of generics, member lookup always returned either a set of members declared solely in classes or a set of members declared solely in interfaces and possibly the type `object`. Member lookup on type parameters changes this somewhat. When a type parameter has both a class constraint and one or more interface constraints, member lookup can return a set of members, some of which were declared in the class, and others of which were declared in an interface. The following additional rules handle this case.

- During member lookup (§20.9.2), members declared in a class other than `object` hide members declared in interfaces.

- During overload resolution of methods (§7.5.5.1) and indexers (§7.5.6.2), if any applicable member was declared in a class other than `object`, all members declared in an interface are removed from the set of considered members.

These rules only have effect when doing binding on a type parameter with both a class constraint and an interface constraint. Informally, members defined in a class constraint are always preferred over members in an interface constraint.

20.7.3 Type Parameters and Boxing
When a struct type overrides a virtual method inherited from `System.Object` (`Equals`, `GetHashCode`, or `ToString`), invocations of the virtual method through an instance of the struct type does not cause boxing to occur. This is true even when the struct is used as a type parameter and the invocation occurs through an instance of the type parameter type. For example

```
using System;

struct Counter
{
    int value;

    public override string ToString() {
        value++;
        return value.ToString();
    }
}

class Program
{
    static void Test<T>() where T: new() {
        T x = new T();
        Console.WriteLine(x.ToString());
        Console.WriteLine(x.ToString());
        Console.WriteLine(x.ToString());
    }

    static void Main() {
        Test<Counter>();
    }
}
```

The output of the program is

```
1
2
3
```

Although it is never recommended for ToString to have side effects, the example demonstrates that no boxing occurred for the three invocations of x.ToString().

Boxing never implicitly occurs when accessing a member on a constrained type parameter. For example, suppose an interface ICounter contains a method Increment that can be used to modify a value. If ICounter is used as a constraint, the implementation of the Increment method is called with a reference to the variable that Increment was called on, never a boxed copy.

```
using System;

interface ICounter
{
    void Increment();
}

struct Counter: ICounter
{
    int value;

    public override string ToString() {
        return value.ToString();
    }

    void ICounter.Increment() {
        value++;
    }
}

class Program
{
    static void Test<T>() where T: new(), ICounter {
        T x = new T();
        Console.WriteLine(x);
        x.Increment();                // Modify x
        Console.WriteLine(x);
        ((ICounter)x).Increment();    // Modify boxed copy of x
        Console.WriteLine(x);
    }

    static void Main() {
        Test<Counter>();
    }
}
```

The first call to Increment modifies the value in the variable x. This is not equivalent to the second call to Increment, which modifies the value in a boxed copy of x. Thus, the output of the program is

```
0
1
1
```

20.7.4 Conversions Involving Type Parameters

The conversions that are allowed on a type parameter T depend on the constraints specified for T. All type parameters, constrained or not, have the following conversions.

- An implicit identity conversion from T to T.

- An implicit conversion from T to object. At runtime, if T is a value type, this is executed as a boxing conversion. Otherwise, it is executed as an implicit reference conversion.

- An explicit conversion from object to T. At runtime, if T is a value type, this is executed as an unboxing conversion. Otherwise, it is executed as an explicit reference conversion.

- An explicit conversion from T to any interface type. At runtime, if T is a value type, this is executed as a boxing conversion. Otherwise, it is executed as an explicit reference conversion.

- An explicit conversion from any interface type to T. At runtime, if T is a value type, this is executed as an unboxing conversion. Otherwise, it is executed as an explicit reference conversion.

If the type parameter T has the interface type I specified as a constraint, the following additional conversions exist.

- An implicit conversion from T to I, and from T to any base interface type of I. At runtime, if T is a value type, this is executed as a boxing conversion. Otherwise, it is executed as an implicit reference conversion.

If the type parameter T has the class type C specified as a constraint, the following additional conversions exist:

- An implicit reference conversion from T to C, from T to any class C is derived from, and from T to any interface C implements

- An explicit reference conversion from C to T, from any class C is derived from to T, and from any interface C implements to T

- An implicit user-defined conversion from T to A, if an implicit user-defined conversion exists from C to A

- An explicit user-defined conversion from A to T, if an explicit user-defined conversion exists from A to C

- An implicit reference conversion from the null type to T

An array type with element type T has the usual conversions to and from object and System.Array (§6.1.4, §6.2.3). If T has a class type C specified as a constraint, then additionally

- An implicit reference conversion exists from an array type A_T with element type T to an array type A_U with element type U, and an explicit reference conversion exists from A_U to A_T, if both the following are true:

  - A_T and A_U have the same number of dimensions.

  - U is one of: C, a class C is derived from, an interface C implements, an interface I that is specified as a constraint on T, or a base interface of I.

The previous rules do not permit a direct explicit conversion from an unconstrained type parameter to a noninterface type, which may be surprising. The reason for this rule is to prevent confusion and make the semantics of such conversions clear. For example, consider the following declaration.

```
class X<T>
{
    public static long F(T t) {
        return (long)t;          // Error, explicit conversion not permitted
    }
}
```

If the direct explicit conversion of t to int were permitted, one might easily expect that X<int>.F(7) would return 7L. However, it would not because the standard numeric conversions are only considered when the types are known to be numeric at compile time. In order to make the semantics clear, the previous example must instead be written as follows.

```
class X<T>
{
    public static long F(T t) {
        return (long)(object)t;   // OK, conversions permitted
    }
}
```

20. Generics

20.8 Expressions and Statements

The operation of some expressions and statements is modified with generics. This section details those changes.

20.8.1 Default Value Expression

A default value expression is used to obtain the default value (§5.2) of a type. Typically, a default value expression is used for type parameters because it may not be known if the type parameter is a value type or a reference type. (No conversion exists from the null literal to a type parameter.)

> *primary-no-array-creation-expression:*
>
>   *...*
>
>   *default-value-expression*
>
> *default-value-expression:*
>   *primary-expression* . default
>   *predefined-type* . default

If a *primary-expression* is used in a *default-value-expression*, and the *primary-expression* is not classified as a type, then a compile-time error occurs. However, the rule described in §7.5.4.1 also applies to a construct of the form `E.default`.

If the left-hand side of a *default-value-expression* evaluates at runtime to a reference type, the result is null converted to that type. If the left-hand side of a *default-value-expression* evaluates at runtime to a value type, the result is the *value-type*'s default value (§4.1.2).

A *default-value-expression* is a constant expression (§7.15) if the type is a reference type or a type parameter that has a class constraint. In addition, a *default-value-expression* is a constant expression if the type is one of the following value types: `sbyte`, `byte`, `short`, `ushort`, `int`, `uint`, `long`, `ulong`, `char`, `float`, `double`, `decimal`, or `bool`.

20.8.2 Object Creation Expressions

The type of an object creation expression can be a type parameter. When a type parameter is specified as the type in an object creation expression, both of the following conditions must hold or a compile-time error occurs.

- The argument list must be omitted.
- A constructor constraint of the form `new()` must have been specified for the type parameter.

Execution of the object creation expression occurs by creating an instance of the runtime type that the type parameter has been bound to and invoking the default constructor of that type. The runtime type may be a reference type or a value type.

20.8.3 The typeof Operator

The typeof operator can be used on a type parameter. The result is the System.Type object for the runtime type that was bound to the type parameter. The typeof operator can also be used on a constructed type.

```
class X<T>
{
    public static void PrintTypes() {
        Console.WriteLine(typeof(T).FullName);
        Console.WriteLine(typeof(X<X<T>>).FullName);
    }
}

class M
{
    static void Main() {
        X<int>.PrintTypes();
    }
}
```

The previous program will print the following.

```
System.Int32
X<X<System.Int32>>
```

The typeof operator cannot be used with the name of a generic type declaration without specifying the type arguments.

```
class X<T> {...}

class M
{
    static void Main() {
        Type t = typeof(X);    // Error, X requires type arguments
    }
}
```

20.8.4 Reference Equality Operators

The reference type equality operators (§7.9.6) may be used to compare values of a type parameter T if T is constrained by a class constraint.

The use of the reference type equality operators is slightly relaxed to allow one argument to be of a type parameter T and the other argument to be null, even if T has no class constraint. At runtime, if T is a value type, the result of the comparison is false.

The following example checks whether an argument of an unconstrained type parameter type is null.

```
class C<T>
{
    void F(T x) {
        if (x == null) throw new ArgumentNullException();
        ...
    }
}
```

The x == null construct is permitted even though T could represent a value type, and the result is simply defined to be false when T is a value type.

20.8.5 The is Operator

The is operator operates on open types largely following the usual rules (§7.9.9). If either the compile-time type of e or T is an open type, then a dynamic type check on the runtime types of e and T is always performed.

20.8.6 The as Operator

The as operator can be used with a type parameter T as the right-hand side only if T has a class constraint. This restriction is required because the value null might be returned as a result of the operator.

```
class X
{
    public T F<T>(object o) where T: Attribute {
        return o as T;        // Ok, T has a class constraint
    }
    public T G<T>(object o) {
        return o as T;        // Error, unconstrained T
    }
}
```

In the current specification for the as operator (§7.9.10), for the expression e as T the final bullet point states that if no explicit reference conversion is available from the compile-time type of e to T, a compile-time error occurs. With generics, this rule changes slightly. If either the compile-time type of e or T is an open type, then no compile-time error occurs in this case; instead, a runtime type check occurs.

20.8.7 Exception Statements

The usual rules for throw (§8.9.5) and try (§8.10) statements apply when used with open types.

- The `throw` statement can be used with an expression whose type is given by a type parameter only if that type parameter has `System.Exception` (or a subclass thereof) as a class constraint.

- The type named in a `catch` clause may be a type parameter only if that type parameter has `System.Exception` (or a subclass thereof) as a class constraint.

20.8.8 The lock Statement

The `lock` statement may be used with an expression whose type is given by a type parameter. If the runtime type of the expression is a value type, the locking will have no effect (because the boxed value could not have any other references to it).

20.8.9 The using Statement

The `using` statement (§8.13) follows the usual rules: The expression must be implicitly convertible to `System.IDisposable`. If a type parameter is constrained by `System.IDisposable`, then expressions of that type may be used with a `using` statement.

20.8.10 The foreach Statement

Given a `foreach` statement of the form

```
foreach (ElementType element in collection) statement
```

If the `collection` expression is a type that does not implement the collection pattern but does implement the constructed interface `System.Collections.Generic.IEnumerable<T>` for exactly one type `T`, then the expansion of the `foreach` statement is

```
IEnumerator<T> enumerator = ((IEnumerable<T>)(collection)).GetEnumerator();
try {
    while (enumerator.MoveNext()) {
        ElementType element = (ElementType)enumerator.Current;
        statement;
    }
}
finally {
    enumerator.Dispose();
}
```

20.9 Revised Lookup Rules

Generics modify some of the basic rules used to look up and bind names. The following sections restate all the basic name lookup rules, taking generics into account.

20. Generics

20.9.1 Namespace and Type Names

The following replaces §3.8.

Several contexts in a C# program require a *namespace-name* or a *type-name* to be specified. Either form of name is written as one or more identifiers separated by . tokens.

> *namespace-name:*
> > *namespace-or-type-name*
>
> *type-name:*
> > *namespace-or-type-name*
>
> *namespace-or-type-name:*
> > *identifier   type-argument-list*$_{opt}$
> > *namespace-or-type-name*   .   *identifier   type-argument-list*$_{opt}$

A *namespace-name* is a *namespace-or-type-name* that refers to a namespace. Following resolution as described below, the *namespace-or-type-name* of a *namespace-name* must refer to a namespace, or otherwise a compile-time error occurs. No type arguments can be present in a *namespace-name* (only types can have type arguments).

A *type-name* is a *namespace-or-type-name* that refers to a type. Following resolution as described below, the *namespace-or-type-name* of a *type-name* must refer to a type, or otherwise a compile-time error occurs.

The meaning of a *namespace-or-type-name* is determined as follows.

- If the *namespace-or-type-name* is of the form I or of the form I<A_1, ..., A_N>, where I is a single identifier and <A_1, ..., A_N> is an optional type argument list.

  - If the *namespace-or-type-name* appears within the body of a generic method declaration and if that declaration includes a type parameter of the name given by I and no type argument list was specified, then the *namespace-or-type-name* refers to that type parameter.

  - Otherwise, if the *namespace-or-type-name* appears within the body of a type declaration, then for each instance type T (§20.1.2), starting with the instance type of that type declaration and continuing with the instance type of each enclosing class or struct declaration (if any)

    - If the declaration of T includes a type parameter of the name given by I and no type argument list was specified, then the *namespace-or-type-name* refers to that type parameter.

- Otherwise, if I is the name of an accessible member in T and if that member is a type with a matching number of type parameters, then the *namespace-or-type-name* refers to the type T.I or the type T.I<A_1, ..., A_N>. Note that nontype members (constants, fields, methods, properties, indexers, operators, instance constructors, destructors, and static constructors) and type members with a different number of type parameters are ignored when determining the meaning of a *namespace-or-type-name*.

- Otherwise, for each namespace N, starting with the namespace in which the *namespace-or-type-name* occurs, continuing with each enclosing namespace (if any) and ending with the global namespace, the following steps are evaluated until an entity is located.

  - If I is the name of a namespace in N and no type argument list was specified, then the *namespace-or-type-name* refers to that namespace.

  - Otherwise, if I is the name of an accessible type in N with a matching number of type parameters, then the *namespace-or-type-name* refers to that type constructed with the given type arguments.

  - Otherwise, if the location where the *namespace-or-type-name* occurs is enclosed by a namespace declaration for N

    - If the namespace declaration contains a *using-alias-directive* that associates the name given by I with an imported namespace or type and no type argument list was specified, then the *namespace-or-type-name* refers to that namespace or type.

    - Otherwise, if the namespaces imported by the *using-namespace-directive*s of the namespace declaration contain exactly one type with the name given by I and a matching number of type parameters, then the *namespace-or-type-name* refers to that type constructed with the given type arguments.

    - Otherwise, if the namespaces imported by the *using-namespace-directive*s of the namespace declaration contain more than one type with the name given by I and a matching number of type parameters, then the *namespace-or-type-name* is ambiguous and an error occurs.

- Otherwise, the *namespace-or-type-name* is undefined, and a compile-time error occurs.

20. Generics

- Otherwise, the *namespace-or-type-name* is of the form N.I or of the form N.I<A$_1$, ..., A$_N$>, where N is a *namespace-or-type-name*, I is an identifier, and <A$_1$, ..., A$_N$> is an optional type argument list. N is first resolved as a *namespace-or-type-name*. If the resolution of N is not successful, a compile-time error occurs. Otherwise, N.I or N.I<A$_1$, ..., A$_N$> is resolved as follows.

    - If N refers to a namespace and if I is the name of a nested namespace in N and no type argument list was specified, then the *namespace-or-type-name* refers to that nested namespace.

    - Otherwise, if N refers to a namespace and I is the name of an accessible type in N with a matching number of type parameters, then the *namespace-or-type-name* refers to that type constructed with the given type arguments.

    - Otherwise, if N refers to a (possibly constructed) class or struct type and I is the name of an accessible type nested in N with a matching number of type parameters, then the *namespace-or-type-name* refers to that type constructed with the given type arguments.

    - Otherwise, N.I is an invalid *namespace-or-type-name*, and a compile-time error occurs.

20.9.2 Member Lookup

The following replaces §7.3.

A member lookup is the process whereby the meaning of a name in the context of a type is determined. A member lookup may occur as part of evaluating a *simple-name* (§20.9.3) or a *member-access* (§20.9.4) in an expression.

A member lookup of a name N in a type T is processed as follows.

- First, a set of accessible members named N is determined.

    - If T is a type parameter, then the set is the union of the sets of accessible members named N in each of the types specified as a class constraint or interface constraint for T, along with the set of accessible members named N in object.

    - Otherwise, the set consists of all accessible (§3.5) members named N in T, including inherited members and the accessible members named N in object. If T is a constructed type, the set of members is obtained by substituting type arguments as described in §20.5.4. Members that include an override modifier are excluded from the set.

- Next, members that are hidden by other members are removed from the set. For every member S.M in the set, where S is the type in which the member M is declared, the following rules are applied.

  - If M is a constant, field, property, event, or enumeration member, then all members declared in a base type of S are removed from the set.

  - If M is a type declaration, then all nontypes declared in a base type of S are removed from the set, and all type declarations with the same number of type parameters as M declared in a base type of S are removed from the set.

  - If M is a method, then all nonmethod members declared in a base type of S are removed from the set, and all methods with the same signature as M declared in a base type of S are removed from the set.

- Next, interface members that are hidden by class members are removed from the set. This step only has an effect if T is a type parameter and T has both a class constraint and one or more interface constraints. For every member S.M in the set, where S is the type in which the member M is declared, the following rules are applied if S is a class declaration other than object.

  - If M is a constant, field, property, event, enumeration member, or type declaration, then all members declared in an interface declaration are removed from the set.

  - If M is a method, then all nonmethod members declared in an interface declaration are removed from the set, and all methods with the same signature as M declared in an interface declaration are removed from the set.

- Finally, having removed hidden members, the result of the lookup is determined.

  - If the set consists of a single member that is not a type and not a method, then this member is the result of the lookup.

  - Otherwise, if the set contains only methods, then this group of methods is the result of the lookup.

  - Otherwise, if the set contains only type declarations, then this group of type declarations in the result of the lookup.

  - Otherwise, the lookup is ambiguous, and a compile-time error occurs.

For member lookups in types other than type parameters and interfaces, and member lookups in interfaces that are strictly single inheritance (each interface in the inheritance chain has exactly zero or one direct base interface), the effect of the lookup rules is simply that derived members hide base members with the same name or signature. Such single-inheritance lookups are never ambiguous. The ambiguities that can possibly arise from member lookups in multiple-inheritance interfaces are described in §13.2.5.

20.9.3 Simple Names

The following replaces §7.5.2.

A *simple-name* consists of an identifier, optionally followed by a type parameter list.

> *simple-name:*
>   *identifier type-argument-list*_{opt}

A *simple-name* of the form I or of the form $I<A_1, \ldots, A_N>$, where I is an identifier and $<A_1, \ldots, A_N>$ is an optional type argument list, is evaluated and classified as follows.

- If the *simple-name* appears within a *block* and if the *block*'s (or an enclosing *block*'s) local variable declaration space (§3.3) contains a local variable or parameter with the name given by I, then the *simple-name* refers to that local variable or parameter and is classified as a variable. If a type argument list was specified, a compile-time error occurs.

- If the *simple-name* appears within the body of a generic method declaration and if that declaration includes a type parameter with the name given by I, then the *simple-name* refers to that type parameter. If a type argument list was specified, a compile-time error occurs.

- Otherwise, for each instance type T (§20.1.2), starting with the instance type of the immediately enclosing class, struct, or enumeration declaration and continuing with the instance type of each enclosing outer class or struct declaration (if any)

  - If the declaration of T includes a type parameter of the name given by I, then the *simple-name* refers to that type parameter. If a type argument list was specified, a compile-time error occurs.

  - Otherwise, if a member lookup (§20.9.2) of I in T produces a match

    - If T is the instance type of the immediately enclosing class or struct type and the lookup identifies one or more methods, the result is a method group with an associated instance expression of `this`. If a type argument list was specified, it is used in calling a generic method (§20.6.3).

    - If T is the instance type of the immediately enclosing class or struct type, if the lookup identifies an instance member, and if the reference occurs within the *block* of an instance constructor, an instance method, or an instance accessor, the result is the same as a member access (§20.9.4) of the form `this.I`. If a type argument list was specified, a compile-time error occurs.

    - Otherwise, the result is the same as a member access (§20.9.4) of the form `T.I` or `T.I<A_1, ..., A_N>`. In this case, it is a compile-time error for the *simple-name* to refer to an instance member.

- Otherwise, for each namespace N, starting with the namespace in which the *simple-name* occurs, continuing with each enclosing namespace (if any) and ending with the global namespace, the following steps are evaluated until an entity is located.

  - If I is the name of a namespace in N and no type argument list was specified, then the *simple-name* refers to that namespace.

  - Otherwise, if I is the name of an accessible type in N with a matching number of type parameters, then the *simple-name* refers to that type constructed with the given type arguments.

  - Otherwise, if the location where the *simple-name* occurs is enclosed by a namespace declaration for N

    - If the namespace declaration contains a *using-alias-directive* that associates the name given by I with an imported namespace or type and no type argument list was specified, then the *simple-name* refers to that namespace or type.

    - Otherwise, if the namespaces imported by the *using-namespace-directive*s of the namespace declaration contain exactly one type with the name given by I and a matching number of type parameters, then the *simple-name* refers to that type constructed with the given type arguments.

    - Otherwise, if the namespaces imported by the *using-namespace-directive*s of the namespace declaration contain more than one type with the name given by I and a matching number of type parameters, then the *simple-name* is ambiguous and an error occurs.

- Otherwise, the name given by the *simple-name* is undefined, and a compile-time error occurs.

20.9.4 Member Access

The following replaces §7.5.4.

A *member-access* consists of a *primary-expression* or a *predefined-type*, followed by a . token, followed by an *identifier*, optionally followed by a *type-argument-list*.

member-access:
    primary-expression . *identifier* *type-argument-list*$_{opt}$
    predefined-type . *identifier* *type-argument-list*$_{opt}$

predefined-type: one of

bool	byte	char	decimal	double	float	int	long
object	sbyte	short	string	uint	ulong	ushort	

A *member-access* of the form E.I or of the form E.I<A$_1$, ..., A$_N$>, where E is a *primary-expression* or a *predefined-type*, I is an *identifier*, and <A$_1$, ..., A$_N$> is an optional *type-argument-list*, is evaluated and classified as follows.

- If E is a namespace and I is the name of a nested namespace in E and no type argument list was specified, then the result is that namespace.

- If E is a namespace and I is the name of an accessible type in E with a matching number of type parameters, then the result is that type constructed with the given type arguments.

- If E is a *predefined-type* or a *primary-expression* classified as a type, if E is not a type parameter, and if a member lookup (§20.9.2) of I in E produces a match, then E.I is evaluated and classified as follows.

  - If I identifies one or more type declarations, then determine the type declaration with the same number of type parameters (possibly zero) as were supplied in the *type-argument-list*, if present. The result is that type constructed with the given type arguments. If no type declaration has a matching number of type parameters, a compile-time error occurs.

  - If I identifies one or more methods, then the result is a method group with no associated instance expression. If a type argument list was specified, it is used in calling a generic method (§20.6.3).

  - If I identifies a static property, a static field, a static event, a constant, or an enumeration member, and if a type argument list was specified, a compile-time error occurs.

  - If I identifies a static property, then the result is a property access with no associated instance expression.

  - If I identifies a static field

    - If the field is readonly and the reference occurs outside the static constructor of the class or struct in which the field is declared, then the result is a value, namely the value of the static field I in E.

    - Otherwise, the result is a variable, namely the static field I in E.

  - If I identifies a static event

    - If the reference occurs within the class or struct in which the event is declared, and the event was declared without *event-accessor-declarations* (§10.7), then E.I is processed exactly as if I was a static field.

    - Otherwise, the result is an event access with no associated instance expression.

  - If I identifies a constant, then the result is a value, namely the value of that constant.

- If I identifies an enumeration member, then the result is a value, namely the value of that enumeration member.

- Otherwise, E.I is an invalid member reference, and a compile-time error occurs.

• If E is a property access, indexer access, variable, or value, the type of which is T, and a member lookup (§7.3) of I in T produces a match, then E.I is evaluated and classified as follows.

- First, if E is a property or indexer access, then the value of the property or indexer access is obtained (§7.1.1) and E is reclassified as a value.

- If I identifies one or more methods, then the result is a method group with an associated instance expression of E. If a type argument list was specified, it is used in calling a generic method (§20.6.3).

- If I identifies an instance property, an instance field, or an instance event, and if a type argument list was specified, a compile-time error occurs.

- If I identifies an instance property, then the result is a property access with an associated instance expression of E.

- If T is a *class-type* and I identifies an instance field of that *class-type*

  • If the value of E is null, then a System.NullReferenceException is thrown.

  • Otherwise, if the field is readonly and the reference occurs outside an instance constructor of the class in which the field is declared, then the result is a value, namely the value of the field I in the object referenced by E.

  • Otherwise, the result is a variable, namely the field I in the object referenced by E.

- If T is a *struct-type* and I identifies an instance field of that *struct-type*

  • If E is a value, or if the field is readonly and the reference occurs outside an instance constructor of the struct in which the field is declared, then the result is a value, namely the value of the field I in the struct instance given by E.

  • Otherwise, the result is a variable, namely the field I in the struct instance given by E.

- If I identifies an instance event

  • If the reference occurs within the class or struct in which the event is declared, and the event was declared without *event-accessor-declarations* (§10.7), then E.I is processed exactly as if I was an instance field.

  • Otherwise, the result is an event access with an associated instance expression of E.

• Otherwise, E.I is an invalid member reference, and a compile-time error occurs.

20.9.5 **Method Invocations**

The following replaces the part of §7.5.5.1 that describes compile-time processing of a method invocation.

The compile-time processing of a method invocation of the form M(A), where M is a method group (possibly including a *type-argument-list*), and A is an optional *argument-list*, consists of the following steps.

- The set of candidate methods for the method invocation is constructed. For each method F associated with the method group M

  - If F is nongeneric, F is a candidate when

    - M has no type argument list, and

    - F is applicable with respect to A (§7.4.2.1).

  - If F is generic and M has no type argument list, F is a candidate when

    - Type inference (§20.6.4) succeeds, inferring a list of type arguments for the call, and

    - Once the inferred type arguments are substituted for the corresponding method type parameters, the parameter list of F is applicable with respect to A (§7.4.2.1), and

    - The parameter list of F, after substituting type arguments, is not the same as an applicable nongeneric method, possibly in expanded form (§7.4.2.1), declared in the same type as F.

  - If F is generic and M includes a type argument list, F is a candidate when

    - F has the same number of method type parameters as were supplied in the type argument list, and

    - Once the type arguments are substituted for the corresponding method type parameters, the parameter list of F is applicable with respect to A (§7.4.2.1).

- The set of candidate methods is reduced to contain only methods from the most derived types: For each method C.F in the set, where C is the type in which the method F is declared, all methods declared in a base type of C are removed from the set.

- If the resulting set of candidate methods is empty, then no applicable methods exist, and a compile-time error occurs. If the candidate methods are not all declared in the same type, the method invocation is ambiguous, and a compile-time error occurs (this latter situation can only occur for an invocation of a method in an interface that has multiple direct base interfaces, as described in §13.2.5).

- The best method of the set of candidate methods is identified using the overload resolution rules of §7.4.2. If a single best method cannot be identified, the method invocation is ambiguous, and a compile-time error occurs. When performing overload resolution, the parameters of a generic method are considered after substituting the type arguments (supplied or inferred) for the corresponding method type parameters.

- Final validation of the chosen best method is performed.

  - The method is validated in the context of the method group: If the best method is a static method, the method group must have resulted from a *simple-name* or a *member-access* through a type. If the best method is an instance method, the method group must have resulted from a *simple-name*, a *member-access* through a variable or value, or a *base-access*. If neither of these requirements is true, a compile-time error occurs.

  - If the best method is a generic method, the type arguments (supplied or inferred) are checked against the constraints (§20.7.1) declared on the generic method. If any type argument does not satisfy the corresponding constraint(s) on the type parameter, a compile-time error occurs.

Once a method has been selected and validated at compile time by the previous steps, the actual runtime invocation is processed according to the rules of function member invocation described in §7.4.3.

20.9.6 Delegate Creation Expressions

The following replaces the part of §7.5.10.3 that describes compile-time processing of a delegate creation expression.

The compile-time processing of a *delegate-creation-expression* of the form new D (E), where D is a *delegate-type* and E is an *expression*, consists of the following steps.

- If E is a method group

  - A single method is selected corresponding to a method invocation (§20.9.5) of the form E(A), with the following modifications.

    - The parameter types and modifiers (ref or out) of D are used as the argument types and modifiers of the argument list A.

    - Conversions are not considered in applicability tests and type inferencing. In instances where an implicit conversion would normally suffice, types are instead required to be identical.

    - The overload resolution step is not performed. Instead, the set of candidates must include exactly one method that is compatible (§15.1) with D (following substitution of type parameters with type arguments), and this method becomes the one to which the newly created delegate refers. If no matching method exists, or if more than one matching method exists, a compile-time error occurs.

20. Generics

521

- If the selected method is an instance method, the instance expression associated with E determines the target object of the delegate.

- The result is a value of type D, namely a newly created delegate that refers to the selected method and target object.

• Otherwise, if E is a value of a *delegate-type*

- D and E must be compatible (§15.1); otherwise, a compile-time error occurs.

- The result is a value of type D, namely a newly created delegate that refers to the same invocation list as E.

• Otherwise, the delegate creation expression is invalid, and a compile-time error occurs.

20.10 Right-Shift Grammar Changes

The syntax for generics uses the < and > characters to delimit type parameters and type arguments (similar to the syntax used in C++ for templates). Constructed types sometimes nest, as in List<Nullable<int>>, but there is a subtle grammatical problem with such constructs: The lexical grammar will combine the last two characters of this construct into the single token >> (the right shift operator), rather than producing two > tokens, which the syntactic grammar would require. Although a possible solution is to put a space between the two > characters, this is awkward and confusing and does not add to the clarity of the program in any way.

In order to allow these natural constructs and to maintain a simple lexical grammar, the >> and >>= tokens are removed from the lexical grammar and replaced with *right-shift* and *right-shift-assignment* productions.

operator-or-punctuator: one of

{	}	[	]	(	)	.	,	:	;
+	-	*	/	%	&	|	^	!	~
=	<	>	?	++	--	&&	||	==	->
!=	<=	>=	+=	-=	*=	/=	%=	&=	|=
^=	<<	<<=							

right-shift:

>   >

right-shift-assignment:

>   >=

Unlike other productions in the syntactic grammar, no characters of any kind (not even white space) are allowed between the tokens in the *right-shift* and *right-shift-assignment* productions.

The following productions are modified to use *right-shift* and *right-shift-assignment*.

shift-expression:
    additive-expression
    shift-expression << *additive-expression*
    shift-expression *right-shift* *additive-expression*

assignment-operator:
    =
    +=
    -=
    *=
    /=
    %=
    &=
    |=
    ^=
    <<=
    right-shift-assignment

overloadable-binary-operator:
    +
    -
    *
    /
    %
    &
    |
    ^
    <<
    right-shift
    ==
    !=
    >
    <
    >=
    <=

21. Anonymous Methods

21.1 Anonymous Method Expressions

An *anonymous-method-expression* defines an **anonymous method** and evaluates to a special value referencing the method.

> *primary-no-array-creation-expression:*
>
>   ...
>
>   *anonymous-method-expression*
>
> *anonymous-method-expression:*
>   `delegate` *anonymous-method-signature*$_{opt}$ *block*
>
> *anonymous-method-signature:*
>   (*anonymous-method-parameter-list*$_{opt}$)
>
> *anonymous-method-parameter-list:*
>   *anonymous-method-parameter*
>   *anonymous-method-parameter-list* , *anonymous-method-parameter*
>
> *anonymous-method-parameter:*
>   *parameter-modifier*$_{opt}$ *type* *identifier*

An *anonymous-method-expression* is classified as a value with special conversion rules (§21.3). The value does not have a type but can be implicitly converted to a compatible delegate type.

The *anonymous-method-expression* defines a new declaration space for parameters, locals, and constants and a new declaration space for labels (§3.3).

21.2 Anonymous Method Signatures

The optional *anonymous-method-signature* defines the names and types of the formal parameters for the anonymous method. The scope of the parameters of the anonymous method is the *block*. It is a compile-time error for the name of a parameter of the anonymous method to match the name of a local variable, local constant, or parameter whose scope includes the *anonymous-method-expression*.

If an *anonymous-method-expression* has an *anonymous-method-signature*, then the set of compatible delegate types is restricted to those that have the same parameter types and modifiers in the same order (§21.3). If an *anonymous-method-expression* does not have an *anonymous-method-signature*, then the set of compatible delegate types is restricted to those that have no `out` parameters.

Note that an *anonymous-method-signature* cannot include attributes or a parameter array. Nevertheless, an *anonymous-method-signature* may be compatible with a delegate type whose parameter list contains a parameter array.

21.3 Anonymous Method Conversions

An *anonymous-method-expression* is classified as a value with no type. An *anonymous-method-expression* may be used in a *delegate-creation-expression* (§21.3.1). All other valid uses of an *anonymous-method-expression* depend on the implicit conversions defined here.

An implicit conversion (§6.1) exists from an *anonymous-method-expression* to any **compatible** delegate type. If D is a delegate type, and A is an *anonymous-method-expression*, then D is compatible with A if and only if the following two conditions are met.

- First, the parameter types of D must be compatible with A.

    - If A does not contain an *anonymous-method-signature*, then D may have zero or more parameters of any type, as long as no parameter of D has the `out` parameter modifier.

    - If A has an *anonymous-method-signature*, then D must have the same number of parameters, each parameter of A must be of the same type as the corresponding parameter of D, and the presence or absence of the `ref` or `out` modifier on each parameter of A must match the corresponding parameter of D. Whether the last parameter of D is a *parameter-array* is not relevant to the compatibility of A and D.

- Second, the return type of D must be compatible with A. For these rules, A is not considered to contain the *block* of any other anonymous methods.

    - If D is declared with a `void` return type, then any `return` statement contained in A may not specify an expression.

    - If D is declared with a return type of R, then any `return` statement contained in A must specify an expression that is implicitly convertible (§6.1) to R. Furthermore, the end point of the *block* of A must not be reachable.

Besides the implicit conversions to compatible delegate types, no other conversions exist from an *anonymous-method-expression*, even to the type `object`.

The following examples illustrate these rules.

```
delegate void D(int x);

D d1 = delegate { };                    // Ok
D d2 = delegate() { };                  // Error, signature mismatch
D d3 = delegate(long x) { };            // Error, signature mismatch
D d4 = delegate(int x) { };             // Ok
D d5 = delegate(int x) { return; };     // Ok
D d6 = delegate(int x) { return x; };   // Error, return type mismatch

delegate void E(out int x);

E e1 = delegate { };                    // Error, E has an out parameter
E e2 = delegate(out int x) { x = 1; };  // Ok
E e3 = delegate(ref int x) { x = 1; };  // Error, signature mismatch

delegate int P(params int[] a);

P p1 = delegate { };                    // Error, end of block reachable
P p2 = delegate { return; };            // Error, return type mismatch
P p3 = delegate { return 1; };          // Ok
P p4 = delegate { return "Hello"; };    // Error, return type mismatch
P p5 = delegate(int[] a) {              // Ok
    return a[0];
};
P p6 = delegate(params int[] a) {       // Error, params modifier
    return a[0];
};
P p7 = delegate(int[] a) {              // Error, return type mismatch
    if (a.Length > 0) return a[0];
    return "Hello";
};

delegate object Q(params int[] a);

Q q1 = delegate(int[] a) {              // Ok
    if (a.Length > 0) return a[0];
    return "Hello";
};
```

21.3.1 Delegate Creation Expression

A *delegate-creation-expression* (§7.5.10.3) can be used as an alternate syntax for converting an anonymous method to a delegate type. If the *expression* used as the argument of a *delegate-creation-expression* is an *anonymous-method-expression*, then the anonymous method is converted to the given delegate type using the implicit conversion rules defined in §21.3. For example, if D is a delegate type, then this expression

```
new D(delegate { Console.WriteLine("hello"); })
```

is equivalent to the following expression.

```
(D) delegate { Console.WriteLine("hello"); }
```

21.4 Anonymous Method Blocks

The *block* of an *anonymous-method-expression* is subject to the following rules.

- If the anonymous method includes a signature, the parameters specified in the signature are available in the *block*. If the anonymous method has no signature, it can be converted to a delegate type having parameters (§21.3), but the parameters cannot be accessed in the *block*.

- Except for `ref` or `out` parameters specified in the signature (if any) of the nearest enclosing anonymous method, it is a compile-time error for the *block* to access a `ref` or `out` parameter.

- When the type of `this` is a struct type, it is a compile-time error for the *block* to access `this`. This is true whether the access is explicit (as in `this.x`) or implicit (as in `x` where `x` is an instance member of the struct). This rule simply prohibits such access and does not affect whether member lookup results in a member of the struct.

- The *block* has access to the outer variables (§21.5) of the anonymous method. Access of an outer variable will reference the instance of the variable that is active at the time the *anonymous-method-expression* is evaluated (§21.6).

- It is a compile-time error for the *block* to contain a `goto` statement, `break` statement, or `continue` statement whose target is outside the *block* or within the *block* of a contained anonymous method.

- A `return` statement in the *block* returns control from an invocation of the nearest enclosing anonymous method, not from the enclosing function member. An expression specified in a `return` statement must be compatible with the delegate type to which the nearest enclosing *anonymous-method-expression* is converted (§21.3).

It is explicitly unspecified whether there is any way to execute the *block* of an anonymous method other than through evaluation and invocation of the *anonymous-method-expression*. In particular, a compiler may choose to implement an anonymous method by synthesizing one or more named methods or types. The names of any such synthesized elements must be in the space reserved for compiler use: The names must contain two consecutive underscore characters.

21.5 Outer Variables

Any local variable, value parameter, or parameter array whose scope includes the *anonymous-method-expression* is called an **outer variable** of the *anonymous-method-expression*. In an instance function member of a class, the `this` value is considered a value parameter and is an outer variable of any *anonymous-method-expression* contained within the function member.

21.5.1 Captured Outer Variables

When an outer variable is referenced by an anonymous method, the outer variable is said to have been *captured* by the anonymous method. Ordinarily, the lifetime of a local variable is limited to execution of the block or statement with which it is associated (§5.1.7). However, the lifetime of a captured outer variable is extended at least until the delegate referring to the anonymous method becomes eligible for garbage collection.

In the example

```
using System;

delegate int D();

class Test
{
    static D F() {
        int x = 0;
        D result = delegate { return ++x; }
        return result;
    }

    static void Main() {
        D d = F();
        Console.WriteLine(d());
        Console.WriteLine(d());
        Console.WriteLine(d());
    }
}
```

the local variable x is captured by the anonymous method, and the lifetime of x is extended at least until the delegate returned from F becomes eligible for garbage collection (which does not happen until the end of the program). Because each invocation of the anonymous method operates on the same instance of x, the output of the example is as follows.

```
1
2
3
```

When a local variable or a value parameter is captured by an anonymous method, the local variable or parameter is no longer considered to be a fixed variable (§18.3) but is instead considered to be a moveable variable. Thus, any `unsafe` code that takes the address of a captured outer variable must first use the `fixed` statement to fix the variable.

21.5.2 Instantiation of Local Variables

A local variable is considered to be *instantiated* when execution enters the scope of the variable. For example, when the following method is invoked, the local variable x is instantiated and initialized three times—once for each iteration of the loop.

```
static void F() {
    for (int i = 0; i < 3; i++) {
        int x = i * 2 + 1;
        ...
    }
}
```

However, moving the declaration of x outside the loop results in a single instantiation of x.

```
static void F() {
    int x;
    for (int i = 0; i < 3; i++) {
        x = i * 2 + 1;
        ...
    }
}
```

Ordinarily, there is no way to observe exactly how often a local variable is instantiated—because the lifetimes of the instantiations are disjoint, it is possible for each instantiation to simply use the same storage location. However, when an anonymous method captures a local variable, the effects of instantiation become apparent. The example

```
using System;

delegate void D();

class Test
{
    static D[] F() {
        D[] result = new D[3];
        for (int i = 0; i < 3; i++) {
            int x = i * 2 + 1;
            result[i] = delegate { Console.WriteLine(x); };
        }
        return result;
    }

    static void Main() {
        foreach (D d in F()) d();
    }
}
```

produces the following output.

```
1
3
5
```

However, when the declaration of x is moved outside the loop

```
static D[] F() {
    D[] result = new D[3];
    int x;
    for (int i = 0; i < 3; i++) {
        x = i * 2 + 1;
        result[i] = delegate { Console.WriteLine(x); };
    }
    return result;
}
```

the output is as follows.

```
5
5
5
```

Note that the three delegates created in the latter version of F will be equal according to the equality operator (§21.7). Furthermore, note that the compiler is permitted (but not required) to optimize the three instantiations into a single delegate instance (§21.6).

It is possible for anonymous method delegates to share some captured variables yet have separate instances of others. For example, if F is changed to

```
static D[] F() {
    D[] result = new D[3];
    int x = 0;
    for (int i = 0; i < 3; i++) {
        int y = 0;
        result[i] = delegate { Console.WriteLine("{0} {1}", ++x, ++y); };
    }
    return result;
}
```

the three delegates capture the same instance of x but separate instances of y, and the output is as follows.

```
1 1
2 1
3 1
```

Separate anonymous methods can capture the same instance of an outer variable. In the example

```
using System;

delegate void Setter(int value);

delegate int Getter();
```

```
class Test
{
    static void Main() {
        int x = 0;
        Setter s = delegate(int value) { x = value; };
        Getter g = delegate { return x; };
        s(5);
        Console.WriteLine(g());
        s(10);
        Console.WriteLine(g());
    }
}
```

the two anonymous methods capture the same instance of the local variable x, and they can thus "communicate" through that variable. The output of the example is as follows.

```
5
10
```

21.6 Anonymous Method Evaluation

The runtime evaluation of an *anonymous-method-expression* produces a delegate instance that references the anonymous method and the (possibly empty) set of captured outer variables that are active at the time of the evaluation. When a delegate resulting from an *anonymous-method-expression* is invoked, the body of the anonymous method is executed. The code in the body is executed using the set of captured outer variables referenced by the delegate.

The invocation list of a delegate produced from an *anonymous-method-expression* contains a single entry. The exact target object and target method of the delegate are unspecified. In particular, it is unspecified whether the target object of the delegate is null, the this value of the enclosing function member, or some other object.

Evaluation of semantically identical *anonymous-method-expression*s with the same (possibly empty) set of captured outer variable instances is permitted (but not required) to return the same delegate instance. The term "semantically identical" is used here to mean that execution of the anonymous methods will, in all cases, produce the same effects given the same arguments. This rule permits code such as the following to be optimized.

```
delegate double Function(double x);

class Test
{
    static double[] Apply(double[] a, Function f) {
        double[] result = new double[a.Length];
        for (int i = 0; i < a.Length; i++) result[i] = f(a[i]);
        return result;
    }
```

```
static void F(double[] a, double[] b) {
    a = Apply(a, delegate(double x) { return Math.Sin(x); });
    b = Apply(b, delegate(double y) { return Math.Sin(y); });
    ...
}
}
```

Because the two anonymous method delegates have the same (empty) set of captured outer variables, and because the anonymous methods are semantically identical, the compiler is permitted to have the delegates refer to the same target method. Indeed, the compiler is permitted to return the same delegate instance from both anonymous method expressions.

21.7 Delegate Instance Equality

The following rules govern the results produced by the equality operators (§7.9.8) and the `Object.Equals` method for anonymous method delegate instances.

* Delegate instances produced from evaluation of semantically identical *anonymous-method-expression*s with the same (possibly empty) set of captured outer variable instances are permitted (but not required) to be equal.

* Delegate instances produced from evaluation of semantically different *anonymous-method-expression*s or having different sets of captured outer variable instances are never equal.

21.8 Definite Assignment

The definite assignment state of a parameter of an anonymous method is the same as for a parameter of a named method. That is, reference parameters and value parameters are initially definitely assigned, and output parameters are initially unassigned. Furthermore, output parameters must be definitely assigned before the anonymous method returns normally (§5.1.6).

The definite assignment state of an outer variable v on the control transfer to the *block* of an *anonymous-method-expression* is the same as the definite assignment state of v before the *anonymous-method-expression*. That is, definite assignment of outer variables is inherited from the context of the *anonymous-method-expression*. Within the *block* of an *anonymous-method-expression*, definite assignment evolves as in a normal block (§5.3.3).

The definite assignment state of a variable v after an *anonymous-method-expression* is the same as its definite assignment state before the *anonymous-method-expression*.

The example

```
delegate bool Filter(int i);

void F() {
    int max;

    // Error, max is not definitely assigned
    Filter f = delegate(int n) { return n < max; }

    max = 5;
    DoWork(f);
}
```

generates a compile-time error because `max` is not definitely assigned where the anonymous method is declared. The example

```
delegate void D();

void F() {
    int n;
    D d = delegate { n = 1; };

    d();

    // Error, n is not definitely assigned
    Console.WriteLine(n);
}
```

also generates a compile-time error because the assignment to n in the anonymous method has no effect on the definite assignment state of n outside the anonymous method.

21.9 Method Group Conversions

Similar to the implicit anonymous method conversions described in §21.3, an implicit conversion exists from a method group (§7.1) to a compatible delegate type.

Given a method group E and a delegate type D, if a delegate creation expression (§7.5.10.3 and §20.9.6) of the form new D(E) is permitted, then an implicit conversion from E to D also exists, and the result of that conversion is exactly equivalent to writing new D(E).

In the example

```
using System;
using System.Windows.Forms;

class AlertDialog
{
    Label message = new Label();
    Button okButton = new Button();
    Button cancelButton = new Button();
```

```
    public AlertDialog() {
        okButton.Click += new EventHandler(OkClick);
        cancelButton.Click += new EventHandler(CancelClick);
        ...
    }

    void OkClick(object sender, EventArgs e) {
        ...
    }

    void CancelClick(object sender, EventArgs e) {
        ...
    }
}
```

the constructor creates two delegate instances using the new operator. Implicit method group conversions permit this to be shortened to

```
public AlertDialog() {
    okButton.Click += OkClick;
    cancelButton.Click += CancelClick;
    ...
}
```

As with all other implicit and explicit conversions, the cast operator can be used to explicitly perform a particular conversion. Thus, the example

```
object obj = new EventHandler(myDialog.OkClick);
```

could instead be written as follows.

```
object obj = (EventHandler)myDialog.OkClick;
```

Method groups and anonymous method expressions may influence overload resolution, but they do not participate in type inferencing. See §20.6.4 for further details.

21.10 Implementation Example

This section describes a possible implementation of anonymous methods in terms of standard C# constructs. The implementation described here is based on the same principles used by the Microsoft C# compiler, but it is by no means a mandated implementation or the only one possible.

The remainder of this section gives several examples of code that contains anonymous methods with different characteristics. For each example, a corresponding translation to code that uses only standard C# constructs is provided. In the examples, the identifier D is assumed to represent the following delegate type.

```
public delegate void D();
```

The simplest form of an anonymous method is one that captures no outer variables.

```
class Test
{
    static void F() {
        D d = delegate { Console.WriteLine("test"); };
    }
}
```

This can be translated to a delegate instantiation that references a compiler generated static method in which the code of the anonymous method is placed.

```
class Test
{
    static void F() {
        D d = new D(__Method1);
    }

    static void __Method1() {
        Console.WriteLine("test");
    }
}
```

In the following example, the anonymous method references instance members of `this`.

```
class Test
{
    int x;

    void F() {
        D d = delegate { Console.WriteLine(x); };
    }
}
```

This can be translated to a compiler generated instance method containing the code of the anonymous method.

```
class Test
{
    int x;

    void F() {
        D d = new D(__Method1);
    }

    void __Method1() {
        Console.WriteLine(x);
    }
}
```

In this example, the anonymous method captures a local variable.

```
class Test
{
    void F() {
        int y = 123;
        D d = delegate { Console.WriteLine(y); };
    }
}
```

The lifetime of the local variable must now be extended to at least the lifetime of the anonymous method delegate. This can be achieved by "lifting" the local variable into a field of a compiler-generated class. Instantiation of the local variable (§21.5.2) then corresponds to creating an instance of the compiler-generated class, and accessing the local variable corresponds to accessing a field in the instance of the compiler-generated class. Furthermore, the anonymous method becomes an instance method of the compiler-generated class.

```
class Test
{
    void F() {
        __Locals1 __locals1 = new __Locals1();
        __locals1.y = 123;
        D d = new D(__locals1.__Method1);
    }

    class __Locals1
    {
        public int y;

        public void __Method1() {
            Console.WriteLine(y);
        }
    }
}
```

Finally, the following anonymous method captures this as well as two local variables with different lifetimes.

```
class Test
{
    int x;

    void F() {
        int y = 123;
        for (int i = 0; i < 10; i++) {
            int z = i * 2;
            D d = delegate { Console.WriteLine(x + y + z); };
        }
    }
}
```

Here, a compiler-generated class is created for each statement block in which locals are captured such that the locals in the different blocks can have independent lifetimes. An

instance of __Locals2, the compiler-generated class for the inner statement block, contains the local variable z and a field that references an instance of __Locals1. An instance
of __Locals1, the compiler-generated class for the outer statement block, contains the
local variable y and a field that references this of the enclosing function member. With
these data structures, it is possible to reach all captured outer variables through an instance
of __Locals2, and the code of the anonymous method can thus be implemented as an
instance method of that class.

```
class Test
{
    void F() {
        __Locals1 __locals1 = new __Locals1();
        __locals1.__this = this;
        __locals1.y = 123;
        for (int i = 0; i < 10; i++) {
            __Locals2 __locals2 = new __Locals2();
            __locals2.__locals1 = __locals1;
            __locals2.z = i * 2;
            D d = new D(__locals2.__Method1);
        }
    }

    class __Locals1
    {
        public Test __this;
        public int y;
    }

    class __Locals2
    {
        public __Locals1 __locals1;
        public int z;

        public void __Method1() {
            Console.WriteLine(__locals1.__this.x + __locals1.y + z);
        }
    }
}
```

22. Iterators

22.1 Iterator Blocks

An iterator block is a *block* (§8.2) that yields an ordered sequence of values. An iterator block is distinguished from a normal statement block by the presence of one or more `yield` statements.

- The `yield return` statement produces the next value of the iteration.

- The `yield break` statement indicates that the iteration is complete.

An iterator block may be used as a *method-body*, *operator-body*, or *accessor-body* as long as the return type of the corresponding function member is one of the enumerator interfaces (§22.1.1) or one of the enumerable interfaces (§22.1.2).

Iterator blocks are not a distinct element in the C# grammar. They are restricted in several ways and have a major effect on the semantics of a function member declaration, but they are grammatically just blocks.

When a function member is implemented using an iterator block, it is a compile-time error for the formal parameter list of the function member to specify any `ref` or `out` parameters.

It is a compile-time error for a `return` statement to appear in an iterator block (but `yield return` statements are permitted).

It is a compile-time error for an iterator block to contain an unsafe context (§18.1). An iterator block always defines a safe context, even when its declaration is nested in an unsafe context.

22.1.1 Enumerator Interfaces

The **enumerator interfaces** are `System.Collections.IEnumerator` and all instantiations of `System.Collections.Generic.IEnumerator<T>`. In this chapter, these interfaces are referenced as `IEnumerator` and `IEnumerator<T>`, respectively.

22.1.2 Enumerable Interfaces

The *enumerable interfaces* are System.Collections.IEnumerable and all instantiations of System.Collections.Generic.IEnumerable<T>. In this chapter, these interfaces are referenced as IEnumerable and IEnumerable<T>, respectively.

22.1.3 Yield Type

An iterator block produces a sequence of values, all of the same type. This type is called the *yield type* of the iterator block.

- The yield type of an iterator block used to implement a function member that returns IEnumerator or IEnumerable is object.

- The yield type of an iterator block used to implement a function member that returns IEnumerator<T> or IEnumerable<T> is T.

22.1.4 This Access

Within an iterator block of an instance member of a class, the expression this is classified as a value. The type of the value is the class within which the usage occurs, and the value is a reference to the object for which the member was invoked.

Within an iterator block of an instance member of a struct, the expression this is classified as a variable. The type of the variable is the struct within which the usage occurs. The variable represents a *copy* of the struct for which the member was invoked. The this variable in an iterator block of an instance member of a struct behaves exactly the same as a *value* parameter of the struct type.

22.2 Enumerator Objects

When a function member returning an enumerator interface type is implemented using an iterator block, invoking the function member does not immediately execute the code in the iterator block. Instead, an *enumerator object* is created and returned. This object encapsulates the code specified in the iterator block, and execution of the code in the iterator block occurs when the enumerator object's MoveNext method is invoked. An enumerator object has the following characteristics.

- It implements IEnumerator and IEnumerator<T>, where T is the yield type of the iterator block.

- It implements System.IDisposable.

- It is initialized with a copy of the argument values (if any) and instance value passed to the function member.

- It has four potential states, *before*, *running*, *suspended*, and *after*, and is initially in the *before* state.

An enumerator object is typically an instance of a compiler-generated enumerator class that encapsulates the code in the iterator block and implements the enumerator interfaces, but other methods of implementation are possible. If an enumerator class is generated by the compiler, the class will be nested, directly or indirectly, in the class containing the function member, the class will have private accessibility, and the class will have a name reserved for compiler use (§2.4.2).

An enumerator object may implement more interfaces than those specified here.

The following sections describe the exact behavior of the `MoveNext`, `Current`, and `Dispose` members of the `IEnumerable` and `IEnumerable<T>` interface implementations provided by an enumerator object.

Note that enumerator objects do not support the `IEnumerator.Reset` method. Invoking this method will throw a `System.NotSupportedException`.

22.2.1 The MoveNext Method

The `MoveNext` method of an enumerator object encapsulates the code of an iterator block. Invoking the `MoveNext` method executes code in the iterator block and sets the `Current` property of the enumerator object as appropriate. The precise action performed by `MoveNext` depends on the state of the enumerator object when `MoveNext` is invoked.

- If the state of the enumerator object is *before*, invoking `MoveNext`

  - Changes the state to *running*.

  - Initializes the parameters (including `this`) of the iterator block to the argument values and instance value saved when the enumerator object was initialized.

  - Executes the iterator block from the beginning until execution is interrupted (as described next).

- If the state of the enumerator object is *running*, the result of invoking `MoveNext` is unspecified.

- If the state of the enumerator object is *suspended*, invoking `MoveNext`

  - Changes the state to *running*.

- Restores the values of all local variables and parameters (including `this`) to the values saved when execution of the iterator block was last suspended. Note that the contents of any objects referenced by these variables may have changed since the previous call to `MoveNext`.

  - Resumes execution of the iterator block immediately following the `yield return` statement that caused the suspension of execution and continues until execution is interrupted (as described next).

- If the state of the enumerator object is *after*, invoking `MoveNext` returns `false`.

When `MoveNext` executes the iterator block, execution can be interrupted in four ways: by a `yield return` statement, by a `yield break` statement, by encountering the end of the iterator block, and by an exception being thrown and propagated out of the iterator block.

- When a `yield return` statement is encountered (§22.4), the following happens.

  - The expression given in the statement is evaluated, implicitly converted to the yield type, and assigned to the `Current` property of the enumerator object.

  - Execution of the iterator body is suspended. The values of all local variables and parameters (including `this`) are saved, as is the location of this `yield return` statement. If the `yield return` statement is within one or more `try` blocks, the associated `finally` blocks are *not* executed at this time.

  - The state of the enumerator object is changed to *suspended*.

  - The `MoveNext` method returns `true` to its caller, indicating that the iteration successfully advanced to the next value.

- When a `yield break` statement is encountered (§22.4), the following happens.

  - If the `yield break` statement is within one or more `try` blocks, the associated `finally` blocks are executed.

  - The state of the enumerator object is changed to *after*.

  - The `MoveNext` method returns `false` to its caller, indicating that the iteration is complete.

- When the end of the iterator body is encountered, the following happens.

  - The state of the enumerator object is changed to *after*.

  - The `MoveNext` method returns `false` to its caller, indicating that the iteration is complete.

- When an exception is thrown and propagated out of the iterator block, the following happens.

  - Appropriate `finally` blocks in the iterator body will have been executed by the exception propagation.

  - The state of the enumerator object is changed to *after*.

  - The exception propagation continues to the caller of the `MoveNext` method.

22.2.2 The Current Property

An enumerator object's `Current` property is affected by `yield return` statements in the iterator block.

When an enumerator object is in the *suspended* state, the value of `Current` is the value set by the last call to `MoveNext`. When an enumerator object is in the *before*, *running*, or *after* states, the result of accessing `Current` is unspecified.

For an iterator block with a yield type other than `object`, the result of accessing `Current` through the enumerator object's `IEnumerable` implementation corresponds to accessing `Current` through the enumerator object's `IEnumerator<T>` implementation and casting the result to `object`.

22.2.3 The Dispose Method

The `Dispose` method is used to clean up the iteration by bringing the enumerator object to the *after* state.

- If the state of the enumerator object is *before*, invoking `Dispose` changes the state to *after*.

- If the state of the enumerator object is *running*, the result of invoking `Dispose` is unspecified.

- If the state of the enumerator object is *suspended*, invoking `Dispose`

  - Changes the state to *running*.

  - Executes any finally blocks as if the last executed `yield return` statement were a `yield break` statement. If this causes an exception to be thrown and propagated out of the iterator body, the state of the enumerator object is set to *after*, and the exception is propagated to the caller of the `Dispose` method.

  - Changes the state to *after*.

- If the state of the enumerator object is *after*, invoking `Dispose` has no effect.

22.3 Enumerable Objects

When a function member returning an enumerable interface type is implemented using an iterator block, invoking the function member does not immediately execute the code in the iterator block. Instead, an *enumerable object* is created and returned. The enumerable object's GetEnumerator method returns an enumerator object that encapsulates the code specified in the iterator block, and execution of the code in the iterator block occurs when the enumerator object's MoveNext method is invoked. An enumerable object has the following characteristics.

- It implements IEnumerable and IEnumerable<T>, where T is the yield type of the iterator block.

- It is initialized with a copy of the argument values (if any) and instance value passed to the function member.

An enumerable object is typically an instance of a compiler-generated enumerable class that encapsulates the code in the iterator block and implements the enumerable interfaces, but other methods of implementation are possible. If an enumerable class is generated by the compiler, the class will be nested, directly or indirectly, in the class containing the function member, the class will have private accessibility, and the class will have a name reserved for compiler use (§2.4.2).

An enumerable object may implement more interfaces than those specified here. In particular, an enumerable object may also implement IEnumerator and IEnumerator<T>, enabling it to serve as both an enumerable and an enumerator. In that type of implementation, the first time an enumerable object's GetEnumerator method is invoked, the enumerable object itself is returned. Subsequent invocations of the enumerable object's GetEnumerator, if any, return a copy of the enumerable object. Thus, each returned enumerator has its own state and changes in one enumerator will not affect another.

22.3.1 The GetEnumerator Method

An enumerable object provides an implementation of the GetEnumerator methods of the IEnumerable and IEnumerable<T> interfaces. The two GetEnumerator methods share a common implementation that acquires and returns an available enumerator object. The enumerator object is initialized with the argument values and instance value saved when the enumerable object was initialized, but otherwise the enumerator object functions as described in §22.2.

22.4 **The yield Statement**

The `yield` statement is used in an iterator block to yield a value to the enumerator object or to signal the end of the iteration.

> *embedded-statement:*
>
> ...
>
> *yield-statement*
>
> *yield-statement:*
> yield return *expression* ;
> yield break ;

To ensure compatibility with existing programs, `yield` is not a reserved word, and `yield` has special meaning only when it is used immediately before a `return` or `break` keyword. In other contexts, `yield` can be used as an identifier.

There are several restrictions on where a `yield` statement can appear, as described in the following list.

- It is a compile-time error for a `yield` statement (of either form) to appear outside a *method-body, operator-body,* or *accessor-body.*

- It is a compile-time error for a `yield` statement (of either form) to appear inside an anonymous method.

- It is a compile-time error for a `yield` statement (of either form) to appear in the `finally` clause of a `try` statement.

- It is a compile-time error for a `yield return` statement to appear anywhere in a `try` statement that contains `catch` clauses.

The following example shows some valid and invalid uses of `yield` statements.

```
delegate IEnumerable<int> D();

IEnumerator<int> GetEnumerator() {
    try {
        yield return 1;     // Ok
        yield break;        // Ok
    }
    finally {
        yield return 2;     // Error, yield in finally
        yield break;        // Error, yield in finally
    }
```

```
        try {
            yield return 3;     // Error, yield return in try...catch
            yield break;        // Ok
        }
        catch {
            yield return 4;     // Error, yield return in try...catch
            yield break;        // Ok
        }

        D d = delegate {
            yield return 5;     // Error, yield in an anonymous method
        };
    }

    int MyMethod() {
        yield return 1;         // Error, wrong return type for an iterator block
    }
```

An implicit conversion (§6.1) must exist from the type of the expression in the `yield return` statement to the yield type (§22.1.3) of the iterator block.

A `yield return` statement is executed as follows.

- The expression given in the statement is evaluated, implicitly converted to the yield type, and assigned to the `Current` property of the enumerator object.

- Execution of the iterator block is suspended. If the `yield return` statement is within one or more `try` blocks, the associated `finally` blocks are *not* executed at this time.

- The `MoveNext` method of the enumerator object returns `true` to its caller, indicating that the enumerator object successfully advanced to the next item.

The next call to the enumerator object's `MoveNext` method resumes execution of the iterator block from where it was last suspended.

A `yield break` statement is executed as follows.

- If the `yield break` statement is enclosed by one or more `try` blocks with associated `finally` blocks, control is initially transferred to the `finally` block of the innermost `try` statement. When and if control reaches the end point of a `finally` block, control is transferred to the `finally` block of the next enclosing `try` statement. This process is repeated until the `finally` blocks of all enclosing `try` statements have been executed.

- Control is returned to the caller of the iterator block. This is either the `MoveNext` method or the `Dispose` method of the enumerator object.

Because a `yield break` statement unconditionally transfers control elsewhere, the end point of a `yield break` statement is never reachable.

22.4.1 **Definite Assignment**

For a `yield return` statement *stmt* of the form

```
yield return expr;
```

- A variable *v* has the same definite assignment state at the beginning of *expr* as at the beginning of *stmt*.

- If a variable *v* is definitely assigned at the end of *expr*, it is definitely assigned at the end point of *stmt*; otherwise, it is not definitely assigned at the end point of *stmt*.

22.5 **Implementation Example**

This section describes a possible implementation of iterators in terms of standard C# constructs. The implementation described here is based on the same principles used by the Microsoft C# compiler, but it is by no means a mandated implementation or the only one possible.

The following `Stack<T>` class implements its `GetEnumerator` method using an iterator. The iterator enumerates the elements of the stack in top to bottom order.

```
using System;
using System.Collections;
using System.Collections.Generic;

class Stack<T>: IEnumerable<T>
{
    T[] items;
    int count;

    public void Push(T item) {
        if (items == null) {
            items = new T[4];
        }
        else if (items.Length == count) {
            T[] newItems = new T[count * 2];
            Array.Copy(items, 0, newItems, 0, count);
            items = newItems;
        }
        items[count++] = item;
    }

    public T Pop() {
        T result = items[--count];
        items[count] = T.default;
        return result;
    }
```

```
        public IEnumerator<T> GetEnumerator() {
            for (int i = count - 1; i >= 0; --i) yield return items[i];
        }
    }
```

The GetEnumerator method can be translated into an instantiation of a compiler-generated enumerator class that encapsulates the code in the iterator block, as shown in the following.

```
    class Stack<T>: IEnumerable<T>
    {
        ...

        public IEnumerator<T> GetEnumerator() {
            return new __Enumerator1(this);
        }

        class __Enumerator1: IEnumerator<T>, IEnumerator
        {
            int __state;
            T __current;
            Stack<T> __this;
            int i;

            public __Enumerator1(Stack<T> __this) {
                this.__this = __this;
            }

            public T Current {
                get { return __current; }
            }

            object IEnumerator.Current {
                get { return __current; }
            }

            public bool MoveNext() {
                switch (__state) {
                    case 1: goto __state1;
                    case 2: goto __state2;
                }
                i = __this.count - 1;
            __loop:
                if (i < 0) goto __state2;
                __current = __this.items[i];
                __state = 1;
                return true;
            __state1:
                --i;
                goto __loop;
            __state2:
                __state = 2;
                return false;
            }
```

```
        public void Dispose() {
            __state = 2;
        }

        void IEnumerator.Reset() {
            throw new NotSupportedException();
        }
    }
}
```

In the preceding translation, the code in the iterator block is turned into a state machine and placed in the MoveNext method of the enumerator class. Furthermore, the local variable i is turned into a field in the enumerator object so it can continue to exist across invocations of MoveNext.

The following example prints a simple multiplication table of the integers 1 through 10. The FromTo method in the example returns an enumerable object and is implemented using an iterator.

```
using System;
using System.Collections.Generic;

class Test
{
    static IEnumerable<int> FromTo(int from, int to) {
        while (from <= to) yield return from++;
    }

    static void Main() {
        IEnumerable<int> e = FromTo(1, 10);
        foreach (int x in e) {
            foreach (int y in e) {
                Console.Write("{0,3} ", x * y);
            }
            Console.WriteLine();
        }
    }
}
```

The FromTo method can be translated into an instantiation of a compiler-generated enumerable class that encapsulates the code in the iterator block, as shown in the following.

```
using System;
using System.Threading;
using System.Collections;
using System.Collections.Generic;

class Test
{
    ...

    static IEnumerable<int> FromTo(int from, int to) {
        return new __Enumerable1(from, to);
    }
```

```
class __Enumerable1:
    IEnumerable<int>, IEnumerable,
    IEnumerator<int>, IEnumerator
{
    int __state;
    int __current;
    int __from;
    int from;
    int to;
    int i;

    public __Enumerable1(int __from, int to) {
        this.__from = __from;
        this.to = to;
    }

    public IEnumerator<int> GetEnumerator() {
        __Enumerable1 result = this;
        if (Interlocked.CompareExchange(ref __state, 1, 0) != 0) {
            result = new __Enumerable1(__from, to);
            result.__state = 1;
        }
        result.from = result.__from;
        return result;
    }

    IEnumerator IEnumerable.GetEnumerator() {
        return (IEnumerator)GetEnumerator();
    }

    public int Current {
        get { return __current; }
    }

    object IEnumerator.Current {
        get { return __current; }
    }

    public bool MoveNext() {
        switch (__state) {
        case 1:
            if (from > to) goto case 2;
            __current = from++;
            __state = 1;
            return true;
        case 2:
            __state = 2;
            return false;
        default:
            throw new InvalidOperationException();
        }
    }

    public void Dispose() {
        __state = 2;
    }
```

```
            void IEnumerator.Reset() {
                throw new NotSupportedException();
            }
        }
    }
```

The enumerable class implements both the enumerable interfaces and the enumerator interfaces, enabling it to serve as both an enumerable and an enumerator. The first time the GetEnumerator method is invoked, the enumerable object itself is returned. Subsequent invocations of the enumerable object's GetEnumerator, if any, return a copy of the enumerable object. Thus, each returned enumerator has its own state, and changes in one enumerator will not affect another. The Interlocked.CompareExchange method is used to ensure thread-safe operation.

The from and to parameters are turned into fields in the enumerable class. Because from is modified in the iterator block, an additional __from field is introduced to hold the initial value given to from in each enumerator.

The MoveNext method throws an InvalidOperationException if it is called when __state is 0. This protects against the use of the enumerable object as an enumerator object without first calling GetEnumerator.

23. Partial Types

23.1 Partial Declarations

A new type modifier, `partial`, is used when defining a type in multiple parts. To ensure compatibility with existing programs, this modifier is different from other modifiers: Like `get` and `set`, it is not a keyword, and it must appear immediately before one of the keywords `class`, `struct`, or `interface`.

class-declaration:
> *attributes*_{opt}   *class-modifiers*_{opt}   `partial`_{opt}   `class` *identifier*
>> *type-parameter-list*_{opt}   *class-base*_{opt}   *type-parameter-constraints-clauses*_{opt}
>> *class-body*   ;_{opt}

struct-declaration:
> *attributes*_{opt}   *struct-modifiers*_{opt}   `partial`_{opt}   `struct` *identifier*
>> *type-parameter-list*_{opt}   *struct-interfaces*_{opt}   *type-parameter-constraints-clauses*_{opt}
>> *struct-body*   ;_{opt}

interface-declaration:
> *attributes*_{opt}   *interface-modifiers*_{opt}   `partial`_{opt}   `interface` *identifier*
>> *type-parameter-list*_{opt}   *interface-base*_{opt}   *type-parameter-constraints-clauses*_{opt}
>> *interface-body*   ;_{opt}

Each part of a partial type declaration must include a `partial` modifier and must be declared in the same namespace as the other parts. The `partial` modifier indicates that additional parts of the type declaration may exist elsewhere, but the existence of such additional parts is not a requirement; it is valid for just a single declaration of a type to include the `partial` modifier.

All parts of a partial type must be compiled together such that the parts can be merged at compile time. Partial types specifically do not allow already compiled types to be extended.

Nested types may be declared in multiple parts by using the `partial` modifier. Typically, the containing type is declared using `partial` as well, and each part of the nested type is declared in a different part of the containing type.

The `partial` modifier is not permitted on delegate or enum declarations.

23.1.1 Attributes

The attributes of a partial type are determined by combining, in an unspecified order, the attributes of each of the parts. If an attribute is placed on multiple parts, it is equivalent to specifying the attribute multiple times on the type. For example, the two parts

```
[Attr1, Attr2("hello")]
partial class A {}

[Attr3, Attr2("goodbye")]
partial class A {}
```

are equivalent to a declaration such as the following.

```
[Attr1, Attr2("hello"), Attr3, Attr2("goodbye")]
class A {}
```

Attributes on type parameters combine in a similar fashion.

23.1.2 Modifiers

When a partial type declaration includes an accessibility specification (the `public`, `protected`, `internal`, and `private` modifiers), it must agree with all other parts that include an accessibility specification. If no part of a partial type includes an accessibility specification, the type is given the appropriate default accessibility (§3.5.1).

If one or more partial declarations of a nested type includes a `new` modifier, no warning is reported if the nested type hides an inherited member (§3.7.1.2).

If one or more partial declarations of a class includes an `abstract` modifier, the class is considered abstract (§10.1.1.1). Otherwise, the class is considered nonabstract.

If one or more partial declarations of a class includes a `sealed` modifier, the class is considered sealed (§10.1.1.2). Otherwise, the class is considered unsealed.

Note that a class cannot be both abstract and sealed.

When the `unsafe` modifier is used on a partial type declaration, only that particular part is considered an unsafe context (§18.1).

23.1.3 Type Parameters and Constraints

If a generic type is declared in multiple parts, each part must state the type parameters. Each part must have the same number of type parameters, and the same name for each type parameter, in order.

When a partial generic type declaration includes type parameter constraints (`where` clauses), the constraints must agree with all other parts that include constraints. Specifically, each part that includes constraints must have constraints for the same set of type parameters, and for each type parameter the set of class, interface, and constructor constrains must be the same. If no part of a partial generic type specifies type parameter constraints, the type parameters are considered unconstrained.

The example

```
partial class Dictionary<K,V>
    where K: IComparable<K>
    where V: IKeyProvider<K>, IPersistable
{
    ...
}

partial class Dictionary<K,V>
    where V: IPersistable, IKeyProvider<K>
    where K: IComparable<K>
{
    ...
}

partial class Dictionary<K,V>
{
    ...
}
```

is correct because those parts that include constrains (the first two) effectively specify the same set of class, interface, and constructor constraints for the same set of type parameters, respectively.

23.1.4 Base Class

When a partial class declaration includes a base class specification, it must agree with all other parts that include a base class specification. If no part of a partial class includes a base class specification, the base class becomes `System.Object` (§10.1.2.1).

23.1.5 Base Interfaces

The set of base interfaces for a type declared in multiple parts is the union of the base interfaces specified on each part. A particular base interface may only be named once on each part, but it is permitted for multiple parts to name the same base interface(s). There must only be one implementation of the members of any given base interface.

In the example

```
partial class C: IA, IB {...}
partial class C: IC {...}
partial class C: IA, IB {...}
```

the set of base interfaces for class `C` is `IA`, `IB`, and `IC`.

Typically, each part provides an implementation of the interface(s) declared on that part; however, this is not a requirement. A part may provide the implementation for an interface declared on a different part.

```
partial class X
{
    int IComparable.CompareTo(object o) {...}
}

partial class X: IComparable
{
    ...
}
```

23.1.6 Members

The members of a type declared in multiple parts is simply the union of the members declared in each part. The bodies of all parts of the type declaration share the same declaration space (§3.3), and the scope of each member (§3.7) extends to the bodies of all the parts. The accessibility domain of any member always includes all the parts of the enclosing type; a `private` member declared in one part is freely accessible from another part. It is a compile-time error to declare the same member in more than one part of the type, unless that member is a type with the `partial` modifier.

```
partial class A
{
    int x;                      // Error, cannot declare x more than once

    partial class Inner         // Ok, Inner is a partial type
    {
        int y;
    }
}

partial class A
{
    int x;                      // Error, cannot declare x more than once

    partial class Inner         // Ok, Inner is a partial type
    {
        int z;
    }
}
```

Although the ordering of members within a type is not significant to C# code, it may be significant when interfacing with other languages and environments. In these cases, the ordering of members within a type declared in multiple parts is undefined.

23.2 Name Binding

Although each part of an extensible type must be declared within the same namespace, the parts are typically written within different namespace declarations. Thus, different `using` directives (§9.3) may be present for each part. When interpreting simple names (§7.5.2) within one part, only the `using` directives of the namespace declaration(s) enclosing that part are considered. This may result in the same identifier having different meanings in different parts.

```
namespace N
{
    using List = System.Collections.ArrayList;

    partial class A
    {
        List x;              // x has type System.Collections.ArrayList
    }
}

namespace N
{
    using List = Widgets.LinkedList;

    partial class A
    {
        List y;              // y has type Widgets.LinkedList
    }
}
```

23. Partial Types

Part III

Appendixes

A. Documentation Comments

C# provides a mechanism for programmers to document their code using a special comment syntax that contains Extensible Markup Language (XML) text. In source code files, comments having a certain form can be used to direct a tool to produce XML from those comments and the source code elements that they precede. Comments using such syntax are called *documentation comments*. They must immediately precede a user-defined type (such as a class, delegate, or interface) or a member (such as a field, event, property, or method). The XML generation tool is called the *documentation generator*. (This generator could be, but does not need to be, the C# compiler itself.) The output produced by the documentation generator is called the *documentation file*. A documentation file is used as input to a *documentation viewer*; a tool intended to produce some sort of visual display of type information and its associated documentation.

This specification suggests a set of tags to be used in documentation comments, but using these tags is not required, and other tags may be used if desired, as long the rules of well-formed XML are followed.

A.1 Introduction

Comments having a special form can be used to direct a tool to produce XML from those comments and the source code elements that they precede. Such comments are single-line comments that start with three slashes (///) or delimited comments that start with a slash and two stars (/**). They must immediately precede a user-defined type (such as a class, delegate, or interface) or a member (such as a field, event, property, or method) that they annotate. Attribute sections (§17.2) are considered part of declarations, so documentation comments must precede attributes applied to a type or member.

Syntax:

> *single-line-doc-comment:*
>   */ / /*   *input-characters$_{opt}$*
>
> *delimited-doc-comment:*
>   */ * **   *delimited-comment-characters$_{opt}$*   ** /*

In a *single-line-doc-comment*, if there is a *whitespace* character following the `///` characters on each of the *single-line-doc-comment*s adjacent to the current *single-line-doc-comment*, then that *whitespace* character is not included in the XML output.

In a *delimited-doc-comment*, if the first non-*whitespace* character on the second line is an *asterisk* and the same pattern of optional *whitespace* characters and an *asterisk* character are repeated at the beginning of each line within the *delimited-doc-comment*, then the characters of the repeated pattern are not included in the XML output. The pattern may include *whitespace* characters after, as well as before, the *asterisk* character. For example

Example:

```
/// <remarks>Class <c>Point</c> models a point in a two-dimensional
/// plane.</remarks>
///
public class Point
{
    /// <remarks>method <c>draw</c> renders the point.</remarks>
    void draw() {…}
}
```

The text within documentation comments must be well formed according to the rules of XML (http://www.w3.org/TR/REC-xml). If the XML is ill formed, a warning is generated and the documentation file will contain a comment saying that an error was encountered.

Although developers are free to create their own set of tags, a recommended set is defined in §A.2. Some of the recommended tags have special meanings.

- The `<param>` tag is used to describe parameters. If such a tag is used, the documentation generator must verify that the specified parameter exists and that all parameters are described in documentation comments. If such verification fails, the documentation generator issues a warning.

- The `cref` attribute can be attached to any tag to provide a reference to a code element. The documentation generator must verify that this code element exists. If the verification fails, the documentation generator issues a warning. When looking for a name described in a `cref` attribute, the documentation generator must respect namespace visibility according to `using` statements appearing within the source code.

- The `<summary>` tag is intended to be used by a documentation viewer to display additional information about a type or member.

- The `<include>` tag includes information from an external XML file.

Note carefully that the documentation file does not provide full information about the type and members (for example, it does not contain any type information). To get such information about a type or member, the documentation file must be used in conjunction with reflection on the actual type or member.

A.2 Recommended Tags

The documentation generator must accept and process any tag that is valid according to the rules of XML. The following tags provide commonly used functionality in user documentation. (Of course, other tags are possible.)

Tag	Section	Purpose
`<c>`	A.2.1	Sets text in a code-like font
`<code>`	A.2.2	Sets one or more lines of source code or program output
`<example>`	A.2.3	Indicates an example
`<exception>`	A.2.4	Identifies the exceptions a method can throw
`<include>`	A.2.5	Includes XML from an external file
`<list>`	A.2.6	Creates a list or table
`<para>`	A.2.7	Permits structure to be added to text
`<param>`	A.2.8	Describes a parameter for a method or constructor
`<paramref>`	A.2.9	Identifies that a word is a parameter name
`<permission>`	A.2.10	Documents the security accessibility of a member
`<remarks>`	A.2.11	Describes a type
`<returns>`	A.2.12	Describes the return value of a method
`<see>`	A.2.13	Specifies a link
`<seealso>`	A.2.15	Generates a *See Also* entry
`<summary>`	A.2.15	Describes a member of a type
`<value>`	A.2.16	Describes a property

A.2.1 <c>

This tag provides a mechanism to indicate that a fragment of text within a description should be set in a special font such as that used for a block of code. For lines of actual code, use <code> (§A.2.2).

Syntax:

```
<c>text</c>
```

Example:

```
/// <remarks>Class <c>Point</c> models a point in a two-dimensional
/// plane.</remarks>
public class Point
{
    // ...
}
```

A.2.2 <code>

This tag is used to set one or more lines of source code or program output in some special font. For small code fragments in narrative, use <c> (§A.2.1).

Syntax:

```
<code>source code or program output</code>
```

Example:

```
/// <summary>This method changes the point's location by
/// the given x- and y-offsets.
/// <example>For example:
/// <code>
/// Point p = new Point(3,5);
/// p.Translate(-1,3);
/// </code>
/// results in <c>p</c>'s having the value (2,8).
/// </example>
/// </summary>
public void Translate(int xor, int yor) {
    X += xor;
    Y += yor;
}
```

A.2.3 <example>

This tag allows example code within a comment to specify how a method or other library member may be used. Ordinarily, this would also involve using the tag <code> (§A.2.2) as well.

Syntax:

```
<example>description</example>
```

Example:

See <code> (§A.2.2) for an example.

A.2.4 <exception>

This tag provides a way to document the exceptions a method can throw.

Syntax:

```
<exception cref="member">description</exception>
```

where

- *member* is the name of a member. The documentation generator checks that the given member exists and translates member to the canonical element name in the documentation file.

- *description* is a description of the circumstances in which the exception is thrown.

Example:

```
public class DataBaseOperations
{
    /// <exception cref="MasterFileFormatCorruptException"></exception>
    /// <exception cref="MasterFileLockedOpenException"></exception>
    public static void ReadRecord(int flag) {
        if (flag == 1)
            throw new MasterFileFormatCorruptException();
        else if (flag == 2)
            throw new MasterFileLockedOpenException();
        // …
    }
}
```

A.2.5 <include>

This tag allows including information from an XML document that is external to the source code file. The external file must be a well-formed XML document, and an XPath expression is applied to that document to specify what XML from that document to include. The <include> tag is then replaced with the selected XML from the external document.

Syntax:

```
<include file="filename" path="xpath"/>
```

A. Comments

where

- *filename* is the filename of an external XML file. The filename is interpreted relative to the file that contains the include tag.

- *xpath* is an XPath expression that selects some of the XML in the external XML file.

Example:

If the source code contained a declaration like the following

```
/// <include file="docs.xml" path='extradoc/class[@name="IntList"]/*' />
public class IntList { … }
```

and the external file docs.xml had the following contents

```
<?xml version="1.0"?>
<extradoc>
<class name="IntList">
        <summary>
            Contains a list of integers.
        </summary>
    </class>
    <class name="StringList">
        <summary>
            Contains a list of integers.
        </summary>
    </class>
</extradoc>
```

then the same documentation is output as if the source code contained.

```
/// <summary>
/// Contains a list of integers.
/// </summary>
public class IntList { … }
```

A.2.6 <list>

This tag is used to create a list or table of items. It may contain a <listheader> block to define the heading row of either a table or definition list. (When defining a table, only an entry for term in the heading need be supplied.)

Each item in the list is specified with an <item> block. When creating a definition list, both *term* and *description* must be specified. However, for a table, bulleted list, or numbered list, only description need be specified.

Syntax:

```
<list type="bullet" | "number" | "table">
    <listheader>
        <term>term</term>
        <description>description</description>
    </listheader>
    <item>
        <term>term</term>
        <description>description</description>
    </item>
        ...
    <item>
        <term>term</term>
        <description>description</description>
    </item>
</list>
```

where

- *term* is the term to define, whose definition is in `description`.

- *description* is either an item in a bullet or numbered list, or the definition of a term.

Example:

```
public class MyClass
{
    /// <remarks>Here is an example of a bulleted list:
    /// <list type="bullet">
    /// <item>
    /// <description>Item 1.</description>
    /// </item>
    /// <item>
    /// <description>Item 2.</description>
    /// </item>
    /// </list>
    /// </remarks>
    public static void Main () {
        // ...
    }
}
```

A.2.7 <para>

This tag is for use inside other tags, such as `<remarks>` (§A.2.11) or `<returns>` (§A.2.12), and permits structure to be added to text.

Syntax:

```
<para>content</para>
```

where *content* is the text of the paragraph.

Example:

```
/// <summary>This is the entry point of the Point class testing program.
/// <para>This program tests each method and operator, and
/// is intended to be run after any nontrivial maintenance has
/// been performed on the Point class.</para></summary>
public static void Main() {
    // ...
}
```

A.2.8 <param>

This tag is used to describe a parameter for a method, constructor, or indexer.

Syntax:

```
<param name="name">description</param>
```

where

- *name* is the name of the parameter.

- *description* is a description of the parameter.

Example:

```
/// <summary>This method changes the point's location to
/// the given coordinates.</summary>
/// <param name="xor">the new x-coordinate.</param>
/// <param name="yor">the new y-coordinate.</param>
public void Move(int xor, int yor) {
    X = xor;
    Y = yor;
}
```

A.2.9 <paramref>

This tag is used to indicate that a word is a parameter. The documentation file can be processed to format this parameter in some distinct way.

Syntax:

```
<paramref name="name"/>
```

where *name* is the name of the parameter.

Example:

```
/// <summary>This constructor initializes the new Point to
/// (<paramref name="xor"/>,<paramref name="yor"/>).</summary>
/// <param name="xor">the new Point's x-coordinate.</param>
/// <param name="yor">the new Point's y-coordinate.</param>
```

```
public Point(int xor, int yor) {
    X = xor;
    Y = yor;
}
```

A.2.10 <permission>

This tag allows the security accessibility of a member to be documented.

Syntax:

```
<permission cref="member">description</permission>
```

where

- *member* is the name of a member. The documentation generator checks that the given code element exists and translates *member* to the canonical element name in the documentation file.

- *description* is a description of the access to the member.

Example:

```
/// <permission cref="System.Security.PermissionSet">Everyone can
/// access this method.</permission>
public static void Test() {
    // ...
}
```

A.2.11 <remarks>

This tag is used to specify overview information about a type. (Use <summary>, described in §A.2.15, to describe the members of a type.)

Syntax:

```
<remarks>description</remarks>
```

where *description* is the text of the remarks.

Example:

```
/// <remarks>Class <c>Point</c> models a point in a
/// two-dimensional plane.</remarks>
public class Point
{
    // ...
}
```

A.

Comments

A.2.12 <returns>

This tag is used to describe the return value of a method.

Syntax:

```
<returns>description</returns>
```

where *description* a description of the return value.

Example:

```
/// <summary>Report a point's location as a string.</summary>
/// <returns>A string representing a point's location, in the form (x,y),
/// without any leading, trailing, or embedded whitespace.</returns>
public override string ToString() {
    return "(" + X + "," + Y + ")";
}
```

A.2.13 <see>

This tag allows a link to be specified within text. Use <seealso>, described in §A.2.14, to indicate text that is to appear in a *See Also* section.

Syntax:

```
<see cref="member"/>
```

where member is the name of a member. The documentation generator checks that the given code element exists and changes member to the element name in the generated documentation file.

Example:

```
/// <summary>This method changes the point's location to
/// the given coordinates.</summary>
/// <see cref="Translate"/>
public void Move(int xor, int yor) {
    X = xor;
    Y = yor;
}

/// <summary>This method changes the point's location by
/// the given x- and y-offsets.
/// </summary>
/// <see cref="Move"/>
public void Translate(int xor, int yor) {
    X += xor;
    Y += yor;
}
```

A.2.14 <seealso>

This tag allows an entry to be generated for the *See Also* section. Use <see> (§A.2.13) to specify a link from within text.

Syntax:

```
<seealso cref="member"/>
```

where *member* is the name of a member. The documentation generator checks that the given code element exists and changes *member* to the element name in the generated documentation file.

Example:

```
/// <summary>This method determines whether two Points have the same
/// location.</summary>
/// <seealso cref="operator=="/>
/// <seealso cref="operator!="/>
public override bool Equals(object o) {
    // ...
}
```

A.2.15 <summary>

This tag can be used to describe a member for a type. Use <remarks> (§A.2.11) to describe the type itself.

Syntax:

```
<summary>description</summary>
```

where *description* a summary of the member.

Example:

```
/// <summary>This constructor initializes the new Point to (0,0).</summary>
public Point() : this(0,0) {
}
```

A.2.16 <value>

This tag allows a property to be described.

Syntax:

```
<value>property description</value>
```

where *property description* is a description for the property.

Example:

```
/// <value>Property <c>X</c> represents the point's x-coordinate.</value>
public int X
{
    get { return x; }
    set { x = value; }
}
```

A.3 Processing the Documentation File

The documentation generator generates an ID string for each element in the source code that is tagged with a documentation comment. This ID string uniquely identifies a source element. A documentation viewer can use an ID string to identify the corresponding metadata/reflection item to which the documentation applies.

The documentation file is not a hierarchical representation of the source code; rather, it is a flat list with a generated ID string for each element.

A.3.1 ID String Format

The documentation generator observes the following rules when it generates the ID strings.

- No whitespace is placed in the string.

- The first part of the string identifies the kind of member being documented via a single character followed by a colon. The following kinds of members are defined.

Character	Description
E	Event
F	Field
M	Method (including constructors, destructors, and operators)
N	Namespace
P	Property (including indexers)
T	Type (such as class, delegate, enum, interface, and struct)
!	Error string; the rest of the string provides information about the error. For example, the documentation generator generates error information for links that cannot be resolved.

- The second part of the string is the fully qualified name of the element, starting at the root of the namespace. The name of the element, its enclosing type(s), and namespace are separated by periods. If the name of the item itself has periods, they are replaced by # (U+0023) characters. (It is assumed that no element has this character in its name.)

- For methods and properties with arguments, the argument list follows, enclosed in parentheses. For those without arguments, the parentheses are omitted. The arguments are separated by commas. The encoding of each argument is the same as a Common Lanugage Infrastructure (CLI) signature: Arguments are represented by their fully qualified name. For example, `int` becomes `System.Int32`, `string` becomes `System.String`, `object` becomes `System.Object`, and so on. Arguments having the `out` or `ref` modifier have an `@` following their type name. Arguments passed by value or via `params` have no special notation. Arguments that are arrays are represented as [*lowerbound* : *size* , ... , *lowerbound* : *size*] where the number of commas is the rank less one, and the lower bounds and size of each dimension, if known, are represented in decimal. If a lower bound or size is not specified, it is omitted. If the lower bound and size for a particular dimension are omitted, the : is omitted as well. Jagged arrays are represented by one [] per level. Arguments that have pointer types other than void are represented using a * following the type name. A void pointer is represented using a type name of `System.Void`.

A.3.2 ID String Examples

The following examples each show a fragment of C# code, along with the ID string produced from each source element capable of having a documentation comment.

- Types are represented using their fully qualified name.

```
enum Color { Red, Blue, Green }

namespace Acme
{
    interface IProcess {...}

    struct ValueType {...}

    class Widget: IProcess
    {
        public class NestedClass {...}

        public interface IMenuItem {...}

        public delegate void Del(int i);

        public enum Direction { North, South, East, West }
    }
}
```

```
"T:Color"
"T:Acme.IProcess"
"T:Acme.ValueType"
"T:Acme.Widget"
"T:Acme.Widget.NestedClass"
"T:Acme.Widget.IMenuItem"
"T:Acme.Widget.Del"
"T:Acme.Widget.Direction"
```

- Fields are represented by their fully qualified name.

```
namespace Acme
{
    struct ValueType
    {
        private int total;
    }

    class Widget: IProcess
    {
        public class NestedClass
        {
            private int value;
        }

        private string message;
        private static Color defaultColor;
        private const double PI = 3.14159;
        protected readonly double monthlyAverage;
        private long[] array1;
        private Widget[,] array2;
        private unsafe int *pCount;
        private unsafe float **ppValues;
    }
}
```
```
"F:Acme.ValueType.total"
"F:Acme.Widget.NestedClass.value"
"F:Acme.Widget.message"
"F:Acme.Widget.defaultColor"
"F:Acme.Widget.PI"
"F:Acme.Widget.monthlyAverage"
"F:Acme.Widget.array1"
"F:Acme.Widget.array2"
"F:Acme.Widget.pCount"
"F:Acme.Widget.ppValues"
```

- Constructors.

```
namespace Acme
{
    class Widget: IProcess
    {
        static Widget() {...}

        public Widget() {...}
```

```
        public Widget(string s) {...}
    }
}
```

```
"M:Acme.Widget.#cctor"
"M:Acme.Widget.#ctor"
"M:Acme.Widget.#ctor(System.String)"
```

- Destructors.

```
namespace Acme
{
    class Widget: IProcess
    {
        ~Widget() {...}
    }
}
```

```
"M:Acme.Widget.Finalize"
```

- Methods.

```
namespace Acme
{
    struct ValueType
    {
        public void M(int i) {...}
    }

    class Widget: IProcess
    {
        public class NestedClass
        {
            public void M(int i) {...}
        }

        public static void M0() {...}
        public void M1(char c, out float f, ref ValueType v) {...}
        public void M2(short[] x1, int[,] x2, long[][] x3) {...}
        public void M3(long[][] x3, Widget[][,,] x4) {...}
        public unsafe void M4(char *pc, Color **pf) {...}
        public unsafe void M5(void *pv, double *[][,] pd) {...}
        public void M6(int i, params object[] args) {...}
    }
}
```

```
"M:Acme.ValueType.M(System.Int32)"
"M:Acme.Widget.NestedClass.M(System.Int32)"
"M:Acme.Widget.M0"
"M:Acme.Widget.M1(System.Char,System.Single@,Acme.ValueType@)"
"M:Acme.Widget.M2(System.Int16[],System.Int32[0:,0:],System.Int64[][])"
"M:Acme.Widget.M3(System.Int64[][],Acme.Widget[0:,0:,0:][])"
"M:Acme.Widget.M4(System.Char*,Color**)"
"M:Acme.Widget.M5(System.Void*,System.Double*[0:,0:][])"
"M:Acme.Widget.M6(System.Int32,System.Object[])"
```

A. Comments

575

- Properties and indexers.

```
namespace Acme
{
    class Widget: IProcess
    {
        public int Width { get {...} set {...} }
        public int this[int i] { get {...} set {...} }
        public int this[string s, int i] { get {...} set {...} }
    }
}
```
```
"P:Acme.Widget.Width"
"P:Acme.Widget.Item(System.Int32)"
"P:Acme.Widget.Item(System.String,System.Int32)"
```

- Events.

```
namespace Acme
{
    class Widget: IProcess
    {
        public event Del AnEvent;
    }
}
```
```
"E:Acme.Widget.AnEvent"
```

- Unary operators.

```
namespace Acme
{
    class Widget: IProcess
    {
        public static Widget operator+(Widget x) {...}
    }
}
```
```
"M:Acme.Widget.op_UnaryPlus(Acme.Widget)"
```

The complete set of unary operator function names used is as follows: op_UnaryPlus, op_UnaryNegation, op_LogicalNot, op_OnesComplement, op_Increment, op_Decrement, op_True, and op_False.

- Binary operators.

```
namespace Acme
{
    class Widget: IProcess
    {
        public static Widget operator+(Widget x1, Widget x2) {...}
    }
}
```
```
"M:Acme.Widget.op_Addition(Acme.Widget,Acme.Widget)"
```

The complete set of binary operator function names used is as follows: `op_Addition`, `op_Subtraction`, `op_Multiply`, `op_Division`, `op_Modulus`, `op_BitwiseAnd`, `op_BitwiseOr`, `op_ExclusiveOr`, `op_LeftShift`, `op_RightShift`, `op_Equality`, `op_Inequality`, `op_LessThan`, `op_LessThanOrEqual`, `op_GreaterThan`, and `op_GreaterThanOrEqual`.

- Conversion operators have a trailing ~ followed by the return type.

```
namespace Acme
{
    class Widget: IProcess
    {
        public static explicit operator int(Widget x) {...}
        public static implicit operator long(Widget x) {...}
    }
}

"M:Acme.Widget.op_Explicit(Acme.Widget)~System.Int32"
"M:Acme.Widget.op_Implicit(Acme.Widget)~System.Int64"
```

A.4 An Example

A.4.1 C# Source Code
The following example shows the source code of a `Point` class.

```
namespace Graphics
{

/// <remarks>Class <c>Point</c> models a point in a two-dimensional plane.
/// </remarks>
public class Point
{

    /// <summary>Instance variable <c>x</c> represents the point's
    /// x-coordinate.</summary>
    private int x;

    /// <summary>Instance variable <c>y</c> represents the point's
    /// y-coordinate.</summary>
    private int y;

    /// <value>Property <c>X</c> represents the point's x-coordinate.</value>
    public int X
    {
        get { return x; }
        set { x = value; }
    }
```

A.

Comments

```
/// <value>Property <c>Y</c> represents the point's y-coordinate.</value>
public int Y
{
    get { return y; }
    set { y = value; }
}

/// <summary>This constructor initializes the new Point to
/// (0,0).</summary>
public Point() : this(0,0) {}

/// <summary>This constructor initializes the new Point to
/// (<paramref name="xor"/>,<paramref name="yor"/>).</summary>
/// <param><c>xor</c> is the new Point's x-coordinate.</param>
/// <param><c>yor</c> is the new Point's y-coordinate.</param>
public Point(int xor, int yor) {
    X = xor;
    Y = yor;
}

/// <summary>This method changes the point's location to
/// the given coordinates.</summary>
/// <param><c>xor</c> is the new x-coordinate.</param>
/// <param><c>yor</c> is the new y-coordinate.</param>
/// <see cref="Translate"/>
public void Move(int xor, int yor) {
    X = xor;
    Y = yor;
}

/// <summary>This method changes the point's location by
/// the given x- and y-offsets.
/// <example>For example:
/// <code>
/// Point p = new Point(3,5);
/// p.Translate(-1,3);
/// </code>
/// results in <c>p</c>'s having the value (2,8).
/// </example>
/// </summary>
/// <param><c>xor</c> is the relative x-offset.</param>
/// <param><c>yor</c> is the relative y-offset.</param>
/// <see cref="Move"/>
public void Translate(int xor, int yor) {
    X += xor;
    Y += yor;
}
```

```
/// <summary>This method determines whether two Points have the same
/// location.</summary>
/// <param><c>o</c> is the object to be compared to the current object.
/// </param>
/// <returns>True if the Points have the same location and they have
/// the exact same type; otherwise, false.</returns>
/// <seealso cref="operator=="/>
/// <seealso cref="operator!="/>
public override bool Equals(object o) {
    if (o == null) {
        return false;
    }

    if (this == o) {
        return true;
    }

    if (GetType() == o.GetType()) {
        Point p = (Point)o;
        return (X == p.X) && (Y == p.Y);
    }
    return false;
}

/// <summary>Report a point's location as a string.</summary>
/// <returns>A string representing a point's location, in the form (x,y),
/// without any leading, training, or embedded whitespace.</returns>
public override string ToString() {
    return "(" + X + "," + Y + ")";
}

/// <summary>This operator determines whether two Points have the same
/// location.</summary>
/// <param><c>p1</c> is the first Point to be compared.</param>
/// <param><c>p2</c> is the second Point to be compared.</param>
/// <returns>True if the Points have the same location and they have
/// the exact same type; otherwise, false.</returns>
/// <seealso cref="Equals"/>
/// <seealso cref="operator!="/>
public static bool operator==(Point p1, Point p2) {
    if ((object)p1 == null || (object)p2 == null) {
        return false;
    }

    if (p1.GetType() == p2.GetType()) {
        return (p1.X == p2.X) && (p1.Y == p2.Y);
    }

    return false;
}
```

```
/// <summary>This operator determines whether two Points have the same
/// location.</summary>
/// <param><c>p1</c> is the first Point to be compared.</param>
/// <param><c>p2</c> is the second Point to be compared.</param>
/// <returns>True if the Points do not have the same location and the
/// exact same type; otherwise, false.</returns>
/// <seealso cref="Equals"/>
/// <seealso cref="operator=="/>
public static bool operator!=(Point p1, Point p2) {
    return !(p1 == p2);
}

/// <summary>This is the entry point of the Point class testing
/// program.
/// <para>This program tests each method and operator, and
/// is intended to be run after any nontrivial maintenance has
/// been performed on the Point class.</para></summary>
public static void Main() {
    // class test code goes here
}
}
}
```

A.4.2 Resulting XML

This following shows the output produced by one documentation generator when given
the source code for class Point, shown previously.

```xml
<?xml version="1.0"?>
<doc>
    <assembly>
        <name>Point</name>
    </assembly>
    <members>
        <member name="T:Graphics.Point">
            <remarks>Class <c>Point</c> models a point in a two-dimensional
            plane.
            </remarks>
        </member>

        <member name="F:Graphics.Point.x">
            <summary>Instance variable <c>x</c> represents the point's
            x-coordinate.</summary>
        </member>

        <member name="F:Graphics.Point.y">
            <summary>Instance variable <c>y</c> represents the point's
            y-coordinate.</summary>
        </member>

        <member name="M:Graphics.Point.#ctor">
            <summary>This constructor initializes the new Point to
        (0,0).</summary>
        </member>
```

```
<member name="M:Graphics.Point.#ctor(System.Int32,System.Int32)">
    <summary>This constructor initializes the new Point to
    (<paramref name="xor"/>,<paramref name="yor"/>).</summary>
    <param><c>xor</c> is the new Point's x-coordinate.</param>
    <param><c>yor</c> is the new Point's y-coordinate.</param>
</member>

<member name="M:Graphics.Point.Move(System.Int32,System.Int32)">
    <summary>This method changes the point's location to
    the given coordinates.</summary>
    <param><c>xor</c> is the new x-coordinate.</param>
    <param><c>yor</c> is the new y-coordinate.</param>
    <see cref="M:Graphics.Point.Translate(System.Int32,System.Int32)"/>
</member>

<member
    name="M:Graphics.Point.Translate(System.Int32,System.Int32)">
    <summary>This method changes the point's location by
    the given x- and y-offsets.
    <example>For example:
    <code>
    Point p = new Point(3,5);
    p.Translate(-1,3);
    </code>
    results in <c>p</c>'s having the value (2,8).
    </example>
    </summary>
    <param><c>xor</c> is the relative x-offset.</param>
    <param><c>yor</c> is the relative y-offset.</param>
    <see cref="M:Graphics.Point.Move(System.Int32,System.Int32)"/>
</member>

<member name="M:Graphics.Point.Equals(System.Object)">
    <summary>This method determines whether two Points have the same
    location.</summary>
    <param><c>o</c> is the object to be compared to the current
    object.
    </param>
    <returns>True if the Points have the same location and they have
    the exact same type; otherwise, false.</returns>
    <seealso
cref="M:Graphics.Point.op_Equality(Graphics.Point,Graphics.Point)"/>
    <seealso
cref="M:Graphics.Point.op_Inequality(Graphics.Point,Graphics.Point)"/>
</member>

<member name="M:Graphics.Point.ToString">
    <summary>Report a point's location as a string.</summary>
    <returns>A string representing a point's location, in the form
    (x,y),
    without any leading, training, or embedded whitespace.</returns>
</member>
```

```xml
        <member
      name="M:Graphics.Point.op_Equality(Graphics.Point,Graphics.Point)">
            <summary>This operator determines whether two Points have the
            same
            location.</summary>
            <param><c>p1</c> is the first Point to be compared.</param>
            <param><c>p2</c> is the second Point to be compared.</param>
            <returns>True if the Points have the same location and they have
            the exact same type; otherwise, false.</returns>
            <seealso cref="M:Graphics.Point.Equals(System.Object)"/>
            <seealso
      cref="M:Graphics.Point.op_Inequality(Graphics.Point,Graphics.Point)"/>
        </member>

        <member
      name="M:Graphics.Point.op_Inequality(Graphics.Point,Graphics.Point)">
            <summary>This operator determines whether two Points have the
            same
            location.</summary>
            <param><c>p1</c> is the first Point to be compared.</param>
            <param><c>p2</c> is the second Point to be compared.</param>
            <returns>True if the Points do not have the same location and
            the
            exact same type; otherwise, false.</returns>
            <seealso cref="M:Graphics.Point.Equals(System.Object)"/>
            <seealso
      cref="M:Graphics.Point.op_Equality(Graphics.Point,Graphics.Point)"/>
        </member>

        <member name="M:Graphics.Point.Main">
            <summary>This is the entry point of the Point class testing
            program.
            <para>This program tests each method and operator, and
            is intended to be run after any nontrivial maintenance has
            been performed on the Point class.</para></summary>
        </member>

        <member name="P:Graphics.Point.X">
            <value>Property <c>X</c> represents the point's
            x-coordinate.</value>
        </member>

        <member name="P:Graphics.Point.Y">
            <value>Property <c>Y</c> represents the point's
            y-coordinate.</value>
        </member>
    </members>
</doc>
```

B. Grammar

This appendix contains summaries of the lexical and syntactic grammars found in the main document and of the grammar extensions for unsafe code. Grammar productions appear in this appendix in the same order that they appear in the main document.

B.1 Lexical Grammar

input:
> *input-section*$_{opt}$

input-section:
> *input-section-part*
> *input-section   input-section-part*

input-section-part:
> *input-elements*$_{opt}$ *new-line*
> *pp-directive*

input-elements:
> *input-element*
> *input-elements   input-element*

input-element:
> *whitespace*
> *comment*
> *token*

B.1.1 Line Terminators

new-line:
> Carriage return character (U+000D)
> Line feed character (U+000A)
> Carriage return character (U+000D) followed by line feed character (U+000A)
> Line separator character (U+2028)
> Paragraph separator character (U+2029)

B.1.2 **Whitespace**

whitespace:
> Any character with Unicode class Zs
> Horizontal tab character (U+0009)
> Vertical tab character (U+000B)
> Form feed character (U+000C)

B.1.3 **Comments**

comment:
> *single-line-comment*
> *delimited-comment*

single-line-comment:
> // *input-characters*$_{opt}$

input-characters:
> *input-character*
> *input-characters   input-character*

input-character:
> Any Unicode character except a *new-line-character*

new-line-character:
> Carriage return character (U+000D)
> Line feed character (U+000A)
> Line separator character (U+2028)
> Paragraph separator character (U+2029)

delimited-comment:
> /* *delimited-comment-characters*$_{opt}$ */

delimited-comment-characters:
> *delimited-comment-character*
> *delimited-comment-characters   delimited-comment-character*

delimited-comment-character:
> *not-asterisk*
> * *not-slash*

not-asterisk:
> Any Unicode character except *

not-slash:
> Any Unicode character except /

B.1.4 **Tokens**

token:
> *identifier*
> *keyword*
> *integer-literal*
> *real-literal*
> *character-literal*
> *string-literal*
> *operator-or-punctuator*

B.1.5 **Unicode Character Escape Sequences**

unicode-escape-sequence:
> \u *hex-digit   hex-digit   hex-digit   hex-digit*
> \U *hex-digit   hex-digit   hex-digit   hex-digit   hex-digit   hex-digit   hex-digit   hex-digit*

B.1.6 **Identifiers**

identifier:
> *available-identifier*
> @ *identifier-or-keyword*

available-identifier:
> An *identifier-or-keyword* that is not a *keyword*

identifier-or-keyword:
> *identifier-start-character   identifier-part-characters_{opt}*

identifier-start-character:
> *letter-character*
> _ (the underscore character U+005F)

identifier-part-characters:
> *identifier-part-character*
> *identifier-part-characters   identifier-part-character*

identifier-part-character:
> *letter-character*
> *decimal-digit-character*
> *connecting-character*
> *combining-character*
> *formatting-character*

letter-character:
> A Unicode character of classes Lu, Ll, Lt, Lm, Lo, or Nl
> A *unicode-escape-sequence* representing a character of classes Lu, Ll, Lt, Lm, Lo, or Nl

combining-character:
>   A Unicode character of classes Mn or Mc
>   A *unicode-escape-sequence* representing a character of classes Mn or Mc

decimal-digit-character:
>   A Unicode character of the class Nd
>   A *unicode-escape-sequence* representing a character of the class Nd

connecting-character:
>   A Unicode character of the class Pc
>   A *unicode-escape-sequence* representing a character of the class Pc

formatting-character:
>   A Unicode character of the class Cf
>   A *unicode-escape-sequence* representing a character of the class Cf

B.1.7 Keywords

keyword: one of

abstract	as	base	bool	break
byte	case	catch	char	checked
class	const	continue	decimal	default
delegate	do	double	else	enum
event	explicit	extern	false	finally
fixed	float	for	foreach	goto
if	implicit	in	int	interface
internal	is	lock	long	namespace
new	null	object	operator	out
override	params	private	protected	public
readonly	ref	return	sbyte	sealed
short	sizeof	stackalloc	static	string
struct	switch	this	throw	true
try	typeof	uint	ulong	unchecked
unsafe	ushort	using	virtual	void
volatile	while			

B.1.8 Literals

literal:
>   *boolean-literal*
>   *integer-literal*
>   *real-literal*
>   *character-literal*
>   *string-literal*
>   *null-literal*

boolean-literal:
> `true`
> `false`

integer-literal:
> *decimal-integer-literal*
> *hexadecimal-integer-literal*

decimal-integer-literal:
> *decimal-digits integer-type-suffix$_{opt}$*

decimal-digits:
> *decimal-digit*
> *decimal-digits decimal-digit*

decimal-digit: one of
> `0   1   2   3   4   5   6   7   8   9`

integer-type-suffix: one of
> `U   u   L   l   UL   Ul   uL   ul   LU   Lu   lU   lu`

hexadecimal-integer-literal:
> `0x` *hex-digits integer-type-suffix$_{opt}$*
> `0X` *hex-digits integer-type-suffix$_{opt}$*

hex-digits:
> *hex-digit*
> *hex-digits hex-digit*

hex-digit: one of
> `0   1   2   3   4   5   6   7   8   9   A   B   C   D   E   F   a   b   c   d   e   f`

real-literal:
> *decimal-digits* `.` *decimal-digits exponent-part$_{opt}$ real-type-suffix$_{opt}$*
> `.` *decimal-digits exponent-part$_{opt}$ real-type-suffix$_{opt}$*
> *decimal-digits exponent-part real-type-suffix$_{opt}$*
> *decimal-digits real-type-suffix*

exponent-part:
> `e` *sign$_{opt}$ decimal-digits*
> `E` *sign$_{opt}$ decimal-digits*

sign: one of
> `+   -`

real-type-suffix: one of
> `F   f   D   d   M   m`

character-literal:
> `'` *character* `'`

character:
> *single-character*
> *simple-escape-sequence*
> *hexadecimal-escape-sequence*
> *unicode-escape-sequence*

single-character:
> Any character except ' (U+0027), \ (U+005C), and *new-line-character*

simple-escape-sequence: one of
> \' \" \\ \0 \a \b \f \n \r \t \v

hexadecimal-escape-sequence:
> \x *hex-digit* *hex-digit*$_{opt}$ *hex-digit*$_{opt}$ *hex-digit*$_{opt}$

string-literal:
> *regular-string-literal*
> *verbatim-string-literal*

regular-string-literal:
> " *regular-string-literal-characters*$_{opt}$ "

regular-string-literal-characters:
> *regular-string-literal-character*
> *regular-string-literal-characters* *regular-string-literal-character*

regular-string-literal-character:
> *single-regular-string-literal-character*
> *simple-escape-sequence*
> *hexadecimal-escape-sequence*
> *unicode-escape-sequence*

single-regular-string-literal-character:
> Any character except " (U+0022), \ (U+005C), and *new-line-character*

verbatim-string-literal:
> @" *verbatim -string-literal-characters*$_{opt}$ "

verbatim-string-literal-characters:
> *verbatim-string-literal-character*
> *verbatim-string-literal-characters* *verbatim-string-literal-character*

verbatim-string-literal-character:
> *single-verbatim-string-literal-character*
> *quote-escape-sequence*

single-verbatim-string-literal-character:
> Any character except "

quote-escape-sequence:
 " "

null-literal:
 `null`

B.1.9 Operators and Punctuators

operator-or-punctuator: one of

{	}	[	]	(	)	.	,	:	;
+	–	*	/	%	&	|	^	!	~
=	<	>	?	++	––	&&	||	<<	>>
==	!=	<=	>=	+=	–=	*=	/=	%=	&=
|=	^=	<<=	>>=	–>					

B.1.10 Preprocessing Directives

pp-directive:
 pp-declaration
 pp-conditional
 pp-line
 pp-diagnostic
 pp-region

conditional-symbol:
 Any *identifier-or-keyword* except `true` or `false`

pp-expression:
 whitespace$_{opt}$ *pp-or-expression* *whitespace*$_{opt}$

pp-or-expression:
 pp-and-expression
 pp-or-expression *whitespace*$_{opt}$ `||` *whitespace*$_{opt}$ *pp-and-expression*

pp-and-expression:
 pp-equality-expression
 pp-and-expression *whitespace*$_{opt}$ `&&` *whitespace*$_{opt}$ *pp-equality-expression*

pp-equality-expression:
 pp-unary-expression
 pp-equality-expression *whitespace*$_{opt}$ `==` *whitespace*$_{opt}$ *pp-unary-expression*
 pp-equality-expression *whitespace*$_{opt}$ `!=` *whitespace*$_{opt}$ *pp-unary-expression*

pp-unary-expression:
 pp-primary-expression
 `!` *whitespace*$_{opt}$ *pp-unary-expression*

pp-primary-expression:
>   true
>   false
>   *conditional-symbol*
>   (*whitespace$_{opt}$ pp-expression whitespace$_{opt}$*)

pp-declaration:
>   *whitespace$_{opt}$* # *whitespace$_{opt}$* define *whitespace conditional-symbol pp-new-line*
>   *whitespace$_{opt}$* # *whitespace$_{opt}$* undef *whitespace conditional-symbol pp-new-line*

pp-new-line:
>   *whitespace$_{opt}$ single-line-comment$_{opt}$ new-line*

pp-conditional:
>   *pp-if-section pp-elif-sections$_{opt}$ pp-else-section$_{opt}$ pp-endif*

pp-if-section:
>   *whitespace$_{opt}$* # *whitespace$_{opt}$* if *whitespace pp-expression pp-new-line*
>   *conditional-section$_{opt}$*

pp-elif-sections:
>   *pp-elif-section*
>   *pp-elif-sections pp-elif-section*

pp-elif-section:
>   *whitespace$_{opt}$* # *whitespace$_{opt}$* elif *whitespace pp-expression pp-new-line*
>   *conditional-section$_{opt}$*

pp-else-section:
>   *whitespace$_{opt}$* # *whitespace$_{opt}$* else *pp-new-line conditional-section$_{opt}$*

pp-endif:
>   *whitespace$_{opt}$* # *whitespace$_{opt}$* endif *pp-new-line*

conditional-section:
>   *input-section*
>   *skipped-section*

skipped-section:
>   *skipped-section-part*
>   *skipped-section skipped-section-part*

skipped-section-part:
>   *skipped-characters$_{opt}$ new-line*
>   *pp-directive*

skipped-characters:
>   *whitespace$_{opt}$ not-number-sign input-characters$_{opt}$*

not-number-sign:
    Any *input-character* except #

pp-diagnostic:
    whitespace$_{opt}$ # *whitespace*$_{opt}$ `error` *pp-message*
    whitespace$_{opt}$ # *whitespace*$_{opt}$ `warning` *pp-message*

pp-message:
    new-line
    whitespace *input-characters*$_{opt}$ *new-line*

pp-region:
    pp-start-region *conditional-section*$_{opt}$ *pp-end-region*

pp-start-region:
    whitespace$_{opt}$ # *whitespace*$_{opt}$ `region` *pp-message*

pp-end-region:
    whitespace$_{opt}$ # *whitespace*$_{opt}$ `endregion` *pp-message*

pp-line:
    whitespace$_{opt}$ # *whitespace*$_{opt}$ `line` *whitespace* *line-indicator* *pp-new-line*

line-indicator:
    decimal-digits *whitespace* *file-name*
    decimal-digits
    `default`
    `hidden`

file-name:
    " *file-name-characters* "

file-name-characters:
    file-name-character
    file-name-characters *file-name-character*

file-name-character:
    Any *input-character* except "

B.2 Syntactic Grammar

B.2.1 Basic Concepts

namespace-name:
    namespace-or-type-name

type-name:
    namespace-or-type-name

namespace-or-type-name:
    identifier
    namespace-or-type-name . identifier

B.2.2 Types

type:
    value-type
    reference-type

value-type:
    struct-type
    enum-type

struct-type:
    type-name
    simple-type

simple-type:
    numeric-type
    `bool`

numeric-type:
    integral-type
    floating-point-type
    `decimal`

integral-type:
    `sbyte`
    `byte`
    `short`
    `ushort`
    `int`
    `uint`
    `long`
    `ulong`
    `char`

floating-point-type:
    `float`
    `double`

enum-type:
    type-name

reference-type:
    class-type
    interface-type
    array-type
    delegate-type

class-type:
    type-name
    `object`
    `string`

interface-type:
    type-name

array-type:
    non-array-type   *rank-specifiers*

non-array-type:
    type

rank-specifiers:
    rank-specifier
    rank-specifiers   *rank-specifier*

rank-specifier:
    [*dim-separators$_{opt}$*   ]

dim-separators:

    ,
    dim-separators   ,

delegate-type:
    type-name

B.2.3 Variables
variable-reference:
    expression

B.2.4 Expressions
argument-list:
    argument
    argument-list   ,   *argument*

argument:
    expression
    `ref`   *variable-reference*
    `out`   *variable-reference*

primary-expression:
  primary-no-array-creation-expression
  array-creation-expression

primary-no-array-creation-expression:
  literal
  simple-name
  parenthesized-expression
  member-access
  invocation-expression
  element-access
  this-access
  base-access
  post-increment-expression
  post-decrement-expression
  object-creation-expression
  delegate-creation-expression
  typeof-expression
  checked-expression
  unchecked-expression

simple-name:
  identifier

parenthesized-expression:
  (*expression*)

member-access:
  primary-expression . *identifier*
  predefined-type . *identifier*

predefined-type: one of
  bool   byte   char   decimal   double   float   int   long
  object   sbyte   short   string   uint   ulong   ushort

invocation-expression:
  primary-expression (*argument-list$_{opt}$*)

element-access:
  primary-no-array-creation-expression [*expression-list*]

expression-list:
  expression
  expression-list , *expression*

this-access:
  this

base-access:
    `base`   `.`   *identifier*
    `base`   `[`   *expression-list*   `]`

post-increment-expression:
    primary-expression   `++`

post-decrement-expression:
    primary-expression   `--`

object-creation-expression:
    `new`   *type*   `(`   *argument-list*$_{opt}$ `)`

array-creation-expression:
    `new`   *non-array-type*   `[`   *expression-list*   `]`   *rank-specifiers*$_{opt}$ *array-initializer*$_{opt}$
    `new`   *array-type*   *array-initializer*

delegate-creation-expression:
    `new`   *delegate-type*   `(`   *expression*   `)`

typeof-expression:
    `typeof`   `(`   *type*   `)`
    `typeof`   `(`   `void`   `)`

checked-expression:
    `checked`   `(`   *expression*   `)`

unchecked-expression:
    `unchecked`   `(`   *expression*   `)`

unary-expression:
    primary-expression
    `+`   *unary-expression*
    `-`   *unary-expression*
    `!`   *unary-expression*
    `~`   *unary-expression*
    pre-increment-expression
    pre-decrement-expression
    cast-expression

pre-increment-expression:
    `++`   *unary-expression*

pre-decrement-expression:
    `--`   *unary-expression*

cast-expression:
    `(`   *type*   `)`   *unary-expression*

multiplicative-expression:
>   *unary-expression*
>   *multiplicative-expression* `*` *unary-expression*
>   *multiplicative-expression* `/` *unary-expression*
>   *multiplicative-expression* `%` *unary-expression*

additive-expression:
>   *multiplicative-expression*
>   *additive-expression* `+` *multiplicative-expression*
>   *additive-expression* `−` *multiplicative-expression*

shift-expression:
>   *additive-expression*
>   *shift-expression* `<<` *additive-expression*
>   *shift-expression* `>>` *additive-expression*

relational-expression:
>   *shift-expression*
>   *relational-expression* `<` *shift-expression*
>   *relational-expression* `>` *shift-expression*
>   *relational-expression* `<=` *shift-expression*
>   *relational-expression* `>=` *shift-expression*
>   *relational-expression* `is` *type*
>   *relational-expression* `as` *type*

equality-expression:
>   *relational-expression*
>   *equality-expression* `==` *relational-expression*
>   *equality-expression* `!=` *relational-expression*

and-expression:
>   *equality-expression*
>   *and-expression* `&` *equality-expression*

exclusive-or-expression:
>   *and-expression*
>   *exclusive-or-expression* `^` *and-expression*

inclusive-or-expression:
>   *exclusive-or-expression*
>   *inclusive-or-expression* `|` *exclusive-or-expression*

conditional-and-expression:
>   *inclusive-or-expression*
>   *conditional-and-expression* `&&` *inclusive-or-expression*

conditional-or-expression:
    conditional-and-expression
    conditional-or-expression || *conditional-and-expression*

conditional-expression:
    conditional-or-expression
    conditional-or-expression ? *expression* : *expression*

assignment:
    unary-expression assignment-operator expression

assignment-operator: one of
    =   +=   -=   *=   /=   %=   &= |=   ^=   <<=   >>=

expression:
    conditional-expression
    assignment

constant-expression:
    expression

boolean-expression:
    expression

B.2.5 Statements

statement:
    labeled-statement
    declaration-statement
    embedded-statement

embedded-statement:
    block
    empty-statement
    expression-statement
    selection-statement
    iteration-statement
    jump-statement
    try-statement
    checked-statement
    unchecked-statement
    lock-statement
    using-statement

block:
    { *statement-list$_{opt}$* }

B. Grammar

statement-list:
  statement
  statement-list   statement

empty-statement:
  ;

labeled-statement:
  identifier   :   statement

declaration-statement:
  local-variable-declaration   ;
  local-constant-declaration   ;

local-variable-declaration:
  type   local-variable-declarators

local-variable-declarators:
  local-variable-declarator
  local-variable-declarators   ,   local-variable-declarator

local-variable-declarator:
  identifier
  identifier   =   local-variable-initializer

local-variable-initializer:
  expression
  array-initializer

local-constant-declaration:
  `const`   *type   constant-declarators*

constant-declarators:
  constant-declarator
  constant-declarators   ,   constant-declarator

constant-declarator:
  identifier   =   constant-expression

expression-statement:
  statement-expression   ;

statement-expression:
  invocation-expression
  object-creation-expression
  assignment

> *post-increment-expression*
> *post-decrement-expression*
> *pre-increment-expression*
> *pre-decrement-expression*

selection-statement:
> *if-statement*
> *switch-statement*

if-statement:
> `if` `(` *boolean-expression* `)` *embedded-statement*
> `if` `(` *boolean-expression* `)` *embedded-statement* `else` *embedded-statement*

boolean-expression:
> *expression*

switch-statement:
> `switch` `(` *expression* `)` *switch-block*

switch-block:
> `{` *switch-sections*$_{opt}$ `}`

switch-sections:
> *switch-section*
> *switch-sections* *switch-section*

switch-section:
> *switch-labels* *statement-list*

switch-labels:
> *switch-label*
> *switch-labels* *switch-label*

switch-label:
> `case` *constant-expression* `:`
> `default` `:`

iteration-statement:
> *while-statement*
> *do-statement*
> *for-statement*
> *foreach-statement*

while-statement:
> `while` `(` *boolean-expression* `)` *embedded-statement*

do-statement:
> `do` *embedded-statement* `while` `(` *boolean-expression* `)` `;`

for-statement:
> `for` (*for-initializer*$_{opt}$ `;` *for-condition*$_{opt}$ `;` *for-iterator*$_{opt}$) *embedded-statement*

for-initializer:
> *local-variable-declaration*
> *statement-expression-list*

for-condition:
> *boolean-expression*

for-iterator:
> *statement-expression-list*

statement-expression-list:
> *statement-expression*
> *statement-expression-list* `,` *statement-expression*

foreach-statement:
> `foreach` (*type identifier* `in` *expression*) *embedded-statement*

jump-statement:
> *break-statement*
> *continue-statement*
> *goto-statement*
> *return-statement*
> *throw-statement*

break-statement:
> `break` ;

continue-statement:
> `continue` ;

goto-statement:
> `goto` *identifier* ;
> `goto case` *constant-expression* ;
> `goto default` ;

return-statement:
> `return` *expression*$_{opt}$;

throw-statement:
> `throw` *expression*$_{opt}$;

try-statement:
> `try` *block catch-clauses*
> `try` *block finally-clause*
> `try` *block catch-clauses finally-clause*

catch-clauses:
    specific-catch-clauses general-catch-clause$_{opt}$
    specific-catch-clauses$_{opt}$ general-catch-clause

specific-catch-clauses:
    specific-catch-clause
    specific-catch-clauses specific-catch-clause

specific-catch-clause:
    `catch` (*class-type identifier$_{opt}$*) *block*

general-catch-clause:
    `catch` *block*

finally-clause:
    `finally` *block*

checked-statement:
    `checked` *block*

unchecked-statement:
    `unchecked` *block*

lock-statement:
    `lock` (*expression*) *embedded-statement*

using-statement:
    `using` (*resource-acquisition*) *embedded-statement*

resource-acquisition:
    local-variable-declaration
    expression

B.2.6 Namespaces

compilation-unit:
    using-directives$_{opt}$ global-attributes$_{opt}$ namespace-member-declarations$_{opt}$

namespace-declaration:
    `namespace` *qualified-identifier namespace-body* ;$_{opt}$

qualified-identifier:
    identifier
    qualified-identifier . *identifier*

namespace-body:
    { *using-directives$_{opt}$ namespace-member-declarations$_{opt}$* }

using-directives:
    using-directive
    using-directives using-directive

using-directive:
    using-alias-directive
    using-namespace-directive

using-alias-directive:
    `using` *identifier* = *namespace-or-type-name* ;

using-namespace-directive:
    `using` *namespace-name* ;

namespace-member-declarations:
    namespace-member-declaration
    namespace-member-declarations namespace-member-declaration

namespace-member-declaration:
    namespace-declaration
    type-declaration

type-declaration:
    class-declaration
    struct-declaration
    interface-declaration
    enum-declaration
    delegate-declaration

B.2.7 Classes

class-declaration:
    attributes$_{opt}$ class-modifiers$_{opt}$ `class` *identifier class-base$_{opt}$ class-body* ;$_{opt}$

class-modifiers:
    class-modifier
    class-modifiers class-modifier

class-modifier:
    `new`
    `public`
    `protected`
    `internal`
    `private`
    `abstract`
    `sealed`

class-base:
    : *class-type*
    : *interface-type-list*
    : *class-type* , *interface-type-list*

interface-type-list:
    interface-type
    interface-type-list , *interface-type*

class-body:
    { *class-member-declarations$_{opt}$* }

class-member-declarations:
    class-member-declaration
    class-member-declarations *class-member-declaration*

class-member-declaration:
    constant-declaration
    field-declaration
    method-declaration
    property-declaration
    event-declaration
    indexer-declaration
    operator-declaration
    constructor-declaration
    destructor-declaration
    static-constructor-declaration
    type-declaration

constant-declaration:
    attributes$_{opt}$ *constant-modifiers$_{opt}$* `const` *type* *constant-declarators* ;

constant-modifiers:
    constant-modifier
    constant-modifiers *constant-modifier*

constant-modifier:
    `new`
    `public`
    `protected`
    `internal`
    `private`

constant-declarators:
    constant-declarator
    constant-declarators , *constant-declarator*

constant-declarator:
    identifier = constant-expression

field-declaration:
    attributes$_{opt}$ field-modifiers$_{opt}$ type variable-declarators ;

field-modifiers:
    field-modifier
    field-modifiers field-modifier

field-modifier:
    `new`
    `public`
    `protected`
    `internal`
    `private`
    `static`
    `readonly`
    `volatile`

variable-declarators:
    variable-declarator
    variable-declarators , variable-declarator

variable-declarator:
    identifier
    identifier = variable-initializer

variable-initializer:
    expression
    array-initializer

method-declaration:
    method-header method-body

method-header:
    attributes$_{opt}$ method-modifiers$_{opt}$ return-type member-name
        (formal-parameter-list$_{opt}$)

method-modifiers:
    method-modifier
    method-modifiers method-modifier

method-modifier:
    `new`
    `public`
    `protected`
    `internal`

```
        private
        static
        virtual
        sealed
        override
        abstract
        extern
```

return-type:
    type
    `void`

member-name:
    identifier
    interface-type . identifier

method-body:
    block
    `;`

formal-parameter-list:
    fixed-parameters
    fixed-parameters , parameter-array
    parameter-array

fixed-parameters:
    fixed-parameter
    fixed-parameters , fixed-parameter

fixed-parameter:
    attributes$_{opt}$ parameter-modifier$_{opt}$ type identifier

parameter-modifier:
    `ref`
    `out`

parameter-array:
    attributes$_{opt}$ `params` *array-type identifier*

property-declaration:
    attributes$_{opt}$ property-modifiers$_{opt}$ type member-name { accessor-declarations }

property-modifiers:
    property-modifier
    property-modifiers property-modifier

property-modifier:
```
new
public
protected
internal
private
static
virtual
sealed
override
abstract
extern
```

member-name:
    identifier
    interface-type   .   identifier

accessor-declarations:
    get-accessor-declaration set-accessor-declaration$_{opt}$
    set-accessor-declaration get-accessor-declaration$_{opt}$

get-accessor-declaration:
    attributes$_{opt}$ get *accessor-body*

set-accessor-declaration:
    attributes$_{opt}$ set *accessor-body*

accessor-body:
    block

    ;

event-declaration:
    attributes$_{opt}$ event-modifiers$_{opt}$ event *type variable-declarators* ;
    attributes$_{opt}$ event-modifiers$_{opt}$ event *type member-name*
        { *event accessor-declarations* }

event-modifiers:
    event-modifier
    event-modifiers event-modifier

event-modifier:
```
new
public
protected
internal
private
```

```
static
virtual
sealed
override
abstract
extern
```

event-accessor-declarations:
  add-accessor-declaration remove-accessor-declaration
  remove-accessor-declaration add-accessor-declaration

add-accessor-declaration:
  attributes$_{opt}$ `add` *block*

remove-accessor-declaration:
  attributes$_{opt}$ `remove` *block*

indexer-declaration:
  attributes$_{opt}$ indexer-modifiers$_{opt}$ indexer-declarator `{` *accessor-declarations* `}`

indexer-modifiers:
  indexer-modifier
  indexer-modifiers indexer-modifier

indexer-modifier:
```
new
public
protected
internal
private
virtual
sealed
override
abstract
extern
```

indexer-declarator:
  type `this` `[` *formal-parameter-list* `]`
  type interface-type `.` `this` `[` *formal-parameter-list* `]`

operator-declaration:
  attributes$_{opt}$ operator-modifiers operator-declarator operator-body

operator-modifiers:
  operator-modifier
  operator-modifiers operator-modifier

operator-modifier:
    `public`
    `static`
    `extern`

operator-declarator:
    unary-operator-declarator
    binary-operator-declarator
    conversion-operator-declarator

unary-operator-declarator:
    type `operator` *overloadable-unary-operator* `(` *type* *identifier* `)`

overloadable-unary-operator: one of
    `+`   `-`   `!`   `~`   `++`   `--`   `true`   `false`

binary-operator-declarator:
    type `operator` *overloadable-binary-operator* `(` *type* *identifier* `,` *type* *identifier* `)`

overloadable-binary-operator: one of
    `+`   `-`   `*`   `/`   `%`   `&`   `|`   `^`   `<<`   `>>`   `==`   `!=`   `>`   `<`   `>=`   `<=`

conversion-operator-declarator:
    `implicit` `operator` *type* `(` *type* *identifier* `)`
    `explicit` `operator` *type* `(` *type* *identifier* `)`

operator-body:
    block

    `;`

constructor-declaration:
    attributes$_{opt}$ constructor-modifiers$_{opt}$ constructor-declarator constructor-body

constructor-modifiers:
    constructor-modifier
    constructor-modifiers constructor-modifier

constructor-modifier:
    `public`
    `protected`
    `internal`
    `private`
    `extern`

constructor-declarator:
    identifier `(` *formal-parameter-list$_{opt}$* `)` *constructor-initializer$_{opt}$*

constructor-initializer:
    : base (*argument-list$_{opt}$*)
    : this (*argument-list$_{opt}$*)

constructor-body:
    block

    ;

static-constructor-declaration:
    attributes$_{opt}$ static-constructor-modifiers identifier ( ) *static-constructor-body*

static-constructor-modifiers:
    extern$_{opt}$ static
    static extern$_{opt}$

static-constructor-body:
    block

    ;

destructor-declaration:
    attributes$_{opt}$ extern$_{opt}$ ~ *identifier* ( ) *destructor-body*

destructor-body:
    block

    ;

B.2.8 Structs

struct-declaration:
    attributes$_{opt}$ struct-modifiers$_{opt}$ struct *identifier struct-interfaces$_{opt}$*
        struct-body ;$_{opt}$

struct-modifiers:
    struct-modifier
    struct-modifiers struct-modifier

struct-modifier:
    new
    public
    protected
    internal
    private

struct-interfaces:
    : *interface-type-list*

struct-body:
    { *struct-member-declarations$_{opt}$* }

struct-member-declarations:
    struct-member-declaration
    struct-member-declarations   struct-member-declaration

struct-member-declaration:
    constant-declaration
    field-declaration
    method-declaration
    property-declaration
    event-declaration
    indexer-declaration
    operator-declaration
    constructor-declaration
    static-constructor-declaration
    type-declaration

B.2.9 Arrays

array-type:
    non-array-type   rank-specifiers

non-array-type:
    type

rank-specifiers:
    rank-specifier
    rank-specifiers   rank-specifier

rank-specifier:
    [*dim-separators$_{opt}$*   ]

dim-separators:
    ,
    dim-separators   ,

array-initializer:
    {   *variable-initializer-list$_{opt}$*   }
    {   *variable-initializer-list*   ,   }

variable-initializer-list:
    variable-initializer
    variable-initializer-list   ,   *variable-initializer*

variable-initializer:
    expression
    array-initializer

B.2.10 Interfaces

interface-declaration:
> *attributes*$_{opt}$ *interface-modifiers*$_{opt}$ `interface` *identifier interface-base*$_{opt}$
>> *interface-body* `;`$_{opt}$

interface-modifiers:
> *interface-modifier*
> *interface-modifiers interface-modifier*

interface-modifier:
> `new`
> `public`
> `protected`
> `internal`
> `private`

interface-base:
> `:` *interface-type-list*

interface-body:
> `{` *interface-member-declarations*$_{opt}$ `}`

interface-member-declarations:
> *interface-member-declaration*
> *interface-member-declarations interface-member-declaration*

interface-member-declaration:
> *interface-method-declaration*
> *interface-property-declaration*
> *interface-event-declaration*
> *interface-indexer-declaration*

interface-method-declaration:
> *attributes*$_{opt}$ `new`$_{opt}$ *return-type identifier* `(` *formal-parameter-list*$_{opt}$ `)` `;`

interface-property-declaration:
> *attributes*$_{opt}$ `new`$_{opt}$ *type identifier* `{` *interface-accessors* `}`

interface-accessors:
> *attributes*$_{opt}$ `get` `;`
> *attributes*$_{opt}$ `set` `;`
> *attributes*$_{opt}$ `get` `;` *attributes*$_{opt}$ `set` `;`
> *attributes*$_{opt}$ `set` `;` *attributes*$_{opt}$ `get` `;`

interface-event-declaration:
> *attributes*$_{opt}$ `new`$_{opt}$ `event` *type identifier* `;`

interface-indexer-declaration:
> *attributes*$_{opt}$ `new`$_{opt}$ *type* `this` `[` *formal-parameter-list* `]` `{` *interface-accessors* `}`

B.2.11 **Enums**

enum-declaration:

 attributes$_{opt}$ *enum-modifiers*$_{opt}$ enum *identifier enum-base*$_{opt}$ *enum-body* ; $_{opt}$

enum-base:

 : *integral-type*

enum-body:

 { *enum-member-declarations*$_{opt}$ }

 { *enum-member-declarations* , }

enum-modifiers:

 enum-modifier

 enum-modifiers enum-modifier

enum-modifier:

 new

 public

 protected

 internal

 private

enum-member-declarations:

 enum-member-declaration

 enum-member-declarations , enum-member-declaration

enum-member-declaration:

 attributes$_{opt}$ *identifier*

 attributes$_{opt}$ *identifier* = *constant-expression*

B.2.12 **Delegates**

delegate-declaration:

 attributes$_{opt}$ *delegate-modifiers*$_{opt}$ delegate *return-type identifier*

  (*formal-parameter-list*$_{opt}$) ;

delegate-modifiers:

 delegate-modifier

 delegate-modifiers delegate-modifier

delegate-modifier:

 new

 public

 protected

 internal

 private

B.2.13 Attributes

global-attributes:
    global-attribute-sections

global-attribute-sections:
    global-attribute-section
    global-attribute-sections   global-attribute-section

global-attribute-section:
    [*global-attribute-target-specifier   attribute-list*   ]
    [*global-attribute-target-specifier   attribute-list*   ,   ]

global-attribute-target-specifier:
    global-attribute-target   :

global-attribute-target:
    `assembly`
    `module`

attributes:
    attribute-sections

attribute-sections:
    attribute-section
    attribute-sections   attribute-section

attribute-section:
    [*attribute-target-specifier*$_{opt}$ *attribute-list*   ]
    [*attribute-target-specifier*$_{opt}$ *attribute-list*   ,   ]

attribute-target-specifier:
    attribute-target   :

attribute-target:
    `field`
    `event`
    `method`
    `param`
    `property`
    `return`
    `type`

attribute-list:
    attribute
    attribute-list   ,   *attribute*

attribute:
    attribute-name   attribute-arguments$_{opt}$

attribute-name:
   type-name

attribute-arguments:
   (*positional-argument-list*$_{opt}$)
   (*positional-argument-list*   ,   *named-argument-list*   )
   (*named-argument-list*   )

positional-argument-list:
   positional-argument
   positional-argument-list   ,   *positional-argument*

positional-argument:
   attribute-argument-expression

named-argument-list:
   named-argument
   named-argument-list   ,   *named-argument*

named-argument:
   identifier   =   *attribute-argument-expression*

attribute-argument-expression:
   expression

B.3 Grammar Extensions for Unsafe Code

class-modifier:
   ...
   ```
   unsafe
   ```

struct-modifier:
   ...
   ```
   unsafe
   ```

interface-modifier:
   ...
   ```
   unsafe
   ```

delegate-modifier:
   ...
   ```
   unsafe
   ```

field-modifier:
   ...
   ```
   unsafe
   ```

method-modifier:

   ...

   unsafe

property-modifier:

   ...

   unsafe

event-modifier:

   ...

   unsafe

indexer-modifier:

   ...

   unsafe

operator-modifier:

   ...

   unsafe

constructor-modifier:

   ...

   unsafe

destructor-declaration:

   attributes$_{opt}$ extern$_{opt}$ unsafe$_{opt}$ ~ *identifier* ( ) *destructor-body*
   attributes$_{opt}$ unsafe$_{opt}$ extern$_{opt}$ ~ *identifier* ( ) *destructor-body*

static-constructor-modifiers:

   extern$_{opt}$ unsafe$_{opt}$ static
   unsafe$_{opt}$ extern$_{opt}$ static
   extern$_{opt}$ static unsafe$_{opt}$
   unsafe$_{opt}$ static extern$_{opt}$
   static extern$_{opt}$ unsafe$_{opt}$
   static unsafe$_{opt}$ extern$_{opt}$

embedded-statement:

   ...

   unsafe-statement

unsafe-statement:

   unsafe *block*

type:

   value-type
   reference-type
   pointer-type

pointer-type:
    unmanaged-type `*`
    `void *`

unmanaged-type:
    type

primary-no-array-creation-expression:

    ...

    pointer-member-access
    pointer-element-access
    sizeof-expression

unary-expression:

    ...

    pointer-indirection-expression
    addressof-expression

pointer-indirection-expression:
    `*` *unary-expression*

pointer-member-access:
    primary-expression `->` *identifier*

pointer-element-access:
    primary-no-array-creation-expression `[` *expression* `]`

addressof-expression:
    `&` *unary-expression*

sizeof-expression:
    `sizeof` `(` *unmanaged-type* `)`

embedded-statement:

    ...

    fixed-statement

fixed-statement:
    `fixed` `(` *pointer-type fixed-pointer-declarators* `)` *embedded-statement*

fixed-pointer-declarators:
    fixed-pointer-declarator
    fixed-pointer-declarators `,` *fixed-pointer-declarator*

fixed-pointer-declarator:
    identifier `=` *fixed-pointer-initializer*

fixed-pointer-initializer:
    `&` *variable-reference*
    expression

local-variable-initializer:
    expression
    array-initializer
    stackalloc-initializer

stackalloc-initializer:
    `stackalloc` *unmanaged-type* `[` *expression* `]`

Index

Symbols

\# character, in keywords,   53

\#define directives, processing,   63, 65–66

\#include directives, requirement for,   6

A

abstract accessors,   325–326, 333

abstract classes
  described,   274–275
  interfaces,   391

abstract methods,   25–28, 311–312, 313–315

access
  array elements,   369
  interface members,   378–380
  members,   79–86
  See also pointer element access; pointer member access; this access

access modifiers, kinds of,   280

access paths, hidden members,   380

access restrictions, namespaces,   78

accessibility
  of class members,   19
  constructed types,   491
  of methods,   74
  See also declared accessibility

accessibility constraints, types,   85

accessibility domains,   81–84

accessible names, hiding,   92

accessing, protected members,   478

accessor declarations, attributes,   417

accessors
  defined,   31, 317
  described,   319–324
  interface property declarations,   377
  See also abstract accessors; event accessors; getaccessor; setaccessors

addition operators,   202–204

additive operators
  described,   13
  precedence of,   150

addresses, fixed pointer initializers,   447

address-of operator,   441–442

alertescapesequence,Unicodeencoding,   59

alias directives, using,   267, 268, 492

aliases. *See* explicit keywords; keywords; reserved words

analysis, lexical,   47–50
  See also lexical grammar; lexical structure

anonymous invocations, delegates,   399

anonymous methods,   525–538
  blocks,   528
  conversions,   526–527, 534–535
  definite assignment states,   533–534
  delegate instance equality,   533
  evaluation,   532–533
  expressions,   525
  generics,   463–466
  implementation example,   535–538

B